Algorithms for Intelligent Systems

This book series publishes research on the analysis and development of algorithms for intelligent systems with their applications to various real world problems. It covers research related to autonomous agents, multi-agent systems, behavioral modeling, reinforcement learning, game theory, mechanism design, machine learning, meta-heuristic search, optimization, planning and scheduling, artificial neural networks, evolutionary computation, swarm intelligence, and other algorithms for intelligent systems.

The book series includes recent advancements, modification and applications of the artificial neural networks, evolutionary computation, swarm intelligence, artificial immune systems, fuzzy system, autonomous and multi agent systems, machine learning, and other intelligent systems related areas. The material will be beneficial for the graduate students, post-graduate students as well as the researchers who want a broader view of advances in algorithms for intelligent systems. The contents will also be useful to the researchers from other fields who have no knowledge of the power of intelligent systems, e.g. the researchers in the field of bioinformatics, biochemists, mechanical and chemical engineers, economists, musicians and medical practitioners.

The series publishes monographs, edited volumes, advanced textbooks and selected proceedings.

Indexed by zbMATH.

All books published in the series are submitted for consideration in Web of Science.

Developing Knowledge Convergence Through Collective Phronesis

Mitsuru Kodama

Developing Knowledge Convergence Through Collective Phronesis

palgrave
macmillan

Mitsuru Kodama
College of Commerce
Nihon University
Tokyo, Japan

ISBN 978-981-96-4402-5 ISBN 978-981-96-4403-2 (eBook)
https://doi.org/10.1007/978-981-96-4403-2

Cover credit: @Maram_shutterstock.com

This Palgrave Macmillan imprint is published by the registered company Springer Nature Singapore Pte Ltd.
The registered company address is: 152 Beach Road, #21-01/04 Gateway East, Singapore 189721, Singapore

Preface

This book will provide new theoretical and practical knowledge for establishing a holistic grand theory in the field of innovation theory. Despite the fact that many management theories have been structured-oriented and neglect process and human subjectivity, the author believes that business studies and innovation theory should be both theoretical and practical. This is because in practice, human subjectivity plays the leading role (e.g., Kodama, 2007, 2011).

The main focus of this book is to incorporate individual subjectivity into theory as much as possible. In reality, practitioner and organizational business behaviors and innovation activities are extremely diverse and chaotic, and management and innovation are both sciences and arts. However, it is thought that the modern corporate workplace is science oriented. Nevertheless, truly excellent management and innovation practice are born from a balance of science and art. When using logic, if you don't have the wisdom to deny logic, it's easy to fall into the analytical paralysis syndrome. Art and science are in a mutually complementary relationship. Therefore, it's necessary to combine both science and art, and the essence of management and innovation activities depends on how a balance is struck between the two.

What is the essence of art in management and innovation? It is not just simple intuition. It's making excellent judgments in situations that can't be rationally calculated. This is an art, and has commonalities with the phronesis and collective phronesis that will be discussed in this book.

Applying theory to reality and iterating through individual cases improves knowledge and turns knowledge into wisdom in practice. Knowledge can refine wisdom, but without knowledge, wisdom is not born. Thus, this practice will enable excellent judgments in the individual contexts of reality. When knowledge is refined and united with subjectivity it becomes wisdom. This is Aristotle's concept of "phronesis"—the wisdom that enables making judgments about what is good—wisdom that is an extremely important element in modern society.

Phronesis is also practical knowledge for making the best judgments and taking the best actions with discretion regarding values and ethics in individual contexts and situations. A collection of this phronesis is "collective phronesis" and is for achieving collective wisdom management. However, the concept of collective phronesis—synergies of phronesis, and its application in the conceptualization of organizations and leadership are un-pioneered themes.

The author of this book and other researchers have recently presented individual theoretical frameworks of the "Dynamic Fractal Organization" (Nonaka et al., 2014), "Holistic Leadership" (Kodama, 2019c), "Boundaries Vision, Boundaries Knowledge and Convergence Knowledge" (Kodama, 2018, 2019b). This book will focus on the new concept of "collective phronesis," which is unseen in similar types of books. Through detailed case studies of global high-tech companies, the book will integrate the separate theoretical frameworks of the "Dynamic Fractal Organization," "Holistic Leadership," and "Boundaries Vision, Boundaries Knowledge and Convergence Knowledge" to provide a new comprehensive theoretical framework and original knowledge.

This book could not have been brought to fruition without the exhaustive and robust interaction of the authors with many practitioners (innovators or creators). The author would like to thank all the practitioners who generously gave their time for interviews and discussions. I would also like to express my gratitude for the support of Faculty of Humanities and Social Sciences at Jissen Women's University and Japan Society for the Promotion of Science (JSPS).

Lastly, I would like to express my deepest thanks to Mr. Jacob Dreyer, Commissioning Editor, and Ms. Uma Vinesh, Project Coordinator of Palgrave Macmillan, for all of their support and efforts.

Tokyo, Japan Mitsuru Kodama

References

Kodama, M. (2007). *Project-based organization in the knowledge-based Society* (Series on Technology Management, Vol. 12). Imperial College Press.

Kodama, M. (2011). *Knowledge integration dynamics: Developing strategic innovation capability*. World Scientific.

Kodama, M. (2018). Boundaries innovation through knowledge convergence-developing triad strategic communities. *Technology Analysis & Strategic Management, 30*(5), 609–624.

Kodama, M. (2019a). Business innovation through holistic leadership-developing organizational adaptability. *Systems Research and Behavioral Science, 36*(4), 365–394.

Kodama, M. (2019b). Boundaries knowledge (knowing)—A source of business innovation. *Knowledge and Process Management, 26*(3), 210–228.

Nonaka, I., Kodama, M., Hirose, A., & Kohlbacher, F. (2014). Dynamic fractal organizations for promoting knowledge-based transformation—A new paradigm for organizational theory. *European Management Journal, 32*(1), 137–146.

Nonaka I., & Takeuchi, H. (1995). *The knowledge-creating company. How Japanese companies create the dynamics of innovation*. Oxford University Press.

Acknowledgments Dr. Ikujiro Nonaka, a world-renowned authority on knowledge creation theory and Professor Emeritus at Hitotsubashi University, passed away on January 25, 2025. As I bring this book to the world, I wish to express my deep sorrow and pay tribute to the esteemed Dr. Nonaka.

Throughout his life, Dr. Nonaka made significant contributions to our field of study, and his research continues to influence many. His passion, insight, and warm personality made him an irreplaceable presence.

Dr. Nonaka's research was filled with originality and profound insights, and served as a guide to gain new knowledge. His teachings and guidance have inspired academic curiosity and have been a beacon for many researchers.

This book is an achievement made possible through the teachings and influence of Dr. Nonaka. With deep gratitude for his efforts and respect for the knowledge and humanity he left in our hearts, I dedicate this book to him.

I sincerely pray for the repose of Dr. Ikujiro Nonaka's soul.

Dr. Ikujiro Nonaka and the author (photographed at Hitotsubashi University ICS on January 17, 2024)

Mitsuru Kodama

Competing Interests The author has no competing interests to declare that are relevant to the content of this manuscript.

Contents

About the Author

Dr. Mitsuru Kodama is Professor of Entrepreneurship and Media Innovation in the Faculty of Humanities and Social Sciences at Jissen Women's University, and Professor Emeritus at Nihon University. He has published 18 books in English—including *Strategic Innovation System* (Routledge, 2023), *Managing IT for Innovation* (Routledge, 2021), *Developing Holistic Strategic Management in the Advanced ICT Era* (World Scientific Europe, 2019), *Sustainable Growth Through Strategic Innovation* (Edward Elgar, 2018), *Developing Holistic Leadership* (Emerald, 2017), *Collaborative Innovation* (Routledge, 2015), *Winning Through Boundaries Innovation* (Peter Lang, 2014), *Competing Through ICT Capability* (Palgrave Macmillan, 2012), *Knowledge Integration Dynamics* (World Scientific, 2011), *Boundary Management* (Springer, 2009), and *Project-Based Organization In The Knowledge-Based Society* (Imperial College Press, 2007)—and articles in several international journals such as *Long Range Planning, Organization Studies, Journal of Management Studies, Technovation, R&D Management, Research Technology Management, Technology Analysis & Strategic Management, Journal of Engineering and Technology Management, International Journal of Information Management and Information Systems Management*, among others. Prior to joining Jissen Women's University and Nihon University, he was working as a project leader at NTT and NTT DoCoMo for around 20 years. In 2003 he received an R&D 100 Award in *R&D Magazine* in United States.

List of Figures

List of Tables

CHAPTER 1

Acquiring Collective Phronesis in the Era of Convergence

1.1 Introduction—Innovation Strategies with Knowledge Convergence

Recent years have also seen new business models created across the boundaries between different industries, with the smartphone-type businesses and Big Data/IoT/AI typified by companies such as Open AI, Microsoft, Apple, Google, Amazon and NVIDIA, and so on. These companies engage in coordination and collaboration with diverse businesses across different industries and business categories to pioneer new and never-before-seen business domains (e.g., Kodama, 2019b). Radical innovation is important for converging other similar businesses to create related business areas separated from the core business and pioneering new businesses in new and different fields with convergence of a company's core business with that of another company.

These fast-paced digital technology and Big Data/IoT/AI developments—digital appliances, e-money, IoT/AI solutions, converged unified communications and various broadcasting, wide-ranging smartphone content delivery, and the new various business models that traverse differing industries and companies—have all been born through knowledge convergence. As well as that, with the new technological and product developments that come about with technical knowledge convergence including ICT/AI, new business networks are forming between

M. Kodama, *Developing Knowledge Convergence Through Collective Phronesis*, https://doi.org/10.1007/978-981-96-4403-2_1

different industries as new value chains emerge with new competition rules and business models that cut across the boundaries between different businesses (see Fig. 1.1).

At the background to the achievement of knowledge convergence in the Big Data/IoT/AI domain, lies the coordination and collaboration between stakeholders, and the value chains that have come about through knowledge convergence between different platforms such as terminals (smartphones, tablets, PCs, smart watch, XR smart glasses, etc.), carrier networks (optical fiber, mobile wireless, and satellite link) and platforms (Finance, transactions, e-commerce, cloud, and AI), through to applications (e.g., distribution and ChatGPT), contents (broadcasting, video, music, and advertising), various SNS and business applications (cloud services, e-learning, remote medicine, software as a service, the smart grid and house, etc.).

These unique value chains have been established business ecosystems such as content businesses and mobile commerce market with smart and

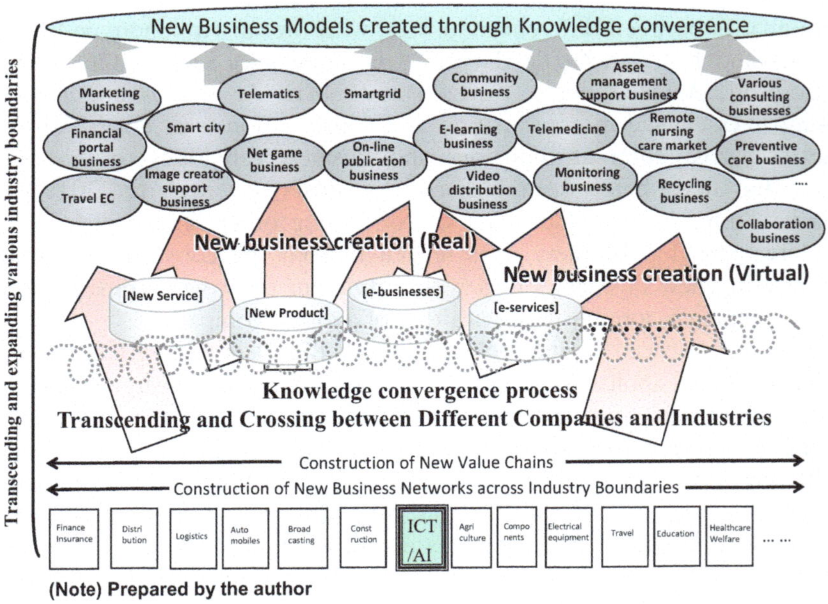

Fig. 1.1 Creating new business through knowledge convergence

mobile telephones. These markets continue to grow rapidly creating co-evolution models in smartphone and mobile phone businesses (Gawer & Cusumano, 2014: Iansiti & Levien, 2004; Kodama, 2009; Moore, 1993). Differing from older types of business structures, these new business networks are examples of how radical innovation moves beyond incremental innovation and simultaneously brings about both new competition and cooperation.

In this way, the phenomenon of knowledge convergence has made competition between companies and industries more complicated. Knowledge convergence has quickly sped up the formation of strategic alliances between companies with the inclusion of their customers and mergers and acquisitions, and triggered massive changes in existing corporate boundaries (both vertical and horizontal). This means corporate strategies that also transcend and focus on alliances between businesses rather than only on competition between differing businesses are becoming increasingly important.

In other words, this means switching away from strategies that focus on competition between companies or between different industries to collaboration strategies between diverse industries that include customers is becoming an important issue for twenty-first-century companies. Modern examples of knowledge convergence that have already been achieved include the new ICT/AI-based markets spanning differing industries and technologies, such as the new smart business models (see Fig. 1.2).

Thus, companies have to put knowledge convergence-based innovation processes at the core of their corporate strategies, and use their core competencies effectively, and continually advance them with incremental innovation, as these are the strengths of their core businesses, while at the same time engage in radical innovation to pioneer peripheral businesses and businesses in differing fields by triggering synergies between these businesses and their core businesses to achieve sustainable competitiveness. Therefore, to raise core competences to a higher level, companies not only need to engage in new strategic activities to converge diverse knowledge across wide-ranging boundaries within themselves, but also need management that can dynamically converge diverse knowledge outside of the company, including that held by customers, to forge ahead with business in differing fields or on the periphery of their core competencies. For this, practitioners need new strategic ways of

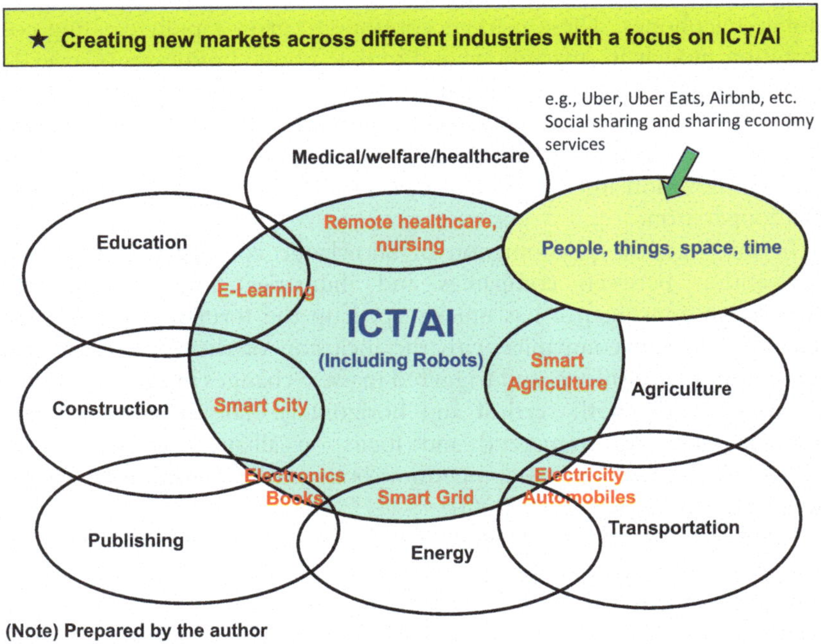

Fig. 1.2 The age of knowledge convergence

thinking and actions—phronesis and collective phronesis to create boundaries knowledge and convergence knowledge, as described in Chapters 2 and 3.

1.2 Strategic Thinking for Knowledge Convergence

Historically, a strategic objective of high-tech companies has been to advance and develop products by sustaining innovation with individual specialized technologies (incremental innovation). However, in recent years, the necessity to develop new products and services through the convergence of dissimilar technologies has increased. The advance of ICT/AI has also compressed the space-time in business processes and supply chains across all kinds of industries, raised the speed at which decisions can be made, raised business efficiency, and brought about new business models that transcend dissimilar industries as mentioned in Figures 1.1 and 1.2. As background to this phenomenon, there are now many cases of never-before-seen new and innovative products and services achieved through the convergence of technologies from one field with those of another.

Diversification and advance of technologies and the rapid advance of ICT/AI are complicating the business models that companies need to provide. Thus, in twenty-first-century companies, the necessity for strategies to respond to convergence and provide customers with new value by integrating dissimilar technologies or services such as ICT, developing products and services, and establishing business models across differing industries has significantly increased. This means companies must not only integrate dissimilar specialized knowledge within themselves, but also means the integration of dissimilar knowledge across the boundaries between companies will form the core of corporate strategy.

A factor of strategic thinking for practitioners in achieving innovation in response to convergence is the aforementioned collective phronesis (Kodama, 2021; Nonaka & Takeuchi, 2019). The acquisition and organizational fostering of holistic leadership (Kodama, 2017, 2019c, 2019b) to be demonstrated by practitioners are necessary conditions for the creation of collective phronesis. Collective phronesis forms dynamic fractal organizations (Nonaka et al., 2014) through practitioners' building of multilayered networks of Ba and communities that include customers both inside and outside of companies. Therefore, the creation of boundaries knowledge through boundaries vision of practitioners to find or form, combine, and bridge these Ba and communities is important (Kodama, 2019a).

From detailed case studies on global high-tech corporations and organizations, this book will present practical theories, insights, and implications for practitioners' collective phronesis, which generates boundaries knowledge and convergence knowledge for convergence(Kodama, 2018). Characteristic of the theoretical model of this book, holistic leadership that brings about excellent collective phronesis creates new convergence knowledge as convergence by inspiring and creating boundaries knowledge through boundaries vision. Thus, the book will clarify how practitioners exercise holistic leadership to bring about collective phronesis, combine various contradictions in and out of companies, build dynamic fractal organizations consisting of multilayered networks of diverse Ba and communities, and achieve boundaries innovation in communities for sustainable innovation to continually generate boundaries knowledge and convergence knowledge.

Individual and diverse boundaries exist between all kinds of things and phenomena. Knowledge boundaries also exist between the areas of specialization of individual people. Foreignness and unique differences exist on these boundaries. Boundaries knowledge is the wisdom to uncover these differences and dissimilarities, and is also the wisdom to be able to determine what type of boundaries to uncover, and how to link them together to inspire new knowledge.

The capability of practitioners to bring about boundaries knowledge is their boundaries vision. The collective phronesis of practitioners brings about boundaries knowledge, and generates convergence knowledge for convergence. Convergence knowledge is the result of the creation of boundaries knowledge (tacit and explicit knowledge uncovered in the dissimilarities and differences on boundaries), and is knowledge born as a result of knowledge converged to achieve the ideals and beliefs of practitioners. While collective phronesis triggers and inspires the boundaries and convergence knowledge of practitioners, this chapter will clarify that the generation of this knowledge is not only required by top management and elites, but is also required by a wide range of middle managers and staff.

This scholarly book will take an original perspective of convergence, boundaries knowledge, convergence knowledge, collective phronesis, dynamic fractal organizations, and holistic leadership, which will be a major feature of the book not found in any similar work to date.

1.3 Developing Collective Phronesis by Dynamic Fractal Organization

Building communities for sustainable innovation is the biggest issue facing corporate management in the twenty-first century. Innovation communities achieve sustainable innovation in knowledge ecosystems of communities of individuals, organizations, companies, and customers that influence corporate activities, rather than operating in markets with an emphasis on the relative value of competitive strategy theory (e.g., Kodama, 2007, 2011; Nonaka & Takeuchi, 1995, 2019). Leading companies are embedded in the broader dynamic relationships of society—relationships that include a wide range of stakeholders outside themselves, and continually generate new knowledge by converging their own knowledge with external knowledge. The critical issue for corporations that globally mobilize knowledge in these ecosystems and sustainably bring about new knowledge is how to mobilize the collective phronesis of the leading people and communities in knowledge ecosystems spanning organizations, companies, and industries.

Collective phronesis is the aggregation of the phronesis (practical knowledge or practical wisdom) of practitioners. Collective phronesis is the aggregate of superior, autonomous and dispersed, and controlled phronesis possessed by people, and is also the integrated practical knowledge for total management by gathering individual pieces of collective knowledge in and across organizations. In other words, collective phronesis is not closed in an enterprise but can also be said to be the good quality wisdom and practical skills consisting of mobilized individual phronesis in knowledge ecosystems that include the environments of people, organizations, companies, communities, and industries. In chains of multilayered "Ba" and communities (multilayered networks of Ba and communities) that transcend the boundaries of environments of diverse organizations and communities that include customers, collective phronesis interdependently acts on environments, people, organizations, and companies, and develops with those while bringing about knowledge ecosystems.

New innovation is not only achieved by certain heroes who hold phronesis but also by diverse practitioners at all levels of organizations including customers and partners bringing together good quality wisdom and practical skills (e.g., Kodama, 2007). Therefore, collective phronesis is also an important factor in creating boundaries knowledge and convergence knowledge through convergence (fusion)—the key drivers of innovation in recent years (Kodama, 2018, 2019a). An important proposition for corporate strategy to adapt to, or to create the convergence worldview, is "management with collective phronesis."

Collective phronesis is quality wisdom and practical capabilities achieved through full mobilization of the phronesis autonomously dispersed (and controlled) of individuals in knowledge ecosystems that include people, organizations, companies, industries, and external environments. In the world of collective phronesis, phronesis is not only carried out by certain heroic types in new knowledge convergence, but also by diverse practitioners in all levels of organizations, including customers, to bring together the best quality knowledge and practical skills to achieve boundaries innovation. This book will clarify that such collective phronesis is a crucial factor in the creation of boundaries knowledge and convergence knowledge, the key drivers of boundaries innovation in recent years.

Moreover, collective phronesis triggers, inspires, and creates the boundaries knowledge and convergence knowledge of leading practitioners. The book will present that such knowledge creation is not only required by elites such as top management, but also required by many middle managers and staff members.

This book will present managerial factors for the creation, sharing, and fostering of practitioners' collective phronesis to generate boundaries knowledge and convergence knowledge to achieve convergence, the managerial factors of the "dynamic fractal organization" (Nonaka et al., 2014) and "leadership (holistic leadership)" (Kodama, 2017, 2019b). Superior collective phronesis of practitioners brought about from the holistic leadership of practitioners in dynamic fractal organizations inspires and creates diverse boundaries knowledge, and dynamically forms multilayered networks of Ba and communities required to create convergence knowledge.

Furthermore, this book presents a new theoretical model and implications for sustainable innovation community companies to perpetually generate boundaries knowledge and convergence knowledge to achieve convergence through collective phronesis, based on detailed case studies of global high-tech corporations (Apple, Cisco Systems, Microsoft, Zoom, TSMC, Nintendo, Toyota, Panasonic, TSMC, and others).

1.4 Conclusion—Building Communities for Sustainable Innovation

Finally, through the case studies of high-tech corporations and organizations presented in detail, the book will summarize how practitioners with excellent collective phronesis use their boundaries vision capabilities to inspire and create boundaries knowledge, and dynamically form multilayered networks of "Ba" and communities required for the creation of convergence knowledge. In "communities for sustainable innovation" that continually bring about boundaries knowledge and convergence knowledge, practitioners use their collective phronesis to combine various contradictions both inside and outside of their companies through their capability to integrate "Ba" and communities to dynamically rebuild multilayered networks of various "Ba" and communities and achieve boundaries innovation.

To achieve new business models, it's crucial that companies dynamically integrate knowledge within themselves linking up their various internal boundaries (between people, organizations and different areas of specialization, etc.) with external knowledge linking up external boundaries (between companies, between companies and their customers, between different industries, etc.). In other words, new convergence knowledge transcending various boundaries comes about by creating boundaries knowledge both inside and outside of companies on their vertical and horizontal boundaries. To achieve boundaries innovation, the creation of new convergence knowledge, sustainable collective phronesis must be acquired through the holistic leadership of practitioners. Through this, practitioners build multilayered networks of dynamic "Ba" and communities to achieve future creation strategies for the common good.

References

Gawer, A., & Cusumano, M. A. (2014). Industry platforms and ecosystem innovation. *Journal of Product Innovation Management, 31*(3), 417–433.

Iansiti, M., & Levien, R. (2004). Keystones and dominators: Framing operating and technology strategy in a business ecosystem. *Harvard Business School, Boston, 3*, 1–82.

Kodama, M. (2007). *Project-based Organization in the Knowledge-based Society* (Vol. 12). World Scientific.

Kodama, M. (2009). Innovation networks in knowledge-based firms: Developing ICT-based integrative competences. In *Innovation networks in knowledge-based firms*. Edward Elgar Publishing.

Kodama, M. (2011). *Knowledge integration dynamics: Developing strategic innovation capability*. World Scientific.

Kodama, M. (2017). *Developing holistic leadership: A source of business innovation*. Emerald Publishing Limited.

Kodama, M. (2018). Boundaries innovation through knowledge convergence-developing triad strategic communities. *Technology Analysis & Strategic Management, 30*(5), 609–624.

Kodama, M. (2019a). Boundaries knowledge (knowing)—A source of business innovation. *Knowledge and Process Management, 26*(3), 210–228.

Kodama, M. (2019b). *Developing Holistic Strategic Management in the Advanced ICT Era*. World Scientific Publishing Co. Pte. Ltd.
Kodama, M. (2019c). Business Innovation Through Holistic Leadership-Developing Organizational Adaptability. *Systems Research and Behavioral Science, 36*(4), 365–394.
Kodama, M. (2021). Knowledge creation through collective phronesis. *Knowledge and Process Management, 28*(3), 223–245.
Moore, J. F. (1993). Predators and prey: A new ecology of competition. *Harvard Business Review, 71*(3), 75–86.
Nonaka, I., & Takeuchi, H. (1995). The Knowledge-Creating Company. How Japanese Companies Create the Dynamics of Innovation.
Nonaka, I., & Takeuchi, H. (2019). *The Wise Company: How Companies Create Continuous Innovation*. Oxford University Press.
Nonaka, I., Kodama, M., Hirose, A., & Kohlbacher, F. (2014). Dynamic fractal organizations for promoting knowledge-based transformation—A new paradigm for organizational theory. *European Management Journal, 32*(1), 137–146.

CHAPTER 2

Boundaries Innovation Through the Creation of Boundaries Knowledge and Convergence Knowledge—Case Studies on Apple, P&G, and NTT DOCOMO

2.1 Innovation Strategy Through Convergence

One point that companies achieving sustainable growth in world markets today have in common is their possession of a core business (mainstay business) based on sound core competence (Hamel & Prahalad, 1994). These companies effectively exploit and sustainably promote their core competence (Zook, 2003). This is equivalent to incremental innovation. Strong core competence for sustainable growth through incremental innovation lies in technological strength based on quality tacit knowledge that forms the core of the value chain.

For example, some companies with worldwide competitiveness that fit this description (which are also presented as case studies in this chapter) are Samsung Electronics in digital home electronics, Canon in business and optical equipment, and FANUC in machine tools. Through incremental innovation these companies accumulate and update on a daily basis their technological expertise in all aspects of their products from component development to final product through the skillful coordination of technological know-how and skills in various functional organizations and different specialized areas within the company and through the convergence of these. In this way, they optimize their value chains as a whole and advance their global strategies. Another example is Apple,

M. Kodama, *Developing Knowledge Convergence Through Collective Phronesis*, https://doi.org/10.1007/978-981-96-4403-2_2

which implements incremental innovation to achieve iPhone improvements and enhancements (miniaturization and quality enhancement) as well as product version upgrades through the convergence of existing and new technologies.

The second common characteristic of companies achieving sustainable growth at present is their advance into peripheral businesses (Zook & Allen, 2001) and different sectors that enable them to demonstrate synergies with core businesses as well as the establishment of new value chains (Kim & Mauborgne, 2005) focusing on the customer. This corresponds to radical innovation. In recent years new forms of competition have arisen from the ambiguity of core business boundaries, the dramatic expansion of peripheral business domains (Zook & Allen, 2001), and the convergence of business in different fields (Kodama, 2009). As a result, considerations such as how to form new markets and redefine their core businesses are becoming increasingly important issues for companies.

For example, the convergence of a business adjacent to the core business may be somewhat distant from the core business but may result in the establishment of a related new business area, or the convergence of a company's core business with the core business of another company may open up a pathway for developing business in a wholly new area. This is the importance of radical innovation. In Japan, major logistics company Yamato Transport set itself apart from other large-lot transporters in the logistics industry where competition is fierce by going into the small-lot freight home delivery service, which is a peripheral business but one where turning a profit is difficult. Focusing on providing meticulous customer service, Yamato succeeded in differentiating itself from other providers. Seven Eleven is another example of the successful development of new business in a field different from the core business. Exploiting the geographical advantage of its stores spread over a wide area in Japan, the company succeeded in developing ATM business as a new financial business providing for the convenience of its customers. In this way, Seven Eleven expanded its business domain from retail to financial business.

The smartphone business of Apple and Google, also detailed in this chapter, is a typical case of a new business model established across boundaries of different industries. Through coordination and collaboration with various companies across different business sectors, business types, and different industries, these companies developed completely new business domains that had never before existed. In Japan, even before the iPhone appeared on the scene, internet delivery of services via mobile telephone services provided by NTT DOCOMO's i-mode, for example, encompassed image and music delivery, mobile commerce, location information, and telematics, and even today Japan's mobile telephone business is a world leader in creating new markets and developing new technologies. The games business, typified by Sony's PlayStation and Nintendo's DS and Wii, also has similarities to the mobile telephone business. Nintendo's DS and Wii game devices in particular are classic examples of the creation of new customer base out of "non-customers" through games that could provide enjoyment to children and adults who hardly ever played before. In this way, these game makers developed so-called blue ocean markets (Kim & Mauborgne, 2005).

In this way, rapid advances in digital technologies and ICT are creating new knowledge in various digital devices, e-money, IC tag solutions, communications and broadcasting integration, diverse content delivery to i-Pods and smartphones, and diverse business models across different industries and between companies. Furthermore, new technologies and new products developed through the convergence of different technologies including ICT as well as new rules in competition and business models that transcend the boundaries of different industries are creating business networks among dissimilar industries through new value chains.

Technologically supporting the realization of convergence in ICT are value chains formed through the convergence of different platforms constructed through the coordination and collaboration of stakeholders. These platforms include terminals (such as smartphones, mobile telephones, tablets, and PCs), communications networks (such as optic fiber communications networks, mobile wireless communications networks), platforms (such as accounting, settlement, e-money), applications (such as delivery systems, IC tags), content (such as broadcasting, images, music, advertising), and business applications (such as cloud services, e-learning, remote healthcare, software as services, smart grids).

These distinctive value chains have already created business ecosystems such as content business and mobile commerce markets using smartphones and mobile telephones. These markets are still growing today as they create co-evolution models for the smartphone and mobile telephone businesses (Gawer & Cusmano, 2004; Iansiti & Levien, 2004; Kodama, 2009; Moore, 1993). The establishment of new business networks such as these is also radical innovation that surpasses incremental innovation by simultaneously creating new competitive and cooperative relationships that differ from conventional business structures.

In this way, the phenomenon of convergence makes competition among conventional companies and industries even more complex. Convergence rapidly accelerates the formation of strategic partnerships and M&A among companies including customers, and becomes a trigger that has the potential to significantly alter existing corporate boundaries (vertical and horizontal boundaries). In this environment, corporate strategies based on "partnerships between different business sectors" which transcend the business axis of simple "competition between different business sectors" is becoming more and more important.

For example, the convergence of the ICT industry with the health care, nursing care, health insurance, and pharmaceutical products industries is creating new business processes and business models such as telemedicine, remote nursing care, tele-healthcare, medical information management, and medication and medical information assistance. This essentially means the transition from a strategy based on competition between companies and different business sectors within the business world or industry to a collaborative strategy with various industries (companies) including customers is an urgent issue for companies to consider. Some examples of convergence that actually already exist at present are e-, e-learning, traceability, smart grids, electric cars, and remote medical care. These new business models are also the results of new market creation across different industries and technologies through convergence centered on ICT.

In this way, a company incorporates the process of innovation based on convergence as a core element of its corporate strategy and must achieve a sustainable competitive advantage by simultaneously implementing incremental innovation and radical innovation, the former referring to the effective use and ongoing development of the company's core competence (which is the company's mainstay business) and the latter referring to the development of peripheral businesses and businesses in different areas that can demonstrate synergies with the core business. Therefore, to enhance its core competence, a company must not only execute new strategy activities for the convergence of knowledge across various boundaries within the company but must also execute new management for the dynamic convergence of knowledge inside and outside the company including its customers in order to develop business in peripheral areas of the company's core competence as well as in different areas.

Through in-depth case studies and new concepts, this chapter describes how boundaries innovation comes about from dynamic knowledge convergence processes that transcend the boundaries (between people, organizations, and different fields of specialization) within and outside of companies (between companies, between companies and customers, and between different industries and so forth). In addition, the chapter offers new perspectives on the "strategic community" (SC), which is the core theory of this chapter, and that inspires practitioners to create boundaries and convergence knowledge as new strategic thinking and actions, and functions to achieve the knowledge convergence process.

The chapter is structured as follows. Firstly, based on existing research, the chapter discusses the knowledge convergence process, which is the process of creating boundaries and convergence knowledge, the core theory of this chapter. Then, the chapter presents the concept of the strategic community (SC), which functions to achieve the knowledge convergence process, and originates from the generation of "Ba." Secondly the chapter discusses its research methodology. Thirdly, the chapter goes into detail of in-depth case studies done on Apple, P&G, and NTT DOCOMO, companies which achieve knowledge convergence. Fourthly, the chapter discusses implications extracted from these case analyses and the theoretical concepts.

2.2 Literature Review and the Theoretical Concept of This Chapter

2.2.1 Creating Boundaries Knowledge and Convergence Knowledge

(1) **The Concept of Boundaries Knowledge**

In the convergence worldview, the critical issue for companies is strategy that applies or creates convergence by sustainable creation of boundaries and convergence knowledge. Knowledge boundaries exist between dissimilar knowledge. This means that essential and unique differences exist in the dissimilar characteristics and details between different types of knowledge.

Generally, as knowledge boundaries become more pronounced between different types of knowledge or novelty in circumstances surrounding individuals, organizations, or companies, both quality and quantity of knowledge boundaries also increases (Carlile, 2004; Kodama,

2007). However, a lot of the new knowledge integration that has come about with innovation to date has occurred on the boundaries between specializations (Leonard-Barton, 1995). This suggests that the thinking and ideas between people and the actions of organizations straddling different fields of specialization are major factors in bringing about innovation success, and therefore factors that contribute to competitive superiority. Leading research also clarifies why it is difficult to generate and maintain innovation (Carlile, 2004).

It has also been reported that the ideas of people and actions of organizations straddling different fields of specialization are constrained by knowledge path dependency (March, 1972; Rosenkopf & Nerkar, 2001). For example, just as past exploratory activities have been easier to carry out with concentration in close relationships between fields of specialization, the communication and collaboration processes between fields of specialization have also been reported to contribute greatly to new innovations (van Rijnsoever & Hessels, 2011).

However, to encourage this kind of communication and collaboration, uncovering the knowledge boundaries perceived by individuals in organizations is critical. In short, this is the capability required to grasp whether the dissimilarities and differences on diverse boundaries will be a source of knowledge convergence.

Generally, most people feel uncomfortable when facing unfamiliar boundaries (contents to which they are unaccustomed), and different people have different perceptive capabilities and awareness when such discomforts occur. "Boundaries knowledge" is thus the capability of practitioners to seek out the differences and discomforts that stem from these dissimilarities on the boundaries, and from them uncover whatever new knowledge is available. Boundaries knowledge is also the capability to figure out what types of boundaries are discovered and how to link them together to trigger knowledge for new ways of perceiving of new things. This means that boundaries knowledge is not static, but is a dynamic, constantly changing capability. It is essential to generate boundaries knowledge for knowledge creation, and boundaries knowledge itself is the most basic element needed to converge different kinds of knowledge to create the "convergence knowledge" described in the following section (see Fig. 2.1).

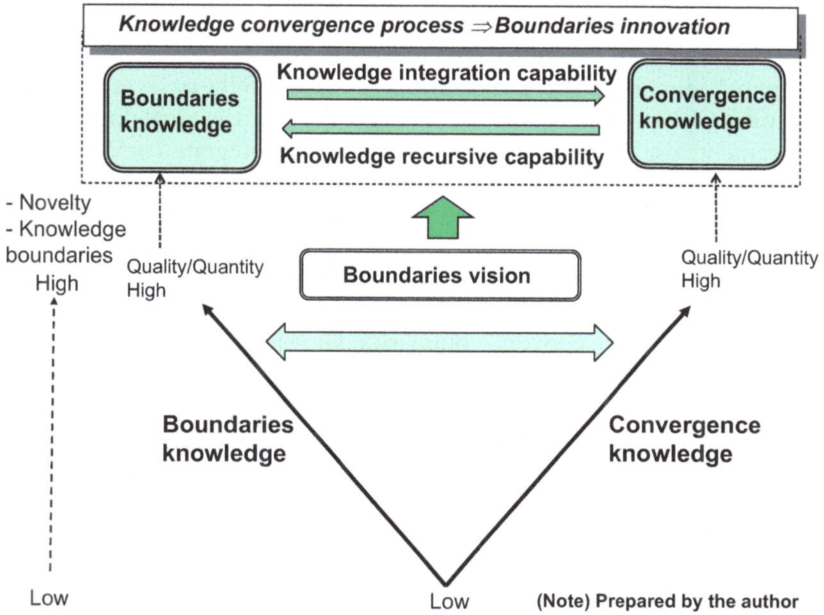

Fig. 2.1 Boundaries knowledge & convergence knowledge

(2) The Concepts of Convergence Knowledge

To succeed with innovation across different specializations, knowledge integration is a must (Klein, 1990; Kodama, 2011a, 2011b; Porter et al., 2006). New innovation happens by bringing together unique knowledge of different types of specializations in the technical convergence process (Hacklin et al., 2009; Rafols & Meyer, 2010), in other words, the knowledge convergence process can be thought of as operating on a level straddling different specialist fields. By its nature, technical convergence happens by bringing together knowledge that once belonged to separate areas of technical expertise. Therefore, to make technical convergence occur, it stands to reason that integration of knowledge from different areas of technical expertise is required.

To succeed with knowledge convergence in this way, the most important factor is the creation of the boundaries knowledge mentioned earlier. The capability to uncover (or create) new boundaries and integrate them when required (in response to condition) to create new convergence knowledge is a crucial capability (called "knowledge integration capability," discussed later). Practitioners purposefully or as a strategic objectives create convergence knowledge, and as the final knowledge achievement, use their boundaries knowledge to integrate (or converge) different and diverse knowledge (existing convergence knowledge). The author calls the capability of practitioners to converge and integrate different knowledge "convergence knowledge." In the same way as boundaries knowledge mentioned earlier, convergence knowledge is not static, but is a constantly and dynamically changing capability.

The capability to convert boundaries knowledge into convergence knowledge is called "knowledge integration capability." Knowledge integration capability is the capability to integrate different and diverse types of boundaries knowledge, and create new convergence knowledge (see Fig. 2.1). To create new convergence knowledge, practitioners have to deeply reflect on convergence knowledge once it has been generated to uncover and create new boundaries knowledge. Thus, the capability to convert convergence knowledge into boundaries knowledge is called "knowledge recursive capability." The spiral (recursive) process of creating boundaries and convergence knowledge the author calls "the knowledge convergence process," and the author describes this process in detail.

2.2.2 *The Knowledge Convergence Process*

In the knowledge economy, diverse human knowledge is the source of valuable products, services, and business models that can give a company new competitiveness. And the structures of knowledge convergence model mentioned earlier bring about new products, services, and business models that transcend various boundaries by convergence of diverse technologies, and/or convergence across different industries, and form value chains as new strategic models.

Accordingly, with respect to the knowledge held by people, groups, and organizations, companies must refresh their perspectives on business processes to create new knowledge by dynamic sharing and integrating across wide-ranging boundaries to build new business. Thus, processes that dynamically achieve knowledge convergence on the boundaries between multiple organizations and knowledge are also the most important capability factors for a company to acquire its competitiveness.

The foresight of practitioners who create these boundaries and convergence knowledge has been described as "peripheral vision" (Day & Schoemaker, 2005) or "boundaries vision" (Kodama, 2011a, 2011b). Especially, boundaries vision is the capability to obtain new insights into the multiple and diverse boundaries that exist both within and outside of companies and organizations. Boundaries vision is the ability to create boundaries and convergence knowledge, drive incremental innovation for existing business, redefine corporate boundaries, and promote radical innovation to achieve new products and business models. In this chapter, incremental and radical innovation brought about by knowledge convergence through the creation of boundaries and convergence knowledge is called "boundaries innovation."

For practitioners, an important perspective is that new boundaries and convergence knowledge is created through boundaries visions owned by individuals, groups, or organizations, and companies are sustainably achieving boundaries innovation to simultaneously grow existing business and create new markets by engaging in both incremental and radical innovation. For this reason, the spiral knowledge convergence process in which boundaries knowledge creation is converted into convergence knowledge creation needs to be embedded in and between companies and must include their customers (see Fig. 2.1).

Through the synergies between convergence and boundaries knowledge, practitioners bring together different and diverse knowledge to continually create the new knowledge needed to achieve their corporate visions and strategic objectives. This is the framework of the knowledge convergence process.

From there, boundaries innovation comes about from dynamic knowledge convergence processes that transcend the boundaries (between people, organizations, and different fields of specialization) within and outside of companies (between companies, between companies and customers, and between different industries and so forth) and it is the "strategic communities" (SCs) that originate from "Ba" mentioned later—that play the lead role in achieving the knowledge convergence process.

2.2.3 Boundaries Innovation Through Strategic Communities(SCs)

Strategic communities (SCs) rooted in "Ba," serve to uncover and create new boundaries knowledge from internal knowledge in companies and external knowledge outside companies (external partners and customers) and create convergence knowledge from these new pieces of boundaries knowledge (see Box 2.1). SCs create a range of knowledge networks—internal knowledge networks and external knowledge networks—to achieve the knowledge convergence process both in and out of companies, and with customers (boundaries knowledge creation → convergence knowledge creation).

SCs, as dynamic human and organizational networks, are organizational platforms through which practitioners drive boundaries innovation with the knowledge convergence process, while at the same time, they act as triggers that dynamically change boundaries of a corporation (its vertical or horizontal boundaries) (see Fig. 2.2).

Additionally, innovative and modest practitioners have a strong tendency to view phenomena from a perspective that transcends the

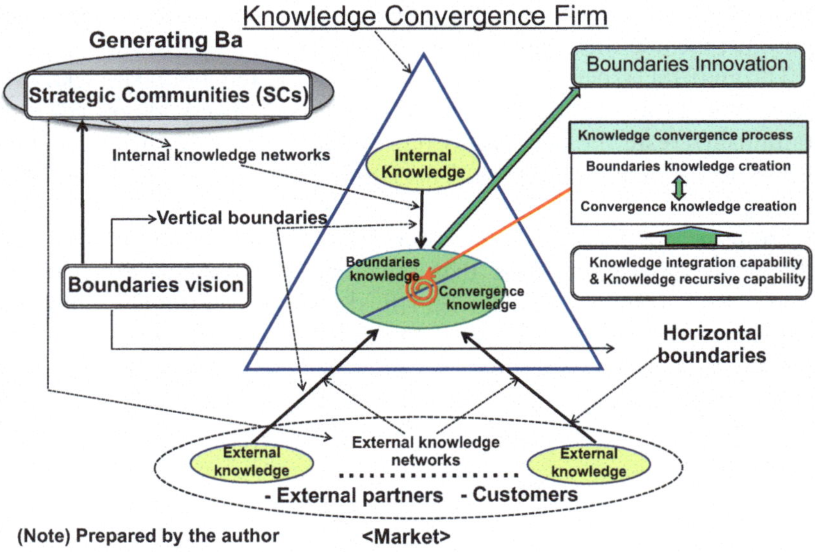

Fig. 2.2 Knowledge convergence process and boundaries innovation—Model of a Knowledge Convergence Firm

framework of different areas of specialization, functions, organizations, corporations, and industries. These people understand mental models and thinking frames different from their own, and they are not averse to absorbing and learning from unfamiliar knowledge. These innovative practitioners have a fundamental "human capability" of creating new knowledge themselves. In particular, to integrate knowledge through external knowledge convergence capabilities achieved through the demonstration of a boundaries vision, collaboration among practitioners through the formation of human networks that cross within organizations and between organizations (and between companies) is essential (e.g., Lin & Kulatilaka, 2006; Owen-Smith & Powell, 2004; Tushman, 1979). "Strategic communities (SCs)," which will be discussed later, are the organizational platform required for forming such networks (e.g., Kodama, 2001, 2002, 2003, 2005a, 2007, 2009).

SCs have characteristics of "Ba" (Nonaka & Konno, 1998; Nonaka & Takeuchi, 1995) and are defined as follows (Kodama, 2005a, p. 28).

> Strategic communities (SCs) are based on the concept of Ba as shared spaces for emerging relationships that serve as a foundation for knowledge creation. Participating in a Ba means transcending one's own limited perspective or boundary and contributing to a dynamic process of knowledge creation. In an SC, members (including customers) who possess different values and knowledge consciously and strategically create Ba in shared contexts that are always changing. New knowledge and competencies are formed by the organic merging and integration of communities to form new Ba to address multiple new eventualities. From a practical aspect, SCs are viewed as informal organizations possessing elements consistent with both the resource-based view of emergent shared-context learning and the planned strategic-based view of planning for a target market position.

Furthermore, noting that SCs have characteristics of small-world structures in network theory, Kodama (2009, p. 469) makes the following remark.

> SCs are groups forming small-world structures where practitioners in diverse specializations realize innovations aimed at solving the issues facing them and implement problem-searching and creative strategies. Short connections between nodes (people are the first unit nodes) and local clustering are features of small-world structures. For example, short paths among nodes of practitioners belonging to heterogeneous organizations

> enable easier access to other practitioners within a firm or based in other firms, including customers. Each node in a small-world structure is embedded in a local cluster. This clustering then enhances the possibility of fostering reliable accessibility. A small-world structure can be formed by either randomly rewiring a portion of an existing regular network or attaching each new node to a "neighborhood" that already exists.

In this way, SCs have characteristics of Ba or small-world structures as networks but in practice they also have characteristics of pragmatic boundaries (Carlile, 2004). For example, Kodama (2005b, p. 40) states that in actual business activities SCs play the following role.

> Boundaries. The third principle is that the SC provides pragmatic boundaries, allowing actors with different contexts to transform existing knowledge. A variety of problems or issues are posed in the pragmatic boundary, and actors need challenges that are aimed at solving these problems and issues and creating new knowledge. The actors of an organization thus require practical yet creative confrontations or conflicts and also political negotiating practice. Innovation or creativity emerges in the boundaries between the disciplines and specializations of different organizations.

On the other hand, Taifi and Passiante, who discuss new products and service development through strategic community creation, note the following in regard to the importance of the formation of SCs in the automotive sector.

> The case study provides and analyzes the structuring characteristics and success factors of an SC of after-sales services firms in the automotive sector. The study shows that it is important to have entities—more precisely SCs—dedicated to the after-sales services firms for the integration of their technical knowledge in the innovation process. The SC plays a key role, which is to contribute to the development of both the products and the services of the automaker. The chapter contributes to the literature on SCs, which is one of the most important entities of inter-organizational collaboration and innovation.

In other words, knowledge integration (convergence) through collaboration between companies is important in service innovation.

From the perspective of previous research, it can be said that SCs are organizational platforms for developing core knowledge within and outside the firm and, at the same time, for actively searching for superior knowledge in the world and achieving convergence of core knowledge within the company.

The creation of new knowledge boundaries is the setting of new corporate boundaries as corporate visions or strategic objectives for adapting to, or creating environments, and the creation of new convergence knowledge from boundaries knowledge to achieve strategies, and achieve new corporate boundaries. For a company to grow sustainably, its corporate boundaries must be dynamically redefined. In other words, that means that companies need to execute spiraling interaction of boundaries knowledge creation with convergence knowledge creation in the knowledge convergence process to grow sustainably.

It's possible to describe the knowledge convergence process in terms of corporate boundaries and the innovation models of leading research. For example, value chains in business (or business models) are decided by vertical boundaries, and the value chains determine how companies execute the knowledge convergence process by employing internal and external knowledge. Open innovation (Chesbrough, 2003) is nothing more than the knowledge convergence process, in which internal and external knowledge are coordinated to achieve new products or services as strategic objectives.

As also discussed in detail in the case studies in this chapter, as seen in P&G of the United States, the "connect & develop strategy" enables greater level of uniqueness to the company services and products through the knowledge convergence process of internal and external knowledge (Huston & Sakkab, 2006). It's also important for strong competitiveness of products and services to absorb customer competencies as external knowledge (Prahalad & Ramaswamy, 2004).

On the other hand, a company can achieve new products and services by executing knowledge convergence processes in which mainly internal knowledge of a company is coordinated and converged in closed innovation with vertical integration (e.g., Kodama, 2006) based on the company's own principles. Samsung electronics, Canon, and Fanuc are typical examples of this. However, new value chains (business models) for challenging new business domains that don't exist are determined by horizontal boundaries. How a company makes use of external knowledge is dependent on how it executes the knowledge convergence process. As discussed in detail in the case studies, Apple strategic transformation from its PC business to music distribution and smartphone businesses, or NTT

DOCOMO's participation in different fields of business are also good examples of this.

The creation of new boundaries knowledge and convergence knowledge through SCs formed along the boundaries between the diverse knowledge and organizations that exist both within and outside of companies and include customers are wellsprings that enable the achievement of boundaries innovation. The practitioners, with their micro existence in organizations, form SCs as dynamic knowledge networks intentionally or unintentionally, and it is the boundaries vision of practitioners that dynamically forms SCs and executes the spiraling knowledge convergence process. This process is the source from which boundaries innovation is born, the results of which are tied in with the capability to bring about sustainable competitiveness.

Into the future, the increasingly important perspectives for practitioners will be the formation of SCs for new strategic activity through the synergies between people across diverse boundaries regardless of whether they be individuals in real or virtual space (by utilizing ICT), and the continuous bringing together of strategic innovation capability for the creation of new boundaries knowledge and convergence knowledge. Innovation companies in the twenty-first century do not just simply seek to reduce transaction costs (e.g., Williamson, 1975) and make their operations run more efficiently, but are characterized by the creation of SCs rooted in "Ba" to continuously and spirally create new boundaries and convergence knowledge—the source of their competitiveness.

Box 2.1: Characteristics of Strategic Communities (SCs)
SCs inside and outside a company including customers create leadership (called "innovative leadership" in this chapter) for the creation of new business models across different corporate and industrial boundaries. Typical examples of communities of boundaries are the smartphone businesses of Apple and Google and the game businesses of Sony and Nintendo, and social networking services (SNS) such as Twitter and Facebook. Through the coordination and collaboration of corporate boundaries achieved through strategic partnerships and M&A across different industries, these companies have opened up completely new business domains. The various services smartphones provide such as mobile internet (such as App Store), image and music delivery, mobile commerce, position information, and telematics are typical examples of these domains

as well as the game business for DS and Wii and various services and social games provided by SNS.

In high-tech industries such as hybrid and electric cars, tooling machinery, electronics, and semiconductors, companies accumulate and update know-how and skills in areas such as marketing, R&D, production technology, and sales, and optimize the overall value chain through skillful coordination and collaboration achieved through the formation of communities of boundaries in and outside the company. SCs and multilayered networks of SCs become organizational platforms for generating new knowledge through coordination and convergence of diverse kinds of knowledge among people, within the community, and between communities. Business models that establish value chains through such SCs exist not only in the hi-tech area but also in logistics, clothing, pharmaceutical products, and financial business.

The strategy view of the dynamic formation of SCs not only has the aspect of efficient business based on a simple, horizontal division of labor, outsourcing, offshoring, and selection and concentration but also has the aspect of pursuing radical innovation in terms of creativity of products, services, and business models. In the business models of Apple and Qualcomm, close coordination and collaboration with companies are required in different specialized areas, and these companies establish a pseudo vertically integrated value chain through virtual integration. In other words, the realization of advanced, high-quality business models (such as music content and application services for Apple's iPod and iPhone) and solutions business (Qualcomm's semiconductor business) that cater to specific customer needs require finely tuned coordination and convergence of knowledge between partners including customers, and SCs and multilayered networks of SCs inevitably exist therein.

2.3 Research Method

The chapter is based on corporate research centered on field research undertaken in Europe, the United States, and Asia over a period of ten years and includes 78 companies such as Apple, Microsoft, Cisco Systems, GE, Procter & Gamble, Qualcomm, IBM, 3M, Samsung, LG, TSMC, Huawei, Virgin, Dyson, SoftBank, and NTT DOCOMO, among others. Following is an explanation of the research methodology and methods of data collection used in preparing this chapter.

We adopted a qualitative research methodology due to the need for rich data that could facilitate the generation of theoretical categories we could not derive satisfactorily from existing theory. In particular, due to the exploratory nature of this research and our interest in identifying the main people, events, activities, and influences that affect the progress of innovation, we selected the grounded theory-based study of data interpretation (Glaser & Strauss, 1967; Strauss, 1987), which was blended with the case study design and with ethnographic approaches (Locke, 2001).

The data analysis for the research consisted of three stages: (1) developing in-depth case history of a big project's activities from the raw data that I could gain all the information, (2) open coding and subsequent selective coding of the in-depth case history for the characteristics and origin of knowledge creation process, and (3) analyzing the pattern of relationships among the conceptual categories.

In the first stage of the data analysis, we constructed chronological descriptions of the project's activities with respect to knowledge convergence process, describing how it came about, when it happened, who was involved, and major outcomes. Through this work, we completed an in-depth case history of the project.

The second stage of analysis involved coding the in-depth case history with respect to its characteristics, origin, and effects. This was a highly iterative procedure that involved moving between the in-depth case history, existing theory, and the raw data (Glaser & Strauss, 1967). Data were subjected to continuous, cyclical, evolving interpretation and reinterpretation that allow patterns to emerge.

The grounded theory approach was adopted based upon the researchers' interpretation and description of phenomena based on the actors' subjective descriptions and interpretations of their experiences in a setting (Locke, 2001). This "interpretation of an interpretation" strives to provide contextual relevance (Silverman, 2000). From the in-depth case history, we initially advanced first-order descriptions based on broad categories that were developed from the existing theory, and then refined these categories by tracing patterns and consistencies (Strauss, 1987). The analysis continued with this interplay between the data and the emerging patterns until the patterns were refined into conceptual categories (Eisenhardt, 1989). The third stage of data analysis was to examine the empirical in-depth case results across the selected categories and the theoretical literature, and to develop the logic of the conceptual framework and generate new theory.

Based on the data obtained from field studies, we first produced an in-depth cases concerning the companies. Next, based on this study, we performed analyses and observations from the viewpoint of knowledge convergence process and boundaries innovation, etc. Various scholars (Eisenhardt, 1989; Pettgrew, 1990; Yin, 1994) have discussed the validity of case studies. Case studies make it possible to explain the relevance and cause-and-effect relationships of a variety of observations through deep and detailed insights with consideration given to qualitative information and subjectivity resulting from the peculiarities of individual cases and the difficulties of general analyses. Case studies not only compensate for the weaknesses of generalities but are also indispensable in new, creative theorization.

2.4 In-Depth Case Studies

2.4.1 Innovation Through Knowledge Convergence at Apple

Apple is a classic example of sustainable and successful "knowledge convergence firm." The company announced iTunes at the MacWorld Expo held in San Francisco in January of 2001, in which Steve Jobs announced the company's digital hub concept. At that time, various digital devices such as PCs, digital cameras, mobile telephones, digital audio players, and so forth were already popular. However, Jobs said that he wanted to make Macintosh the digital hub connecting these various devices.

It was this digital hub concept that later led to the innovation of the iPod, iPhone and iPad series of products and services—convergence of diverse digital devices with diverse content and applications. As well as that, the strategy transformation that Apple underwent by redefining its corporate boundaries with horizontal expansion of its Macintosh PC business into the music distribution and smartphone fields was indicative of its advanced corporate vision.

At first, Apple's iMac global hit product was not supplied with jukebox/CD burner software to handle digital music. At the time, file-sharing networks such as Napster enabled users to load CDs into their PC and share the pieces of music on them over the Internet, and consumer interest during this period was in music capabilities more so than iMac's powerful digital video editing functions. Thus, Apple had at the time failed to grasp this latent demand for music. Napster was enabling tens of millions of users to swap music over the net, and Windows had enabled users to easily copy music and burn it on CD-R, but Apple had taken no action. In later interview with Fortune magazine, Jobs said that he realized at the time that the company was about to let the music market opportunity go to waste.

Thus, the thing that triggered Apple's strategy transformation into the music distribution business was the inspiration and discoveries of the boundaries knowledge that stemmed from Steve Jobs' realization. Jobs then began to warm to the idea of an online music store blending a portable music player and contents with the iTunes developed earlier (transformation from boundaries knowledge to convergence knowledge). To this end, Jobs and his business team developed a music player with a unique and superior human interface that surpassed existing mobile music players, and thus had great ambition to do a never-before-seen great thing by seamlessly linking up this product with the already-commercialized iTunes.

Right after announcing iTunes, the executive at Apple began studying the details of the music distribution business, and they began to get hints of a potential music distribution market. And what's more, they soon realized that they would be able to take advantage of the strengths of Apple to develop this market. In other words, the Apple executives including Jobs believed that they could develop a superior portable music player if they could deploy the product development capabilities of Apple to design a much easier-to-use interface, and deal with all elements of product construction from hardware, OS, applications, software, and design. This thinking and action meant the germinated and created new boundaries knowledge leading to new convergence knowledge.

In this way, the leaders at Apple uncovered new boundaries knowledge from the dissimilar contexts and information surrounding jukebox software, portable music players, music content, Internet distribution and billing, and organically tied these types of boundaries knowledge together to create new convergence knowledge straddling the boundaries of dissimilar knowledge areas, to bring about the company's unique online music store (iTunes Music Store).

The iPod and iTunes developments were achieved through knowledge convergence of the superior product development and design capabilities and the excellent technical capabilities of leaders both in and outside of Apple—personnel spread around the globe. This resulted in the music distribution business model that seamlessly combined the iPod hardware and software technologies with the iTunes software technology. With its iPod and iTunes developments, Apple focused on non-technical aspects such as marketing and design strategies to set their product development goal, while at the same time drove the knowledge convergence process to uncover new boundaries knowledge not only from knowledge within the company, but also from external knowledge, and bring these new types of boundaries knowledge together organically to create new convergence knowledge.

Specifically, this meant Apple purchasing the rights to the sound jam MP software developed by Jeffrey Robin et al. at Casady & Greene (the development team including Robin) on which iTunes was built, software that made it easier and simpler for users to read music from CDs, and encode, replay, and manage their music. Furthermore, for its iPod development, Apple scouted for personnel with rich experience in planning and developing mobile music players. A key contributor to the iPod development was Anthony Fadell. It was his wealth of empirical knowledge that contributed greatly to the creation of iPod—a revolutionary product. Thus, it was the effects of knowledge convergence with excellent leadership brought in from outside the company that lay behind the success of iTunes and iPod.

Moreover, the iPod/iPhone/iPad business developments were characterized by multilayered networks of SCs as shared organizational platforms for these businesses. Apple mobilized the best external knowledge in the knowledge ecosystem that existed in a wide range of businesses and customers including partner companies (EMS, component development manufacturers, etc.), contents businesses (music, video, games, E books, etc.), and consumers developing diverse applications to achieve user innovation, and converged this external knowledge with Apple's own internal core knowledge (product design, marketing, and development capabilities) to achieve its new business models. The key to the success of this convergence knowledge was the formation of multilayered networks of SCs by applying strategic innovation capability across all the knowledge in Apple's ecosystem. Taking diverse knowledge from various dissimilar and dynamic contexts, Apple achieved a unique business model through close dialogue and practice across and between wide-ranging companies and industries, including customers, to accomplish its corporate vision (the digital hub concept) and strategic objectives (to create customer value with new experiences).

Apple not only expanded the vertical boundaries of its value chains upstream and downstream (from product planning, developmental designed to manufacturers sales), but also achieved dynamic expansion of its horizontal boundaries into the unfamiliar domains of the music distribution and smartphone businesses. SCs were created not only from Apple's top management centered on Jobs, but also the company was successful in creating multilayered SCs for collaboration with new product development teams (project organizations) (for iPod/iPhone/iPad) and existing organizations (line organizations), and these company-internal SCs were also networked with the multilayered SCs connecting Apple stores working as the hub for selling and marketing company's products with EMS partners focusing on manufacture, and with leading component manufacturers to create value chains with the company's business model centered on Apple. Apple also created SCs to include content providers and application developers central to the creation of these new business domains, and created value chains with new businesses centered on Apple.

It's possible to classify the multilayered SCs in Apple as follows. As well as the formation of SCs as project networks centered on the new project organizations charged with developing the new products, services, and business models of iTunes, iPod and iTunes Music Store, and so on (called "exploration SCs," discussed later), there are also SCs as line networks centered on existing organizations mainly charged with the operations management involved with launching these new businesses with a commercial base (called "exploitation SCs," discussed later). As well as those, there are also SCs between new project organizations and existing business divisions centered on leader teams that include top management centered on the Apple CEO (called "synthesis SCs," discussed later), that make decisions about important resource allocations such as investments for developing new business and personnel assignment.

These dynamic vertically and horizontally changing multilayered networks of SCs contributed greatly to Apple's execution of the knowledge convergence process (see Fig. 2.3).

2.4.2 *Innovation Through Knowledge Convergence at P&G*

Founded in 1837 and with a long, more than 170 year history, Procter & Gamble is a global household goods manufacturer with an aggregate

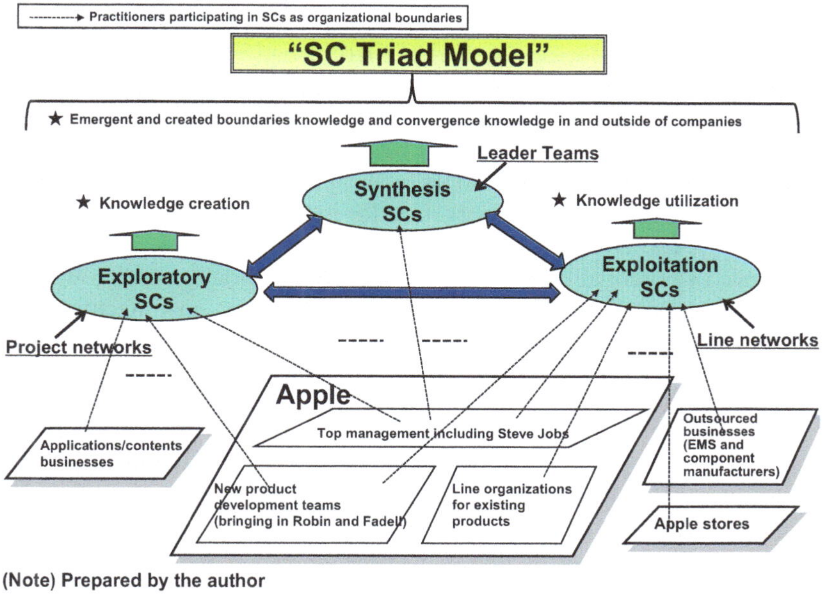

Fig. 2.3 Multilayered SCs in Apple's iPod & iTunes development

value ranking it 20th in the world. Employing around 106,000 people worldwide, the company is a global major both in terms of economic growth and health. This company has become highly distinguished by the strategy that CEO A.G Lafley introduced during the serious financial crisis that hit the company in 2000. Lafley's mantra is "consumer is boss"—he declared that all business at P&G must begin by understanding customers. Through sweeping reforms of the company's technology-biased business systems, Lafley made major achievements by doubling sales and tripling net profits in 7 years.

In particular in product development, based on its policy of realizing innovative ideas to answer the wishes of ordinary citizens, P&G remains proactive in promoting collaboration through communities that include scientists, engineers, designers, and citizens from all over the world, and crowd sourcing (contracting work to third parties of undetermined numbers), making it a groundbreaking knowledge convergence firm.

Looking back to 2000, P&G sales and profits were down since the company had lost a lot of the market share it had enjoyed with its core brands and products, and the company faced a serious financial crisis as its shares plummeted by almost 50% over six months. Before the crisis, P&G's innovation systems had been the "closed innovation" systems, in which the company depended on its own capabilities and trusted supplier network for R&D, sales, and marketing for its new products and services. Accordingly, the company didn't go out of its way to link up with the excellence of potential external partners, the technologies and know-how developed by P&G were entirely used for development, manufacture, and sales of P&G products, and the company engaged in almost no licensing of its technologies to other companies. These are the main reasons why the company was unable to respond to changing business circumstances.

Then when CEO A.G. Lafley took the helm, he set down the objectives of having half of P&G's new products created in the company's laboratories and the other half coming through P&G's labs. This strategic objective of having half of P&G's innovation sourced externally with the objective of having half of P&G's new products created in the company's laboratories and the other half of P&G's new products born through company labs was in essence a strategy to continue making effective use of staff capabilities rather than deploying 7500 of P&G's research staff outside the company.

P&G calls this novel R&D strategy "Connect + Develop." Currently, the Connect + Develop strategies lie at the base of ideas to accelerate innovation with external individuals, or in partnerships with other companies—the company applies this strategy over a wide area including product developments both within and outside of itself, and with branding (trademarks, packaging, marketing models, engineering, business services, design, and technologies).

Under the CEO's direction, the strategy is executed top down across the entire company, and specialist executives positioned. Furthermore, the company engages in new businesses as exploration activity by actively creating new specialist organizations. As a result of this, 45% of the company's product development projects have grown from innovations discovered outside the company, which has also enabled reductions in innovation costs. P&G has successfully shifted its organizational culture away from one that stuck to closed innovation and was resistant to "NIH" (Not Invented Here) innovation—innovation that was not the company's own, to "PFE" (Proudly Found Elsewhere) culture that is receptive to innovations from outside the company.

Major factors of success of P&G's strategy transformation have been the formation of SCs based on pragmatic "Ba" to share new strategic contexts, and the switch from closed innovation to the company's "Connect + Develop" open innovation strategy that uncovers and supplies knowledge assets while driving the knowledge convergence process.

SCs at P&G are created from 70 technology entrepreneurs positioned all around the globe from leadership centered on top management through the company's Connect + Develop strategy, that search out new knowledge assets all around the world and provide them to development communities within the company, while at the same time promote dynamic linking of SCs created on secure IT platforms to make available and share important technical materials, and promote the spanning of the bridges between these boundaries (both organizational and knowledge boundaries). In this way, P&G's activities greatly contribute to new knowledge convergence processes.

To make the Connect + Develop strategy work smoothly, P&G also has autonomous organizations within its organizational system. For example, P&G has a "corporate innovation fund" overseen by the CTO, and set up with the direct support of the CEO and CFO to finance high-risk ideas. The main objective of this enterprise is to provide seed money to create brand-new business and potentially bring about disruptive innovation. Moreover, the ideas funded may originate either inside or outside the company.

As well as that, the company has its "Future Works" organization—an organization characterized by its spanning of departments within the company with the objective of seeking out opportunities for innovation to bring about new kinds of consumption, and is thus charged with promoting the creation of new and novel business. This organization is not bound by existing categories, but rather aims to create new business or product categories, and thus requires discontinuous ideas to pioneer neighboring territories while spanning existing business categories. These kinds of approaches include new business models development and strategic partnerships including joint ventures needed to pioneer novel enterprises. In other words, the organizational function of Future Works is to uncover and create new boundaries knowledge, and link up the boundaries knowledge to transform it into convergence knowledge.

The individual projects carried out through Future Works are sponsored by a business unit in their early stages. Then, once the organization has verified initial concepts, the business unit takes responsibility for turning these ideas into businesses and products. This means that Future Works has to find a business unit to act as a sponsor early on, and once an idea has taken shape, that unit takes up responsibility for it.

As well as that, P&G has "New Business Development (NBD)" organizations that drive innovation within particular business units by focusing on both disruptive and incremental innovation in particular categories. Innovations that start out in NBD can be based on ideas, products, or technologies from within a business unit or can come from external resources. In some cases proposals that require supply of seed money from CIF are introduced. Most of P&G's incremental innovation is carried out within these business units.

The company also has "External Business Development (EBD)" organizations, broker-type organizations that the company uses for strategic partnering with external resources that do not conclude in a single business unit. This organization executes and supports all business units in the deal making process from seeking out external organizations through to finalizing contracts. In contrast to low-risk projects that are sent to business units by EBD, the company's Future Works mechanisms handle high-risk innovation.

It's possible to classify the multilayered SCs in P&G as follows. As well as the formation of SCs as project networks centered on the new project organizations such as Future Works, NBD, and EBD charged with developing the new businesses, products, services, and business models (called "exploration SCs," discussed later), there are also SCs as line networks centered on existing organizations mainly charged with the operations management involved with launching these new businesses with a commercial base (called "exploitation SCs," discussed later). As well as those, there are also SCs between new Future Works, NBD, and EBD project organizations and existing business divisions centered on leader teams that include top management (called "synthesis SCs," discussed later), that make decisions about important resource allocations such as investments for developing new business and personnel assignment.

The important point about this organizational system, with its organizational systems of existing business units and Future Works, NBD, and EBD mechanisms that P&G use to drive new businesses and new innovation, is it offers new knowledge about the so-called ambidextrous organization (e.g., O'Reilly & Tushman, 2004). Even with new business brought about by the company's new organizations such as Future Works, the company focuses on thoroughly scrutinizing the relationships of new business with existing business, and whether the peripheral domains or resources of existing business can be used effectively with new business. In other words, the company's Connect + Develop strategies do not only enable close contact with external resources, but also triggers enabling sufficient depth of contact between new and existing organizations, enabling developers to discover and create new boundaries knowledge and create new convergence knowledge to drive the knowledge convergence process.

2.4.3 NTT DOCOMO's Forays into Dissimilar Businesses

(1) NTT DOCOMO's Project and Line Organizations

NTT DOCOMO (DOCOMO hereinafter) is a company that leads with innovation through convergence by structuring fractal community organizations as multilayered networks of SCs that stretch across and outside of the company. Japan is a country that leads the world in mobile telephone services—it was the i-mode service provided by DOCOMO, a pioneering mobile Internet company, that was a precursor to the iPhone business model.

DOCOMO has noteworthy characteristics as an internal integrated organization. It consists of line organizations (bureaucratic organizations) that are charged with exploitation to develop existing business, and agile project organizations charged with exploration to develop new businesses on newly defined horizontal boundaries, and synthesis functions that combine these two aspects.

Project organizations specialize in service planning and developing new businesses, and make use of the existing organizational capabilities that line organizations in the company have for other related business. For example, in the case of i-mode (Kodama, 2002), it was project organizations at DOCOMO that came up with business model for the new service concept and repeatedly experimented with networks while coordinating with external software developers and content providers, while it was the line organizations with their development, technology and facilities departments that developed the mobile telephone terminals and the i-mode servers, and the sales and service department line organization that commenced sales of the new service. In other words, project organizations that are good at creating knowledge were charged with the conceptualization of new business, while the line organizations with their ability to use existing knowledge efficiently were charged with executing it. Thus, the optimization of value chains across the entire business was carried out by internal integrated organizations.

Project organizations operate in environments of uncertainty to inspire and create new boundaries knowledge for boundaries innovation based in creativity and imagination and bring about new business model concepts (new products, services, business frameworks, etc.) through trial and error. Then, project networks (exploration SCs) are formed as multilayered network SCs with strategic business partners outside the company to take up knowledge from both inside and outside the company in high-risk environments to drive radical innovation through creative strategies and the strategic practice of entrepreneurs. Individual project organizations are individual projects in network organizations (Kodama, 2003) and act autonomously and are dispersed, but business activities are always monitored by an organizational chief and the direction and objectives of business are controlled across entire project organizations. In this way, various new concepts and prototypes for new products and services are brought forth and incubated one after the other through project organizations.

Currently, DOCOMO is working toward the creation of new markets with a focus on smartphones to carve out the next i-mode "S-curve." For this, the company has optimized its vertical boundaries while simultaneously defining horizontal boundaries to push forth into new business areas. DOCOMO's "Osaifu-keitai" (wallet phone) and mobile phone credit businesses are purely the result of the company getting a foothold into the finance business through knowledge convergence. DOCOMO has also executed strategies to create new convergence knowledge as previously unseen markets by inspiring and creating new boundaries knowledge through the formation of project networks (exploration SCs) that combine dissimilar business types to enable boundaries innovation through knowledge convergence, such as the convergence of broadcasting and mobile telecommunications, automotive telematics businesses, ubiquitous businesses, new personalized and social services, as well as the company's medical and healthcare businesses, environmental and ecology businesses and businesses concerned with safety and security.

These kinds of organizational activities will continue to spread out DOCOMO's horizontal boundaries into the future, and will trigger the forging of new business models. Not only does the company optimizes its smartphone and i-mode value chains through vertical integration for its stakeholders, but also places the utmost importance on creating business ecosystems that enable win–win relationships with stakeholders by presenting new mobile business visions on its horizontal boundaries.

Practitioners go about their business in project networks mainly according to "timely time." Timely time is the subjective and quality time that human beings feel psychologically, and that enables them to achieve business development and find solutions to problems by demonstrating creativity in particular contexts by asking questions such as who, what, why, with whom, when, and how. Strategic activity processes are incorporated into project networks through timely time, the need for speed, and improvisation.

Nevertheless, business processes of facilities construction, sales, distribution and after support, and so forth are crucial for efficiently introducing, popularizing, and spreading new products and services in a timely manner. It's the line organizations and infrastructure at DOCOMO that take charge of these business processes (facilities, maintenance and sales departments, etc.). The line organizations commercialize new services with confirmed marketability following the conceptualization, marketing, trial development, and incubation processes carried out by the project networks with good timing, and drive the spiral of spreading and penetrating the market.

In line organizations, "line networks" (exploitation SCs) are created to draw up plans for high performance and efficient facilities to meet projected demand of new services, to set up new network operation systems to maintain high service quality, and to collaborate with group companies and to outsource strategically. These line networks drive efficient business process management cycles such as establishing nationwide sales, maintenance, and after-care systems.

Based in knowledge assets accumulated over many years, line organizations, as bureaucratic organizations, drive incremental innovation through the practice of improving and upgrading by forming line networks (exploitation SCs) as multilayered networks of SCs with group companies and strategic outsourcing partners. Well orchestrated strategic planning based on strategic rules is adopted by line organizations, and they proceed with routine business activities to pursue efficiency in business processes and incremental improvements and upgrades. These organizations make efforts to promptly and efficiently get results from the innovative new products and service concepts, and introduce them, spread them, and expand their markets. This also involves the linking of exploration and exploitation SCs (or the shifting of exploration SCs to exploitation SCs).

Practice in line networks in this way requires thorough productivity and efficiency. In contrast to the timely time of project networks mentioned earlier, these processes require the execution of organizational management that follows objectivity, rules, and "clock time." To convert the creativity of the project networks into the routine business of upgrades and improvements, line networks function according to clock time for planned strategic activity.

(2) **Leader Teams as Synthesis SCs**

In DOCOMO, two types of organizations (the project organizations as opposed to line organizations) and two types of multilayered network of SCs (project networks (exploration SCs) as opposed to the line networks (exploitation SCs)) exist, which are markedly different, in that one of these types deals with practice in timely time with the creatively and autonomously, whereas the other has the contrasting elements of practice in clock time with the efficiency and systematization. Thus, there is always a certain degree of conflict and friction that exists between these two types of organizations, which can inhibit integration of the knowledge of practitioners in organizations. This is because line organizations and project organizations differ in many respects such as their ways of thinking, priorities, their values systems, the degree of uncertainty that they allow, etc. However dialectical dialogue enables contradictions to be sublated through creative abrasion and productive friction, and it's the leader teams as synthesis SCs that drive this integration. At DOCOMO, leader teams are formed at all management levels (at top management levels, middle management levels, staff layers, and management teams for project organizations as well as line organizations, and informal cross-functional teams and task forces, etc.), in the executive (CEO, board members, and divisional managing directors), senior management (departmental managing directors, directors), and among other managers (managers and assistant managers) and staff.

Between DOCOMO's project and line organizations, discussions, judgments, and decision-making are performed through leader teams formed among leaders of respective task organizations, such as research, marketing, service development, sales, facilities, after support, and maintenance services, about emergent strategies, entrepreneur strategies, services based on these strategies, and the timing of execution of these strategies and services, plans, mechanisms, and resources needed to execute these. Leaders in leader teams engage in dialectical dialogue to select strategies and plans that will genuinely enable marketing innovation to flourish, which are then moved on to be executed by the innovative leadership of the company's leaders. Including the CEO and executives, leaders at all management levels collaborate through interaction of their synergy of innovative leadership, to promote dialectical dialogue, drive finely detailed planning strategies for carefully selected emergent or entrepreneurial strategies, and achieve synthesis of knowledge with strategy through the formation of multilayered networks of SCs.

Leader teams synthesize knowledge in these organizations, and take the lead in bringing about integrative network capability in SCs throughout DOCOMO. To achieve this integrative network capability in SCs, it is essential that leader teams combine and integrate the seemingly contradictory strategic methods of simultaneously being creative and planning. For these leader teams, the existence of multilayered networks of SCs is key to combining sustainable innovation with radical innovation in their innovation processes. And through the formation of fractal community organizations in which project networks are combined with line networks, leader teams combine contradictory creative and planned processes by merging the knowledge in those respective networks to bring out SCs integrative network capability across the entire company. This SCs integrative network capability creates new boundaries knowledge, and brings about convergence knowledge as new markets or environments.

As described above, the leader teams formed in DOCOMO as synthesis SCs act as contact points or hubs and nodes in network space, and driving the networking of multiple SCs outside of the company (project networks (exploration SCs) and line networks (exploitation SCs)). Networking individual SCs that have dissimilar contexts and knowledge brings about new boundaries and convergence knowledge and drives the knowledge convergence process. DOCOMO uses its boundaries vision to create new

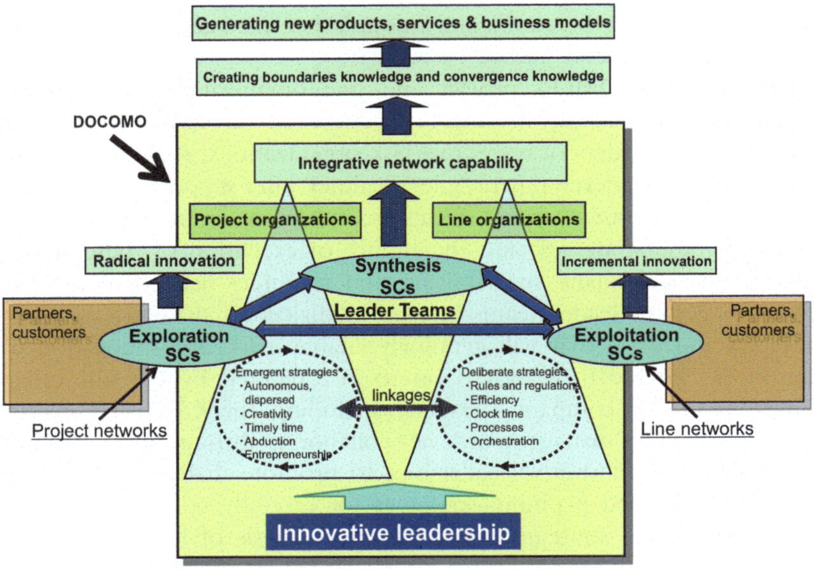

Fig. 2.4 NTT DOCOMO as knowledge convergence firm

boundaries and convergence knowledge, and creates the "SC triad model (discussed later)," which optimizes vertical and horizontal boundaries by dynamically reconfiguring multilayered networks of SCs, and thus sustainably produce boundaries innovation through knowledge convergence (see Fig. 2.4).

2.5 Discussion and Implications

2.5.1 Knowledge Convergence Firm

This chapter discussed from a micro viewpoint the context of strategies and organizations in the creation of boundaries knowledge and convergence knowledge to enable a company's sustainable generation of boundaries innovation for strategic management activities centered on innovation processes (incremental innovation and radical innovation) in a company. At present, many companies consider "knowledge" the most important element as the wellhead for maintaining an enduring competitive advantage. In the future, the knowledge convergence processes practiced by individuals, groups, and organizations inside and outside the company will form the basis of dynamic innovation activities that continually create new boundaries knowledge and convergence knowledge as well as the organizational capability for these.

The process of strategically acquiring new boundaries knowledge and convergence knowledge to generate boundaries innovation becomes an important element in acquiring dynamic organizational capability for rapidly establishing a company's market position in new markets and technologies. The "knowledge convergence firm" this chapter proposes is a new corporate model that achieves sustainable boundaries knowledge by promoting creative, productive friction among people, within the community, and among communities and by implementing knowledge convergence processes at diverse boundaries within and outside the company (see Fig. 2.2).

The driving forces of boundaries innovation in companies are the boundaries vision of people and communities, boundaries and convergence knowledge, the innovative leadership of top and middle management, and the mechanisms of practical processes that actually execute business. A company formulates and implements a dynamic strategy and achieves boundaries innovation while people and communities, the boundaries vision, boundaries knowledge and convergence knowledge, innovative leadership, and practice processes have an impact on each other. Of particular importance is the focus on constructing knowledge networks of people and organizations and the generation of boundaries innovation through the implementation of new knowledge convergence processes based on "dynamic network thinking" purposefully implemented by practitioners as the microorganisms of the company. Boundaries innovation lies in practice processes people create together and is also a form of teamwork and group game. The unofficial organizations that realize such boundaries innovation are the SCs discussed in this chapter.

Kaplan and Norton (2008) indicate that strategy and operational breakdowns are the cause of stagnating corporate results. While it is vital to have in place a management system as a strategy manual of explicit knowledge to reinforce workplace activities and forge strong links between specific strategy aims and strategic tools supporting practical corporate activities, this is not the entire essence of strategy or innovation activities. The key focus is not only innovation strategy planning but a comprehensive view including the "human system" comprising operations, technologies, and the actions and leadership of practitioners (including customers who are closely connected with the organization) working inside and outside the corporation. If the "human system" is ignored, the expectation of an outstanding management system will be pie in the sky. Strategy and innovation activities are organically living objects and really look more like "human processes." Hence, the dynamic SC formations of practitioners, and the practice processes therein are these kinds of human systems and processes.

In this regard, Jack Welch, one of the world's leading business practitioners, wrote in his book (Welch & Welch, 2005):

> I know that strategy is a living, breathing, totally dynamic game... In real life, strategy is actually very straightforward. You pick a general direction and implement like hell. If you want to win, when it comes to strategy, ponder less and do more... Obviously, everyone cares about strategy. You have to. But most managers I know see strategy as I do – an approximate course of action that you frequently revisit and redefine, according to shifting market conditions. It is an iterative process and not nearly as theoretical or life-and-death as some would have you believe.

In sum, strategy and innovation activity are dynamic practice process through the formation of SCs that involves practitioners recognizing and managing the dynamic relationships among people through daily practice, producing concepts and ideas to build new values while developing corporate visions and strategy aims through trial and error, and then reliably implementing them. Then the new value creation activities arising out of this practice process deliver superior products and services while returning general satisfaction to the community. Amid the time-axis flow running from past to future, the essence of boundaries innovation lies in dynamic practice process through the formation of SCs that continuously pursues new strategic positioning with the aims of adapting to changes in the external environment (or creating environmental change oneself), realizing the ideal shape of the company, and creating new value.

2.5.2 *Knowledge Convergence Through the SC Triad Model*

From these case studies it can be seen that in companies that generate incremental innovation (exploitation) and radical innovation (exploration), which are elements of boundaries innovation, simultaneously, and achieve knowledge convergence through the dynamic synthesis of exploration and exploitation, the SC triad model exists as multilayered networks. This chapter offers a new organizational model perspective called the "SC triad," taking cues from the characteristics of the SC triad model.

Formally structured organizations form the foundation of SCs, while SCs can be perceived as dynamic organizational forms when viewed from the perspective of practitioner behaviors. SCs and formal organizations are in mutually complementary relationships. From an element reduction process perspective, formal organizations in a company can be generally classified as project organizations, line organizations, overhead organizations, etc. If informal organizations are viewed as overlapping networks of multilayered and diverse SCs, SCs form from formalized organizations, which are also groups of people.

From this interpretation, organizations such as the new product development teams at Apple, P&G's Future Works, NBD and EBD organizations, and the project organizations at DOCOMO form exploration SCs that mainly deal with driving innovation activities that include various partner companies. Similarly, line organizations form exploitation SCs that mainly deal with driving improvement and upgrade of existing businesses that include many partner companies. Also, overhead organizations such as the top management teams at Apple, the top management team overseeing the Corporate Innovation Fund (CIF) at P&G, and the top management team at DOCOMO form synthesis SCs that make decisions to execute appropriate resource allocation across the entire company to combine both exploration and exploitation activities. In this way, project, line, and overhead formal organizations form the SC triad model through the mutual coordination and cooperation.

It's possible to interpret the SC triad model from the perspective of strategic exploration and exploitation activities, as follows—Synthesis SCs have a shared context of linking (to build and sustainably maintain value chains), and combining (to simultaneously concentrate on new business innovation and main business) exploration and exploitation. Exploration

SCs share the contexts of a focus on creative activity (e.g., radical innovation), while exploitation SCs share the contexts of focusing on business upgrades and improvement (e.g., incremental innovation).

The so-called project organizations involved in new product and business development execute new knowledge convergence processes through the formation of exploration SCs to achieve knowledge convergence as innovation. Furthermore, to bring new ideas and concepts born through activities in project organization-centered exploration SCs to fruition, new value chains are built by coordinating business processes through the formation of exploitation SCs centered on line organizations. As well as that, synthesis SCs between project and line organizations that include overhead organizations, enable building and combining value chains by linking these exploration and exploitation SCs and smoothly shifting business output through the practices in both of these SCs.

Also, incremental knowledge convergence processes are executed through the formation of exploitation SCs in line organizations to bring about product lineups, and to upgrade and improve existing products. There are also many cases where clever combination of existing knowledge assets accumulated over many years through exploitation SCs form new project organization-centered exploration SCs to drive the knowledge convergence process (Apple's new product versions are examples of this).

Furthermore, rather than engage in specific strategy executions, overhead organizations such as headquarters set down comprehensive company-wide strategies for dynamic synthesis of exploration and exploitation to set visions and strategic objectives and establish long and short-term corporate strategy for the whole company, through the formation of the SC triad model. The important mission of these organizations is to properly allocate the resources needed to set down and execute specific strategies in project and line organizations, make evaluations, and get feedback.[1]

On the other hand, in the synthesis SCs observed in the Apple, P&G, and DOCOMO cases, leader teams (LTs) are formed at all management layers (top, middle, staff) in the project, line, and overhead organizations. "Leader teams" are formed from executives (CEO, board members, divisional directors, etc.), middle management and senior staff, etc., at all management levels (these are mixed management teams formed in all project, line, and overhead organizations from top and middle management and staff layers, and informal cross-functional teams (CFTs) and task forces (TFs), sometimes including external partners).[2]

Leader teams in knowledge convergence firms turn strategically targeted projects into business by converging knowledge related to exploration and exploitation through the formation of the SC triad model. Members of leadership teams demonstrate leadership to turn corporate visions into a reality and achieve strategic objectives. At the same time, they recognize the role and value of each other's jobs through collaboration and practice where thoroughly understanding and sharing of problems and issues are promoted by dialectic dialogue through healthy mutual discussions. Moreover, leaders and managers combine wide-ranging contradictions through dialogue and practice by going back and forth between the realities and ideas of top management and frontend staff in the workplace.

In analyzing Apple, P&G, and DOCOMO's organizational systems and strategies from the perspective of the knowledge convergence process, the multilayered SCs networks as the SC triad model are due to the existence of the Ba triad model. The Ba triad model was presented from case studies of the leading companies and organizations of Toyota, Fujifilm, and Apple, as "dynamic fractal organizations for promoting knowledge-based transformation"—a new paradigm for organizational theory" of Nonaka et al. (2014). For example, the case of the Prius new product development at Toyota was a radical innovation (exploration) involving the convergence of a wide range of technologies and required incremental innovation (exploitation) to continually upgrade and improve this new product, which is a dynamic synthesis of exploration and exploitation. For these reasons, Toyota's various project teams and existing line organizations had to form multilayered networked Ba both horizontally and vertically within and between organizations to simultaneously pursue the creation and utilization of knowledge.

What draws attention in this case, is that Ba to drive exploration activities for the knowledge creativity of radical innovation (called exploration Ba) are responsible for processes to share tacit knowledge and convert it to explicit knowledge, while in contrast, Ba that drive exploitation activities to commercialize the products a continually upgrade and improve commercialized products with knowledge efficiency (called exploitation Ba) are responsible for processes of synthesis of explicit knowledge, and internalization through personal experience. In other words, exploration

Ba strongly leaned toward tacit knowledge and exploitation Ba strongly leaned toward explicit knowledge. Nevertheless, both tacit knowledge and explicit knowledge are intrinsically linked in the spirals synthesis of the third type of knowledge, practical knowledge (phronesis) (Nonaka's so-called SECI process). Driving this spiral process to simultaneously achieve the creation and accumulation of knowledge is the "synthesis Ba." In actual fact, Teece (2014) sites dynamic capabilities as complementary to "phronetic" leadership (Nonaka & Toyama, 2007), where is in contrast, phronesis is in the background of source factors of knowledge convergence that manages different knowledge characteristics at the same time in simultaneous pursuit of exploration and exploitation (see Fig. 2.5).

Hence, synthesis Ba which dynamically synthesize exploration Ba and exploitation Ba are mutually connected, which forms the Ba triad model. Then, the Ba triad model also brings about the SC triad model which is multilayered network of SCs with characteristics of Ba. Accordingly, since the Ba triad model forms the basis for the SCs tried model, the SCs tried

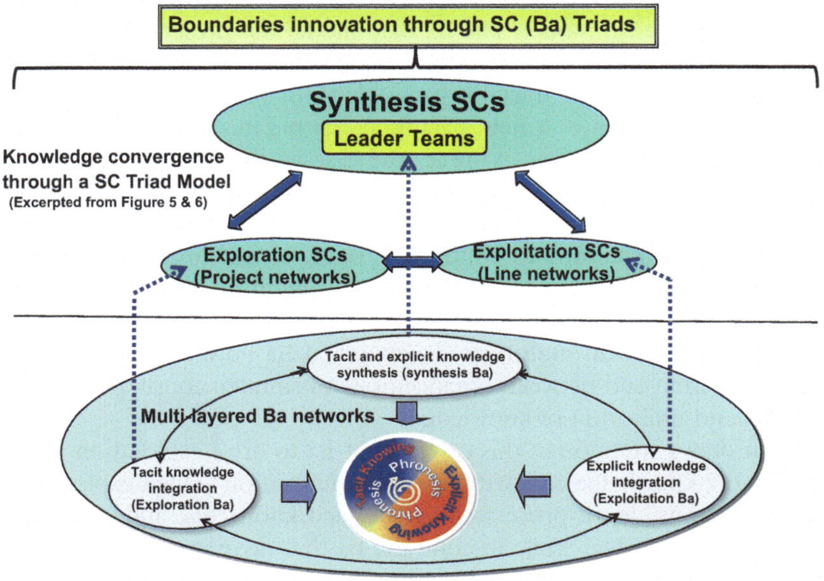

Source: Excerpted from Figure 4, Nonaka, et al. (2014)

Fig. 2.5 Boundaries innovation based on a Ba and SC triad model

model is also a framework to achieve knowledge convergence process (see Fig. 2.5).

Thus, the author offers the following new perspectives on the similarities of the SC triad model with the "ambidextrous organization" (O'Reilly & Tushman, 2004; Tushman & O'Reilley, 1997). In ambidextrous organizations, it's asserted that clear strategic objectives are set down for new business development organizations and organizations developing existing business, and the interaction between these organizations is heavily restricted at the operational level while upper management is responsible for both. In contrast, in the SCs triad model, close collaboration and interaction of exploration SCs consisting of project networks aiming to pursue new R&D and build new business development, and exploitation SCs consisting of line networks that continually improve and upgrade commercialized products and services are driven by synthesis SCs centered around leader teams. Practitioners at levels of management (top, middle, and staff) drive smooth shifting between the domains with the SC triad model and combine exploration and exploitation. This perspective also contributes a new theoretical framework for the ambidextrous organization.

At Apple, P&G, and DOCOMO, leader teams synthesize the knowledge of these organizations (project networks & line networks), and play the role of bringing about boundaries innovation by knowledge convergence process throughout the entire company. To achieve knowledge convergence process, it's important that leader teams simultaneously combine and synthesize the apparently contradictory creative and planned strategic methods. Thus, for leader teams, the configuration of the SC triad model to combine both incremental and radical innovation is key.

From the perspective of network theory, (e.g., Barabasi, 2002; Watts, 2003) the leader teams as synthesis SCs formed internally in Apple, P&G, and DOCOMO act as hubs and nodes in network space (in other words connections), and act to network multiple SCs both inside and outside of the company, and configure the SC triad model with project networks (exploration SCs) and line networks (exploitation SCs). Then, the new contexts and knowledge that are brought about through the SC triad model promotes boundaries innovation (see Fig. 2.5).

2.5.3 *The SC Triad Model for Combining Exploration and Exploitation*

Much of the leading research to date has discussed how organizations charged with radical innovation (e.g., Leifer et al., 2000) in a company should be physically and culturally separated from the existing organizations (or line or mainstream organizations), or set up as independent venture organizations (e.g., Benner & Tushman, 2003; Burgelman & Sayles, 1986; Hill & Rothaermel, 2003; Kanter, 1985). Also, most of the discussion on observations of the 2 archetypes of exploration and exploitation, or of incremental or radical innovation (e.g., Greenwood & Hinings, 1993; Tushman & O'Reilly, 1997), or on the ambidextrous organization (e.g., O'Reilly & Tushman, 2004), has dealt with structural and functional aspects of managerial processes, or how organizational structures should be applied.

Regarding this, this chapter presents the characteristics of the "SC triad model" as a new organizational form to achieve sustainable knowledge convergence process by enabling dynamic synthesis of exploration and exploitation through the formation of SCs. The SC triad model is structured not only in order to combine both exploration and exploitation in the establishment and execution of corporate strategy, but are also configured as organizations (leaders and managers) that demonstrate strategic innovation capability to propel the dynamic view of strategy that brings about synergies between dissimilar or similar types of exploration and exploitation, that shifts from exploration to exploitation, that shifts back from exploration to exploitation, and that brings about synergies between exploration and exploitation. This dynamic view of strategy ensures growth by combining both the dissimilar modes of exploration and exploitation, not only in the short but also in the long term (e.g., Benner & Tushman, 2003; March, 1991; Tushman & O'Reilly, 1997).

Exploration and exploitation are not dichotomous strategic activities. It is necessary to strike a clever balance between these strategic activities in corporations and execute these two strategies in a way in which they complement each other (He & Wong, 2004). Accordingly, the SCs triad model, which brings about boundaries innovation in knowledge convergence firms as strategy across multiple projects and in line organizations that are smoothly and dynamically linked through the activities of overhead organizations or leadership teams, and in which synergies between strategies are uncovered, is a candidate for a new organizational model.

In addition, close collaboration between multiple organizations structured as the SC triad model and organic collaboration with customers and partners in business environments as knowledge ecosystems is a requisite part of the dynamic view of strategy, and it is the dynamic configuration of multilayered networked SCs with the SC triad model that achieves this kind of diverse collaboration.

2.6 Conclusion

This chapter has considered the important strategic management themes of exploration and exploitation and related issues from the perspective of organizational theory, and has described the SC triad model as a new organizational model for achieving boundaries innovation through the sustainable knowledge convergence process. A common organizational activity in companies that achieve the boundaries innovation needed to sustainably and dynamically synthesize exploration and exploitation is the formation of multilayered networked SCs with the SCs triad model. The SC triad model converges the different knowledge necessary for the strategic activities of exploration and exploitation, and achieves a robust SC triad model that can respond to changing business environments and create new business environments.

The ability to configure the SC triad model brings about boundaries innovation, and is a driving force that can create new business models by advancing new rules and synthesizing dissimilar technologies through dynamic knowledge convergence of internal and external knowledge. Therefore, the practical implications of this are that companies aiming for sustainable growth must consciously create multilayered networked SCs based on the SC triad model within and between all kinds of organizations, and both within and outside of themselves, as knowledge convergence firms.

Notes

1. Arker (2011) indicated the necessity to simultaneously consider the distinctly different aspects of "dynamic strategic commitment" to drive the "exploitation" activities of incremental innovation, "selective opportunism" to drive the "exploration" activities of radical innovation, as well as "centralized resource allocation" capabilities required to execute those activities appropriately. The establishment

of the SC triad model through overhead organizations indicated in this chapter can achieve the three conditions cited by Arker (2011).

2. Even in leading research on ambidextrous organizations, the importance of leader-centric or team-centric team structures has been indicated, in order to manage the paradoxical strategies of exploration and exploitation (Smith et al., 2010). Here, top management and senior leaders play the central role in combining paradoxical strategies, but the role or influence of middle management and below, and of the whole organization itself were not clarified (Christensen & Raynor, 2003; Smith et al., 2010).

References

Arker, D.(2011). *Brand relevance: Making competitors irrelevant*. Jossey-Bass.

Barabasi, A. (2002). *Linked: The new science of networks*. Perseus Books Group.

Benner, M., & Tushman, M. (2003). Exploitation, exploration, and process management: The productivity dilemma revisited. *Academy of Management Review, 28*(2), 238–256.

Burgelman, R., & Sayles, R. (1986). *Inside corporate innovation: Strategy, structure, and managerial skills*. Free Press.

Carlile, P. (2004). Transferring, translating, and transforming: An integrative framework for managing knowledge across boundaries. *Organization Science, 15*(5), 555–568.

Chesbrough, H. (2003). *Open innovation*. Harvard Business School Press.

Christensen, C. M., & Raynor, M. (2003). *The innovator's solution*. Harvard Business School Press.

Day, G., & Schoemaker, J. (2005). Scanning the periphery. *Harvard Business Review*, 135–148.

Eisenhardt, K. (1989). Building theories from case study research. *Academy of Management Review, 14*, 532–550.

Gawer, A., & Cusmano, M. A. (2004). *Platform leadership*. Harvard Business School Publishing.

Glaser, B., & Strauss, A. (1967). *The discovery of grounded theory: Strategies for qualitative research*. Aldine.

Greenwood, R., & Hinings, C. (1993). Understanding strategic change: The contribution of archetypes. *Academy of Management Review, 36*(5), 1052–1081.

Hacklin, F., Marxt, C., & Fahrni, F. (2009). Coevolutionary cycles of convergence: An extrapolation from the ICT industry. *Technological Forecasting and Social Change, 76*(6), 723–736.

Hamel, G., & Prahalad, C. K. (1994). *Competing for the future*. Harvard Business School Press.

He, Z., & Wong, P. (2004). Exploration vs. exploitation: An Empirical test of the ambidexterity hypothesis. *Organization Science, 15*(4), 481–494.

Hill, C., & Rothaermel, F. (2003). The performance of incumbent firms in the face of radical technological innovation. *Academy of Management Review, 28*(2), 257–247.

Huston, L., & Sakkab, N. (2006). Connect and develop inside procter & gamble's new model for innovation. *Harvard Business Review, 84*(3), 58–66.

Iansiti, M., & Levien, R. (2004). *The keystone advantage: What the new dynamics of business ecosystems mean for strategy, innovation, and sustainability*. Harvard Business School Press.

Kaplan, R., & Norton, D. (2008). Mastering the management system. *Harvard Business Review, 86*(1), 62–77.

Klein, J. T. (1990). *Interdisciplinarity: History, theory, and practice* (1st ed.). Wayne State University Press.

Kim, W. C., & Mauborgne, R. (2005). *Blue ocean strategy*. Harvard Business School Publishing.

Kodama, M. (2001). Creating new business through strategic community management. *International Journal of Human Resource Management, 11*(6), 1062–1084.

Kodama, M. (2002). Transforming an old economy company through strategic communities. *Long Range Planning, 35*(4), 349–365.

Kodama, M. (2003). Strategic innovation in traditional big business. *Organization Studies, 24*(2), 235–268.

Kodama, M. (2005a). Knowledge creation through networked strategic communities: Case studies in new product development. *Long Range Planning, 38*(1), 27–49.

Kodama, M. (2005b). How two Japanese high-tech companies achieved rapid innovation via strategic community networks. *Strategy & Leadership, 33*(6), 39–47.

Kodama, M. (2006). Innovation through boundary managing—Case of Matsushita Electric reforms. *Technovation, 27*(1–2), 15–29.

Kodama, M. (2007). *The strategic community-based firm*. Palgrave Macmillan.

Kodama, M. (2009). Boundaries innovation and knowledge integration in the Japanese firm. *Long Range Planning, 42*(4), 463–494.

Kodama, M. (2011a). *Knowledge integration dynamics—Developing strategic innovation capability*. World Scientific Publishing.

Kodama, M. (2011b). *Interactive business communities—Accelerating corporate innovation through boundary networks*. Gower Publishing.

Leifer, R., McDermott, M., O'Connor, C., Peters, S., Rice, M., & Veryzer, W. (2000). *Radical innovation: How mature companies can outsmart upstarts*. Harvard Business School Press.

Leonard-Barton, D. (1995). *Wellsprings of knowledge: Building and sustaining the sources of innovation*. Harvard Business School Press.

Lin, L., & Kulatilaka, N. (2006). Network effects and technology licensing with fixed fee, royalty, and hybrid contracts. *Journal of Management Information Systems, 23*(2), 91–118.

Locke, K. (2001). *Grounded theory in management research*. Sage.

March, J. (1972). Model bias in social action. *Review of Educational Research, 42*(4), 413–429.

March, J. (1991). Exploration and exploitation in organizational learning. *Organization Science, 2*(1), 71–87.

Moore, J. (1993). Predators and prey: A new ecology of competition. *Harvard Business Review, 71*(3), 75–86.

Nonaka, I., & Konno, N. (1998). The concept of "ba": Building a foundation for knowledge creation. *California Management Review, 40*(3), 40–54.

Nonaka, I., & Takeuchi, H. (1995). *The knowledge-creating company*. Oxford University Press.

Nonaka, I., & Toyama, R. (2007). Strategic management as distributed practical wisdom (phronesis). *Industrial and corporate change, 16*(3), 371–394.

Nonaka, I., Kodama, M., Hirose, A., & Kohlbacher, F. (2014). Dynamic fractal organizations for promoting knowledge-based transformation—A new paradigm for organizational theory. *European Management Journal, 32*(1), 137–146.

Owen-Smith, J., & Powell, W. W. (2004). Knowledge networks as channels and conduits: The effects of spillovers in the Boston biotechnology community. *Organization Science, 15*(1), 5–22.

O'Reilly III, C., & Tushman, M. (2004, April). The ambidextrous organization. *Harvard Business Review, 82*, 74–82.

Pettigrew, A. M. (1990). Longitudinal field research on change: Theory and practice. *Organization Science, 1*(1), 267–292.

Porter, A. L., Roessner, J. D., Cohen, A. S., & Perreault, M. (2006). Interdisciplinary research: Meaning, metrics and nurture. *Research Evaluation, 15*(3), 187–195.

Prahalad, C. K., & Ramaswamy, V. (2004). *The future of competition: Co-creating unique value with customers*. Harvard Business School Press.

Rafols, I., & Meyer, M. (2010). Diversity and network coherence as indicators of interdisciplinarity: Case studies in bionanoscience. *Scientometrics, 82*(2), 263–287.

Rosenkopf, L., & Nerkar, A. (2001). Beyond local search: Boundary-spanning, exploration, and impact in the optical disk industry. *Strategic Management Journal, 22*(4), 287–306.

Silverman, D. (2000). *Doing qualitative research*. Sage.

Smith, W., Binns, A., & Tushman, M. (2010). Complex business models: Managing strategic paradoxes simultaneously. *Long Range Planning, 43*(2–3), 448–461.

Strauss, A. (1987). *Qualitative analysis for social scientists*. Cambridge University Press.

Teece, D. J. (2014). The foundations of enterprise performance: Dynamic and ordinary capabilities in an (economic) theory of firms. *Academy of Management Perspectives, 28*(4), 328–352.

Tushman, M. (1979). Work characteristics and subunit communication structure: A contingency analysis. *Administrative Science Quarterly, 24*(1), 82–98.

Tushman, M. L., & O'Reilly, C. A. (1997). *Winning through innovation*. Harvard Business School Press.

van Rijnsoever, F. J., & Hessels, L. K. (2011). Factors associated with disciplinary and interdisciplinary research collaboration. *Research Policy, 40*(3), 463–472.

Watts, J. (2003). *Six degrees: The science of a connected age*. W.W. Norton and Company.

Welch, J., & Welch, S. (2005). *Winning*. Harper Business.

Williamson, O. E. (1975). *Markets and hierarchies: Analysis and antitrust implications*. Free Press.

Yin, R. K. (1994). *Case study research: Design and methods* (2nd ed.). Sage.

Zook, K. (2003). *Beyond the core: Expand your market without abandoning your roots*. Harvard Business School Press.

Zook, C., & Allen, C. (2001). *Profit from the core: Growth strategy in an era of turbulence*. Harvard Business School Press.

CHAPTER 3

Creating Dynamic Fractal Organization Through Collective Phronesis by Apple

3.1 Creating Collective Phronesis, Boundaries Knowledge and Convergence Knowledge Across Boundaries

The factor that achieves innovation in response to convergence is the collective phronesis described in Chapter 2. The root of creation of collective phronesis requires the practical wisdom (phronesis) (Nonaka et al., 2008) demonstrated by practitioners which must be acquired and fostered organizationally. Collective phronesis promotes the formation by practitioners of multilayered networks of Ba within and across companies including customers. Therefore, the creation of boundaries knowledge is crucial to the way that practitioners form or uncover Ba and bridge them (Kodama, 2019, 2020). Diverse boundaries exist between wide-ranging things and phenomena. Knowledge boundaries also exist between areas of specialization of individual people.[1] In other words, foreign content and unique differences exist on these boundaries. Boundaries knowledge is the wisdom to uncover such foreignness and dissimilarities, and is also the wisdom to be able to determine what type of boundaries to uncover, and how to link them together to inspire new knowledge.

The capability of practitioners to bring about boundaries knowledge is their boundaries vision (Kodama, 2019; Kodama & Shibata, 2016). The collective phronesis of practitioners brings about boundaries knowledge, and generates convergence knowledge for convergence. Convergence

M. Kodama, *Developing Knowledge Convergence Through Collective Phronesis*, https://doi.org/10.1007/978-981-96-4403-2_3

knowledge is the result of the creation of boundaries knowledge (tacit and explicit knowledge uncovered in the dissimilarities and differences on boundaries), and is knowledge born as a result of dissimilar knowledge fused (synthesized) to achieve the ideals and beliefs of practitioners. Collective phronesis triggers, inspires, and creates the boundaries knowledge and convergence knowledge of practitioners—knowledge creation not only required by elites such as top management, but also by many middle managers and staff members.

Practitioners demonstrate boundaries vision through collective phronesis based in phronesis to create new boundaries knowledge. Moreover, through Ba synthesizing capabilities, collective phronesis creates multilayered networks of Ba to synthesize diverse dynamic contexts. Practitioners know what to do for the common good, have high aspirations, determine what is good for society as a whole, and through multilayered networks of Ba, build the knowledge creation company model (Nonaka & Toyama, 2005) to organically tie together the individual elements of their knowledge visions, driving objectives, dialogue and practice, SECI, knowledge assets and environments to generate convergence knowledge as convergence (see Fig. 3.1).

This paper presents elements of the collective phronesis for the creation of convergence knowledge as convergence by the practical knowledge (or practical wisdom) of practitioners. Superior collective phronesis entails the use of boundaries vision to inspire and create boundaries knowledge, and Ba synthesizing capabilities to dynamically form the multilayered networks of Ba required for the creation of convergence knowledge. From an in-depth case study of the high-tech company such as Apple, this chapter analyzes and discusses knowledge creating companies that continuously bring about boundaries knowledge and convergence knowledge as sustainable innovation communities. The chapter identifies that knowledge creating companies drive collective phronesis to combine various contradictions both inside and outside of themselves, to dynamically configure and reconfigure multilayered networks of Ba through their Ba synthesizing capabilities to achieve boundaries innovation.

This chapter is organized as follows. First, while reviewing a series of major studies on Nonaka theory (e.g., Nonaka & Takeuchi, 1995, 2019; Nonaka et al., 2008), the following points are provided as the core

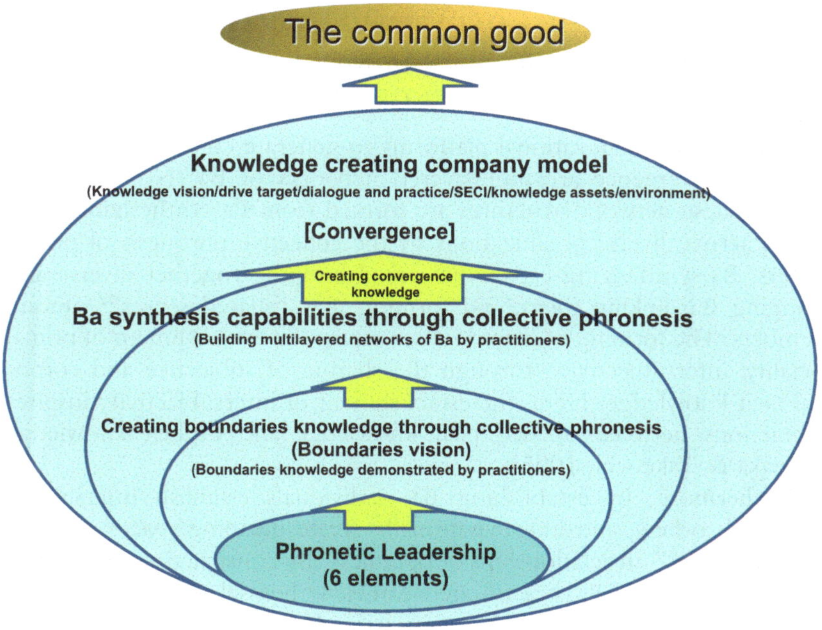

(Note) Prepared by the author

Fig. 3.1 Framework for knowledge creation through convergence

frame of this chapter through a case study of Apple Inc. in the United States. The first point is in the conceptual frame of creating boundaries knowledge and convergence knowledge. The second point is the process of creating boundaries knowledge and convergence knowledge through collective phronesis. Furthermore, a model of dynamic fractal organization based on Ba triad and knowledge triad relationships is derived. Finally, as a summary of this chapter, some insights obtained through the case studies and future research issues related to the "construction of an innovation community model for convergence" are discussed.

3.2 The Conceptual Framework for Creating Boundaries Knowledge and Convergence Knowledge

The intangible organizational platforms to generate convergence knowledge as convergence are multilayered networks of Ba (Nonaka et al., 2000). These network structures are formed from Ba synthesizing capabilities across diverse organizations by the collective phronesis of practitioners. Ba synthesizing capabilities entail bringing together diverse and changing Ba, linking them, and forming new "shared senses"[2] among members. The forming of shared senses means the establishment of primal sociality, intersubjectivity, through the sharing of subjective and corporeal tacit knowledge. Here, the establishment of intersubjectivity inspires interactions between opened tacit knowledge and explicit knowledge (Nonaka & Takeuchi, 1995).

Furthermore, by establishing Ba, individuals establish intersubjectivity with others, and improvisationally create meaning spaces as "self-transcendence"[3] in relationships of openness. By constructing new multilayered networks of Ba, practitioners can view themselves from inside the world (e.g., their profession or position) and also view themselves from the higher or different perspectives from the outside (e.g., the professional field or position of another person) at the same time. Building multilayered networks of Ba and committing to them leads to transcendence of one's own limited views or boundaries (in other words knowledge) by the sharing of diverse contexts. This process is required in the creation of convergence knowledge through convergence, and is the capability to synthesize dissimilar contexts and knowledge.

Also, in the creation of convergence knowledge through convergence, "self organization"[4] to balance independence of individuals with the independence of the whole is required. If multilayered networks of Ba are perceived vertically (e.g., from upstream to downstream on the value chain, from the top management level down to the lower layers) or horizontally (e.g., between different business domains, networks between different types of business, etc.) as evolving knowledge platforms deployed both vertically and horizontally, self-organizing multilayered networks of Ba enable the dynamic combination of both creativity and efficiency to respond with agility and achieve innovation creating convergence knowledge through convergence.

Ba architect (design) capabilities to discover or create Ba and connect them require practitioners' boundaries vision not only to inspire and create boundaries knowledge by bridging the boundaries between different organizations and forming new Ba but also to uncover boundaries knowledge between Ba (Kodama, 2019, 2020). For practitioners to acquire boundaries vision, phronetic leadership for the demonstration of phronesis is required. The six capabilities of practitioners' phronetic leadership (Nonaka et al., 2008) promote the recognition, discovery, exploration, and creation of boundaries knowledge through collective phronesis. Moreover, Ba synthesizing capabilities through collective phronesis inspires the building of multilayered networks of Ba which leads to the creation of convergence knowledge from the creation of boundaries knowledge.

New, dynamically formed multilayered networks of Ba are the existential spaces where the SECI process actually takes place. Knowledge creating companies consist of the seven elements of a "knowledge vision" based on absolute values, which gives SECI direction and are the power source driving SECI, "driving objectives" for specific value creation, "new convergence knowledge creation through the SECI process" expressed in the close interactions of "dialogue" and "practice" across different types of business and diverse corporations, the SECI process inputs and outputs of "knowledge assets" (resources and know-how), and the "environments" as the knowledge ecosystems of various stakeholders and different business types, which are multilayered networks of Ba, and aggregations of Ba (Nonaka et al., 2008). Practitioners then repeatedly engage in dialogue and practice and interconvert tacit knowledge and explicit knowledge (SECI) to synthesize dissimilar knowledge from multiple layers of dynamic contexts to create new convergence knowledge as convergence to achieve their shared knowledge visions and driving objectives (see Fig. 3.2).

3.2.1 Convergence Innovation by Apple

Apple is a classic example of a knowledge creating company that sustainably brings about convergence knowledge through convergence. In January of 2001, Apple announced iTunes at the MacWorld Expo held in San Francisco, and Steve Jobs announced the company's digital hub strategy. At that time, various digital devices such as PCs, digital cameras, mobile telephones, digital audio players, and so forth were already

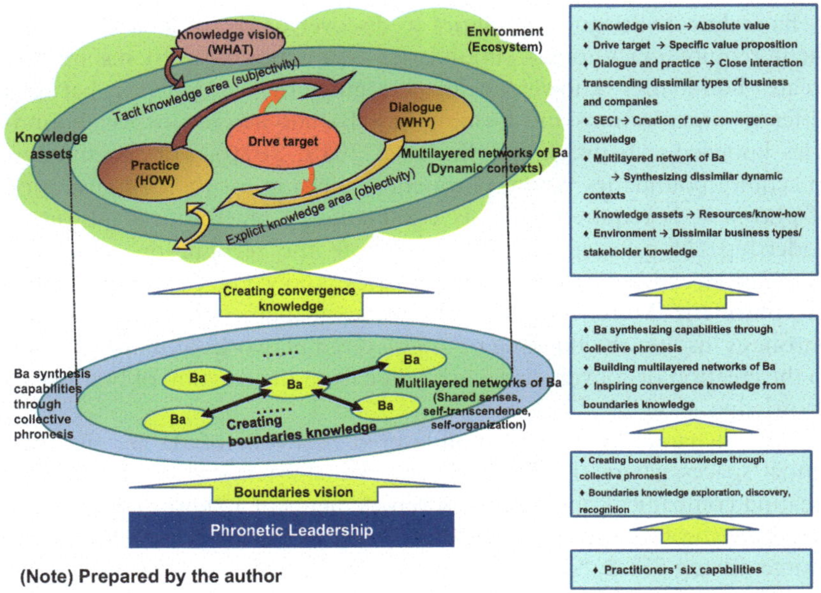

Fig. 3.2 Conceptual framework for creating boundaries and convergence knowledge

popular. However, Jobs said that he wanted to make Macintosh the digital hub connecting these various devices. It was this digital hub concept that later led to the innovation of the iPod, iPhone, and iPad products that converged diverse digital devices, content, and applications. Meanwhile, Apple's redefinition of its corporate boundaries with horizontal expansion of its Macintosh PC into the music distribution and smartphone fields was indicative of its advanced knowledge vision for its strategy transformation.

At first, Apple's hit iMac product was not supplied with the jukebox CD burner[5] software to handle digital music. At the time, file-sharing networks such as Napster enabled users to load CDs into their PC and share tunes on the Internet. Consumer interest during this period was in music, more so than the iMac's powerful digital video editing functions. Thus, Apple had at the time failed to grasp the latent demand for music. Using Napster enabled tens of millions of users to swap music over the net, and Windows enabled users to easily copy music and burn it onto CD-R, but Apple had taken no action. In later interview with Fortune magazine, Jobs said he had realized that the company was about to let the music market opportunity go to waste.

The trigger for Apple's strategy transformation into the music distribution business was Jobs' awareness. Jobs was warming to the idea of an online music store that brought together portable music players and content through iTunes, which had already been developed. Jobs and his business team had big ambitions to accomplish a great thing that nobody else had ever achieved by developing a music player with a unique and superior human interface that surpassed existing mobile music players, and seamlessly linking up the product with the already-commercialized iTunes.

Right after announcing iTunes, the executive at Apple began studying the details of the music distribution business, and sensed the latent existence of the music distribution market. This is where they could use Apple's strength. In other words, the Apple executives including Jobs believed that they could develop a superior portable music player if they could deploy the product development capabilities of Apple to deal with all elements of product construction—an interface that was much easier to use, hardware, OS, applications, software, and design. In this way, the practitioners at Apple uncovered new boundaries knowledge from the dissimilar contexts and information of the jukebox software, portable music players, music content, Internet distribution and billing, and organically tied these pieces of boundaries knowledge together to create the company's unique online music store (iTunes Store) as new convergence knowledge straddling the boundaries of dissimilar knowledge.

In this, iPod and iTunes were achieved through the synthesis of the product development and design capabilities of practitioners in and out of Apple and technical capabilities spread around the globe. This was the music distribution business model that seamlessly linked the iPod hardware and software technologies with the iTunes software technologies. With its iPod and iTunes developments, Apple established its product development theme while focusing on non-technical aspects such as marketing and design strategies while using collective phronesis by proactively absorbing and synthesizing not only knowledge from within itself, but also knowledge from outside the company.

Specifically, this meant Apple purchasing the rights to the Sound Jam MP software developed by Jeffrey Robin et al. at Casady & Greene (the development team including Robin) to achieve iTunes, software based on Sound Jam MP that made it simpler and more friendly for users to read music from CDs, and encode, replay, and manage their music. For its iPod development, Apple scouted for personnel with rich experience in planning and developing mobile music players. Among these, a key person was Antony Fadell who later made a huge contribution to the iPod development. His experiential knowledge contributed greatly to the creation of iPod—a revolutionary product. Thus, it was the major impact of the collective phronesis of practitioners from outside the company that lay behind the success of iTunes and iPod. And Jobs, as CEO, drove the development of iTunes and the iPod toward the realization of a product concept that pursued creativity. At the same time, the iPod development project team took the lead in pursuing thorough efficiency through intense collaboration with existing functional organizations within the company.

Another point worthy of mention is the existing product development processes at Apple until then were for the most part based on a closed innovation model (Kodama, 2011) of vertical integration as exemplified by the development of the Mac, for example. In the music delivery business, however, rather than R&D-driven closed innovation led by an internal organization, Apple focused on promoting open innovation (Chesbrough, 2003) that aggressively imported superior external knowledge. O'Connor insists that radical innovation must be open innovation, and case studies of U.S. firms indicate that an open innovation approach facilitates radical innovation. The strategy for developing technology for Apple's iTunes and iPod at the time was close to that approach.

The iPod/iPhone/iPad business developments were characterized by multilayered networks of Ba as shared organizational platforms for these businesses. Apple mobilized the best external knowledge in the knowledge ecosystem consisting of a wide range of businesses and customers including partner companies (EMS, component development manufacturers, etc.), contents businesses (music, video, games, books, etc.), and consumers as application developers achieving user innovation, and synthesized this external knowledge with the company's own internal core knowledge (its product design, marketing, and development capabilities) to achieve its new business model. The key to the achievement of this convergence knowledge was the formation of multilayered networks through Ba synthesizing capabilities across the knowledge ecosystem around Apple. Using diverse knowledge from such varied dissimilar and dynamic contexts, Apple achieved a unique business model through close dialogue and practice across and between wide-ranging companies, including customers, to accomplish its knowledge vision (the digital hub concept) and driving objective (to create customer value as new experiences).

Rather than only expand the vertical boundaries of its Apple-centered value chains upstream and downstream (from product planning, development design through to manufacturer and sales), Apple achieved dynamic expansion of its horizontal boundaries into the unfamiliar domains of the smartphone and music distribution businesses. In Apple, hypertext organizations (discussed later) functioned for new product development, and as well as the management top team Ba centered on jobs, multilayered Ba for collaboration between existing organizations (line organizations) and the new product development teams (project organizations) (iPod/iPhone/iPad) were configured. These multiple in-house Ba were also networked as multilayered Ba with Apple stores, the sales and marketing hubs of Apple products, Ba with EMSs at the core of manufacturing, and Ba with capable component manufacturers to create the value chain for Apple-centered business model. In the formation of its new business domains, Apple also formed Ba as communities of Apple and core partners including content providers and application developers to create its new business value chains. As discussed above, these dynamically changing vertical and horizontal multilayered networks of Ba contributed greatly to Apple's creation of new convergence knowledge as convergence (see Fig. 3.3).

Without even savoring a moment's pleasure when the iPod took the world by storm, Jobs immediately began to brood over what might be a potential threat to this stunning device. A mobile telephone equipped with a music player was one such possibility. Almost immediately, even at the risk of the iPod being "cannibalized" by another Apple product, the internal iPod development team embarked on another project to commence development of the iPhone. There seemed to be a sense of crisis with Jobs that unless Apple "cannibalized" its own product, its fate would be at the mercy of another company. In other words, he deliberately averted a high-end disruptive innovation dilemma (Christensen, 1997; Kodama & Hashimoto, 2024).

Apple then plunged into the applied development of a mobile telephone device, later named the iPhone, as a new creation. Later, after repeated trial production, development, verification, and assessment, Apple went on to develop various innovative technologies and in 2007

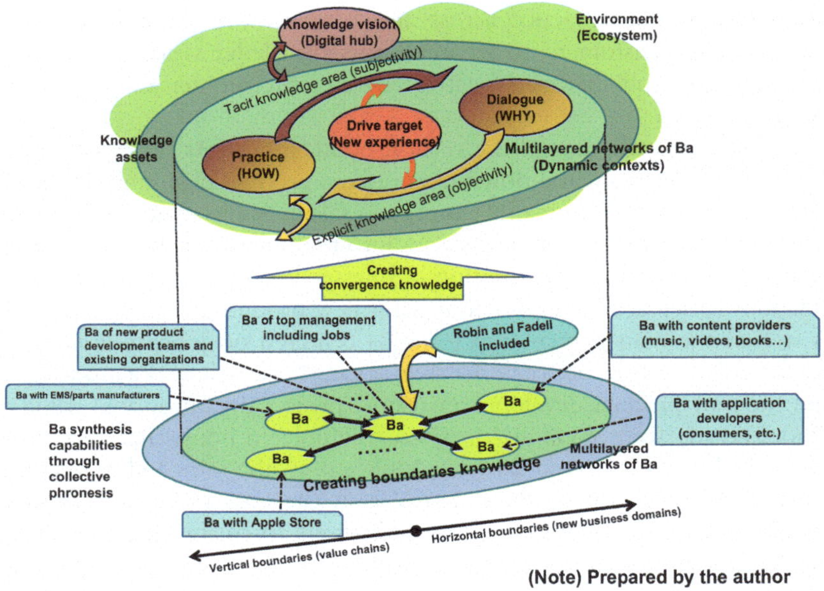

Fig. 3.3 Creating multilayered networks of Ba, boundaries knowledge and convergence knowledge centered on Apple

finally released the iPhone as an innovative mobile telephone (smartphone) that incorporated a music delivery service function based on the iPod.

As in the case of Apple's knowledge creation process, to achieve new business models, it's crucial that companies dynamically synthesize their internal knowledge combining their various internal boundaries (between people, organizations, different areas of specialization, etc.), with external knowledge combining external boundaries (between companies, between companies and their customers, between different industries, etc.). In other words, new convergence knowledge transcending various boundaries is created by the knowledge creation process through the creation of boundaries knowledge both inside and outside of companies on both their vertical and horizontal boundaries. In this paper, innovation brought about by this knowledge creation process is called "boundaries innovation" (Kodama, 2009a, 2009b, 2014).

3.2.2 Boundaries Innovation

The variety of e-businesses and new content industries that have appeared alongside the smartphones and tablets released by the highly influential global ICT company Apple are not only due to technological aspects as the development of ICT but are also boundaries innovations as markets created anew through the convergence of the knowledge of a wide range of players. Furthermore, developments like NTT DOCOMO's i-mode, the example business model for the iPhone, etc., Sony and Nintendo's gaming devices (PlayStation/DS/Wii/Switch) and the recent rapid expansion of SNS services like Facebook, Twitter, and social games are characterized by not only technological aspects as product developments, but also boundaries innovations of the creation of new markets (for contents, applications, games software) through the convergence of the knowledge of players across various boundaries in knowledge ecosystems. These boundaries innovations have driven co-creation and co-evolution across the entire ICT industry, and have formed dynamic knowledge ecosystems as new value chains.

To bring about new products, services, and business models through boundaries innovation across various industries or through the convergence of dissimilar technologies, many high-tech companies and global corporations face a multitude of challenges such as figuring out the strategic and organizational actions that a company should take, and the forms that management and leadership should take.

Nevertheless, while the details of strategy vary from individual industry and company, the creation of boundaries knowledge through the phonetic leadership of practitioners is the first important point for corporate strategy to adapt to the boundaries innovation strategy view of convergence or create it. This requires boundaries vision through collective phronesis, the aggregation of the autonomous and decentralized phronesis of practitioners. The boundaries vision encourages the discovery and creation of the boundaries knowledge required for the creation of convergence knowledge as convergence. The second point is the Ba synthesizing capabilities through collective phronesis required to create the convergence knowledge required for convergence by dynamically synthesizing diverse and dissimilar contexts and knowledge. The crucial organizational platform and corporate model to achieve this is the knowledge creating company model achieved through the creation of multilayered networks of Ba, as shown in Figure 3.3.

In practice, in the creation of convergence knowledge, not only is it necessary to synthesize a wide variety of dissimilar knowledge across different organizations and different areas of specializations within a company—the greatest challenge is boundaries innovation synthesizing the knowledge of a company with the leading knowledge decentralized around the globe by building global networks of leading partner companies around the world that include customers such as consumers. The following describes these key concepts in detail.

3.3 The Process of Creating Boundaries Knowledge and Convergence Knowledge Through Collective Phronesis

In the knowledge economy, diverse human knowledge is the source of valuable products, services, and business models that can give a company new competitiveness (Kodama, 2007; Nonaka & Takeuchi, 1995). As in the case of product development at Apple mentioned above, new value chains are formed as new strategic models by converging diverse technologies and different industries to bring about new products, services, and business models that transcend various boundaries. Accordingly, regarding the knowledge held by people, groups, and organizations, companies must re-recognize the importance of processes to create new convergence knowledge by transcending various organizational boundaries in knowledge ecosystems and synthesizing dissimilar contexts and knowledge to build new business.

New convergence knowledge has a strong tendency to occur on the boundaries between dissimilar fields or professions (Leonard-Barton, 1995; Nonaka & Takeuchi, 1995). Various functional organizations and specialist fields are separated from each other in corporations and various business types and functions are separated from each other between corporations and industries. Thus, among these, moving from the macro to the micro, many visible and invisible boundaries exist. In the rapidly changing circumstances and competitiveness in the businesses and industries of the convergence era, corporations have to transcend dissimilar industries at the global level to create new convergence knowledge and boundaries innovation. Thus, companies have to execute wide-ranging knowledge synthesis strategies across the various boundaries within and between themselves, including their customers. Certainly, knowledge is a source of competitiveness for companies, however, it is not only the sectionalism between businesspeople in companies that exist as organizational boundaries—knowledge boundaries also stem from the individual values systems of business people, and their backgrounds and specializations at the micro level. In other words, fixed mental models and path-dependent knowledge of practitioners are a hindrance to innovation (Brown & Duguid, 2001; Carlile, 2002; Kogut & Zander, 1992; Leonard-Barton, 1995; Nonaka & Takeuchi, 1995).

Many practitioners recognize that there are "unseen walls" between specialist organizations in companies, and between companies including customers. The problems and issues that relate to new business in relationships with external partners and customers are further complicated by the far greater degrees of tension than the contexts within a company. How to dynamically bring about new convergence knowledge from the dissimilar contexts and knowledge of diverse practitioners surmounting organizational and knowledge boundaries? This requires collective phronesis, aggregations of phronesis of practitioners, which creates boundaries knowledge through boundaries vision, and Ba synthesizing capabilities to form the multilayered networks of Ba required for the creation of new convergence knowledge. The dynamic knowledge creation process of collective phronesis, boundaries knowledge, and convergence knowledge occurring recursively in knowledge ecosystems is the origin of dynamically changing corporate boundaries and generating new boundaries innovation as convergence and business ecosystems.

3.3.1 Boundaries Vision Dynamically Changing Corporate Boundaries

In the creation of convergence knowledge, practitioners require network thinking capabilities (Kodama, 2019) to gain new insights from diverse and complicated boundaries by demonstrating boundaries vision and create boundaries knowledge by bridging diverse boundaries both inside and outside of companies, including customers. Boundaries vision is also the thinking and insight for designing new business and corporate strategies by recognizing wide-ranging boundaries and bridging them. From the perspective of corporate strategy theory, boundaries vision is also a capability that should be acquired by corporate leaders as well as many managers and staff to enable a corporation to bring about new convergence knowledge by generating boundaries knowledge by designing (being the architect of) its optimal vertical and horizontal boundaries and by not only adjusting its boundaries to adapt to changes in environments (markets) but also willfully changing the boundaries of the corporation to create new environments (markets).

On the other hand, Day and Schoemaker (2005) point to the importance of "Peripheral Vision (sensing weak signals from the boundaries of existing mainstream businesses)" as a sub-capability of sensing. Peripheral vision is the ability to identify early signs of potential business opportunities and threats before competitors do (see Fig. 3.4). As with human vision, the out-of-focus periphery is a fuzzy zone. Degradation of the signal-to-noise ratio (the so-called S/N ratio) prevents companies from seeing and scrutinizing peripheral areas. Information overload, dispersion of expertise, and uncertainty and confusion in the corporate environment are serious impediments to the functioning of peripheral vision.

"Sensing" in dynamic capabilities (Teece, 2014) is the ability to explore, filter, and analyze business opportunities and relies on the "cognitive capabilities" (Helfat & Peteraf, 2015) of individual practitioners,

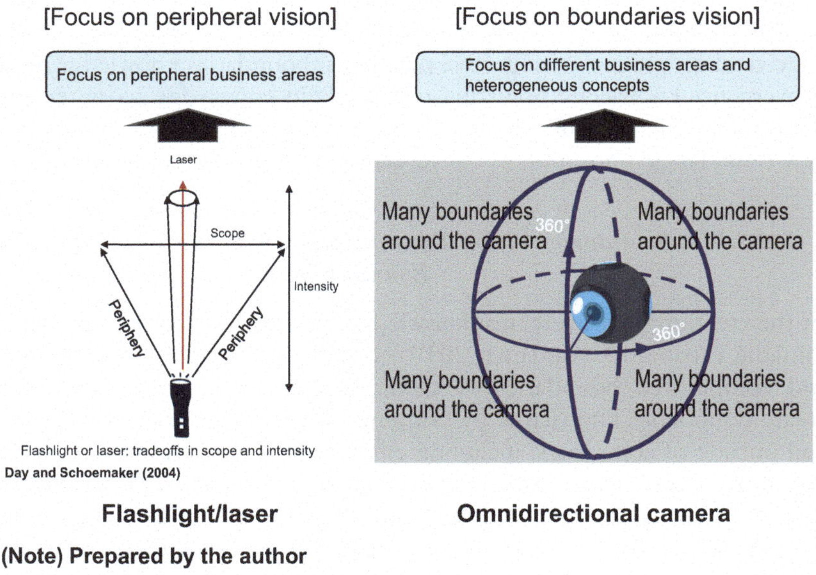

Fig. 3.4 Difference between boundaries vision and peripheral vision

particularly executives and middle management. In the process of R&D activities and selection of new technologies to realize innovation, the presence of appropriate cognitive capabilities at the management level to respond to the dynamic external environment, including the identification of business opportunities, is an extremely important factor. Helfat and Peteraf (2015) have argued that, in recent years, heterogeneity in cognitive capabilities among top executives leads to managerial performance gaps under highly uncertain or dynamically changing conditions. According to their reviews of the theories of cognitive psychology, cognitive science, social psychology, cognitive neuroscience, and behavioral decision theory, cognitive capabilities entail important aspects that are rooted in certain contexts or expertise. It has also been argued in existing research that these aspects can affect heterogeneity in cognitive capabilities (e.g., Ericsson & Lehmann, 1996).

Helfat and Peteraf (2015) assert that, in many years of research into management, cognitive capabilities that are the basis for mental processes (or mental models) (e.g., Grinyer & McKiernan, 1994), have been an important attribute of managers at the top of organizations, and present a number of cases of evidence such as research by Rosenbloom (2000) into NCR, and research by Tripsas and Gavetti (2000) into Polaroid. Furthermore, they also suggest that top managers need to strengthen "paradoxical cognition" (Kodama, 2003; Smith & Tushman, 2005) to be able to pursue exploration and exploitation (March, 1991) simultaneously, and at the same time, take heed of the warnings that there are many cases of hindrance caused by empirical knowledge, because when companies search for new technologies and strategies they often unwittingly or inappropriately rely on specialist knowledge (assets) of the past. As confirmed by leading research into the field of management, heterogeneity in the cognition of top management teams affects the heterogeneity of approaches to corporate transformation and strategic change and their outcomes in management activities.

The role played by the non-cognitive capability of the "intuition" (e.g., Kodama, 2011) of practitioners is large, and brings about awareness and flashes of insight through their deep interaction with a wide range of stakeholders (including customers and partners). For practitioners to demonstrate intuition, practitioners must have capabilities of boundaries vision (Kodama, 2011; Kodama & Shibata, 2016) to be able to acquire new insights from complex and diverse boundaries. The concept of boundaries vision drives "external knowledge convergence capabilities"—the ability to orchestrate different tangible and intangible (knowledge) assets[6] (Kodama, 2011; Kodama & Shibata, 2016).

The aforementioned peripheral vision is required to have the dynamic vision and sensitivity to respond to the speed of environmental change. Driving this vision enables risk management without missing signs, capturing opportunities, and surviving in times of change. On the other hand, boundaries vision encompasses the concept of peripheral vision and also includes knowledge acquired not only from the peripheral areas of the company's core business domain, where peripheral vision is fully used, but also from business domains in different industries that separated by diverse heterogeneous boundaries and had no relationship with the company in the past (or the company was not interested in at all) and various customer knowledge (customer knowledge and customer competence) (e.g., Prahalad & Ramaswamy, 2000, 2004).

Jack Welch, the legendary CEO who brought a lot of wealth to General Electric, said:

> The second characteristic is the ability to see around corners. Every leader has to have a vision and the ability to predict the future, but good leaders must have a special capacity to anticipate the radically unexpected. In business, the best leaders in brutally competitive environments have a sixth sense for market changes, as well as moves by existing competitors and new entrants. (Welch & Welch, 2005, p. 89)

The ability to foresee what is just around the corner (the sixth sense) corresponds to boundaries vision. Figure 3.4 shows an image of the difference between peripheral and boundary vision. Peripheral vision means only the peripheral area, the fuzzy zone where light such as that from a flashlight or laser does not easily reach. Boundaries vision, on the other hand, is closer to the view from an omnidirectional camera. An omnidirectional camera has two lenses, one in the front and one in the back. Each lens covers one side of the camera, and by combining the images from the two lenses, the camera can capture a 360-degree image from the sky to the ground. An omnidirectional camera is a photographic device that can take 360-degree panoramic photos and 360-degree videos in all directions, and is also called a 360° camera, VR camera, or full dome camera.

Prior research has shown that practitioners who share diverse (knowledge) assets and create new assets exhibit behavioral patterns of network thinking with boundaries vision to bridge diverse boundaries within and outside companies (Kodama, 2019, 2021). Boundaries vision is a philosophy and insight possessed by practitioners who recognize diverse boundaries, bridge boundaries to realize asset orchestration to design new business and corporate strategies.

In other words, boundaries vision is the capability of practitioners to find various discomforts and differences in the heterogeneity at boundaries, and moreover, the capability of practitioners to find new ideas and knowledge such as new hints and ideas from such boundaries. Boundaries vision also corresponds to capabilities that inspire "boundaries knowledge" (Kodama, 2019)—a new way of seeing and perceiving things by discovering boundaries and connecting them. Boundaries vision is not static, but is a cluster of dynamic, constantly changing capabilities. Such boundaries vision must be demonstrated as the source of new "knowledge convergence processes" (Kodama & Shibata, 2016) through the fusion (integration) of different knowledges (assets). Thus, such boundaries vision is the most fundamental element for convergence (i.e., asset orchestration) of different assets.

To achieve dynamic knowledge convergence across multiple diverse boundaries, practitioners need to demonstrate boundaries vision and create additional "external knowledge convergence capabilities" (Kodama & Shibata, 2016). In practice, executives and managers must create new innovations (new products, services, and business models) by integrating different assets through external knowledge convergence capabilities that focus on diverse boundaries.

External knowledge convergence capability by boundaries vision is the ability to go beyond peripheral vision to perceive heterogeneous assets that have little (or no) relationship with each other or with one's assets, find the relationship with one's own assets, and merge them together. The intersection and fusion of heterogeneous assets is a source of new innovation (e.g., Johansson, 2004). Therefore, for practitioners, the ability to find relationships among multiple heterogeneous assets, or between existing assets and heterogeneous assets, and to find new meanings and assets from these relationships, is the first important trigger for demonstrating external knowledge convergence capabilities as a component of "sensing").

Boundaries vision triggers dynamic execution of the optimization of value chains for a company's core business by changing internal and external vertical boundaries. In addition, boundaries vision is the ability to search out and arouse[7] business in different business domains, not only in those around the periphery of core businesses, and radically alter a company's horizontal boundaries to uncover boundaries knowledge that relates to knowledge different from the knowledge of the company. Boundaries knowledge created through boundaries vision is an enabler for the creation of new convergence knowledge by the synthesis of dissimilar knowledge. For example, as mentioned, Apple's move from the PC business into the smartphone and music distribution business with its strategy transformation, or the ventures of Japanese 7-Eleven and NTT DOCOMO into the finance business are examples of massive changes in the horizontal boundaries of companies.

In contrast, traditional innovation in mature industries has been carried out mainly in company laboratories and product development divisions as closed, hierarchical, and autonomous systems, in which innovation processes are controlled by the company. In closed innovation systems like these, the governance mechanisms generate the company's unique core competences, and are the origin of the company's competitiveness. However, companies were able to raise business efficiency across the board by changing the vertical boundaries that determine their corporate value chains through joint development with other countries, or knowledge transfer from other companies to acquire knowledge that they didn't have.[8] Under conditions where environmental change is soft, it's advantageous for a company to configure value chains with vertical integration within the company or with group companies through coordination and close interdependency of technical resources between related internal business units.[9] The "keiretsu"-type of business grouping in the traditional automobile industry is a good example of this.

However, in rapidly changing market environments and in the environments of convergence, focus has also been put on dynamic processes to proactively bring in knowledge from outside the company from knowledge ecosystems to adapt to environmental changes (or create environmental changes), and flexibly execute knowledge recombination while strengthening and maintaining conventional core competencies. This means greater necessity for the "knowledge creating company model" (see Fig. 3.1) to synthesize knowledge both inside and outside of the company and create new products, services, and business models, by dynamically incorporating external core competencies, including those of customers, while improving, upgrading, and strengthening the core competencies of the company.

For this to happen, companies need to engage in the dynamic processes of synthesizing knowledge decentralized within and outside the company and reconfiguring it as the situation demands. Thus, companies have to constantly reconfigure the vertical and horizontal boundaries that form the company's business models to respond to environmental changes (or to intentionally create environmental changes as convergence).[10] To achieve a new business model, it's important for companies to create convergence knowledge by dynamically synthesizing internal knowledge acquired with multilayered networks of Ba joining their internal boundaries (people, organizations, different technical specializations, etc.) with external knowledge acquired with multilayered networks of Ba joining boundaries outside the company (between companies, between companies and customers, between different industries, etc.)—this is the "knowledge creating company model" shown in Fig. 3.1.

In the knowledge creating company model, to not only grow core business but also acquire opportunities for new business, boundaries vision on vertical and horizontal boundaries functions to proactively develop management methods such as strategic partnering, strategic outsourcing, joint development, joint ventures, and M&A, regardless of whether it's company in-house, between companies, group companies, similar businesses, dissimilar business types or customers. In this process, knowledge creating companies demonstrate capabilities to create new knowledge (convergence knowledge) by building multilayered networks of Ba vertically and horizontally and skillfully synthesizing diverse contexts and knowledge.

3.3.2 Boundaries Vision Elements

It's important for practitioners to have "context architect capability"—the ability to respond to diverse and complex contexts, and design new ones. To create boundaries knowledge and convergence knowledge, practitioners have to have boundaries vision—boundaries knowledge to design contexts from complex and diverse boundaries and gain new insight. For practitioners to demonstrate boundaries vision to enable the creation of boundaries knowledge, the 3 phronetic leadership factors of a broad perspective, Ba creation and human capabilities are required. These 3 main factors require the 4 management capabilities of (1) external knowledge synthesizing capabilities,[11] (2) strategic synthesizing capabilities,[12] (3) organizational synthesizing capabilities,[13] and (4) situational practical skills,[14] which are the management elements of boundaries vision. The following sections describe the relationship between the 3 main factors of phronetic leadership and the 4 capabilities required for boundaries vision (see Fig. 3.5).

(1) Broad Perspectives, External Knowledge Synthesizing Capabilities, and Strategic Synthesizing Capabilities

The broad perspective is the capability to grasp the essence of matters by looking directly at reality through the spiraling between the micro and macro, and from there, to draw concepts of the future. This capability requires the phronetic leadership elements of the ability to create

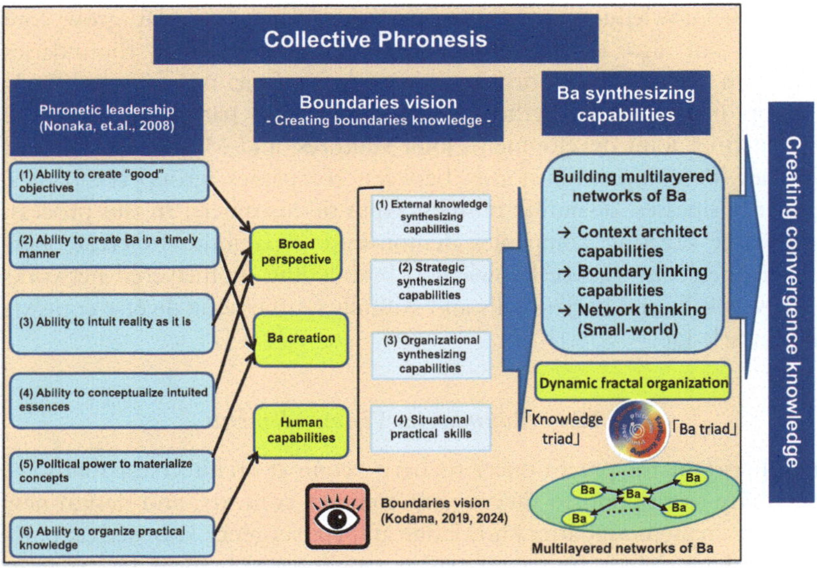

Fig. 3.5 Creating boundaries knowledge and convergence knowledge through collective phronesis

"good" objectives, the ability to intuit reality as it is, and the ability to form concepts of those intuited essences. Determining what is "good"—in other words what is true, wholesome, and beautiful—begins with the values of individual people. Since knowledge is created from these values, the achievement of knowledge creation management is based on and influenced by the values of practitioners (their ideas of truth, goodness, and beauty). If an individual has a well-established values system and philosophy, the individual can judge what is "good," and can therefore create "good products" with his or her external knowledge synthesizing capability—the capability to synthesize various contexts and dissimilar knowledge.

Furthermore, the ability to intuit reality as it is and to see the essence of matters is the ability to intuitively see through meanings and truths that are presented by people, things, and events. This is the ability to see all the way through to the background of various phenomena, feel things, and quickly recognize situations and imagine a future and draw up the details of it. This is the situation recognition capability that enables practitioners to intuitively see through to the underpinnings of dynamic and complex phenomena at the micro level as occasion calls. This capability has a major effect on strategy formation.

Situational recognition is demonstrated in strategy creation in the sense of the purely emergent, in other words, strategy from ideas that bubble up suddenly from the thoughts of people, in discovery and invention processes such as science or new product development. These are also called "incidental emergent strategies," and are often the birthplace of new inventions and products that stem from the intuition, sense, recognition or serendipity, etc., of scientists and researchers in the process of sustained learning through coincidence and failure (see Fig. 3.6). Some of these include new product developments such as 3 M's Post-It products, P&G's Ivory Soap, and Pfizer's Viagra, or new scientific discoveries and inventions such as Fleming's penicillin, Pasteur's vaccines, and Leo Esaki's tunnel diode.

In addition, there are "intentional emergent strategies" that differ from intentional or planned strategies that are executed by planning and decision-making at the top level of companies, but are strategic proposals that originate from the business frontline or often from middle management (see Fig. 3.6). In the process of intentional emergent strategies, originators intentionally anticipate, foresee, and predict new meaning

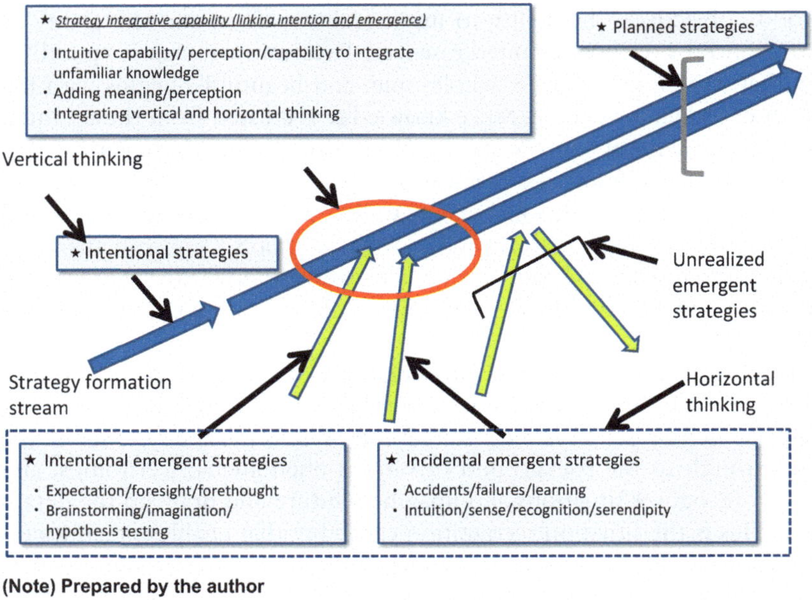

Fig. 3.6 Strategic synthesizing capabilities

from the relationships between dissimilar knowledge and existing knowledge (or empirical knowledge), and repeatedly verify hypotheses by taking advantage of flashes of inspiration and the imagination to create new strategies. For example, these are products and services that have come about through convergence and new product developments such as NTT DOCOMO's i-mode, Sharp's mobile phone with built-in camera, Panasonic's anti-shake digital camera, Nintendo's Wii/DS, and so on, and corporate strategy transformations such as those seen at Intel (memory → logic), Microsoft (OS → Internet business), or Apple (PC → music distribution/smartphone businesses).

New product developments and strategy transformations like these are heavily reliant on conceptualizing intuitive essences, and require capabilities to go back and forth from the micro (the individual specifics) to the macro (the universal). This entails representation and conceptualization of intuitions gained at the micro level through dialogue, description of these conceptualized in relationships using the power of imagination at the macro level (as historical views, visions, scenarios, etc.), and persuasion—it's also the ability to create product concepts or corporate objectives. i-mode, mobile phone with built-in camera, Wii/DS, and iPod/iPhone/iPad are good examples of this kind of product development. These processes do not only entail vertical methodologies such as deduction and induction, but also take advantage of analogical horizontal methodologies such as metaphors, analogies, and stories. Therefore, it is important to embed the concepts and actions of incidental emergent strategies and intentional emergent strategies within organizations so that all members of staff can demonstrate "strategic synthesizing capabilities" (see Fig. 3.6).

(2) Ba Creation, and Situational Practical Skills

The second point, Ba creation, requires phronetic leadership elements of the ability to create Ba at the right time to conceptualize and realize the future by dynamically perceiving the relationships both within and outside of organizations, and changing these relationships, and the political capabilities to materialize the concept by getting people and organizations to move through the force of strong personal will. The capability to share contexts is the capability to create Ba so that the knowledge of the emotions fundamental to the human being—delight, anger, sorrow, and joy—can be directly shared. Ba are shared dynamic contexts, and are dynamic psychophysical conditions as platforms on which Ba participants create and share knowledge. To achieve this, capabilities to create Ba in which individuals can go beyond themselves to connect with others, care for, love, and develop mutual trust for one another to generate knowledge assets, and capabilities to move and connect multiple Ba in multilayered structures are fundamental.

However, it is not enough to simply see through to the essence of matters, and convey that to people through the formation of Ba. The next step requires orienting the Ba toward objectives while enveloping others and bringing together capabilities. This is the ability to get people and organizations moving in directions judged to be toward "the good," and the ability to achieve objectives by combining measures selected to suit the situation, and using political power sometimes extemporarily and cleverly taking advantage of Machiavellian approaches. In this step, to link together dissimilar contexts to create new contexts, practitioners spontaneously create new Ba that transcend knowledge boundaries and also draw other practitioners as stakeholders into the Ba.

By creating multilayered networks of Ba in this way, and as necessary, through the interactions with customers and external partners, practitioners strengthen their boundaries vision to bring about new knowledge. It is the context architect capability of practitioners that draws practitioners into a specific Ba. To create high-quality new knowledge, leading practitioners form specific Ba and draw specific other practitioners into the specific Ba as required. Moreover, practitioners take the initiative to create and participate in multiple dissimilar Ba, disseminate contexts and knowledge between dissimilar Ba, and act to inspire and share these contexts and knowledge among practitioners. This is the boundaries consolidation capability of practitioners, and is a capability that enables practitioners to network multiple dissimilar Ba (build multilayered networks of Ba). As important Ba creation capabilities, context architect, and boundaries consolidation capabilities bring about new ideas and solutions required to formulate and execute strategic objectives, and give rise to the dynamic practical process of practitioners of going back and forth between networks of multilayered Ba and formal organizations.

Thus, the new common sense and self-transcendence that are brought forth with the formation of these new multilayered networks of Ba simultaneously promote new self-organization. Here, practitioners do not merely convey information or formally transfer knowledge, but also act beyond the role of the so-called "boundary spanner"[15] by forming pragmatic Ba and driving specific practical actions.

Executing strategic processes is dynamic and dependent on situations and is therefore fraught with chaos and inconsistencies. The methodology needed in such situations is dialectical thinking and action that extracts dynamic order by nullifying dichotomies with commitment, and practically sublates contradiction, rather than conforming without good reason, or passively making compromises on logical dichotomies. This process is in reality the political process of achieving objectives through social interactions with others with political judgment at its heart. In everyday, run-of-the-mill verbal and non-verbal communications, political judgment capability is used through an understanding of the feelings of others—their anger, delight, sorrow and pleasure, empathy, sensitivity toward the subtleties of emotions, and consideration of the timing and limitations of interventions between oneself and others. Thus, practitioners require situational practical skills consisting of the capabilities to create Ba in a timely manner, and the political skills to materialize concepts using their situational judgment capabilities.

(3) **Human Capabilities, and Organizational Synthesizing Capabilities**

The third point is human capabilities, and requires a phronetic leadership element of the capability to organize phronesis to foster the next generation of phronetic leaders. Human capabilities reinforce organizational synthesizing capabilities, organize phronesis, and foster the next generation of phronetic leaders. Then, the wisdom embedded in the personalities of individuals is transmitted and nurtured in practice, and systematized as autonomous and decentralized phronesis. This is the most important process in the creation of the aforementioned "collective phronesis,"—the aggregation of autonomous and decentralized phronesis. This enables the configuration of resilient organizations that can flexibly and creatively respond in real time to whatever happens such as dramatically changing environments (the "dynamic fractal organizations" having the structure of multilayered networked Ba discussed in Chapter 2).

(4) **Ba Synthesizing Capabilities**

Practitioners uncover valuable boundaries necessary for boundaries innovation through convergence among a variety of dissimilar boundaries through external knowledge synthesizing capabilities by taking advantage of their broad perspectives. It is important to uncover knowledge differences (Kodama, 2019)[16] between dissimilar contexts and knowledge using boundaries vision to create boundaries knowledge. The ability to recognize knowledge differences is a capability that inspires the creation of new boundaries knowledge bridging boundaries.

Moreover, at the same time, strategic synthesizing capabilities entailing flexible thinking and practical skills for creating strategies based in the broad perspective, situational practical skills for creating Ba, and organizational synthesizing capabilities demonstrating human capabilities are the capabilities that create Ba bridging specific boundaries, and promote dialogue and practice to give meaning to certain boundaries. This process enables the creation of boundaries knowledge, the basis of boundaries innovation as convergence. Boundaries vision is the capability to see invisible things and also the capability to inspire and discover new boundaries knowledge and convergence knowledge on a variety of dissimilar boundaries.

In knowledge convergence, the larger the scale and more complex corporate driving objectives are, the greater the number of boundaries, and the more decentralized and numerous the Ba bridging those boundaries in time and space. Networking these decentralized Ba to achieve driving objectives enables synthesis of diverse and complex dynamic contexts. Joining together Ba is also joining boundaries (between Ba), and is starting point for the creation of new objects and events. Practitioners that create boundaries knowledge determine the type of Ba that are created or discovered and networked by using their boundaries vision, while the practical capability to network these is their Ba synthesizing capability. Ba synthesizing capabilities are also dynamic context architecture capabilities and boundaries consolidation capabilities. It is this Ba synthesizing capability that achieves multilayered networks of Ba, which have commonalities with the "small-world networks" of network theory, discussed later.

The above "phronetic leadership," "boundaries vision," and "Ba synthesizing capability" are the core elements of "collective phronesis. The formation of a "dynamic fractal organization" by the "knowledge triad relationship" and the "Ba triad relationship" through the "Ba synthesizing capabilities" will produce boundaries knowledge and convergence knowledge (see Fig. 3.5).

3.4 Dynamic Fractal Organizations—A New Organizational Model for Synthesizing Capability

Regarding the proposition that "innovative corporations that maintain growth through knowledge creation and utilization have organizational structures that achieve dynamic synthesis of exploration and exploitation," I touch on the problems and limitations with the information processing model and contingency theory that form the basis of these ideas, and consider a new organizational model.

3.4.1 The New Model, and Limitations to the Information Processing Model and Contingency Theory

Business studies that have made propositions about "exploration and exploitation" base their arguments on the information processing model and contingency theory proposed by the Carnegie school. Neoclassical economics assumed that people knew all information and made rational decisions (the so-called homo economics model) (e.g., Mele et.al., 2014). In contrast, the Carnegie school assumed that people have knowledge limitations, and therefore can only have limited rationality, and that their behaviors are influenced by circumstances (Cyert & March, 1955; March & Simon, 1958; Simon, 1969). There is also the so-called "Homo Adaptivus" model in which people make decisions depending on how they process information acquired from the environment.

Thus, in order to effect economic activity at a level of rationality that exceeds the limited level of the individual, organizations are required, because organizations are able to address circumstantial uncertainties through the process of gathering and transferring information and decision-making processes (Simon, 1969).

The Carnegie school is characterized by the exclusion of value premises by making abstractions of the value and meaning of information, and attempts to make a science out of decision-making in an organization by only dealing with factual premises. In other words, both individual people and organizations can be thought of as information processing systems that make decisions by gathering and analyzing information.

Continuing this idea, contingency theory assumes that circumstantial uncertainty regulates an organization (Burns & Stalker, 1961). Put differently, there are no optimum organizational structures or principles that can be universally applied to any organization, because organizations change as they respond to the circumstances facing them. Thus, it is in the way that organizations change and apply appropriate structures in response to circumstances that enable them to raise performance (e.g., Galbraith, 1973; Lawrence & Lorsch, 1967).

Accordingly, an organization can be said to be highly effective if there is a match between information processing requisites to accommodate circumstances and the organization's information processing capability. In other words, pre-existing information becomes the subject of exploration and exploitation, and individuals or organizations are merely mechanisms that process information passively and in a fixed manner.

In the Carnegie school, because of the given environment, the aspect of environmental adaptability in which individuals or organizations exist passively is given the focus, but there is no context for environmental creation in which individuals or organizations exert influence on the environment, in other words actively work the environment with their own beliefs and thoughts for creating something new. Similarly, information already exists in the external world, and people are merely information processors, but there is no notion that people can create it anew. Also, the subjectivity of the individual is completely removed in analysis of information, and thus does not provide a sufficient description of corporate organizational action in the complex and dynamically changing environment of the modern world.

The information processing model and contingency theory contributed to the development of economic and business studies of the twentieth century in which operational efficiency and effectiveness were pursued, however in the knowledge society twenty-first century, in which value creation and innovation are pursued (Drucker, 1993), it has to be said that these ideas are out of step with the times. Thus, we believe that the most important aspect of the economic and business studies of the future will be a focus on knowledge and the subjectivity of the humans creating and utilizing it.

As criteria required for a new theoretical model that embraces environmental creation based on human subjectivity, firstly are organizations that have enough diversity within themselves to accommodate diverse circumstantial change to adapt in complex and dynamically changing environments. Secondly, just like the Apple case mentioned at the beginning of this paper, is the creation of new markets and environmental diversity, through new knowledge creating activities (Nonaka & Takeuchi, 1995). Put differently, it is necessary for an organization to acquire "requisite variety" (Ashby, 1956), because "only diversity can beat (absorb) diversity."

Requisite variety is the capability for prompt, flexible, and dynamic synthesis of the diverse contexts and different knowledge possessed by members of an organization into a variety of forms, and is the basis for the formation of "dynamic fractal organizations based on dynamic 'Ba' formation," discussed later. Organizational bodies that pursue requisite variety are in extreme cases spherical, because the facets they acquire are potentially ever-increasing.

It is not possible for organizational members to pursue this requisite variety in an organization structured in such a way that can be reduced to its elements. The key here is the "formation of 'Ba'" (Nonaka & Takeuchi, 1995), described below. In other words, a viewpoint that sees an organization as an organically arranged multiplicity of diverse and mutually interleaved "Ba" (multilayered networks of "Ba") as opposed to an organization as a structure is required.

3.4.2 The Multilayered Relationships of "Ba Triad Relationships" and "knowledge triad relationships"

In knowledge creation theory, knowledge has the 2 dimensions of tacit knowledge and explicit knowledge, and it is the continuous interconversion of these 2 types of knowledge that enables the creation of knowledge. Knowledge creating activities are interconversion processes in which the tacit knowledge originating in the body, thoughts, and beliefs of an individual is put into words and transformed into explicit knowledge.

Although these two types of knowledge contrast each other they are on a continuum. When an individual's tacit knowledge is shared with another person it becomes explicit knowledge, and when this is merged with other explicit knowledge it becomes new explicit knowledge, which in turn can then be converted into the tacit knowledge of an individual and thus link with the subsequent conversion process. It is the spiraling of this conversion process from which innovation is born, and Phronesis is the 3rd factor that promotes this spiraling (the synthesis and sublation of tacit and explicit knowledge).

Phronesis is a concept first put forward by the ancient Greek philosopher Aristotle in the "Nicomachean Ethics," and is translated as prudence or practical wisdom (Aristotle, 1980). Phronesis is a method of practical understanding that accompanies objectives, values, and actions, and is the practical knowledge that accompanies physicality to enable optimum on-the-spot decision-making in individual contexts, while holding to standards of common good. Phronesis is characterized by contemplation in action—thinking things through while engaged in activity—and quick decision-making within a context with timely, finely tuned balance.

In the past, the idea of Phronesis has been thought of as separate from the idea of mutual interaction between tacit and explicit knowledge, however, we freshly position Phronesis as the third knowledge factor required to drive the spiraling of tacit and explicit knowledge. We call the synthesis of these 3 types of knowledge the “knowledge triad relationship (see Fig. 3.7).”

The conventional economic view is that an organization is an aggregation of agreements and resources, but in knowledge creating theory (Nonaka & Takeuchi, 1995), organizations are perceived as mutually interleaved multilayered networks of diverse “Ba.” “Ba” are interactions of circumstances, structures, and actors in a “here and now” relationship, and are thus born and developed through mutual interfusion. Therefore, the actions in “Ba” or relationships between “Ba” also form the environments, structures, and actions by actors. In other words, synergies occur between people, and between people and the environment based on the knowledge that they possess in addition to the meanings that they generate, then the “Ba” of these newly built relationships move into action, and these “Ba” are mutually linked with one another. In this way, by perceiving organizations as multilayered networks of “Ba” as opposed to structured aggregations of resources, we can more clearly understand an organization as flows of knowledge rather than as an organizational schematic.

As mentioned, generally in the organizational theory put forth by the Carnegie school with its information processing model and contingency theory, organizational structures were defined by the environment, and organizational structures defined the actions of individuals as a linear dependency through adaptation to the environment. However, in

Fig. 3.7 Phronesis drives the conversion of tacit and explicit knowing

knowledge creation theory, the relationships between organizations as environments and structures, and individuals as actors are dialectic and composite relationships that are constantly changing through "Ba" as repeating cycles of forming and dissolving relationships.

Thus, the behaviors of individuals stemming from their own beliefs and thoughts comprise the medium through which "Ba" are formed, which enables both adaptation to the environment as well as work to be actively done on the environment to create new environments, because through the formation of "Ba," individuals are endowed with a practical power that enables them to transform environments by their own actions (Giddens, 1984).

In circumstances where the formation and use of knowledge is desirable, "Ba" enable free and open exchange of knowledge, and mutual stimulation and synthesis of knowledge across wide-ranging existing knowledge boundaries. These sorts of boundaries in "Ba" are self-organizing and have an open and porous character.

In leading organizations, multiple "Ba" are intertwined at many levels, "Ba" are connected together flexibly, communication and collaboration occur, and new "Ba" are formed. In effective "Ba," participants maintain diversity while mutually deepening their relationships, and at the same time, members broaden their reach into the circumstances.

If we view "Ba" as knowledge enablers that are deployed both horizontally and vertically, self-organizing "Ba" enable agile response to any kind of circumstantial change, effectively creation of new environments at will, and dynamic, creative, and efficient integration of knowledge. In this perspective, "Ba" can be said to be dynamic "invisible organizations" from the point of view of action.

Usually, we think of organizations as having static structures in which the roles of members are controlled. However, "Ba" and organizations have supplementary relationships with each other, and interconvert. The structural characteristics of organizations are one factor that promotes the generation and invigoration of "Ba." For instance, as "Ba" grow both horizontally and vertically, they could become stably structured, or they could be dismantled by self-organizing groups or teams. In this way, the "invisible organizations" defined in the "Ba" perspective are on multilayered networks of diverse and mutually interleaved "Ba." Accordingly, the degree to which "Ba" are strategically or autonomously bound together, and what sorts of synergies occur will determine the quality of knowledge that is created.

The case of the Toyota Prius (Nonaka, et al., 2014) was a case of "dynamic synthesis of exploration and exploitation,"—innovation through convergence—the fusion of diverse technologies (exploration) that was subsequently commercialized as a specific product with ongoing improvements and upgrades (exploitation). For these reasons, Toyota's various project teams and existing line organizations had to form "Ba" as multilayered networks both horizontally and vertically within and between organizations to simultaneously bring about the creation and utilization of knowledge.

In cases like these, the focus is on "Ba" that drive exploratory activities to create knowledge for innovation (exploration "Ba"), in which tacit knowledge is shared and converted into explicit knowledge (SE in the SECI process), and on the "Ba" that drive exploitative activities (exploitation "Ba"), to first realize a commercial product and then carry out upgrades and improvements embodied in condensed explicit knowledge and personal experience (CI in the SECI process). In short, the level of tacit knowledge is high in exploration "Ba," while explicit knowledge is high in exploitation "Ba." However, tacit and explicit knowledge exist on a continuum and both are synthesized in a spiraling manner, and in this spiraling, Phronesis (practical wisdom) (synthesis "Ba") is created and built up, and Phronesis drives spiraling.

From many of the detailed case studies of corporations we have made (e.g., Kodama, 2007, 2011a; Nonaka & Takeuchi, 1995; Nonaka et al., 2008), we have identified the existence of multilayered networks of "Ba" that achieve a "knowledge triad relationship" and "Ba triad relationship" in corporations that realize "dynamic synthesis of exploration and exploitation" through the knowledge dialectics of tacit knowledge, explicit knowledge, and Phronesis (practical wisdom).

Next, we would like to present perspectives for a new organizational model based on the clues offered by these "knowledge triad relationships," and "Ba triad relationship" through multilayered networked "Ba."

3.4.3 Dynamic Fractal Organizations

Organizations that accomplish requisite variety (multilayered networks of "Ba" that achieve knowledge triad relationship and Ba triad relationship) are multifaceted aggregates of "Ba" that make use of knowledge creation and exploitation dynamically, and at their extreme, are spherically configured "invisible organizations."

On the time access, these invisible organizations expand the knowledge ecosystem both inside and outside of the company while driving knowledge creation activities, and dynamically enlarge the scope of their multilayered networks of "Ba" while maintaining Ba triad and knowledge triad relationships and the metaphorical "sphere" of requisite variety. Thus, in the internal systems within this sphere, knowledge triad relationships of tacit knowledge, explicit knowledge, and practical wisdom (Phronesis) are established as multifaceted aggregations of "Ba triad relationship," which dialectically sublate (synthesis—the formation of Phronesis) the exploratory Ba (SE in SECI) with the exploitative Ba (CI in SECI), and which are in turn dynamically reconfigured by the synergies between people and organizations, within and between the various organizations within a company, between other organizations, and across entire environments as knowledge ecosystems. This is the "fractal organization phenomenon"—a new perspective[17]—and forms the basis of the concept of the new "dynamic fractal organization" organizational theory described below (see Fig. 3.8).

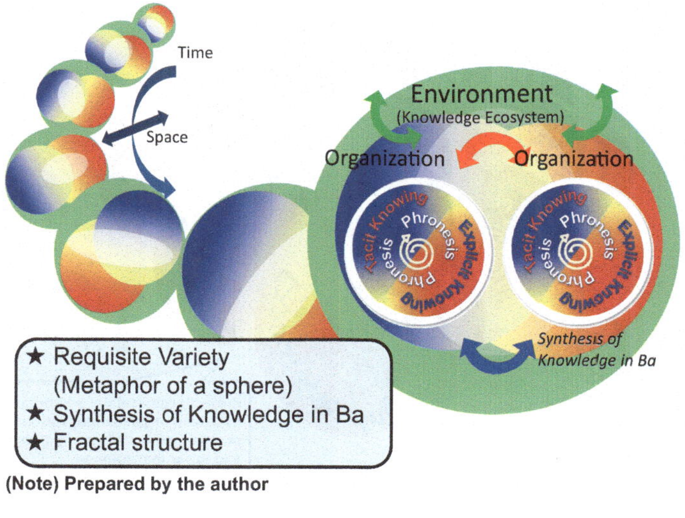

Fig. 3.8 Dynamic fractal organizations

Structured organizations provide the foundations for the formation of "Ba," whereas "Ba" are dynamic organization systems when viewed from a behavioral perspective. "Ba" and structured organizations form mutually supplementing relationships and interconvert. In this way, these ba triad and knowledge triad relationships observed between structured organizations can also be observed within the individual organizations in a company, between organizations, and across the boundaries between companies.

In other words, it is possible to find a multilayered organizational fractal characteristic that emerges in project, line, and overhead organizations, at the various management levels (top, middle, and lower management), among different specialties and job types, and between organizations and companies (see Fig. 3.9).

The word fractal (Mandelbrot, 1983) is a word used in complex adaptive systems theory, in which the whole consists of parts that resemble the whole or the creation of the whole by assembling those parts and

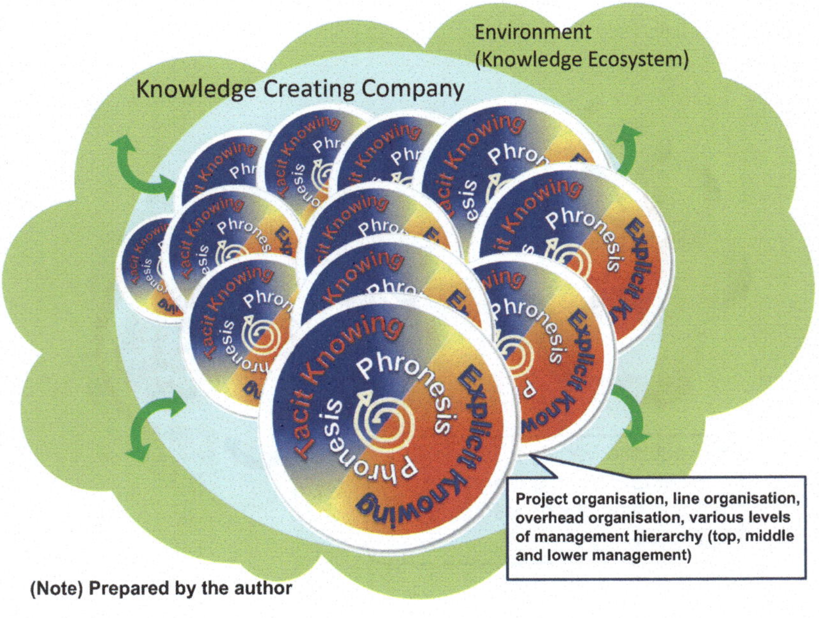

Fig. 3.9 Dynamic fractal organization in knowledge creating companies

ending up with the same basic shape. In corporations, because organizations have fractal characteristics in that any part could be extracted and expanded to form the same shape as the whole, it is possible to assign the same standards to decision-making and knowledge creation at any level (c.f. Christian, 2011). The supply chain mechanisms that comprise systems affiliated with automobile manufacturing businesses also have fractal characteristics.

Multilayered "Ba" networks that achieve Ba triad and knowledge triad relationships drive a dynamic view of strategy in corporations by their capability to dynamically synthesize exploration and exploitation, and enable companies to adapt to circumstances and create environments, while at the same time sustainably advance new and existing knowledge resources.

The structure of dynamic fractal organizations enables corporations to demonstrate phronetic or practical leadership and achieve innovation through the creation of new knowledge.

3.4.4 *Practical Wisdom Leadership Producing Dynamic Fractal Organizations*

Much of the previous research has addressed the argument that organizations within a company charged with radical innovation (e.g., Leifer et al., 2000) should be physically or culturally separated from existing organizations (or line organizations) (the mainstream), or alternatively set up as independent venture businesses (e.g., Benner & Tushman, 2003; Burgelman & Sayles, 1986; Hill & Rothaermel, 2003; Kanter, 1985). Also, the majority of the previous research has addressed the structural and functional issues surrounding management processes and organizational configurations, such as the ambidextrous organizations (e.g., O'Reilly & Tushman, 2004), as two separate and different archetypes of "exploration" and "exploitation," or of the "incremental" and "radical" (e.g., Greenwood & Hinings, 1993; Tushman & O'Reilly, 1997). In contrast, this paper considers how an organizational form should be configured to enable leadership that possesses practical wisdom to sustainably create knowledge through capabilities that dynamically synthesis exploration and exploitation.

This paper differs from the various elemental and reductive structural models put forth by previous research, in that it presents the fractal character of organizations in a new organizational model. Being based on the concept of a unified or integrated organizational model, this organizational model is a departure from the structural perspective of the older information processing model and contingency theory.

In the dynamic and fractal organizations in this model, corporations and organizations integrate the diverse contradictions both inside and outside of themselves, and achieve dynamic synthesizing of exploration and exploitation through knowledge triad relationships to sustainably create new knowledge and efficiency.

"Dynamic fractal organizations" are structured so that they do not only take advantage of both exploration and exploitation in setting down and executing corporate strategy, but also enable leaders with practical wisdom to demonstrate synthesizing capabilities as they drive the interaction of exploration and exploitation entailed in their dynamic view of strategy by effecting synergies between different types of exploration and exploitation as well as driving shifts from exploration to exploitation and vice versa. In this way, the dynamic view of strategy encompasses synthesis of different modes of exploration and exploitation through the Ba triad and knowledge triad relationships of tacit knowledge, explicit knowledge, and Phronesis, not only to achieve short-term corporate growth, but also to ensure growth in the long term (e.g., Benner & Tushman, 2003; March, 1991; Tushman & O'Reilly, 1997).

In this model, there is no dichotomy between exploration and exploitation in strategic activity; rather, strategies must be executed in which Ba triad and knowledge triad relationships are built while finding a robust balance and mutually supplementary relationship between the two strategic activities (He & Wong, 2004).

Accordingly, dynamic fractal organizations that possess Ba triad and knowledge triad relationships to simultaneously improve the performance of exploration and exploitation by successfully and dynamically integrating strategies in multiple organizations, or seeking out synergies between strategies can be said to be candidates for a new organizational model to achieve sustainable innovation.

To achieve a dynamic view of strategy like this, dense collaboration between the multiple organizations comprising a dynamic fractal organization and organic collaboration with customers and partners in the knowledge ecosystem of the environment is required. Achieving this type of diverse collaboration lies in the formation of dynamic multilayered networks of "Ba" to create Ba triad and knowledge triad relationships, and the key to these multilayered networks of "Ba" is in the creation of autonomous and distributed phronesis of leaders with practical wisdom (distributed phronesis), and the aggregation of these to gather together their collective intelligence (collective phronesis).

It is here where Apple's practical wisdom leaders came to the fore. From the dissimilar information and contexts surrounding jukebox software, portable music players, music content, Internet distribution, accounting, and so forth, tacit knowledge emerged, and Apple synthesized this tacit knowledge across these different knowledge boundaries to create its proprietary online music store (iTunes music store) as new explicit knowledge.

Furthermore, with the development of iPod and iTunes, Apple created a "Ba" of exploration to integrate the tacit knowledge that the company had built up over the years with the tacit knowledge of its external partners (experts and partners in different business categories), and accomplished a novel business model with the emergence of new tacit knowledge in its "Ba" integrating the non-technological aspects of marketing and design strategies.

Also, in the production of iPod, Apple formed "Ba" of exploitation to achieve integration of explicit knowledge not only within the company, but also with the company's best outsourcing partners for horizontal integration all the way from upstream through to downstream in the value chain.

Furthermore, the "Leader Team" within the company's management hierarchy, which integrates the "exploration Ba" and the "exploitation Ba" has formed a "synthesis Ba" (Kodama, 2004, 2017).

Behind Apple's successful knowledge transformation with iTunes and iPod (and then with iPhone and iPad later on), is the configuration of multilayered networks of "ba" that enable Ba triad and knowledge triad relationships of the tacit knowledge, explicit knowledge and Phronesis inside and outside of the company. This is what gives Apple its dynamic synthesizing capability, and what enabled it to bring about a completely new business model that merges dissimilar knowledge both within and outside of the company. Apple Inc. built a new business model through the teamwork of its leader, Steve Jobs, senior executive vice presidents, and excellent subordinates (see Fig. 3.10).

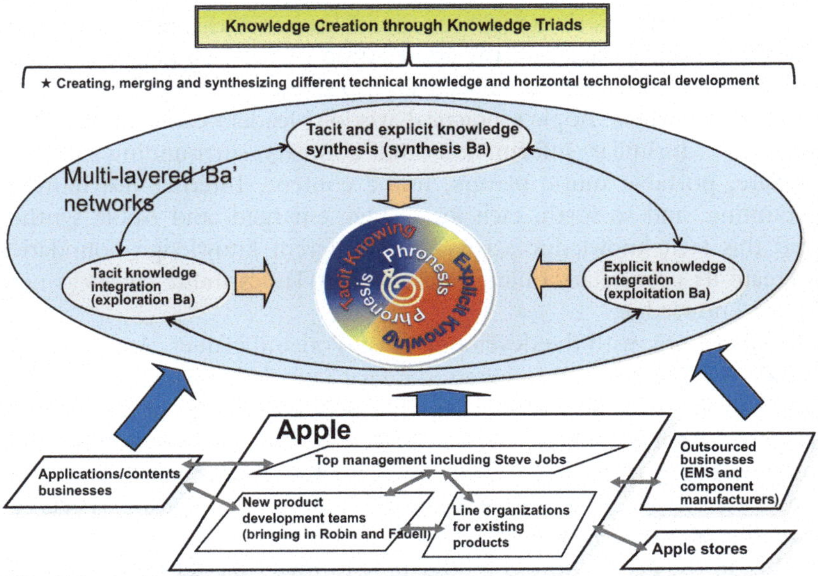

Fig. 3.10 Knowledge transformation via knowledge triads in Apple

3.5 Building the Innovation Community Model for Convergence

As Drucker (1993) identified, knowledge has become the only significant resource in the modern age. As an economic resource, Drucker pointed out that the way that knowledge is accumulated, distributed, and used is not yet completely understood. Nonaka and Takeuchi (1995, 2019) stated that the most prominent characteristic of knowledge is that it is a resource created in human relationships. Unlike a natural resource, knowledge is not a physical self-sufficient resource waiting to be discovered and collected by someone, but rather is created by people in their relationships with each other and the environment, and is a resource whose meaning and value changes depending on the characteristics of the people who use it (by their thoughts, ideals, subjectivity, emotions, etc.), and the situations in which it is used. Innovation through convergence is also brought about from such close relations between people and organizations. Continually generating knowledge in this way is the knowledge creating company model presented in Fig. 3.3, which is a corporate model that requires phronetic management through collective phronesis for it to function sustainably.

3.5.1 The Knowledge Creating Company Models Through Collective Phronesis

Currently, as shown in the case of Apple, what is required in innovation companies that will create the future as convergence is to use the autonomous and decentralized phronetic leadership of individual practitioners, and collective phronesis, the aggregation of this, to practice collective wisdom management across knowledge ecosystems. This entails the specific issues of having ideas and taking actions to understand what needs to be done to achieve the common good, having higher ambitions, and figuring out what is good for society overall while thinking on the front line, keeping an eye on specific changes in details, and bringing about a historical broad perspective. This kind of broad perspective brings about external knowledge synthesizing capability and strategy synthesizing capability. Ba must be created to dynamically perceive the relationships both inside and outside of organizations and change these relations to achieve future concepts. Specifically, this means situational practical skills based on diverse ideas and actions including political capabilities to respond to situations, make decisions while knowing that everything is dependent on context, discern while knowing that everything is in the midst of change, and knowing that everything is dependent on timing. This also means that organizational systems typical of hypertext organizations in which practitioners with this kind of phronesis are fostered on the site of practice and that human capabilities are organizationally accumulated, and that organizational synthesizing capabilities to combine both creativity and efficiency must be demonstrated.

Collective phronesis, the aggregation of this phronesis, promotes the creation of convergence knowledge as convergence. Individual practitioners require boundaries vision to bring forth new inspiration from diverse boundaries in and out of their companies using collective phronesis, and Ba synthesizing capabilities for diverse contexts and knowledge. Creating collective phronesis, requires an organizational broad perspective, Ba creation and human capabilities—elements that accumulate external knowledge synthesizing capabilities, strategic synthesizing capabilities, organizational synthesizing capabilities, and situational practical skills to bring about boundaries knowledge using boundaries vision, the foundation of the achievement of convergence. Moreover, the creation of boundaries knowledge by practitioners, and their Ba synthesizing capabilities achieves convergence as the creation of convergence knowledge.

Based on phronetic leadership and collective phronesis, knowledge integration companies organically tie together the 7 factors of a knowledge vision, driving objectives, dialogue and practice, the SECI process, knowledge assets, multilayered networks of Ba, and environment to synthesize dissimilar knowledge from multilayered dynamic contexts and create new convergence knowledge as convergence. This knowledge integration company model is the basis for the innovation community model that sustainably achieves boundaries innovation through convergence.

3.5.2 *The Knowledge Creation Process and the "space/Time/Resources" Axes*

Nonaka et al. (2008) presented that the sustainable innovation community model develops through the knowledge creation process in three dimensions of space–time, "space/time/resources." As observed in the Apple case, Apple sustainably developed their business models of their products and services for their knowledge visions and driving objectives for boundaries innovation as convergence.

For its knowledge vision of the digital hub concept and its driving objective of creating customer value as new experiences, Apple greatly evolved from the social reality level synthesizing the intersubjectivity of its Apple Computer PC specialized business and Apple users through the development of the iPod/iPhone/iPad products. The company changed its name to Apple, triggered by its strategy transformation in the music distribution business while developing toward into a collective subjectivity—the building of new knowledge ecosystems as music distribution communities and expanded social reality. Moreover, the company independently formed the new smartphone and tablet markets, bringing about social structures synthesizing global "ultra subjectivity" as the smartphone culture at a higher level.

Furthermore, observed on the time axes of timely time and clock time, Apple had created the unique organizational structures of dynamic fractal organizations. The combination of project organizations pursuing creativity with timely time and line organizations pursuing efficiency with clock time enables a company to efficiently achieve a business model as the knowledge creating company business model to create creative convergence knowledge in a spiral manner and practice convergence knowledge required for convergence.

Also, from the perspective of the third resource axis, both companies drove the SECI process pivoting on dialogue and practice. Empathizing with reality through direct experience, condensing essences of awareness into concepts, relating and systemizing concepts, turning concepts into value as technology, products, software, services, and experience, and fleshing out knowledge at the same time as triggering new knowledge in organizations, markets, and environments leads back to socialization. Accelerating the SECI process brings about synthesizing capabilities to dynamically combine creativity and efficiency in the aforementioned hypertext organizations. This sustainable spiraling process enables qualitative and quantitative expansion of knowledge assets.

As described above, the sustainable innovation community model entails the development of knowledge creation processes in the 3 space–time dimensions of time, space, and resources, and the knowledge organizational platforms that sustainably bring about new knowledge as convergence are the aforementioned multilayered networks of Ba.

3.5.3 *Small-World Networks and Multilayered Networks of Ba*

This section discusses multilayered networks of Ba consisting of practitioners across various boundaries from the knowledge of network theory (e.g., Barabasi, 2002; Watts, 2003). Networks of people, groups, and organizations at the micro level, which have complimentary relationships with formal corporate organizations, are important platforms that promote the knowledge creation processes, and thus, the form of these networks has a profound influence on the transfer of information and knowledge (e.g., Lin & Kulatilaka, 2006; Owen-Smith & Powell, 2004). Also, for a company to acquire sustainable organizational capabilities, it is essential that it can dynamically configure networks (Kodama, 2005) and be able to dynamically reconfigure networks to respond to changing environments and strategic actions.

Network theory provides valuable knowledge and insights into practitioner actions both in and between companies and relationships between practitioners. The formation of human networks is an important trigger to make the boundaries vision of practitioners function to inspire and create boundaries knowledge and convergence knowledge. Network forms are broadly divided into centralized networks and decentralized networks. Centralized networks are appropriate for processing information and passing knowledge efficiently (knowledge and information is passed from a central node to peripheral nodes) (e.g., Albert & Barabasi, 2000; Tushman, 1979). Formal organizations with so-called multilayered structures are equivalent to centralized networks.

In contrast, decentralized networks consist of localized clusters (the close relationships between practitioners). Between these dissimilar clusters, dissimilar practitioners in these clusters are linked together by shortcuts (bypasses). This networked topology has been called the "small-world network" (Watts & Strogatz, 1998), and according to the definition in network theory, it is characterized by nodes that can connect to any other node via a small number of nodes so that nodes that connect to a specific node are thus connected each other. Technically, a small-world network is defined as a network having a short average path length[18] and a high cluster coefficient.[19] In a typical small-world network, adjacent nodes (the joining points—e.g., individuals in a society) are connected according to rules, while nodes that are far apart on the network can be linked by random shortcuts or bypasses.

As decentralized networks, small-world networks (Watts, 2003) are appropriate network structure in uncertain situations or when facing new challenges and issues such as boundaries innovation through convergence. In small-world networks, while there is adjacent networking of individuals who are closely connected (e.g., practitioners in the same formal organizations), there are also practitioners who are organizationally decentralized and are able to access each other via the shortcuts available, expand the limits of individual knowledge, and use resources (knowledge) more efficiently across entire organizations. Small-world networks are robust networks that are resilient against information concentration, excessive overload or bottlenecks within organizations, sudden circumstantial changes such as unexpected problems and accidents, or destruction (e.g., Newman, 2004; Shah, 2000).

From the perspective of social network theory, Ba are examples of clusters or cliques[20] formed from the smallest nodes—the individual. Cliques are collectives of closely linked practitioners that exchange and share information, contexts, and knowledge, whereas Ba are not simply collectives for exchange of information, but instead are pragmatic collectives formed as a matrix of meaning forms and practical contexts, and are space–time for the dynamic creation of new contexts and knowledge in response to changing contexts. Also, driving organizational small-world networking, a Ba is space–time in which practitioners with diverse expertise use ICT to create new boundaries knowledge and convergence knowledge to solve the challenges they are facing and realize new creative strategies. In this perspective, a knowledge creating company consists of multilayered networks of Ba—decentralized networks of cliques formed by many shortcuts of practitioners—and formal organizations as centralized networks of many clusters. The overall network form of these is an example of a small-world network.

We place particular focus on multilayered networks of Ba, which are dynamically changing decentralized networks, whose network forms are examples of group-interlocked networks (Watts, 2003). Duncan Watts (2003) said given that actors have a relationship with a particular context, business people proactively form Ba as particular contexts in the real business world, while at the same time other practitioners are brought in (in other words links are created with other practitioners, or they are pulled onto the aforementioned knowledge boundaries). Accordingly, Ba change dynamically in response to context, and at the same time multilayered networks of Ba—the Ba network form—are also formed and change dynamically, as seen in the Apple case.

As part of daily practice, Ba are dynamically reconfigured by practitioners. Then, multiple practitioners participate in multiple Ba to share knowledge and information, and transfer this information and knowledge to the other Ba in which they participate to share it among practitioners. This is the process through which multilayered networks of Ba are formed as the aforementioned group-interlocked networks. In the framework of the group-interlocked network, Ba are examples of nodes or hubs.[21] Practitioners who belong to hub or node Ba inside and outside of companies create networks among those Ba by dynamically bridging multiple and dissimilar Ba. New contexts and knowledge are created as these multiple Ba are linked together by networks. To build new business models or develop new products for convergence, practitioners intentionally network multiple Ba in and out of their companies and deeply connect them to build multilayered networks of Ba.

3.5.4 *Multilayered Networks of Ba as Macro and Micro Linkages*

For businesspersons, multilayered networks of Ba are knowledge organizational platforms for bringing about new knowledge through the sharing of dynamic contexts (time, places, relationships among people). Multilayered networks of Ba are examples of space–time that are generated and changed by practitioners by sharing and changing contexts with others as they interact. This does not only entail sharing tacit knowledge—multilayered networks of Ba are also space–time for creative dialogue and the practical processes of strategic activities.

Organizations and individuals are in dialectical relationships, and while the space–time of "here and now" as multilayered networks of Ba and dynamic practical consciousness are cyclically involved with organizations, practitioners change organizations using their broad perspectives and human capabilities. As discussed in the Apple case, practitioners have the practical power to transform organizations and environments with their own behaviors while being subject to the restriction of the organizations and environments that they themselves have brought about (Giddens, 1984; Giddens & Pierson, 1998).

In other words, multilayered networks of Ba are platforms that bridge practitioners and organizations (companies). Multilayered networks of Ba are also the space–time in which practitioners come together to practice strategic action through collective phronesis both inside and outside of companies. Dynamic contexts are born from the various daily episodes and events that occur on multilayered networks of Ba and practitioners share these contexts. Then, practitioners continue practical processes to create boundaries knowledge and convergence knowledge through formal and informal practical processes. As micro existences, the strategic actions of practitioners affect the macro structures of organizations, companies, industries, and society as a whole through the formation (or elimination) of Ba (see Fig. 3.11).

Accordingly, multilayered networks of Ba are not only important as micro–macro linkages in the networks in society—practitioners affect corporate performances by forming and linking multilayered networks of Ba, and generating and accumulating social capital (e.g., Cohen & Prusak, 2000) in the relationships of practitioners—organizations—multilayered networks of Ba—corporations—industries. Conversely, from the perspective of how practitioners themselves are influenced, multilayered networks of Ba are important analytical units.

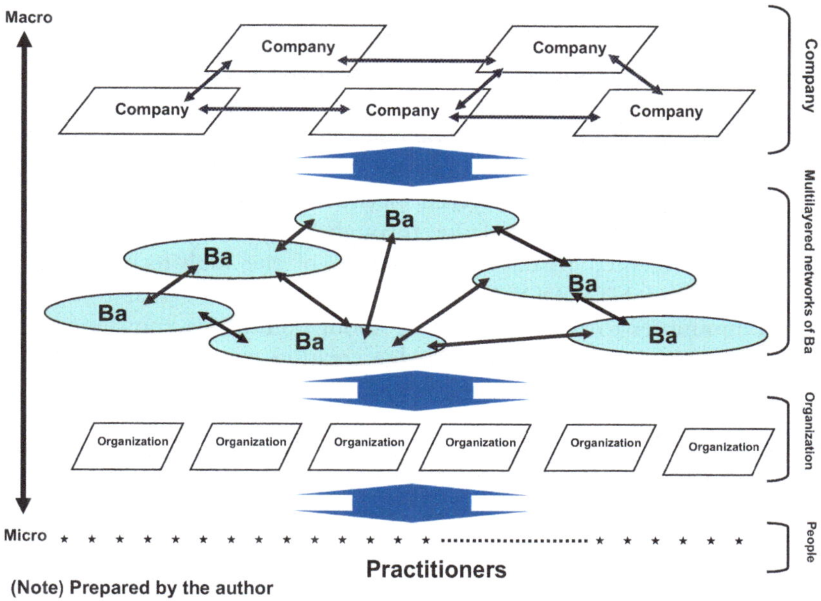

Fig. 3.11 Practitioners and multilayered networks of Ba

Meanwhile, from the perspective of knowledge management theory, social capital that has value as knowledge capital comes about on multilayered networks of Ba, just like the case of Apple. Also, from the perspective of clarifying the processes of synthesizing various knowledge through multilayered networks of Ba, the existence of multilayered networks of Ba is important. These are things that practitioners create and link by proactively persuading others in the environment (such as customers), and inside and outside of organizations. Thus, going forward, the architecture (design thinking) of multilayered networks of Ba that are pivotal to business models involving convergence will become increasingly important. Also, for practitioners, from the perspective that the formation and linking of multilayer networks of Ba leads to new knowledge generation, the concept of multilayered networks of Ba is a significant and practical one.

3.6 Implications and Conclusion

This paper has presented the elements of collective phronesis for the creation of convergence knowledge as convergence by the phronetic leadership of practitioners. Superior collective phronesis entails the use of boundaries vision to inspire and create boundaries knowledge, and dynamically form the multilayered networks of Ba required for the creation of convergence knowledge through Ba synthesizing capabilities, which was presented through case studies of the high-tech organizations Apple and NTT DOCOMO. As a model for sustainable innovation communities to continually bring about boundaries knowledge and convergence knowledge, the knowledge creating company model drives collective phronesis to combine various contradictions both inside and outside of companies, through Ba synthesizing capabilities to dynamically configure and reconfigure a variety of multilayered networks of Ba and achieve boundaries innovation.

To achieve new business models, it's crucial that companies dynamically synthesize knowledge within themselves linking up their various internal boundaries, between people, organizations, different areas of specialization, etc., with external knowledge linking up external boundaries (between companies, between companies and their customers, between different industries, etc.). In other words, new convergence knowledge transcending various boundaries is created in the process of knowledge creation through the creation of boundaries knowledge both inside and outside of companies on both their vertical and horizontal boundaries. To achieve boundaries innovation, the creation of new convergence knowledge as convergence, the creation of sustainable collective phronesis through the phronetic leadership of leading practitioners enables them to build dynamic multilayered networks of Ba and achieve future creation strategies for the common good.

This chapter has considered issues surrounding the important strategic management themes of exploration and exploitation from the perspectives of organizational theory and knowledge creation theory, and has presented the "dynamic fractal organization" as a new organizational model to achieve innovation through sustained knowledge creation. In the understanding of organizations based on the information processing model and contingency theory, exploration and exploitation of knowledge is separated and these concepts stop at integration at the management level, which cannot explain dynamic knowledge creation and innovation. However, from the perspective of knowledge creating theory, it is clear that companies that sustainably achieve dynamic synthesis of exploration and exploitation commonly have multilayered networks of "Ba" that produce the Ba triad and knowledge triad relationships of tacit knowledge, explicit knowledge, and Phronesis, and these knowledge triad relationships bring together the activities of exploration Ba, exploitation Ba, synthesis Ba and achieve robust dynamic fractal organizations which enable environmental adaptation and creation simultaneously.

Ba triad and knowledge triad relationships in dynamic fractal organizations set down and define new rules for dynamic synthesis of internal and external knowledge, and enable convergence of different technologies and the creation of new business models. Thus it is the Phronesis of the leaders with their practical wisdom that effect and propel these successes, and it must exist at all levels of an organization.

Therefore, as a practical implication, companies that aim to achieve sustainable growth must proactively configure multilayered networks of "Ba" to achieve Ba triad and knowledge triad relationships within and between all kinds of organizations both inside and outside of the company. Companies must also foster leadership with practical wisdom and infuse it into their organizations.

As remaining research challenges, detailed analysis and clarification of strategy formulation and organizational characteristics required to achieve dynamic synthesis of exploration and exploitation needs to be addressed, and the questions of how Ba triad and knowledge triad relationships with fractal characteristics should be formed across the knowledge ecosystems within and between diverse organizations, and between companies and industries needs to be answered.

How should the multilayered networks of "Ba" be designed?

It is crucial that the architecture of a "Ba" for realizing Ba triad and knowledge triad relationships is structured so that the dynamic synthesizing process through autonomous and distributed phronesis of leaders with practical wisdom (distributed phronesis) and their collective intelligence (collective phronesis) is achieved.

In innovative organizations, all kinds of knowledge are dynamically synthesized in knowledge triad relationships and networks of multilayered

"Ba." This is a fractal structure, and its driving force lies in the capabilities and practical wisdom of their leaders. Regardless of the size of an organization, the knowledge creation process is characterized by spiraling at all levels, and in all dimensions. Into the future, there are prospects for further elaboration and empirical analysis of theoretical models in these fields.

Notes

1. Refer to Brown and Duguid (2001), Dougherty (1992), and Grinyer and McKiernan (1994) regarding knowledge boundaries, thought worlds, and mental models respectively.
2. To generate shared senses, it's necessary to put oneself in the position of another, and to understand the other it's necessary to grasp its behavior directly with one's own body, rather than indirectly by inferring internalities from externalities of the other's behavior. This leads to empathy, residence, and inclusion with the other.
3. In the process of dynamically sharing contexts, the opportunities for dialectical sublation to re-perceive oneself in the entirety of relationships with others increase, rather than individuals only looking at things in a self-centered way. Nishida's concept of "absolute nothing" is not that nothing exists, but that the new "self in all" appears in the relationships that exists when one abandons the self. Participating in Ba leads to transcendence of one's own limited views or boundaries by the sharing of contexts.
4. Like elementary particles, life has a duality of particles (localization) and waves (ubiquity), and self-organization in this case has been identified as the creation of self-other non-separable relationships like the generation of one wave with a large amplitude through the interactions of waves of differing wavelengths (Nonaka et al., 2014). Knowledge boundaries are generated through self-organization, and have an open and porous character. Primarily, a knowledge network is an open system and can be set freely according to the vision or objective of the subject. Perhaps requisite variety is the Ba boundary setting principle for both optimizing a diversity of individual parts, and thus optimize the whole. Taken to the extreme, self-organization can be perceived through the metaphor of a sphere. Spheres are characterized by having the lowest surface area to volume ratio of any object. In good Ba,

participants maintain diversity while mutually deepening their relationships as each member maximizes the scope of their territories in the environment.

5. Leading software that easily and efficiently enabled writing to CD (jukebox software).
6. In this paper, so-called "knowledge" is generally referred to as "assets." Tangible and intangible (knowledge) assets correspond to explicit and tacit knowledge, respectively.
7. Boundary vision embraces the concept of "peripheral vision." Refer to Day and Schoemaker (2005) for more about peripheral vision.
8. For example, refer to Teece (1982) for discussions on transaction cost theory and corporate boundaries.
9. While close in-house integration with path dependency can be a strength, it can also be a weakness in cases where serious issues arise with such close interdependency when environments change (e.g., Hargadon and Sutton, 1997; Henderson & Clark, 1990; Siggelkow, 2001). While unique technologies and value chains are a strength, strengths can become weaknesses due to changes in the market or disruptive technology (Christensen, 1997) (e.g., Levitt and March, 1988; Leonard-Barton, 1992, 1995; Martins & Kambil, 1999).
10. Here, horizontal boundaries mean the drivers that determine strategic domains for businesses related to the core businesses of a company or new business. Refer to Kodama (2009a, 2009b).
11. External knowledge synthesizing capability is the ability to detect dissimilar contexts and knowledge that are only loosely related or entirely unrelated, and uncover relationships with one's own contexts and knowledge and synthesize them. Much of the leading research to date has reported that the crossing or convergence with dissimilar knowledge is a source of new innovation. Accordingly, for phronimos, to demonstrate external knowledge synthesizing capabilities, uncovering the relationships between dissimilar and existing knowledge, and discovering new meanings is the first important trigger. Refer to Johansson (2004) for more information about crossover innovation with dissimilar knowledge.
12. Strategic synthesizing capabilities are integrative strategy-making capabilities that aim to combine the paradox of being simultaneously intentional and creative. Emergent strategies are rooted in

the sharing of introspection and tacit knowledge among individuals, and are formed in the creation of concepts through abduction. In multilayered networks of Ba, phronimoses share a wide range of dynamic concepts, and produce new knowledge through improvisation. Emergent concepts are crystallized into explicit knowledge as products and services, and intentional strategies are executed through company-wide decision-making. The essence of the process of forming strategy by integrating the emergent with the intentional involves the interplay of creativity and imagination through dialectical dialogue, creative abrasion, and productive friction, repeated self-correction of formalized hypotheses, and finally steady and planned achievement of these hypotheses by phronimoses in multilayered networks of Ba. Being able to combine these two different strategy-making processes simultaneously in a company is an important element of the capability of boundaries vision.

13. In innovating companies, organizational actions commonly require synthesizing capability to connect multiple organizations within the company (between existing and new organizations, and projects, etc.), and make connections between companies (with external partners and customers). While the relationships between such organizations and companies differ depending on the strengths or weaknesses of connections, and the degree of sharing of information and knowledge, for organizations and companies to bring about new innovation, organizational synthesizing capability to make connections between organizations and companies through close collaboration with existing organizations in companies, parent companies, and external partners and customers is crucial. Multilayered networks of Ba form the foundations of this organizational synthesizing capability. Leader teams, groups of supervisors in management layers throughout a company, play the role of forming multilayered networked Ba, and demonstrate the practical knowledge leadership needed to bring about organizational synthesizing capability. The significance of forming multilayered networks of Ba is not only the enabling of the formation of the "community of practice" or the production of cohesive relationships between companies maintaining business relationship over the long term, but also the enabling of the formation of small-world structures for companies to acquire diverse knowledge by

shortcutting those cohesive networks. These small-world structures are examples of Ba and multilayered networks of Ba.

14. Situational practical skills are deeply related to leadership behaviors based on contingency theory. Refer to von Krogh, Nonaka and Rechsteiner (2012).
15. Much previous research has identified the necessity of smooth communications and the importance of "boundary spanners" (Brown and Eisenhardt, 1995) on the cross-functional boundaries (e.g., Allen, 1977; Tushman, 1977; Tushman and Nadler, 1978) that lay in the background of successful product development. The main concept of these theories is the information processing model (Carlile, 2002, 2004) on syntactic boundaries, which focuses on efficient processing, transfer, storage, and retrieval of large amounts of information and knowledge. Obviously, as a fundamental of corporate activity, the information processing approach is important for company procedures based on rules and to execute project management or business processes efficiently. However, because innovation has a tendency to occur on the boundaries between businesspersons from organizations with distinct rules or different specializations (Leonard-Barton, 1995; Nonaka and Takeuchi, 1995), the information processing approach, with its focus on efficiency of information and knowledge processing, cannot sufficiently explain the innovation processes that occur on boundaries.
16. In the technical sense, knowledge differences can be theoretically broken down as a combination of the appropriation of existing knowledge assets, the improvement of existing knowledge assets, and new developmental elements (ideas). Based on existing tacit knowledge (the experience and know-how of engineers and engineering groups) and existing explicit knowledge, the ability to break down, analyze and reconfigure elements (ideas) of the objective product development as new factors (including improvements to existing knowledge) and existing factors (knowledge) is required by engineers. Thus, knowledge differences is one of the abilities to recognize the 3 categories of (1) the appropriation of existing knowledge, (2) the improvement of existing knowledge, and (3) elements (ideas) of new development to achieve new concepts through thorough discussions among engineers (Kodama, 2006). However, from the viewpoint of marketing, to bring about new

objects or events by integrating different products, services, or business models, knowledge differences refer to ideas and concepts that fill in the gaps between them.

17. Christian (2011) stated the following:

    In contrast to the pyramidical or hierarchical structures of companies or scale-projects, there are many cases where you can think of parts as fractals, in that if you remove one and expand it, it has the same shape as the whole. Decision-making and artistic standards should be the same on whatever scale you look at them.

    For details, see Christian (2011).
18. The average shortest distance between any nodes.
19. The cluster coefficient describes the level of clustering of nodes on a network.
20. A clique describes a group of nodes on a network that are directly connected to each other.
21. A hub refers to any of an extremely small number of nodes that have huge numbers of links on the network.

References

Ahn, J. H., Lee, D. J., & Lee, S. Y. (2006). Balancing business performance and knowledge performance of new product development. Lessons from ITS Industry. *Long Range Planning, 39*(6), 525–542.

Albert, R., & Barabasi, A. (2000). Topology of evolving networks: Local events and universality. *Physical Review Letters, 85*(24), 5234–5237.

Allen, T. J. (1977). *Managing the flow of technology*. MIT Press.

Aristotle. (350 BCE/1980). *The Nicomachean Ethics* (David Ross, trans.). Oxford University Press.

Ashby, R. (1956). *An introduction to cybernecs*. Chapman and Hall.

Barabasi, A. (2002). *Linked: The new science of networks*. Perseus Books Group.

Benner, M., & Tushman, M. (2003). Exploitation, exploration, and process management: The productivity dilemma revisited. *Academy of Management Review, 28*(2), 238–256.

Brown, J. S., & Duguid, P. (2001). Knowledge and organization: A social-practice perspective. *Organization Science, 12*(2), 198–213.

Brown, S. L., & Eisenhardt, K. M. (1995). Product development: Past research, present findings, and future directions. *Academy of Management Review, 20*(2), 343–378.

Burgelman, R., & Sayles, R. (1986). *Inside corporate innovation: Strategy, structure, and managerial skills*. Free Press.
Burns, T., & Stalker, G. (1961). *The management of innovation*. Tavi-stock.
Carlile, P. (2002). A pragmatic view of knowledge and boundaries: Boundary objects in new product development. *Organization Science, 13*(4), 442–455.
Carlile, P. (2004). Transferring, translating, and transforming: an integrative framework for managing knowledge across boundaries. *Organization Science, 15*(5), 555–568.
Chesbrough, H. W. (2003). *Open innovation: The new imperative for creating and profiting from technology*. Harvard Business Press.
Christensen, C. (1997). *The innovator's dilemma: When new technologies cause great firms to fail* (p. 288). Harvard Business Review Press.
Christian, B. (2011). *The most human human*. Penguin Books.
Cohen, D., & Prusak, L. (2000). *In good company: How social capital makes organizations work*. Harvard Business School Press.
Cyert, R., & March, J. (1955). Organizational structure and pricing behavior in an oligopolistic market. *The American Economic Review, 45*(1), 129–139.
Day, G. S., & Schoemaker, P. J. (2005). Scanning the periphery. *Harvard Business Review, 83*(11), 135.
Dougherty, D. (1992). Interpretive barriers to successful product innovation in large firms. *Organization Science, 3*(2), 179–202.
Drucker, P. F. (1993). *Post-capitalist society* Harper Business.
Ericsson, K. A., & Lehmann, A. C. (1996). Expert and exceptional performance: Evidence of maximal adaptation to task constraints. *Annual Review of Psychology, 47*(1), 273–305.
Galbraith, J. (1973). *Designing complex organizations*. Addison-Wesley.
Giddens, A. (1984). *The constitution of society. Outline of the theory of structuration*. Polity Press.
Giddens, A., & Pierson, C. (1998). *Conversation with Anthony Giddens: Making sense of modernity*. Blackwell Publishers.
Greenwood, R., & Hinings, C. (1993). Understanding strategic change: The contribution of archetypes. *Academy of Management Review, 36*(5), 1052–1081.
Grinyer, P., & McKiernan, P. (1994). Triggering major and sustained changes in stagnating companies. In *Strategic groups, strategic moves and performance* (pp. 173–195).
Hargadon, A., & Sutton, R. I. (1997). Technology brokering and innovation in a product development firm. *Administrative Science Quarterly*, 716–749.
He, Z., & Wong, P. (2004). Exploration vs. exploitation: An Empirical test of the ambidexterity hypothesis. *Organization Science, 15*(4), 481–494.

Helfat, C. E., & Peteraf, M. A. (2015). Managerial cognitive capabilities and the microfoundations of dynamic capabilities. *Strategic Management Journal, 36*(6), 831–850.

Henderson, R. M., & Clark, K. B. (1990). Architectural innovation: The reconfiguration of existing product technologies and the failure of established firms. *Administrative Science Quarterly*, 9–30.

Hill, C. W., & Rothaermel, F. T. (2003). The performance of incumbent firms in the face of radical technological innovation. *Academy of Management Review, 28*(2), 257–274.

Johansson, F. (2004). *The medici effect*. Harvard Business School Press.

Kanter, R. (1985). Supporting innovation and venture development in established companies. *Journal of Business Venturing, 1*(1), 47–60.

Kodama, M. (2003). Strategic innovation in traditional big business: Case studies of two Japanese companies. *Organization Studies, 24*(2), 235–268.

Kodama, M. (2004). Strategic community-based theory of firms: Case study of dialectical management at NTT DoCoMo. *Systems Research and Behavioral Science: THe Official Journal of the International Federation for Systems Research, 21*(6), 603–634.

Kodama, M. (2005). Knowledge creation through networked strategic communities: Case studies in new product development. *Long Range Planning, 38*(1), 27–49.

Kodama, M. (2006). Knowledge-based view of corporate strategy. *Technovation, 26*(12), 1390–1406.

Kodama, M. (2007). *The strategic community-based firm*. Palgrave Macmillan.

Kodama, M. (2009a). Boundaries innovation and knowledge integration in the Japanese firm. *Long Range Planning, 42*(4), 463–494.

Kodama, M. (2009b). Innovation networks in knowledge-based firms: Developing ICT-based integrative competences. In *Innovation networks in knowledge-based firms*. Edward Elgar Publishing.

Kodama, M. (2011). *Knowledge integration dynamics—Developing strategic innovation capability*. World Scientific Publishing.

Kodama, M. (2014). *Winning through boundaries innovation: Communities of boundaries generate convergence*. Peter Lang.

Kodama, M. (2017). *Developing holistic leadership: A source of business innovation*. Emerald Publishing Limited.

Kodama, M. (2019). Boundaries knowledge (knowing)—A source of business innovation. *Knowledge and Process Management, 26*(3), 210–228.

Kodama, M. (2020). Developing knowledge communities through video-based information networks. *Knowledge and Process Management, 27*(2), 103–122.

Kodama, M. (2021). Knowledge creation through collective phronesis. *Knowledge and Process Management, 28*(3), 223–245.

Kodama, M., & Hashimoto, K. (2024). Research on high-end disruptive innovations - Analysis and insights from the video conferencing systems market. *Technology in Society, 77*, 102576.

Kodama, M., & Shibata, T. (2016). Developing knowledge convergence through a boundaries vision—A case study of Fujifilm in Japan. *Knowledge and Process Management, 23*(4), 274–292.

Kogut, B., & Zander, U. (1992). Knowledge of the firm, combinative capabilities, and the replication of technology. *Organization Science, 3*(3), 383–397.

Lawrence, P., & Lorsch, J. (1967). *Organization and environments.* Harvard Business School Press.

Leifer, R, McDermott, M, O'Connor, C, Peters, S., Rice, M., & Veryzer, W. (2000). *Radical innovation: How mature companies can outsmart upstarts.* Harvard Business School Press.

Leonard-Barton, D. (1992). Core capabilities and core rigidities: A paradox in managing new product development. *Strategic Management Journal, 13*(S1), 111–125.

Leonard-Barton, D. (1995). *Wellsprings of Knowledge: Building and sustaining the sources of innovation.* Harvard Business School Press.

Levitt, B., & March, J. G. (1988). Organizational learning. *Annual Review of Sociology, 14*(1), 319–338.

Lin, L., & Kulatilaka, N. (2006). Network effects and technology licensing with fixed fee, royalty, and hybrid contracts. *Journal of Management Information Systems, 23*(2), 91–118.

Mandelbrot, B. (1983). *The fractal geometry of nature.* Freeman.

March, G., & Simon, A. (1958). *Organization.* Wiley.

March, J. (1991). Exploration and exploitation in organizational learning. *Organization Science, 2*(1), 71–87.

Martins, L. L., & Kambil, A. (1999). Looking back and thinking ahead: Effects of prior success on managers' interpretations of new information technologies. *Academy of Management Journal, 42*(6), 652–661.

Melé, D., Cantón, C. G. (2014). The homo economicus model. In: *Human foundations of management. IESE Business Collection.* Palgrave Macmillan.

Newman, M. E. J. (2004). Fast algorithm for detecting community structure in networks. *Physical Review E, 69*(6), 1–5.

Nonaka, I., & Takeuchi, H. (1995). *The Knowledge Creating Company.* Oxford University Press.

Nonaka, I., Kodama, M., Hirose, A., & Kohlbacher, F. (2014). Dynamic fractal organizations for promoting knowledge-based transformation—A new paradigm for organizational theory. *European Management Journal, 32*(1), 137–146.

Nonaka, I., & Takeuchi, H. (1995). *The knowledge-creating company.* Oxford University Press.

Nonaka, I., & Takeuchi, H. (2019). *The wise company: How companies create continuous innovation*. Oxford University Press.

Nonaka, I., & Toyama, R. (2005). The theory of the knowledge-creating firm: Subjectivity, objectivity and synthesis. *Industrial and Corporate Change, 14*(3), 419–436.

Nonaka, I., Toyama, R., & Hirata, T. (2008). *Managing flow: A process theory of the knowledge-based firm*. Palgrave Macmillan.

Nonaka, I., Toyama, R., & Konno, N. (2000). "Ba" and leadership: A unified model of dynamic knowledge creation. *Long Range Planning, 33*, 5–34.

Owen-Smith, J., & Powell, W. W. (2004). Knowledge networks as channels and conduits: The effects of spillovers in the Boston biotechnology community. *Organization Science, 15*(1), 5–22.

O'Reilly, C., & Tushman, M. (2004, April). The ambidextrous organization. *Harvard Business Review, 82*, 74–82.

Prahalad, C. K. & Ramaswamy, V. (2000). Co-opting customer competence. *Harvard Business Review, 78*(1), 79–87.

Prahalad, C. K. & Ramaswamy, V. (2004). *The future of competition: Co-creating unique value with customers*. Harvard Business School Press.

Shah, P. (2000). Network destruction: The structural implications of downsizing. *Academy of Management Journal, 43*(1), 101–112.

Siggelkow, N. (2001). Change in the presence of fit: The rise, the fall, and the renaissance of Liz Claiborne. *Academy of Management Journal, 44*(4), 838–857.

Simon, H. A. (1969). *The sciences of the artificial*. MIT Press.

Smith, W., & Tushman, M. (2005). Managing strategic contradictions: A top management model for managing innovation streams. *Organization Science, 16*(5), 522–536.

Teece, D. J. (1982). Towards an economic theory of the multiproduct firm. *Journal of Economic Behavior & Organization, 3*(1), 39–63.

Teece, D. J. (2014). The foundations of enterprise performance: Dynamic and ordinary capabilities in an (economic) theory of firms. *Academy of Management Perspectives, 28*(4), 328–352.

Tushman, M. (1979). Work characteristics and subunit communication structure: A contingency analysis. *Administrative Science Quarterly, 24*, 82–98.

Tushman, M. L., & O'Reilly, C. A. (1997). *Winning trough innovation*. Harvard Business School Press.

Tushman, M., & Nadler, D. (1978). Information Processing as an integrating concept in organizational design. *Academy of Management Review, 3*(3), 613–624.

Tushman, M. L. (1977). Special boundary roles in the innovation process. *Administrative Science Quarterly, 22*(2), 587–605.

von Krogh, G., Nonaka, I., & Rechsteiner, L. (2012). Leadership in organizational knowledge creation: A review and framework. *Journal of Management Studies, 49*(1), 240–277.

Watts, J. (2003). *Six degrees: The science of a connected age*. W. W. Norton and Company.

Watts, J., & Strogatz, S. (1998). Collective dynamics of "small-world" networks. *Nature, 393*(4), 440–442.

Welch, J., & Welch, S. (2005). *Winning*. Harper Business

CHAPTER 4

Innovation by Technology Convergence Through High-End Disruption by Cisco, Microsoft, and Zoom

4.1 Introduction—Video Conferencing Systems Market Evolution and Current Status

Due to the impact of the novel coronavirus (COVID-19), an infectious disease, the digital transformation of work styles around the world has been progressing faster than ever. Corporate strategies regarding "with corona," and looking ahead to "after corona," have been facing major changes on a global scale. In these circumstances, digital shifts (digital transformation: DX) away from conventional work styles are getting enormous attention and demands for them are rising in societies. Moreover, the spread of IoT, 5G, cloud services, etc., is further accelerating these digital transformations.

In particular, the global scale of the spread of novel coronavirus infections has increased demands for cloud services all over the world. Notable in this expansion are demands for videoconferencing tools, which are indispensable for telework (e.g., Kodama, 2012, 2020a, 2020b, 2021b). For example, interest in online learning and online healthcare is rapidly increasing, and the introduction of telework and online seminars, etc., is rapidly progressing. After the novel coronavirus spread, the stock price of "Zoom" (NASDAQ: ZM), a video conferencing software developer, rose sharply.

M. Kodama, *Developing Knowledge Convergence Through Collective Phronesis*, https://doi.org/10.1007/978-981-96-4403-2_4

In China, Ali Baba offered chat and video conferencing services to 10 million companies free of charge and increased its memberships to 200 million. Other that those, companies such as Baidu, Tencent, and ByteDance that offer TikTok have been providing various telework tools for free with over 18 million companies and more than 300 million people doing telework. In this way, global demand for video conferencing tools skyrocketed—downloads of Zoom in the second week of March 2020 were 14 times higher in the United States, 20 times higher in the United Kingdom, 27 times higher in Spain, and 55 times higher in Italy, compared to the weekly average for the fourth quarter of 2019.

Looking back at the history of the videoconferencing system market, momentum for the development of videoconferencing systems grew in Japan, Europe, and the United States after the appearance of the world's first videoconferencing system realized using color television transmission lines in Japan around the 1980s. After the systems featuring proprietary standards in the 1980s, the 1990s saw an upsurge in international standardization, perhaps as a reaction to that trend, and hardware-based videoconferencing systems that support H.320[1] were born. Subsequently, with the advent of the Internet, which spread concurrently with the spread of H.320, international standardization based on IP (Internet Protocol) began in earnest. In the late 1990s and early 2000s, cloud service-based unified communications led by Microsoft and Cisco Systems emerged, along with the penetration of the international standard SIP[2] protocol, which led to the current cloud-based video conferencing services. This transformed video conferencing systems into the era of software-based cloud video conferencing services.

In this chapter, we will discuss products, services, technologies, and business strategies related to the video conferencing system market as a case of technology convergence. The realization of cloud video conferencing services, which are an aggregation of technology convergence, has revolutionized the traditional hardware-based video conferencing system market and created a new market. Through detailed case studies of high-end disruption (e.g., Carr, 2005; van der Rhee et al., 2012; Van Orden et al., 2011) led by companies such as Microsoft, Cisco Systems, and Zoom, which continue to pioneer and drive this new market, we will analyze and examine the success factors of these companies from the perspective of dynamic capabilities and the SECI process.

The structure of this chapter is as follows. First, I will detail the strategic analysis of the video conferencing system market from the perspectives of product architecture, business models, and organizational strategies. Second, I will analyze and consider the relationship between dynamic capabilities and the SECI process that drive technology convergence. Finally, I will discuss the implications and conclusions.

4.2 Business Ecosystems: The Visual FMC Era (2011–Present)

Nearing 2010, the industry was changing with keywords such as communication system integration (unified communications), HD, and Telepresence. In addition, the aforementioned entry of Cisco Systems and Microsoft, which acquired web conferencing vendors, had a significant impact on the video conferencing market. This was the catalyst and accelerator for the move to a new software architecture: cloud videoconferencing services with today's unified communications capabilities (see Fig. 4.1). It was also around this time that the shadow of the traditional dedicated hardware terminal-based VCS manufacturers began to show.

The new architecture of unified communication not only allows different means of communication to work together flexibly, but also enables seamless communication between different devices such as IP phones, PCs, mobile phones, smartphones, and tablets. By linking these multiple communications methods, corporations can enjoy the advantages of more efficient management and greater productivity. From the old telephone and fax machines to e-mail, instant messaging, videoconferencing, and web conferencing, today's companies and organizations are able to utilize a wide variety of communication methods. These communication methods were used for different purposes and were achieved by individual devices, terminals, applications, etc. The integration of this group of differing communications on the IP network, and the achievement of flexible intercommunications is called "unified communications" (see Fig. 4.1).

Until around 2010, many companies incorporated various groupware and ERP tools, etc., to facilitate communications and information sharing among organizations and promote best practices in daily operations. However, even in companies that had already transformed their corporate culture with the uptake of these tools, the problems of being unable to sufficiently strengthen communications in and between organizations with e-mail and groupware alone and speed up decision-making began to surface. Therefore, the ultimate practical ICT tools to completely solve

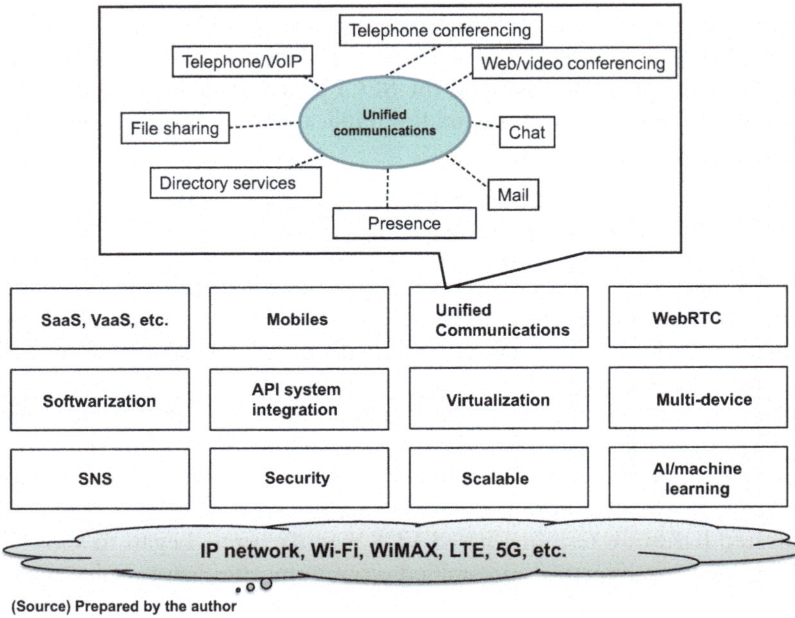

Fig. 4.1 Cloud videoconferencing service architecture

the kind of "blockage" that prevents individual intentions and thoughts from being adequately communicated through e-mail and groupware, and to lead companies toward innovation, are "unified communications" using the cloud.

In other words, such tools enable full discussion of contents and quick decision-making. Looking at this from the perspective of the knowledge creation process, which is central to corporate business transformation activities, in the linking and improved efficiency of explicit knowledge (e.g., knowledge that has already been documented), e-mail, various types of groupware, application sharing, and databases has shown great power. On the other hand, unified communications, which integrate video, voice, and text data, is a new approach to tacit knowledge (e.g., knowledge that cannot be verbalized, such as human beliefs, thoughts, sensations, images, etc.) in the interactions and collaborations in a world where cyberspace (online) and real space merge. At the level of tacit knowledge, these have the potential to inspire and trigger new ideas, thoughts, sensations, and emotions in humans. Therefore, unified communications in the cloud era will bring about an era of creation in which a wide variety of information and knowledge that are unevenly distributed throughout the world are collected, analyzed, and linked to create new knowledge and value (e.g., creation of rich tacit knowledge and formalization of tacit knowledge to explicit knowledge) (Kodama, 2012).

Led by Microsoft, Cisco Systems, Avaya, HP, IBM, Broadsoft, Mitel, and others, the integration of various communication tools for unified communications has been accelerated. Although the market was led by Polycom and Tandberg in the era of dedicated hardware VCS, the market is led by Microsoft, Cisco, Google, and Zoom. This led to the videoconferencing industry becoming a fairly high-profile industry and, as a result, the opportunity to surpass the business models of Polycom, Tandberg, and others based on dedicated hardware VCS.

During this period, cloud, mobile, low-cost videoconferencing, and WebRTC[3] also encouraged venture companies to enter the market. In addition to traditional venture capital-based startups, there are also examples (High Five, Inc.) that utilize crowdfunding. Meanwhile, more and more companies from China, India, and Eastern Europe are entering the market. One reason for this is that the proliferation of the Internet, PCs, and devices, and the realization of VCSs and MCUs through software architecture have lowered the threshold for new entrants. Providers advocating cloud-based web conferencing services began to emerge around 2009, and now cloud video services have become a major trend. In addition, system integration with CRM, groupware, and other business systems has increased through business-to-business alliances, and the formation of business ecosystems centered on platforms such as Zoom, Microsoft, and Google have been observed (see Box 4.1). Platforms have shifted to cloud-based and multi-vendor ecosystem strategies, depending on users' usage and objectives (see Fig. 4.2).

As mentioned by Kodama (2002), we can say that a "visual fixed-mobile convergence (FMC)" environment has been created in which video communications are possible seamlessly without being aware of fixed terminals (PC, dedicated VCS), mobile terminals (smartphones, tablets, etc.), or network types (IP network, Wi-Fi, WiMAX, LTE, 5G, etc.) (see Fig. 4.1). Put differently, the era of ubiquitous and seamless broadband has arrived.

The entry of Zoom, Microsoft, Cisco Systems, and Google, continues to have a significant impact on the video conferencing industry. Notably,

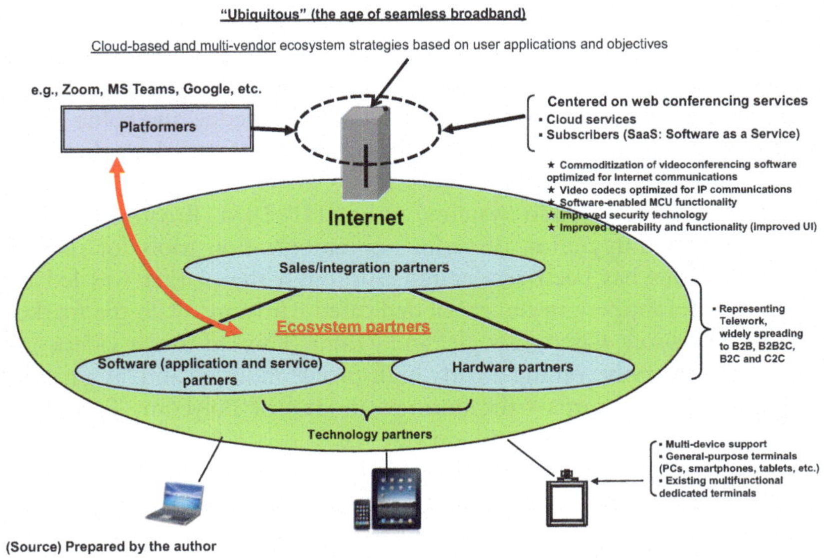

Fig. 4.2 Business ecosystem (visual FMC era)

the number of acquisitions increased during the entry of Microsoft and Cisco (since 2004). Cisco Systems acquired WebEx, a U.S. web collaboration service, in 2007. Hardware videoconferencing manufacturers (VCS, MCU, etc.) from the early ISDN/IP era (Polycom, Tandberg) and related service providers (WireOne, BlueJeans) had all been acquired by other companies by 2022. At the same time, early web conferencing service providers are exiting the market, starting with Cisco's acquisition of Webex.

In the aftermath of this trend, a number of mergers, acquisitions, and partnerships led to the acquisition of major manufacturers in the 1990s and 2000s. For example, Polycom expanded its corporate scale through a number of acquisitions to survive, but it has been in two or three phases: acquired by a fund (2016), later by Plantronics (2018), and then by HP (2022), effectively turning from a traditional hardware terminal (VCS) and MCU manufacturer to a brand of speaker microphones, headsets, and other products.

After 2020, Zoom, MS Teams, and Cisco Webex have been at the center of their respective ecosystems, with more acquisitions as part of adding or enhancing product features (AI, encryption, translation capabilities, etc.). Acquisitions reached 14 in the two and a half years since 2020 and could grow to more than 20 by 2024.

In the present, from around 2010, high-end encroachment (e.g., van der Rhee et al., 2012; Van Orden et al., 2011) by cloud videoconferencing services occurred simultaneously in the existing hardware-type VCS market and had a significant impact on the videoconferencing market in the global market.[4] Figure 4.3 shows the actual market size of the high-end encroachment of cloud video conferencing services in the Americas, EMEA, and APAC market. The market for cloud videoconferencing services began to emerge in 2011, the cloud accounted for about 40% of the total market. By 2019 the market share was comparable to that of the hardware-type VCSs. On entering 2019, the market showed remarkable growth and overtook the existing market for the hardware-type VCSs by 2020.

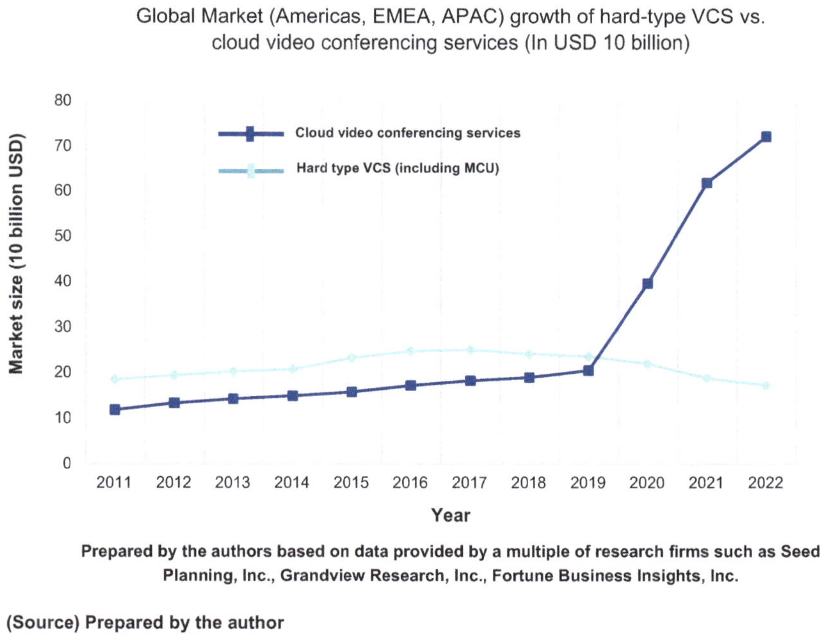

Fig. 4.3 High-end encroachment of cloud video conferencing services (Global market)

Meanwhile, the rapid high-end encroachment (e.g., Carr, 2005; van der Rhee et al., 2012; Van Orden et al., 2011) and erosion by these cloud videoconferencing services has led to companies exiting or declining from the existing hardware-type VCS market. For example, Poly (that acquired Polycom), the world's largest hardware-type VCS manufacturer, was acquired by HP and will not develop or sell any new hardware-type VCSs, but will invest its resources in peripheral equipment such as cameras and speaker microphones. Major global videoconferencing manufacturers have been forced to end production and sales of their products, with Sony discontinuing its PCS series in August 2018, NEC discontinuing its MEDIAPOINT HD in February 2020, and Panasonic discontinuing its HD Com in December 2022.

Box 4.1. Zoom's Platform Strategy and Ecosystem Strategy Roadmap
Zoom, a company that has attracted global attention in recent years, was founded in 2011 and spent 18 months in beta with 40 engineers who were originally from WebEx with the goal of developing software suitable for the smartphone and cloud era. In May 2012, the company changed its name from SaaSbee to Zoom Video Communications. In August of the same year, a beta version was released. This version achieved HD quality group video chat with 15 people participating simultaneously. In November of the same year, the company's first customer signed a contract with the university, and by December the number of users had reached 1000.

In January 2013, the company announced the cloud-based Unified Meeting Experience (UMX) Zoom 1.0, which enabled up to 25 people to participate in HD video conferencing. The free version allowed calls up to 40 minutes. In June of the same year, the company released Zoom 2.0, a cloud video collaboration system. The concept for this version was "affordable, unified, cross platform meeting experience for everyone." Additional features, such as an H.323 connector, were also added for integration with existing videoconferencing systems from other companies.

In July of the same year, the company launched the Works with Zoom partner program with the participation of 12 companies, including Aver Information and Logitech (Logicool). Zoom achieved 2 million users (meeting participants), 5500 meetings/day, and 100 million meetings. In December of the same year, Zoom 2.5 was released, adding enhancements for iPhone/iPad, 100 participants/meeting, 25 gallery view, connection to H.323/SIP devices, passcodes, personal meeting IDs, and other features. Then in FY2013, the company achieved 5000 corporate contracts.

From 2014, Zoom steered its development strategy toward a joint development strategy with development partners aiming for an ecosystem strategy. In April of the same year, the company introduced Zoom Presence (Zoom Rooms as of 2022) for conference rooms, offering an all-in-one touch screen, monitor, Mac mini, camera, and speakerphone. In June, ARRNet (Australia), an inter-school Internet service with 2000 participating schools, adopted Zoom, and has exceeded 1 million users.

In July of the same year, the number of users (conference participants) reached 10 million. This represents an increase of 8 million users in one year. In August of the same year, Zoom 3.0 was released, adding group messaging, co-annotation (simultaneous writing), and a new service, Zoom Webinar was released. In December, five months after launching Zoom 3.0, the company released Zoom 3.5, the first to support cloud recording (MP4), mobile screen sharing (iPad/iPhone app to Mac/PC), and mobile screen sharing, ahead of its competitors. The ability to transfer files through group messaging and other functions were also added.

Poly (formerly Polycom), Logitech, Sure, Yamaha, Yealink, Aver, DTEN, Jabra, Lenovo, Personify, and Revolve Robotics participated as hardware partners (technology partners) in the Zoom-centric ecosystem. The aforementioned Zoom Rooms are dedicated Zoom hardware terminals with built-in microphones, cameras, and speakers that are used with the Zoom service and are intended for conference rooms and home teleworkers. Currently, Zoom Rooms services are widespread around the globe. Zoom entered a partnership with Polycom (offering bundled products). Polycom, a long-established codec manufacturer, shifted its focus to selling webcams and speakerphones, which is a major turning point in the company's business model.

In addition, the ecosystem's software (applications and services) partners (technology partners) include Salesforce, Miro, and Slack, as well as Google Workplace, Calendar, Documents, Microsoft Teams (Schedule), Dropbox, Evernote, Zendesk (for help desk), Qumu (video streaming), Otter.ai (voice AI, minutes, etc.), and others. For example, with 1500 applications registered, the Zoom App Marketplace is a convenient application that can be used in conjunction with Zoom meetings. Linking with other companies' services such as Slack and Salesforce enables you to start a Zoom meeting from a Slack chat or from a Salesforce user's screen (customer data and other information). Apps range from those that summarize the contents of meetings (ToDo lists) to other applications. These are used to improve the quality of Zoom meetings and reduce operational stress.

The apps are intended to improve the quality of Zoom meetings, but conversely, API and SDK offerings have also been actively developed recently through the execution of the Zoom Developer Program to integrate Zoom into users' business systems. In April 2021, Zoom launched the $100 million Zoom Apps Fund. The purpose of Zoom Apps (Zoom integration apps) is to promote the growth of the company's ecosystem, consisting of integration with other companies' services, developer platforms, and compatible hardware. The fund invests in developer partners that have developed profitable products and are new to the market, with an initial investment of $250,000 to $2.5 million in each portfolio company. There are also more than 1000 reseller and integrator partners worldwide.

In 2015, to accommodate the rapid user expansion associated with three consecutive years of triple-digit hyper growth, Zoom entered into a partnership with Equinox, a data center, and contracted 13 data centers worldwide, reaching 450,000 subscribing businesses, 5800 educational institutions, and 15 billion annual meeting minutes. In 2017, the company announced apps one after the other, including Zoom for Telehealth, a cloud-based telehealth service in February, Zoom Connector for Polycom for Polycom terminals in May, and One Zoom One Tap Connector for Cisco for Cisco terminals in June. The company also partnered with Samsung Electronics Korea to offer the Samsung Dex mobile dock, a mobile-to-desktop meeting experience. In addition, in July 2020, the company released the hardware subscription "Zoom Hardware as a Service" (HaaS) and announced "Zoom for Home" for remote workers. We are entering an era of subscriptions not only for cloud computing, but also for hardware.

These hardware partners (technology partners), software service partners (applications and services) (technology partners), as well as reseller partners and integrator partners form a business ecosystem around the Zoom service platform, which has been the backbone of the company's rapid growth (see Fig. 4.2).

4.3 Factors that Prevent Existing Leader Companies from Responding to High-End Disruptive Innovation and Strategies for Responding—From the Perspective of Knowledge Theory and Capability Theory

So why can't existing leader companies respond to high-end disruptive innovation?

Knowledge has been noted as both a source of, and a barrier to innovation (Carlile, 2002, p. 442). Much innovation occurs between disciplines and specialties (Leonard-Barton, 1995), which is not only why work done across boundaries is a major source of competitive advantage, but also why innovation is so difficult to generate and retain. The reason for this difficulty is the existence of knowledge boundaries (Brown & Duguid, 2001) between the market environments facing corporate leaders (Kodama, 2019b). On the boundaries between corporate leaders' knowledge of existing products and knowledge of new products when novel new product architecture or business models emerge, corporate leaders often lack the common knowledge to adequately share and evaluate their field-specific knowledge (Carlile, 2004).

Company leaders tend to misidentify new things (in this case, a new product architecture or business model) as something known, in a "competency trap" (Levitt & March, 1988; Martins & Kambil, 1999) or dismiss new things as meaningless (Arrow, 1994; Perrow, 1994). Camerer et al. (1989) call these tendencies the curse of knowledge. This means existing corporate leaders have difficulty discarding path-dependent knowledge—such issues highlight the challenges corporate leaders face in identifying important things when new situations emerge (Weick et al., 1999).

On the other hand, according to the literature on core capabilities, a company's unique strengths, which other companies cannot easily imitate, can become strengths if these core capabilities are compatible with its business environment. However, when the business environment and technology change and conventional management behavior no longer works, the problem in management is that these capabilities paradoxically turn into core rigidities. In other words, a company's strengths are simultaneously its weaknesses. Core capabilities can certainly be transformed into core rigidities, and knowledge-generating activities by core capabilities can, in turn, impede the flow of knowledge (Leonard-Barton, 1992).

In addition, whether the existing leader companies demonstrate rigidity in their core capabilities depends on whether senior management has grasped a new innovation as a threat or an opportunity. Gilbert (2005) decomposes the structure of inertia into two distinct categories: resource rigidity (not changing resource investment pattern) and routine rigidity (not changing the organizational processes using those resources). While a strong perception of threat helps overcome resource rigidity, it also reveals that it amplifies everyday rigidity.

According to the interview data mentioned above, there are elements that hardware vendors decided too late to shift their business to cloud video conferencing, in addition to the increase in development costs. In addition, it was difficult for the company to switch to a cloud provider in the situation where the brand as a hardware manufacturer was established. On the other hand, the management decided that continuing the development of hardware products utilizing video and audio technology with thousands of patents would be a more realistic solution. These reflect the commitment to past knowledge assets.

Such "competency traps," "the curse of knowledge," and "core rigidities" make it difficult for existing corporate leaders to abandon path-dependent knowledge and transform to new product architectures and business models to accommodate high-end disruptive innovation. This is one of the factors that leads to the decline and withdrawal of existing products or acquisition of existing companies. However, Zuckerman (2016) mentions that "disruptive innovation" is not a direct factor affecting the "competency trap."

The second point is the problem of internal competition and external relationships in related industries with other companies. Internal competition is when a firm's business units compete within the firm for the same business (Zuckerman, 2016). Internal issues include development system issues such as development resources, and difficulty in sharing common resources such as brands and sales channels. On the other hand, in terms of external relationships, in the case of this chapter, as in the interview data mentioned above, in order to maintain a good partnership with Microsoft in different or related business areas, it has reached a political management decision to refrain from (cannibalizing) similar businesses and participate in the ecosystem formed by Microsoft and Zoom. On the other hand, as will be described later, Cisco Systems has achieved both hardware VCS and cloud conferencing technology as a business development system, and successfully promoted services using different technologies through coordination between business units within the company.

Third, as pointed out by Christensen and Bever (2014) and Zuckerman (2016), incumbents have a higher hurdle rate for development investment in new technologies than new entrants (expected rate of return above which they will invest). The reason for this is that the pressure on management to maintain and grow market share with current technologies (products) may discourage them from pursuing smaller market opportunities with new technological developments. As in the interview data mentioned above, the top management chose to select and concentrate on the business because the volume and scale of the company's video conferencing business were small. They decided not to invest in new development and to downsize or withdraw from existing businesses. In this business environment, Zuckerman (2016) points out that business development investment in niche markets may reduce commitment to existing stakeholders (customers, employees, investors).

The fourth reason is the quality of the lens through which a company's top management sees future strategy, as well as the dynamic capabilities (hereinafter referred to as DC) (e.g., Teece, 2007, 2014) that implement the future strategy. In strategy formation, excessive bias from the business environment and business conditions surrounding a company takes effect, and the logic of "selection and concentration" prevails. As is this case, the videoconferencing systems market is certainly a niche market today, and understandably it is logical that it would be a lower priority than a large company's core business for resource allocation in strategic planning. However, there is a possibility that as ICT tools, video conferencing systems will go beyond the framework of conference use and in future transform into ICT tools with new-normal cultural elements at the level of the current telephone, e-mail, and even SNS. This will make video communications a core platform that supports social and economic activities, and this platform may further evolve and create new business opportunities by integrating different technologies such as AI, XR, IoT, real-time translation, meta, and sensory communications. Anticipating such contexts, leaders of existing companies will need to decide on and quickly implement strategic shifts to new product architectures and business models.

DC exist, in part, along with individual managers and top executives (Adner & Helfat, 2003; Teece, 2014). At certain critical junctures, the ability of the CEO and top management to recognize important developments and trends, devise responses, and guide the entire company as it moves forward is the most prominent characteristic of DC in a company. An organization's values and culture, as well as its ability to quickly implement new business models and other changes as one group, are also factors that determine the strength or weakness of a company's DC. Bartlett and Ghoshal (2002, p. 14) state that "As major global competitors achieve parity in the scale of their operations and their international market positions, the ability to link and leverage knowledge is increasingly the factor that differentiates the winners from the losers and survivors" (Teece, 2014).

In other words, knowledge as the aforementioned core capabilities is difficult to imitate and usually needs to be created by a company itself. Teece (2014) asserts that orchestration of knowledge and capabilities requires entrepreneurial capabilities, but many business executives simply do not have them. Therefore, the process of "coordination/integration" of asset orchestration through entrepreneurial behavior possessed not only by top management but also by good middle managers becomes especially important (Teece, 2007). A company's commitment to its accumulated past knowledge assets will never be a factor in creating (driving) DC but will only demonstrate "Ordinary Capabilities (OC)" that facilitate the improvement and refinement of normal routines.

In contrast, Zoom refined the evolution of its software architecture and promoted its platform strategy with a cloud-based business model. Microsoft also acquired Skype and released platform services (Skype for Business to Teams) for its new communications and collaboration strategies. The common denominator of these two companies' strategies is a thorough software strategy. For Zoom and Microsoft, the coherence element of software strategy has become an important driver within companies (organizations) to realize the business model of cloud videoconferencing services.

This coherence is achieved primarily through the integration of attention (Ocasio & Joseph, 2018) through company communication channels (Joseph & Ocasio, 2012) and communications that occur between organizational members within those channels (Ocasio et al., 2017). Coherence across an organization's channels avoids ambiguity regarding the interpretation of strategic opportunities and threats and increases the likelihood of providing members of the organization with a consistent understanding of what a business solution should look like to solve a business challenge or problem.

Meanwhile, Ocasio and Joseph (2018) compare Apple and Motorola's new product development in terms of capabilities that sustain attention over time. Despite starting from similar strategic ideas about smartphones, the performance levels achieved by the two companies have been very different. In other words, the suggestion of a clear mechanism by which these strategic action processes—the transformation and framing of ideas into concrete, successful strategic agendas, and then solutions—are made possible by DC.

For good strategy, a company uses its identity, which allows it to focus on a strategic agenda and continuously direct attention toward driving organizational processes that correspond to its strategic goals (Ocasio & Joseph, 2018). Identity brings commonality in the focus of attention among members of an organization, which is an important determinant of a company's attention perspective (Ocasio, 2011). Such identity is the source of a company's unique capabilities, embodied in its institutional commitments and repeated patterns of decision-making.

Although Apple and Motorola shared a common identity as high-tech product leadership companies, their identities were, in many other respects, quite different. Apple's strong organizational identity was based on designing and developing superior products with the goal of changing the world. Focus on digital design, obsession with improving the customer experience, and delighting and surprising customers as well as meeting their expectations are all part of Apple's organizational identity. On the other hand, Motorola, which focused on superior products but had a more traditional organizational identity as an engineering company, did not share the same organizational identity as Apple (Ocasio & Joseph, 2018). At Zoom and Microsoft, this is interpreted as the significance of having an organizational identity of implementing a superior cloud video strategy with a consistent software architecture, a focus on software strategy, a focus on creating customer value, and sustained attention to organizational members.

This structured interaction of the two elements of "attention control and problem-solving" through the "attention-based view" (Ocasio, 1997, 2011), called "integration of attention," increases the potential to transform existing OC and realize the generation of DC (Schulze & Brusoni, 2022).

Meanwhile, Cisco Systems acquired Norway's Tandberg, a leading hardware VCS company, and WebEx, a web conferencing service company, to promote its "ambidextrous development strategy" of hardware and software. Typical studies of this ambidextrous development strategy are the cases of technology conversion from electro-hydraulic pulse motors to DC servo motors and technology conversion from hard-wired to soft-wired by FANUC in Japan (Shibata & Kodama, 2008; Kodama & Shibata, 2014). The implementation of such an ambidextrous strategy is one element of DC and corresponds to organizational capabilities to respond to dynamic market changes.

O'Reilly and Tushman (2016) argue that existing leaders can use organizational duality (dual organizational structures, processes, subcultures, and cognitively flexible executive teams) to simultaneously pursue different types of innovation and manage assumed conflicts. As O'Reilly and Tushman (2008) point out, ambidextrous management (ambidexterity) relies in part on top management DC (Adner & Helfat, 2003) (of Cisco Systems) to perform the integration of new and mature businesses (in this case, existing product architecture and business models with new product architecture and business models). Helfat and Winter (2011, p. 1248) identify that there are some types of capabilities that enable ambidexterity (e.g., the dynamic capabilities of top management). The DC of managers can contribute to organizational level integrated capabilities for ambidexterity.

In addition, existing companies such as Cisco Systems and Microsoft took up disruptive entrants (e.g., WebEx and Skype) through mergers and acquisitions as they try to establish leadership in new markets (e.g., Christensen et al., 2011; McDonald & Eisenhardt, 2017). Particularly in the IT industry, once a startup's technology reaches a certain threshold, it is important to redefine the meaning and value of technology and new businesses through disruptive innovation, either by partnering, licensing, acquiring new entrants outright, or introducing new platforms (Marx et al., 2014; Raffaelli, 2019).

In particular, companies with weaker capabilities need a different strategy than those with stronger capabilities. For example, in a culture that is resistant to change, new capabilities needed to execute strategy should be acquired from outside rather than developed internally and acquired capabilities should be managed separately in a way that minimizes conflicts with current business units. Achieving ultimately good performance through acquisitions requires a good strategy in conjunction with strong DC for sensing, seizing, and transforming (Teece, 2014). Cisco Systems and Microsoft can be considered examples of successful acquisition strategies demonstrating excellent DC.

It is assumed that top and middle management need to demonstrate entrepreneurial spirit to overcome various knowledge boundaries, and at the same time, demonstrate DC including acquisition strategies and ambidextrous development strategies, with "coherence" through "integration of attention" within their companies and organizations for existing leader companies to respond to high-end disruptive innovation, although detailed research is a future issue.

4.4 Dynamic Capabilities for Technology Convergence

As mentioned in the case analysis, an element of the successful product strategy by Microsoft, Cisco Systems, and Zoom through high-end disruption is the demonstration of DC. From the opposite perspective, there is still room for existing companies, by properly exercising their DC, to be the first to develop products with high-end disruption and succeed in fast-changing technological evolution, where there is a high degree of uncertainty (indeterminacy) in the market and technical aspects of products.

It is important for companies to have the internal diversity to respond to the diversity of complex, uncertain, and dynamic environmental changes (technology and markets) caused by high-end disruption. Nonaka et al. (2014) point out that companies (organizations) in diversified environments need to acquire "requisite variety" (Nonaka et al., 2014), which means that "only diversity can destroy (absorb) diversity."

Requisite variety is also the ability of an organization's members to synthesize diverse contexts and heterogeneous knowledge flexibly, rapidly, and dynamically in a variety of forms. Therefore, the most important factor for the mindset of top management (including middle managers) in existing companies is not to downsize or withdraw from business to avoid the risks associated with high-end disruption, but rather to work quickly on product development through high-end disruption on their own.

On the other hand, from a strategic theory perspective (Grant, 2021), strategy has an aspect of "competing today (current strategic positioning)" as well as "responding to future readiness (new strategic positioning)." This corresponds to the challenging dilemma (or paradox) of "managing dual strategy" (Abell, 1993), a theme of strategic management theory. This is also the management challenge of "exploitation" and "exploration" (March, 1991).

After surveying the strategy typologies of many commentators, Hart (1992), who discussed the need for an integrative framework for the strategy-making process, addressed the issue of how firms can manage the paradox of strategy in a balanced manner, proposed that one of the management challenges for the future is "integrative strategy theory," which states that the greater a company's ability to construct multiple modes of strategy making, the better its performance will be. The key point is whether multiple heterogeneous or contradictory modes of strategy making can coexist within a single enterprise. The formulation and execution of strategies that are different from (or contradictory to) existing businesses and that respond to disruptive innovation is also an "integrative strategy" concept.

Therefore, existing companies need to formulate integrative strategies that embrace "strategic diversity" to respond to future readiness (new strategic positioning) and embark on their own high-end disruptive innovation that goes beyond the boundaries of existing products (businesses). This section discusses in detail DC as an organizational capability to realize high-end disruption by existing companies.

4.4.1 Dynamic Capabilities and the Asset Orchestration View

DC (Teece, 2007, 2014), whose theory has been refined in recent years, has become a framework for elucidating the mechanism of sustainable growth through corporate strategic innovation. Teece et al., (1997, p. 516) give DC the following meaning: "The firm's ability to integrate, build, and reconfigure internal and external competences to address rapidly changing environments."

Teece et al. (1997) argued that DC are important in creating sustainable corporate-level competitive advantage in fast-changing markets. Strong DC enables companies to innovate in response to changes in the market and, more generally, in business environments by favorably building and updating internal and external resources (knowledge assets) and reconfiguring DC as needed (Rose, 2013; Teece, 2007). The use of DC allows companies and their top management to make inferences about customer needs, business challenges, and technology advancements, validate those inferences, and implement measures by adjusting and reforming existing knowledge assets and management activities to ensure continuous innovation and change (Teece, 2014).

These micro-core functions of DC can be broadly classified into three clusters: (1) identifying, developing, co-developing, and evaluating technological opportunities in relation to customer needs (sensing); (2) mobilizing resources to address needs and opportunities and realize value (seizing); and (3) continuously updating (transforming) (Teece, 2007). Continuous or semi-continuous sensing, seizing, and transforming is important for a company to sustainably grow in response to changes in customers, competitors, and technologies (Teece, 2007) (see Fig. 4.5).

On the other hand, the central concept of DC, the "asset orchestration" function (Teece, 2007, 2014) is reinforced by three organizational processes: (1) coordination/integration, (2) learning, and (3) reconfiguration (Teece et al., 1997). Coordination and integration routines link various knowledge assets in an entrepreneurial manner for the purpose of, for example, new product development. Learning is an outcome of practice and experimentation and enables more efficient task performance. Reconfiguration or transformation is associated with recombination, modification, or conversion of existing knowledge assets. Regarding the three main clusters (subsystems) of DC, Teece (2014, p. 333) notes that asset orchestration is most relevant in supporting seizing and transforming.

With regard to such asset orchestration, Teece (2014, p. 340) addresses the comments of U.S. Army General Stanley McChrystal, noting that resources alone were insufficient during the U.S. Army's involvement in Iraq, as follows. "We had a culture in our forces, of excellence. It was how good can I be at my task?... But that's not as important as how well those pieces mesh together... The real art is... cooperating with civilian agencies, it's cooperating with conventional forces, it's tying the pieces together. That's the art of war, and that's the hard part" (Rose, 2013, p. 6).

In addition, the late Steve Jobs of Apple Inc. had the following to say about new product development: "...designing a product is keeping 5,000 things in your brain these concepts and fitting them all together in kind of continuing to push to fit them together in new and different ways to get what you want and every day you discover something new that is a new problem or a new opportunity to fit these things together a little differently and it's that process that is the magic and… (Jobs, 1995)".

The asset orchestration function for realizing innovation is essentially about how skillfully to combine individual pieces and how to recombine a large number of concepts through trial and error and connect them in new ways to create what you want. However, the dynamic mechanism of such asset orchestration is largely unknown in previous studies. From the next section, we will present the main components of the three overarching clusters of DC micro-core functions: sensing, seizing, and transforming.

4.4.2 Sensing in Fast-Changing and/or Uncertainty Environments

Day and Schoemaker (2016) point to the importance of "Peripheral Vision (sensing weak signals from the boundaries of existing mainstream businesses)" as a sub-capability of sensing. Peripheral vision is the ability to identify potential business opportunities and early signs of threats before competitors do (see Fig. 4.5). Sensing is the ability to explore, filter, and analyze business opportunities and relies on the "cognitive capabilities" (Helfat & Peteraf, 2015) of individual practitioners, particularly executives and middle management. In the process of R&D activities and selection of new technologies to realize innovation, the presence of appropriate cognitive capabilities of executives and middle managers to respond to the dynamic external environment, including the identification of business opportunities, is an important factor.

Helfat and Peteraf (2015) have shown that heterogeneity in cognitive capabilities among top executives leads to managerial performance gaps in situations of high uncertainty or dynamic change in recent years. Helfat and Peteraf (2015) note that there are important aspects of cognitive capabilities that are rooted in specific contexts and domains of expertise, and that these aspects may affect the heterogeneity of cognitive capabilities.

Helfat and Peteraf (2015) mention that cognitive capabilities, on which mental models (Grinyer & McKiernan, 1994; Spender, 1990) are based, are an important attribute of managers and entrepreneurs. For example, previous studies on NCR (Rosenbloom, 2000) and Polaroid (Tripsas & Gavetti, 2000) fall into this category. Thus, managers need to strengthen their "paradoxical cognition" (Kodama, 2003; Smith & Tushman, 2005) so that they can pursue "exploration and exploitation" (March, 1991) simultaneously. In addition, as companies explore new technologies and strategies, they often unwittingly and inappropriately rely on past expertise (knowledge assets), which means past experiential knowledge may be detrimental. The high-end disruption in the videoconferencing market in this chapter's cases may be due to this heterogeneity in cognitive capabilities.

The "intuition" (Kodama, 2011a, 2011b), a non-cognitive capability possessed by practitioners, plays a major role, and many of the insights and inspirations generated by the intuition come from deep interactions with various stakeholders (customers, partners, etc.). For practitioners to demonstrate intuition, they must have capabilities of boundaries vision (Kodama, 2011a, 2011b, 2020c; Kodama & Shibata, 2016) to be able to acquire new insights from complex and diverse boundaries. The concept of boundaries vision drives "external knowledge convergence capabilities"—the ability to orchestrate different tangible and intangible (knowledge) assets.

The aforementioned peripheral vision is required to have the dynamic vision and sensitivity to respond to the speed of environmental change. Driving this vision enables risk management without missing signs, capturing opportunities, and surviving in times of change. On the other hand, boundaries vision encompasses the concept of peripheral vision and is not limited to the peripheral areas of a company's own core business domains that make use of peripheral vision. Boundaries vision includes knowledge from diverse and heterogeneous boundary-separating business domains and different technical areas of expertise, as well as diverse customer knowledge and customer competence, which in the past had nothing to do with the company (or in which the company had no interest).

Jack Welch, the legendary CEO who brought a lot of wealth to General Electric, said

> The second characteristic is the ability to see around corners. Every leader has to have a vision and the ability to predict the future, but good leaders must have a special capacity to anticipate the radically unexpected. In business, the best leaders in brutally competitive environments have a sixth sense for market changes, as well as moves by existing competitors and new entrants. (Welch & Welch, 2005, p. 89)

The ability to foresee what is just around the corner (the sixth sense) corresponds to boundaries vision. Figure 4.4 shows an image of the difference between peripheral and boundary vision. Peripheral vision means only the peripheral area, the fuzzy zone where light does not easily reach such as that from a flashlight or laser. Boundaries vision, on the other hand, is closer to the view from an omnidirectional camera. An omnidirectional camera has two lenses, one in the front and one in the back. With this mechanism, each lens covers one side of the camera, and by combining the images from the two lenses, the camera can capture a 360-degree image from the sky to the ground. An omnidirectional camera is a photographic device that can take 360-degree panoramic photos and 360-degree videos in all directions, and is also called a 360° camera, VR camera, or full dome camera. Such boundaries vision and peripheral vision are complementary to each other, and both should be used according to the environment and other circumstances faced by the company. Both are key sub-capabilities of "sensing" (see Fig. 4.5).

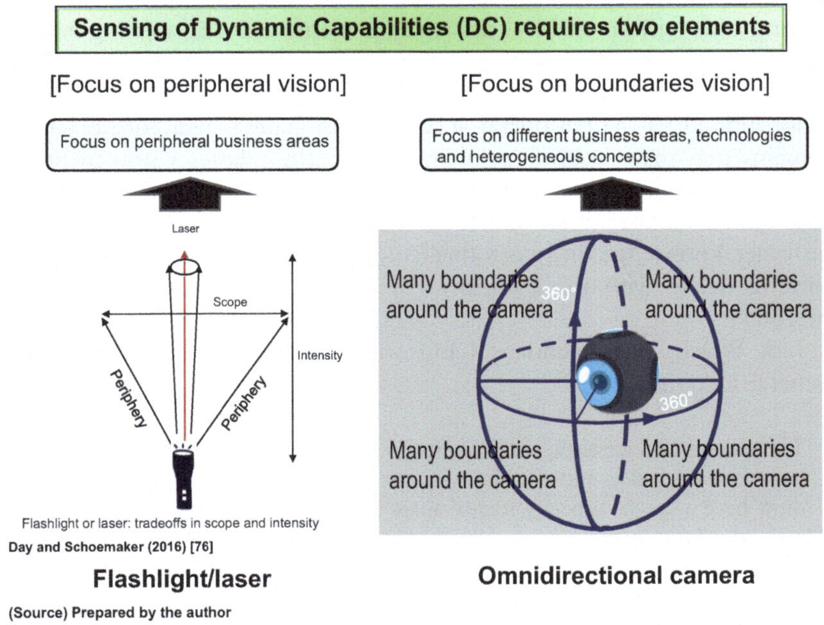

Fig. 4.4 Sensing through boundaries vision and peripheral vision

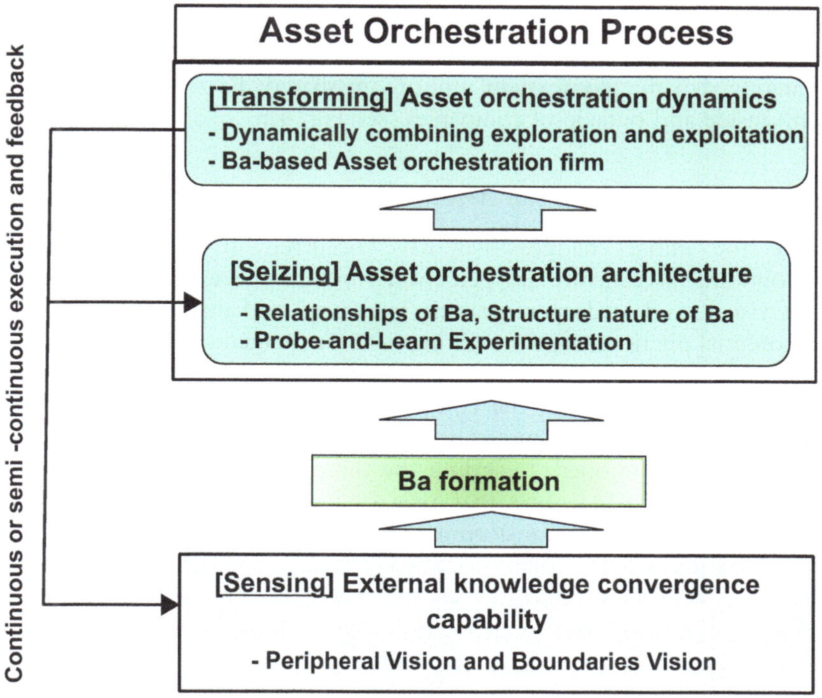

(Source) Prepared by the author

Fig. 4.5 DC and asset orchestration framework

In the aforementioned cases, having such a boundaries vision gives practitioners of existing companies the opportunity to detect technological evolution (hardware to software, product to service, ownership to cloud, PC to mobile device, etc.) and market changes (from business use to various consumer usage patterns) against high-end disruption, and triggers transformational thinking to adapt and cope with these changes.

To integrate different knowledge assets through external knowledge convergence capabilities by demonstrating a boundaries vision, collaboration among practitioners through the formation of human networks within and across organizations (and even across companies) is essential for seizing and transforming the knowledge assets mentioned in the next section. The platform necessary for the formation of human networks that generate such collaboration is the "Ba" (Kodama, 2021b; Nonaka & Konno, 1998; Nonaka et al., 2000), in which constantly changing dynamic contexts in motion are shared. Ba are formed across both inside and outside of companies (see Fig. 4.5).

4.4.3 Asset Orchestration Architecture Based on Seizing Through Ba

Once the initial changes that have occurred in the environment surrounding a company are perceived through the exercise of boundaries vision, and as deeper meaning is entered and understood for new or potential phenomena, the next important management issue is what to do with new knowledge. There, as the practitioners' managerial actions and commitments occur, the companies deal with the pursuit of risky strategies that are full of uncertainty or based on biased information. In particular, as mentioned, regarding the three main clusters (subsystems) of DC, Teece (2014) notes that asset orchestration is most relevant in supporting seizing and transforming. The function of asset orchestration by DC requires practitioners to actively create it by driving seizing to develop new business opportunities and new technologies. However, little is known about this asset orchestration in previous studies.

In recent years, there have been increasing demands to design open innovation (Chesbrough, 2003) and even hybrid innovation (Kodama, 2011a, 2011b), an intermediate between open and closed innovation. In this chapter's cases, the key management element for existing companies is to build a new architecture and business model of high-end disruption by exercising their boundaries vision to draw a grand design with a new asset orchestration architecture to integrate and optimize the knowledge assets inside and outside the company. To achieve this, executives and managers must orchestrate different knowledge assets and create new innovations through strategic thinking and actions that focus on diverse boundaries.

A representative example is Apple's foray into the music distribution service and smartphone business (Kodama, 2014, 2017, 2018b). In Apple's development of new products such as the iPod and iPhone, the asset orchestration of new products and services was realized through strong collaboration by forming Ba of practitioners from inside and outside the company who had different knowledge assets (Kodama, 2014, 2017, 2018b).

Tim Cook, a longtime Apple executive and current CEO, said in February 2013 in reference to the company's integration of hardware, software, and services that "Apple has the ability to innovate in all three of these spheres and create magic.... This isn't something you can just write a check for. This is something you build over decades" (AFP, 2013). The iPhone business model is based on the orchestration of various assets, including mobile phone development, technology platform development, application and content development, and service development. Also, Fujifilm's foray into new businesses such as the cosmetics business in Japan (Kodama & Shibata, 2016) is the result of demonstrating such superior (1) boundaries vision and (2) asset orchestration architecture.

The concept of asset orchestration architecture has something in common with the "knowledge integration architecture" of previous studies on the knowledge integration process (Kodama, 2009, 2011a, 2011b). In addition, a new perspective obtained from previous case studies on knowledge creation theory (Nonaka et al., 2008, 2014) is that to create new knowledge assets, there always exist various multilayered Ba in different contexts, as well as network structures of these Ba. Knowledge assets emerge from such dynamic contexts (time, location, human relationships). Ba are time–space generated and transformed as individuals share and transform their context with others through interaction and are also informal organizational platforms necessary to facilitate the spiral interconversion of tacit and explicit knowledge. Ba are formed and linked together as practitioners proactively approach others in their environments (customers, etc.) or inside and outside of their companies (organizations). What patterns of Ba formation and linkage (networking) are practitioners consciously (or unconsciously) engaging in? Here, we present two new perspectives: (1) Relationships between Ba and (2) The structural nature of Ba.

(1) **Relationships Between Ba**

The key issue is "how to orchestrate different distributed knowledge assets" (from a technological perspective, it is the issue of how to technologically integrate knowledge assets in different technological fields). Dispersed knowledge assets are embedded in organizations and Ba dispersed across time and space. To orchestrate knowledge assets, individual assets must transcend the boundaries of Ba and be networked together. Put differently, distributed Ba must be joined together in networks, and the knowledge assets dispersed throughout those Ba must be deeply embedded in the networks. Practitioners commit to multiple Ba play a central role in tying Ba with other Ba for knowledge asset orchestration. For different knowledge assets to be orchestrated, practitioners need to deeply understand and share the different knowledge assets (tacit and explicit knowledge) in each Ba, and the shared knowledge assets must be deeply embedded in a broad network across Ba boundaries. Especially in the sharing of tacit knowledge, the context must be deeply shared in a network-like manner, and Ba must be connected with other Ba by strong ties.

On the other hand, according to the teachings of social network theory, it is also possible to bridge new dissimilar information with weak ties (Granovetter, 1973). Also, Burt (1992) identified the high possibility of acquiring new business opportunities by practitioners accessing new information through weak ties with "structural holes." An important point is the organizational architecture to realize the orchestration of knowledge assets (this does not only mean the formal organizational structure of a company, but also the design policy of what kind of organizational boundary should be formed to realize such orchestration), in addition to building a network of Ba with strong ties, building a network of Ba with weak ties is also an important issue in the development of new business. Practitioners need to consciously consider how to simultaneously reconcile (or use differently) such Ba relationships of strong ties and weak ties at the same time. Innovative companies maintain Ba with strong ties and also form networks of Ba with weak ties, bridging structural holes in a timely manner and orchestrating heterogeneous knowledge assets (see Fig. 4.6).

(2) **Structural Nature of Ba**

The structural nature of Ba can be divided into vertical integration of Ba and horizontal integration of Ba (see Fig. 4.6).

"Vertical integration of Ba" is a hierarchy of Ba, a structure in which practitioners in various sections within a company form multiple Ba with cross-functional characteristics, and at the same time, form hierarchical networks of these Ba at the management level. Such vertical integration of Ba can be an effective organizational architecture, especially in the process of new product development where orchestration of various technologies is required.

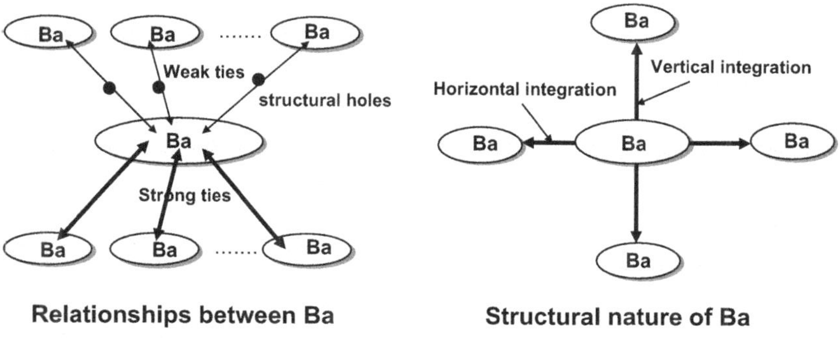

(Source) Prepared by the author

Fig. 4.6 Ba-based asset orchestration architecture

On the other hand, "horizontal integration of Ba" means collaborative Ba with equal relationships with customers and external partners, in which there are fewer characteristics of hierarchy as seen in vertical integration of Ba. Horizontal integration of Ba entails cases of disseminating common knowledge assets with partners, and engaging in joint development of new products and services, etc., on an equal footing. By balancing the duality of vertical and horizontal integration of Ba, companies can demonstrate their ability to integrate scale, scope, and speed in new markets. In the sensing process, companies need to use boundaries vision to analyze and evaluate the elements of seizing—superior intangibles and tangible knowledge assets—through Ba-based asset orchestration architecture.

Day and Schoemaker (2016) assert that in the slow environmental changes or uncertain environments observed in the early stages of innovation, in the creation process stage of new technologies through ideas, business concepts, and discovery and invention, the exploration process by "probe-and-learn experimentation" through various types of "real options" is driven. Through Ba-based asset orchestration architecture, trial-and-error learning requires leaders to actively foster and support a culture that allows, and in some cases, encourages failure. Management leaders need to foster climates in which failure is tolerated, organizational members learn from their mistakes, and experimentation is the norm (see Fig. 4.5).

In the aforementioned cases in this chapter, many Japanese firms were unable to adapt to high-end disruption and withdrew from the market. These Japanese companies should have commercialized new videoconferencing services for cloud-based business by building domestic and international business networks and forming strategic alliances with leading development partners around the world to conduct trial experiments by devising new knowledge asset architecture.

It is important for practitioners to consciously and proactively formulate and connect with potential Ba, including partners and customers, who are the contextual source of knowledge assets hidden behind existing formal organizations, companies, and industry structures, as well as among different industries, and to focus their thinking and actions on asset orchestration architecture based on Ba, without being bound by existing paradigms of thinking.

4.4.4 Transforming Internal and External Shaping Through Asset Orchestration Dynamics

(1) **Asset Orchestration Dynamics**

New business opportunities for companies are created by sensing with boundaries vision and seizing with architectural thinking by building and driving an asset orchestration architecture. However, the proper execution of the new strategy of continuous transformation and innovation requires action through transforming (this function is called "asset orchestration dynamics"). This requires the ability to steer and shape environments, including external environments, in addition to the ability to adjust and restructure the design of organizations internally (Day & Schoemaker, 2016). In companies, asset orchestration dynamics is needed to demonstrate transformational power, build an agile and entrepreneurial mindset, and develop a dynamic approach to building Ba (and multilayered Ba) inside and outside the company.

The first characteristic of asset orchestration dynamics is the driving force that changes the vertical boundaries of a company and dynamically executes the optimization of the value chains of existing core businesses. The second characteristic is the ability to search not only the peripheral areas of the company's core business, but also different business areas using boundaries vision to stimulate the development of new business and new technologies, to significantly change the company's horizontal boundaries, and to find relationships with knowledge assets that are different from the company's own knowledge assets. In other words, asset orchestration dynamics is not only the management activity of exploitation that promotes the growth and development of existing businesses by refining existing knowledge assets, but also the management activity of exploration that acts as an enabler for the creation of new business through convergence of heterogeneous knowledge assets.

From the perspective of knowledge management (Kodama, 2021b), to realize a new business model, it is important to dynamically integrate internal knowledge assets through the formation of Ba that crosses and combines internal boundaries of a company (people, organizations, different expertise, etc.) of a company, and external knowledge assets through the formation of Ba that span and combine the external boundaries of a company (between companies, between companies and customers, between different industries, etc.).

For a company's ability to transform itself to create new businesses, it is important not only to redesign and restructure the company's internal environment, but also to interact with the company's external environment to form an ecosystem around its own company, just as Microsoft, Cisco Systems, and Zoom have done. Specifically, this means joint lobbying with partners, developing new technical industry standards, and redeveloping the business ecology of the company (Day & Schoemaker, 2016). In restructuring a business ecology, building Ba not only within a company, but also outside a company is particularly powerful driver of change.

In the aforementioned cases in this chapter, the exercising of DC by existing companies generates technological evolution for high-end disruption (from hardware to software, from ownership to cloud, from products to services, from PC to mobile devices, etc.) and market change (from business use to various forms of use by consumers), and in terms of technology, existing hardware-oriented companies need to converge heterogeneous knowledge assets of software and heterogeneous knowledge assets of various applications in different fields with their own knowledge assets.

From the perspective of innovation management, there are two innovation processes: "incremental innovation," which is exploitation, and "radical innovation," which is exploration (the word "radical" is used here to mean "not incremental"). The former pursues the efficiency of a company's existing business (core business) knowledge assets, while the latter pursues the creativity of the company's future business development knowledge assets. The process of strategic innovation (Dixon et al., 2014; Kodama, 2018b), in which these two different innovation processes, exploitation and exploration, are managed simultaneously (and sometimes used differently, depending on the situation) and integrated into the core of the corporate strategy, is necessary in innovative companies.

The process of asset orchestration dynamics, which simultaneously executes these two different management activities (or uses them differently depending on the situation), is an excellent corporate strategy for pursuing and developing unique new strategic positions and achieving a sustainable competitive advantage (Markides, 1999).

In this chapter, we refer to a corporate entity that uses such asset orchestration dynamics to achieve strategic innovation as a "Ba-based Asset Orchestration Firm," The ability to combine the management activities of incremental innovation (exploitation) and radical innovation (exploration) to build a "Ba-based asset orchestration firm" is the key element of transforming (asset orchestration dynamics) (see Fig. 4.5).

(2) **Ba-Based Asset Orchestration Firm**

Here, we discuss the specific organizational form of an asset orchestration firm that uses asset orchestration dynamics to achieve strategic innovation. Ultimately, what is needed for productive and creative transformation that leads to corporate growth are new routines and entrepreneurial actions to introduce new activities in parallel with existing business areas. However, Teece (2007, 2014) mentions the tendency of many organizations to have a set of routines readily available for downsizing to improve operational efficiency in the company, but generally no routines that would grow the company.

Companies often face contradictions and paradoxes among the various management elements as they continue to grow sustainably into the future (Kodama, 2003). For example, in a situation where a company is exploring new future business opportunities while taking advantage of current business opportunities, a number of potentially incompatible activities must be conducted simultaneously. For example, as in this chapter's cases, it is the activity of planning and developing new products and services while improving and enhancing existing products in response to technological evolution and market changes for high-end disruption. There are also activities such as developing new clients at the same time as committing to existing ones, acquiring talented people while retraining current staff, and introducing new business processes while improving operations.

The "ambidextrous organization" mentioned by O'Reilly and Tushman (2008, 2016) as an organizational form to ease the tension between exploitation and exploration suggested by March (1991) is likely to be the engine of an organization that produces DC, although separation of organizations can lead to success or failure of new strategic initiatives. In addition, ambidextrous organizations may disperse company resources and not help strengthen core competitiveness.

A number of other problems with ambidextrous organizations have been identified. Issues raised with driving innovation businesses through separated organizational structures are in the long-term perspectives related to fusing and harmonizing new and old organizational culture (Markides, 1998, 1999). Even if innovation is achieved with a new organization with a new culture, the company-wide problem of reforming the mindset of traditional organizations with their outdated values still remains. Govindarajan and Trimble (2005) assert that exchange at the general and senior managers level should be minimized, since this is often the epicenter of discord, and suggest the importance of resources exchange at the workplace level (middle management and below), and thus challenge the ambidextrous organization.

However, depending on each case, how much independence is needed depends on how factors such as the magnitude of technological discontinuity, the speed of environmental change, and the value of existing assets in the core business, are reviewed under the new strategy (Day & Schoemaker, 2016). Then, what should be the specific organizational form to realize such asset orchestration dynamics?

Kodama (2003, 2004, 2019b) discusses five patterns shown in Fig. 4.8 regarding organizational forms that promote both exploitation and exploration activities. In the "integrated organization" shown in "Pattern E" (Kodama, 2019b), the work is divided between the new organization responsible for exploration and the existing organization responsible for exploitation, and business is conducted based on the formation of Ba-based communities within the company consisting of leader teams (LT) at each management level. Existing and new organizations work together to achieve both exploitation and exploration through deep interaction and collaboration between different organizations. Kodama (2019b) notes that this organizational form is an element of successful innovation. In other words, the integrated organization form is similar to the Ba-based asset orchestration firm proposed in this chapter.

To mitigate and reconcile the tension between exploitation and exploration, organizational design must encompass the opposing qualities of creativity and efficiency, meaning creation (knowledge creation), and information processing, in a dynamic structure (Kodama, 2003, 2004). The asset orchestration process requires the formation and integration of multiple Ba with heterogeneous and different characteristics, where the emergent Ba with heterogeneous and new knowledge assets and the traditional Ba with accumulated knowledge assets over many years must be balanced and integrated (see Fig. 4.8).

Emergent Ba continually create new knowledge assets that can constantly create new business model (new products, new services, new business frameworks) concepts based on creativity for new innovations in uncertain and dynamic environments. In this context, emergent organizations form multilayered "Ba" (external convergence networks) with external strategic business partners, including customers, to incorporate internal and external knowledge assets in uncertain and high-risk environments, and to promote emergent and entrepreneurial strategies. Individual projects within an emergent organization behave in autonomous decentralized organizational manner as a networked organization or a semi-structured organization between tightly coupled and loosely coupled organizations, and they generate concepts and prototypes of new products and services one after another through abduction, and perform numerous incubations.

On the other hand, business processes such as production, sales, distribution, product improvement and enhancement, and after-sales support are important to commercialize these new products and services, and to release, promote, and expand them in the market in a timely and efficient manner. The "traditional Ba" is responsible for these business processes. A traditional organization with a hierarchical structure with a well-defined chain of command and order executes deliberate strategies as orchestration with certainty based on strategic discipline and knowledge assets accumulated over many years. Business processes are then streamlined and further incrementally refined and improved through the creation of multiple, multilayered Ba (external convergence networks), centered on traditional organizations, with external strategic business partners. Then, the results of innovative new products and service concepts created by the emergent Ba are quickly, efficiently, and reliably introduced to the market for dissemination and expansion through the traditional Ba.

Generally, these two types of Ba have paradoxical elements in that the emergent Ba pursue creativity and autonomy while the traditional Ba pursue efficiency and control, although such contradictions are sublated through creative abrasion (Carlile, 2002; Leonard-Barton, 1995) and productive friction (Hagel & Brown, 2005) through creative and dialectical dialogue (Kodama, 2004) between both types of Ba. In a Ba-based asset orchestration firm, leadership Ba (leader teams (LT) in Fig. 4.7) as multilayered Ba (internal convergence networks) are formed at each management level (top management, middle management, mixed management teams, cross-functional teams, task forces, etc., in emergent and traditional organizations). Each Ba is composed of its own leaders (CEOs, directors, division heads, department heads, project leaders, and other practitioners).

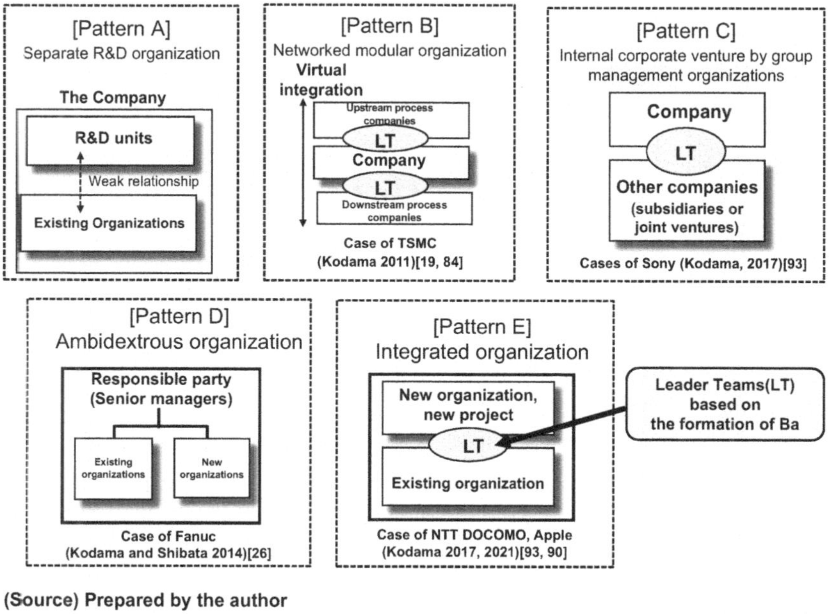

Fig. 4.7 The formation of innovative organizations

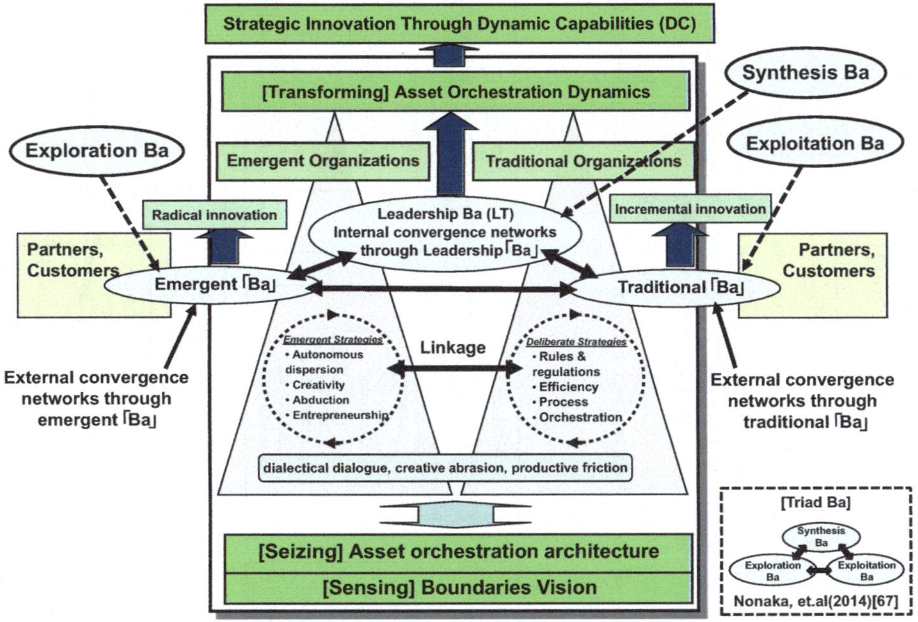

(Source) Prepared by the author

Fig. 4.8 Ba-based asset orchestration firm

Through the construction of emergent Ba, traditional Ba, and leadership Ba in emergent and traditional organizations, diverse knowledge assets are fused and integrated, and transforming through asset orchestration dynamics is implemented. Through these practices, companies drive the balancing of exploration and exploitation by creating superior radical innovation through the creation of new knowledge assets, and at the same time, maintaining competitiveness through incremental innovation in existing core businesses by utilizing existing knowledge assets (Kodama, 2011a, 2011b).

Leadership Ba play a role in orchestrating assets in these two types of organizations and the Ba, and bringing about "transforming" for the entire company. To achieve transforming, it is important for leadership Ba to balance and synthesize the seemingly contradictory strategies of creativity and planning at the same time. A leadership Ba is a multilayered network of Ba that balances the innovation processes of incremental and radical innovation (see Fig. 4.8).

The Ba triad model was presented from short cases of the leading companies and organizations of Toyota, Fujifilm, and Apple, in the "Dynamic fractal organizations for promoting knowledge-based transformation—A new paradigm for organizational theory" of Nonaka et al. (2014). For example, Toyota's Prius new product development case was an innovation that required the convergence of various technologies (exploration) which were commercialized and continuously improved (exploitation), making it necessary to have dynamic synthesis of exploration and exploitation. For those reasons, Toyota's various project teams and existing line organizations formed multilayered networked Ba both horizontally and vertically within and between organizations to simultaneously pursue the creation and utilization of knowledge.

What draws attention in these cases, is that Ba to drive exploration activities for knowledge creativity of innovation (called exploration Ba, equivalent to the emergent Ba mentioned above) are responsible for processes to share tacit knowledge and convert it to explicit knowledge, while in contrast, Ba that drive exploitation activities for knowledge efficiency to commercialize, and upgrade and improve products (called exploitation Ba, equivalent to the traditional Ba mentioned above) are responsible for processes of synthesis of explicit knowledge, and internalization of it through personal experience. In other words, exploration Ba have a strong tendency toward tacit knowledge, while exploitation Ba strongly lean toward explicit knowledge. Nevertheless, both tacit knowledge and explicit knowledge are intrinsically linked in the spirals synthesis of the third type of knowledge, practical knowledge (phronesis) (Nonaka's so-called SECI process). Driving this spiral process to simultaneously achieve the creation and accumulation of knowledge is the "synthesis Ba (the leadership Ba mentioned above)."

Thus, there exists a "Ba triad model" that interconnects synthesis Ba that realize the dynamic synthesis of exploration Ba and exploitation Ba. This "Ba triad model" inspires the external knowledge convergence capabilities of boundaries vision and can also be a model for realizing knowledge convergence from different specialties. The presence of a Triad Ba is also observed in the case study of Fujifilm's technology integration by Kodama and Shibata (2016) and the case study of new business development by NTT DOCOMO by Kodama (2018b). Therefore, the Ba-based asset orchestration firm proposed in this chapter is similar to the organizational model of Nonaka et al. (2014) (see Fig. 4.8).

On the other hand, such a "Ba-based asset orchestration firm" is similar to an "ambidextrous organization" (O'Reilly & Tushman, 2008, 2016), but differs in the following respects. It's asserted that, in ambidextrous organizations, clear strategic objectives are set down for new business development organizations and organizations developing existing business, and the interaction between these organizations is heavily restricted at the operational level while upper management is responsible for both. In contrast, the Ba-based asset orchestration firm realizes dense interaction and collaboration between the emergent Ba (exploration Ba) consisting of emergent organizations that pursue new products and build fundamental technologies, and the traditional Ba (exploitation Ba) consisting of traditional organizations that pursue business-directed development and current business. In addition, the formation of a synthesis Ba (Leadership Ba) promotes interaction and collaboration at each management level (top management, middle management, and lower management) and serves as an efficient and effective bridge between R&D processes (and even commercialization processes).

In such an "SC-based Asset Orchestration Firm," the formation of a "Ba" across the company (organization) toward the business achievement of strategic innovation promotes the resonance of the values of each practitioner, including top management (Kodama, 2001), and the integrated synergy effect of leadership possessed by each practitioner can form a solid new business value chain, and furthermore, create new customer value.

4.5 Relationship Between SECI Model and DC Framework to Realize Technology Convergence

Although knowledge can be broadly defined as either tacit knowledge or explicit knowledge, these are not completely separate but in a mutual complementary relationship. Explicit knowledge is accumulated, and knowledge is used by combining it and associating it with other knowledge. Tacit knowledge is accumulated in individuals or in organizations in activities through the creation and usage of knowledge. Then, tacit knowledge is conceptualized, systemized, and extracted as new explicit knowledge. This mutual cycling of tacit and explicit knowledge is the SECI model.

Such knowledge transformation activities do not necessarily take place within a single person, but within social processes between humans. When recognizing things, it is difficult to be completely isolated from social interactions, hence, knowledge transformation, the mutual cycling between tacit knowledge and explicit knowledge, takes place with the social processes between humans as the main stage. Knowledge transformation in social processes enables effective increase of tacit knowledge both qualitatively and quantitatively.

According to Nonaka and Takeuchi (1995), the SECI model consists of the four knowledge transformation modes of (1) "Socialization" that entails creation of group tacit knowledge from individual tacit knowledge. (2) "Externalization" that entails creation of explicit knowledge from tacit knowledge, (3) "Combination" that entails creation of systemized explicit knowledge from individual pieces of explicit knowledge, and (4) "Internalization" that entails the creation of tacit knowledge from explicit knowledge.

Socialization is the process of creating tacit knowledge such as mental models or skills by sharing experiences. In this activity, words may not necessarily be required—the important aspect is shared experience, like learning skills through observation, imitation, practice, etc., in OJT used in corporate training and so forth. The tacit knowledge of individuals is gradually shared through such shared experiences. The origin of the idea of the mobile phone with built-in camera described by Kodama (2019b) was the acquisition and sharing of tacit knowledge in the field.

The formation of "Ba" plays a major role in innovation-oriented experience sharing that includes elements of pragmatic boundaries. The formation of Ba for sharing tacit knowledge is a trigger in the process of socialization. Within Ba, the socialization process is promoted as members share their experiences and mental models. Nonaka et al. (2016) associate such socialization processes with the sensing of the DC framework. In such shared experience, "tacit knowledge integration" (the integration or convergence of different tacit knowledge) is realized by the process of boundaries knowledge through boundaries vision (see Fig. 4.9).

Externalization is the process of expressing tacit knowledge as clear concepts. In this step, tacit knowledge to be conveyed to multiple people is converted into explicit knowledge. In externalization process, creative learning is based on meaningful creative dialogue and learning is the trigger. Since it is difficult to create explicit knowledge purely with an analytical approach, it is possible to conceptualize tacit knowledge that is difficult to convey using metaphors and analogies. Tacit knowledge is made into concepts through dialogue and learning using metaphors, analogies, concepts, hypotheses, models, etc., to give it form.

The abduction process is an important method that is often used to generate concepts through combination of deduction and induction.

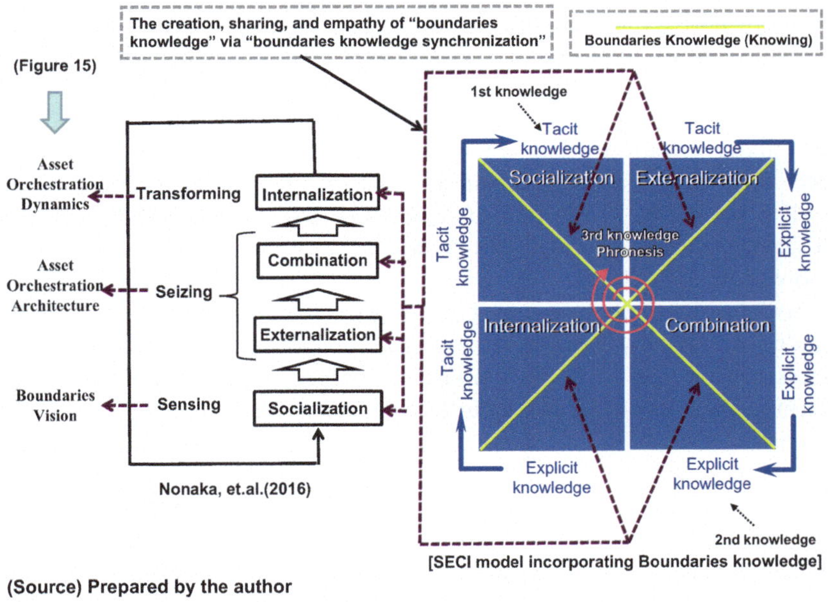

Fig. 4.9 Relationship between the DC framework and the SECI model

For example, this could mean taking a deductive approach to generating concepts from such things as business philosophy or strategy, or inductively being guided by target customers or market research, etc. However, there are cases in which it's not possible to generate appropriate concepts from deductive or inductive approaches, and so a non-analytical approach is required. This could be the use of metaphors or analogies.

Metaphors have been described as a method of sensing something different or intuitive understanding by painting a picture in the mind as a symbol of a thing. Donnellon et al. (1986) point out that metaphors generate new interpretations of experiences by urging whoever is listening to see things differently, and hence they are a communication mechanism that has the function of harmonizing mismatches in meaning. Using metaphors effectively enables thinking about similarities between concepts, and enables awareness of contradictions and imbalances between concepts. This can contribute to the generation of new meaning. In this way, the function of boundaries vision includes the use of metaphors.

In addition, analogies enable reduction of parts that cannot be understood by focusing on commonalities of different objects. Although metaphors and analogies are often confused, association by metaphor uses images and is more intuitive, but is not something that will reveal knowledge differences between individual specific objects. In contrast, association by analogy is done with logical thinking, and enables clarification of knowledge differences by focusing on similarities of the structure and function of the objects. Thus, using the analytical, deductive approach, the functional approach, and non-analytic metaphors and analogies is an effective way of deriving explicit concepts from tacit knowledge. This way, the use of metaphors and analogies is involved in driving the process of boundaries knowledge through boundaries vision.

Combination is a process for creating knowledge systems by combining concepts, and is also the process of creating new explicit knowledge by combining dissimilar explicit knowledge (explicit knowledge integration). Through externalization, tacit knowledge is transformed into explicit knowledge, systematization is enabled which makes knowledge transmission and sharing easier, and leads to rapid accumulation of explicit knowledge. Combination involves combining accumulated explicit knowledge. In fact, combination is contact with explicit knowledge through documentation, meetings, telephone calls, or the Internet, and combining that explicit knowledge to reassemble it as a relation of explicit knowledge. Also, it entails putting knowledge into words, accumulating it in a database, turning it into a theoretical model, etc., so that anybody can use it. The processing, modification, and search of explicit knowledge can be promoted more effectively by using the advanced ICT of recent years that utilizes the AI, IoT, and big data. These are also typical processes used in workplaces for education, training, etc.

Combination of explicit knowledge is not only a matter of arriving at a single summarized knowledge system, but also entails generation of new concepts and new knowledge. Often seen in the combination process is the introduction of business and product concepts into specific forms in middle management. On the other hand, when combination is used in top management, it creates a new meaning with company-wide concepts such as corporate strategy and vision in combination with medium-range concepts such as those handled by middle management. According to Kodama (2019b), the process of "boundaries knowledge through boundaries vision" is key, even in such explicit knowledge integration.

Nonaka et al. (2016) associate the externalization and combination stages to the seizing function of the DC framework. On the other hand, externalization and combination are equivalent to the building processes of asset orchestration architecture as shown in Fig. 4.6, insofar as they entail the formation of specific theories (or frameworks), prototypes, or business models from concepts (see Fig. 4.9).

Finally, internalization is the process in which individuals acquire new tacit knowledge from explicit knowledge. Organizations or individuals must behave in specific ways in this process. Thus, by such behaviors, they gain experience and internalize explicit knowledge to make it their own tacit knowledge. Up to this point, practitioners come into contact with the tacit knowledge of others through accumulated dialogue, extract explicit knowledge from tacit knowledge, create documentation and prototypes, etc., for combination of such knowledge in the processes of collaboration, externalization, and combination. Then, practitioners are able to internalize such knowledge by viewing documentation or actual prototyped items and their actual use.

Having shared experiences with others and follow-up experiences and knowing explicit knowledge leads the individual to convert what he or she knows to his or her own tacit knowledge, which triggers the sharing of values and leads back to socialization once again. The important thing with internalization is expanding the scope of experience, which entails efficiently acquiring and sharing the tacit knowledge of individuals and organizations by forming Ba that span in and out of organizations (and between companies), and that have their origins in many diverse ba. For example, this does not mean just driving existing business through existing organizations, but also promoting wide-ranging experiences that transcend specialized job functions to bring about diverse tacit knowledge in individuals, teams, and organizations by building new business development organizations, cross-functional teams, and transformation (or innovation) teams. Expanding the scope of experience (e.g., new business development for radical innovation) is extremely effective for internalization. For example, this could mean practicing exploitation and exploration to combine existing business and new business. Here, "learning by doing" is the trigger—this process is "asset orchestration dynamics," which is the transforming function of the DC framework.

Put differently, the internalization stage is equivalent to practicing asset orchestration architecture built through trial and error in the externalization and combination stages, through asset orchestration dynamics. Through this practice, boundaries knowledge through boundaries vision born of the gaps between the acquired introspection and reality serves to expand the scope of experience and transform it, and internalize explicit knowledge. Nonaka et al. (2016) associate this process with the transforming function of the DC framework. In terms of learning through specific practice and transformation, the internalization stage is equivalent to the execution of asset orchestration dynamics (see Fig. 4.9). Additionally, the core element that promotes the driving of the SECI process lies in the dynamic process and the following sections as "Creation, Sharing, and Empathy of Boundaries Knowledge through Boundaries Knowledge Synchronization among Stakeholders" (see Fig. 4.9).

4.6 Creation, Sharing, and Empathy of Boundaries Knowledge Through Boundaries Knowledge Synchronization Among Stakeholders

In the progress of product development projects, Cisco, Microsoft, and Zoom promoted the four phases of the knowledge creation process (SECI process) through deep dialogues with internal stakeholders (various organizational members). As shown in Fig. 4.9, "boundaries knowledge synchronization," which involves the creation, sharing, and empathy of boundaries knowledge through "boundaries synchronization" among different stakeholders, synchronizes the dynamic execution of the SECI process for each stakeholder. Consequently, stakeholders create new knowledge to achieve new strategic goals and promote the organizational sharing and accumulation of this knowledge. For example, the SECI process through the creation, sharing, and empathy of boundaries knowledge via "boundaries knowledge synchronization" at Cisco, Microsoft, and Zoom can be explained as follows (see Fig. 4.10).

(1) The Stage of "Socialization (S)" (Tacit Knowledge → Tacit Knowledge: Tacit Knowledge Integration Process)

To realize the targeted tacit knowledge, it was crucial for Cisco, Microsoft, and Zoom to integrate various tacit knowledge based on their

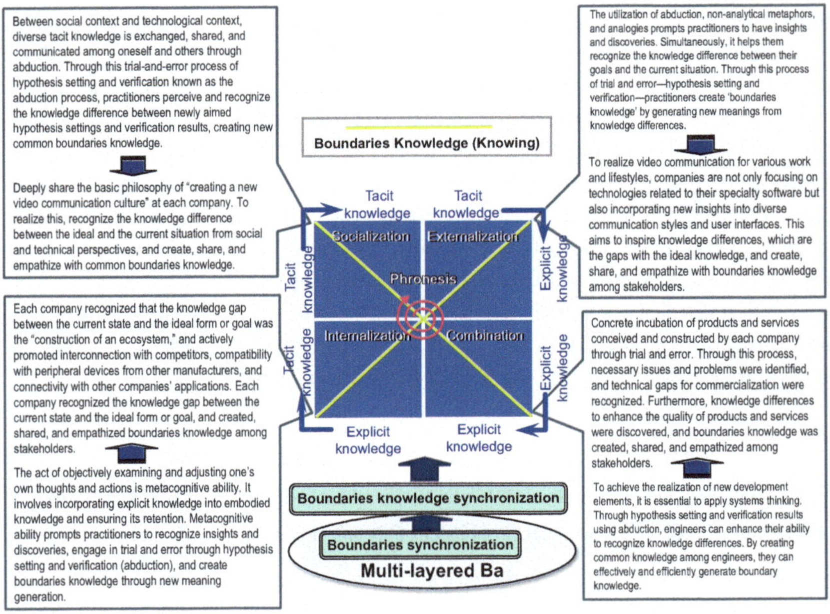

Fig. 4.10 The creation, sharing, and empathy of boundaries knowledge in Cisco, Microsoft, Zoom

accumulated experiences and know-how through the "knowledge integration process" (tacit knowledge → tacit knowledge). It was also important for them to appropriately recognize "knowledge differences" and generate "boundaries knowledge" from them. In other words, "boundaries knowledge" became a driving factor for the new "(Tacit) knowledge integration process." These newly generated "boundaries knowledge" were incorporated into new hypothesis settings, leading to the discovery and creation of new tacit knowledge through the reconstruction and reintegration of diverse tacit knowledge, aiming for a significant refinement/renewal of hypotheses.

Polanyi (1962) refers to the process of relating dispersed elements of tacit knowledge, inferring a consistent and comprehensive whole inductively from the bottom up, and creating new comprehensive meanings as "tacit knowledge integration." On the other hand, Nonaka (2016) mentions that the act and method of "knowing" by practitioners are all generated by the capabilities of "tacit knowledge integration," which can be considered skills of invention, discovery, and creation. For such "tacit knowledge integration," it is important to create new meanings through the creation of "boundaries knowledge" by recognizing the previous "knowledge differences." There, the generation of "boundaries knowledge" enables the integration of diverse tacit knowledge (tacit knowledge → tacit knowledge) and plays a role in creating new tacit knowledge (see "Socialization" in Fig. 4.10).

From this perspective, Cisco, Microsoft, and Zoom demonstrated the capabilities of "boundaries vision" (Kodama & Shibata, 2016), which involves discovering, perceiving, recognizing, and creating new "boundaries knowledge" through spiral interactions by abduction between social and technical contexts (and between these contexts at macro and micro levels) aimed at realizing a video communication culture (see Fig. 4.9). Questions and creative dialectical dialogues (Kodama, 2007) such as "What are the images and product concepts that enable video communication anytime, anywhere, with anyone?", "How can we refresh the traditional product image?", and "Wouldn't it work if we did this?" were conducted through direct experiences in the abstract space (life world domain) at each company (Kodama, 2019b). There, the beliefs and thoughts of Cisco, Microsoft, and Zoom clashed in the abstracted time and space of images. Through the formation of multilayered Ba, Cisco, Microsoft, and Zoom realized "boundaries synchronization," which converged on pragmatic boundaries among different stakeholders.

Specifically, the fundamental concept of "creating a new video communication culture" was deeply shared within Cisco, Microsoft, and Zoom. To achieve this, Cisco, Microsoft, and Zoom recognized the knowledge differences between the ideal and the current situation from the perspectives of social and technical contexts and promoted the creation, sharing, and empathy of common boundaries knowledge among various stakeholders through "boundaries knowledge synchronization."

(2) The Stage of "Externalization (E)" (Tacit Knowledge → Explicit Knowledge: Knowledge Transformation Process)

The use of metaphors and analogies prompted awareness and discoveries for Cisco, Microsoft, and Zoom, while simultaneously making them recognize "knowledge differences." The generation of new meanings from these "knowledge differences" led Cisco, Microsoft, and Zoom to create "boundaries knowledge" through the abduction process of hypothesis setting and verification by trial and error, aiming for convergence on pragmatic boundaries through "boundaries synchronization."

In particular, to realize the targeted explicit knowledge, it was crucial for Cisco, Microsoft, and Zoom to appropriately recognize the "knowledge differences" based on their accumulated experiential knowledge, such as past experiences and know-how, and further generate "boundaries knowledge." In other words, the "boundaries knowledge" derived from the interpretation of technical possibilities (e.g., differences from the product and service development processes realized by traditional hardware-centric companies: also a knowledge difference) became a driving factor for the new "knowledge transformation process" (see "Externalization" in Fig. 4.10).

Specifically, in creating plans for video communication that incorporate various work styles and lifestyles, not only were the software-related technologies that Cisco, Microsoft, and Zoom excel at included, but also insights into communication forms such as B2B/B2C/B2B2C/C2C and user interface usage patterns. The "boundaries knowledge" inspired by the knowledge gap with the ideal (knowledge difference) was created, shared, and empathized through "boundaries synchronization" and "boundaries knowledge synchronization" aimed at convergence on pragmatic boundaries among different stakeholders, facilitated by the formation of multilayered Ba within Cisco, Microsoft, and Zoom

(3) The Stage of "Combination ©" (Explicit Knowledge → Explicit Knowledge: explicit Knowledge Integration Process)

To realize new development elements, it is necessary to discover and create boundaries knowledge from the knowledge differences between different explicit knowledge. To identify such new development elements, it is important to base the process on systems thinking (e.g., Kodama, 2019b) and to engage in the abduction process of hypothesis setting and verification, which stimulates knowledge differences between hypotheses and verification results. As a result of this process, companies create boundaries knowledge based on formalized knowledge differences, driving the "(explicit) knowledge integration process" (explicit knowledge → explicit knowledge) (see "Combination" in Fig. 4.10).

The ability to accurately identify new development elements in the "Combination" domain and the creativity to generate boundaries knowledge are related to "common knowledge" (e.g., Carlile, 2002; Star, 1989). The existence of common knowledge is necessary for Cisco, Microsoft, and Zoom to acquire domain-specific knowledge required for the development of new products and services they target. Common knowledge promotes knowledge sharing and knowledge inspiration (Kodama, 2007) among diverse stakeholders with different technical expertise. At the same time, Cisco, Microsoft, and Zoom enhanced their ability to recognize knowledge differences and effectively and efficiently generated boundaries knowledge through "boundaries synchronization" and "boundaries knowledge synchronization" aimed at convergence on pragmatic boundaries.

Thus, the discovery and creation of boundaries knowledge enabled the integration of diverse explicit knowledge. Combination is achieved by incorporating boundaries knowledge into the integration process of accumulated diverse explicit knowledge. The integration of explicit knowledge not only forms a cohesive knowledge system but also leads to the creation of new knowledge and concepts for cloud video conferencing services by combining diverse explicit knowledge.

Specifically, the concrete incubation of products and services conceived and constructed by Cisco, Microsoft, and Zoom was carried out through trial and error. Through this process, necessary issues and problems were identified, and technical gaps for commercialization were recognized. As a result of this process, new services such as the business model of public cloud called SaaS (Software As A Service) and on-premises private cloud were born. Furthermore, boundaries knowledge derived from knowledge differences to enhance the quality of products and services was discovered, and within Cisco, Microsoft, and Zoom, boundaries knowledge was created, shared, and empathized through "boundaries synchronization" and "boundaries knowledge synchronization" aimed at convergence on pragmatic boundaries among diverse stakeholders through the formation of multilayered Ba.

(4) **The Stage of "Internalization (I)" (Explicit Knowledge → Tacit Knowledge: Knowledge Transformation Process)**

To accumulate high-quality tacit knowledge within individuals and organizations, the process of abduction through "reflective practice" (Nonaka & Takeuchi, 1995) is crucial. Ichiro Suzuki, a renowned Major League Baseball player, mentioned that he feels as if there is another self watching his batting and bunting form. This suggests that he continuously improves by logically and objectively assessing his actual movements, imagining his ideal form and body movements, and providing feedback through the differences (also "knowledge differences") to generate boundaries knowledge (Kodama, 2019b).

The act of objectively observing and correcting one's thoughts and actions is known as "metacognitive ability" (e.g., Haynie et al., 2016), which allows the theoretical explicit knowledge to be internalized as bodily knowledge. This metacognitive ability encourages new awareness and discoveries for practitioners, simultaneously making them recognize "knowledge differences." The generation of new meanings from these "knowledge differences" led Cisco, Microsoft, and Zoom to create "boundaries knowledge" through the abduction process of hypothesis setting and verification by trial and error, aiming for convergence on pragmatic boundaries through "boundaries synchronization" and "boundaries knowledge synchronization." The knowledge differences and boundaries knowledge generated through reflective practice in this "Internalization" phase drive the "knowledge transformation process," leading to the accumulation of high-quality tacit knowledge, which is the source of differentiation, among the practitioners of Cisco, Microsoft, and Zoom (see "Internalization" in Fig. 4.10). Thus, the "boundaries knowledge" generated from new meanings derived from "knowledge differences" becomes an element that creates high-quality tacit knowledge, which is the source of differentiation.

Meanwhile, Cisco, Microsoft, and Zoom needed to further expand the adoption of their cloud video conferencing services. They recognized that the knowledge gap between the current state and the ideal form or goal was the "construction of an ecosystem," and actively promoted interconnection with competitors, compatibility with peripheral devices from other manufacturers, and connectivity with other companies' applications. To deepen such collaboration, they promoted "boundaries synchronization" aimed at convergence on pragmatic boundaries through the formation of multilayered Ba. Through "boundaries knowledge synchronization," boundaries knowledge was created, shared, and empathized.

4.7 Implications and Conclusion

This chapter clarified that the emergence of cloud-based videoconferencing systems as a technology convergence is a "high-end disruptive innovation"—a phenomenon that revolutionized the market for traditional hardware videoconferencing services, opening and driving not only the existing videoconferencing market, but also new markets.

As a theoretical contribution, analyzing the evidence from the viewpoints of knowledge theory and capabilities theory, the threat of high-end disruptive innovation has a negative impact on the path-dependent core capabilities of incumbent leader firms, leading to the decline (or withdrawal) of existing businesses. Thus, the emergence of novelty, in cases of radical innovation through new product architectures or the emergence of innovative business models, the path-dependent knowledge of existing firms becomes a factor in the creation of "competency traps," the "curse of knowledge," and "core rigidities." This makes it difficult for existing firms to discard path-dependent knowledge, transform to new product architectures and innovative business models to accommodate high-end disruptive innovation. This has been shown to be a factor that leads to the decline or withdrawal of existing products or to the acquisition of existing firms by other companies. This phenomenon is a point that has not been discussed at all in previous studies on high-end disruptive innovation and represents a new theoretical contribution.

Second, as a theoretical contribution, we present a new framework of the key elements of dynamic capabilities (DC) (sensing [boundaries vision], seizing [asset orchestration architecture], transforming [asset orchestration dynamics]) necessary for existing leader firms to demonstrate their own DC with respect to the potential for high-end disruptive innovation, thereby providing new theoretical insights to previous studies of DC. In addition, the relationship between the SECI process and the DC framework to realize technology convergence was presented.

As the first characteristic point about DC, we present the new concept of boundaries vision, a function of sensing. Practitioners who share diverse knowledge and create new knowledge have a behavioral pattern of network thinking with boundaries vision that bridges diverse boundaries inside and outside of companies. Boundaries vision is the philosophy and insight of practitioners who recognize various boundaries, realize knowledge convergence (transformation) by bridging these boundaries, and design new business and corporate strategies. And the act of creating "boundaries knowledge through boundaries vision" in the four phases of the SECI process drives the SECI process and produces outcomes as new technology convergence.

As in this case, we found that a group of companies (mainly in the United States) that have succeeded in high-end disruptive innovation have demonstrated successful acquisition strategies and ambidextrous development strategies through the demonstration of DC using boundaries vision to create new product architectures (radical innovation) and innovative business models. Such boundaries vision not only searches the peripheral areas of a company's core businesses but also different business areas, stimulates new business, drastically changes the company's corporate boundaries, and creates new innovations (new products, services, and business models).

As the second characteristic, we present a new theoretical perspective on "Ba architecture" regarding the mechanism of asset orchestration, which has rarely been reported in previous studies. It is known that new tacit and explicit knowledge is created through the formation of Ba, according to the knowledge creation theory of Nonaka and Takeuchi (2019). However, because Ba are formed from a complex process of practice by a diverse group of practitioners, in many case studies, the explanation of the formation of Ba remains as the abstract expression, "multilayered Ba formation." However, in contrast to previous studies, this research provides a new theoretical contribution to knowledge creation theory by presenting a specific form of Ba in which assets (knowledge assets) are orchestrated.

The concept of "knowledge integration" by Grant (1996) relies on the idea of a knowledge-based view, and the process of combining different knowledge within and outside an organization (company) and the capabilities needed in that process have been researched (Berggren et al., 2011). However, prior research has not sufficiently interpreted the mechanism of knowledge integration itself (Zahra et al., 2020). However, in this study, Ba architecture, which realizes integration by combining various types of knowledge to bring about new products and services, provides a new theoretical contribution, as a concrete form, to the concept of "knowledge integration" by Grant (1996).

Furthermore, as an organizational form to realize the "transforming" process, we presented a new organizational form called "Ba-based asset orchestration firm" and provide new theoretical contributions on its differences and advantages compared to the existing concept of the ambidextrous organization.

Meanwhile, the first point as a practical implication is that three subtypes of high-end disruptive innovation (immediate, new attribute, and new market) are likely to occur simultaneously when product architecture and business models undergo major changes due to technological evolution of existing products. Therefore, the chapter has pointed out that marketing and product planners, and developers need to constantly monitor technological evolution, including ICT (in recent years, there has been much interest in AI), to see how it will affect existing businesses.

Second, the chapter identified that to respond to potential high-end disruptive innovation, existing companies need to function with "boundaries vision," the "sensing" component of DC, and develop "the ability to see the invisible" and "the ability to sense new threats." It is also important for existing leader companies to continue to explore new strategic positions without becoming bogged down in their current core businesses. To achieve this, the chapter identifies that different management activities of exploitation and exploration must be balanced, and that potential high-end disruptive innovation businesses must be sought and realized through a trial-and-error process. This process is also the reason why leaders and managers of existing companies continue to demonstrate DC rooted in entrepreneurship.

In this chapter, I analyzed detailed case studies of high-end disruptive innovation and presented the elements that promote high-end intrusion. At the same time, to answer the research questions "why can't existing leader companies immediately respond to high-end disruptive innovation?" and "what strategies and organizational management are needed to respond?" the chapter presented new findings from the viewpoints of knowledge theory and capabilities theory (especially dynamic capabilities).

Future research issues include the collection and analysis of case studies from other fields related to high-end disruptive innovation. In particular, the recent knowledge convergence among different industrial sectors, including the ICT sector (Kodama, 2014) is creating diverse products, services, and business models. Knowledge convergence between different specialties is an important research issue in the field of innovation and technology management. Furthermore, technological convergence between different specialties is an element that generates radical innovation in the form of architecture for new products and services.

For example, new markets and business models are forming as ICT merges into diverse industrial sectors and businesses and new hybrid fields such as AI, microelectronics, mechatronics, robotics, and nanobiotechnology. Particularly in a platform economy, disruptive innovation from digital platforms is likely to come from the high end. In the ICT industry, causing technological convergence across entire industries can act as a major trigger to the formation of business ecosystems covering new business environments and markets in which many companies are involved. The phenomenon of knowledge convergence is adding new layers of complexity to the traditional model of corporate and industry competitiveness.

Knowledge convergence is accelerating M&A and strategic partnering between corporations, includes customers, and is triggering dramatic changes to existing corporate boundaries (vertical and horizontal boundaries). Therefore, corporate strategy through "collaborative innovation" (Kodama, 2015) that transcends the business axis of competition in different industries and links up different businesses has become an increasingly important issue. Knowledge convergence between the ICT industry and the medical, nursing, healthcare, and pharmaceutical industries is creating new business processes and business models such as telemedicine, telecare, tele-healthcare, medical information management, and drug medicine information support (Kodama, 2015, 2021b). These new service architectures and business models will invade the operations of existing industries as high-end disruptive innovation.

Therefore, going forward, more in-depth exploratory research on high-end disruptive innovation originated from knowledge convergence will be necessary, from the perspective of innovation and technology management and strategic management theory including product architecture, service architecture, digital platform, business model, dynamic capability, etc.

Notes

1. H.320 is a comprehensive recommended standard established by the International Telecommunication Union Telecommunication Standardization Sector (ITU-T) for multimedia (voice, video, and data) communications over ISDN-based networks. H.221, H.230, and H.242 are used as the primary protocols, G.711 and G.723 as audio codecs, and H.261 and H.263 as video codecs.
2. One of the VoIP standards, a protocol for real-time communication of voice and video over a network.
3. An open framework for real-time communication via the Internet in a browser. It defines the network, voice, and video technologies involved, it is a P2P communication API technology that does not require conventional web conferencing software or applications and allows high-quality video and audio communication with a browser, and its source code is open to the public. The term WebRTC began to attract attention in 2013. The widespread use of HTML technology on the Internet and the availability of APIs for communication functions have made it easier to develop software. Currently, WebRTC standardization is underway at W3C and IETF. It has already been implemented in major browsers.
4. For a detailed description and discussion of high-end encroachment by high-end disruption, see the following references: Kodama and Hashimoto (2024).

References

AFP. (2013). Apple still has "magic," innovation, says CEO Cook. *afp.com*. Retrieved February 12, from http://www.globalpost.com/dispatch/news/afp/130212/apple-still-has-magic-innovation-says-ceocook-0

Abell, D. F. (1993). *Managing with dual strategies: Mastering the present, preempting the future*. The Free Press.

Adner, R., & Helfat, C. E. (2003). Corporate effects and dynamic managerial capabilities. *Strategic Management Journal, 24*(10), 1011–1025.

Arrow, K. J. (1994). Methodological individualism and social knowledge. *The American Economic Review, 84*(2), 1–9.

Bartlett, C. A., & Ghoshal, S. (2002). *Managing across borders: The transnational solution*. Harvard Business Press.

Berggren, C., Bergek, A., Bengtsson, L., & Söderlund, J. (2011). Exploring knowledge integration and innovation. In *Knowledge integration and innovation: Critical challenges facing international technology-based firms* (pp. 3–19). Oxford University Press.

Brown, J. S., & Duguid, P. (2001). Knowledge and organization: A social-practice perspective. *Organization Science, 12*(2), 198–213.

Burt, S. (1992). *Structural holes: The social structure of competition*. Harvard University Press.

Camerer, C., Loewenstein, G., & Weber, M. (1989). The curse of knowledge in economic settings: An experimental analysis. *Journal of Political Economy, 97*(5), 1232–1254.

Carlile, P. R. (2002). A pragmatic view of knowledge and boundaries: Boundary objects in new product development. *Organization Science, 13*(4), 442–455.

Carlile, P. R. (2004). Transferring, translating, and transforming: An integrative framework for managing knowledge across boundaries. *Organization Science, 15*(5), 555–568.

Carr, N. (2005). Top-down disruption. *Strategy and Business, 39*, 1–5.

Chesbrough, H. (2003). *Open innovation*. Harvard Business School Press.

Christensen, C., & Van Bever, D. (2014). *The capitalist's dilemma*. Harvard Business Review.

Christensen, C. M., Alton, R., Rising, C., & Waldeck, A. (2011). The new M&A playbook. *Harvard Business Review, 89*, 48–57.

Day, G. S., & Schoemaker, P. J. (2016). Adapting to fast-changing markets and technologies. *California Management Review, 58*(4), 59–77.

Dixon, S., Meyer, K., & Day, M. (2014). Building dynamic capabilities of adaptation and innovation: A study of micro-foundations in a transition economy. *Long Range Planning, 47*(4), 186–205.

Donnellon, A., Gray, B., & Bougon, M. G. (1986). Communication, meaning, and organized action. *Administrative Science Quarterly*, 43–55.

Gilbert, C. G. (2005). Unbundling the structure of inertia: Resource versus routine rigidity. *Academy of Management Journal, 48*(5), 741–763.

Govindarajan, V., & Trimble, C. (2005). *Ten rules for strategic innovations*. Harvard Business School Press.

Granovetter, M. (1973). The strength of weak ties. *American Journal of Sociology, 78*(6), 1360–1380.

Grant, R. M. (1996). Toward a knowledge-based theory of the firm. *Strategic Management Journal, 17*(S2), 109–122.

Grant, R. M. (2021). *Contemporary strategy analysis*. John Wiley & Sons.

Grinyer, P., & McKiernan, P. (1994). Triggering major and sustained changes in stagnating companies. In H. Daems & H. Thomas (Eds.), *Strategic groups, strategic moves and performance* (pp. 173–195). Pergamon.

Hagel, J., III., & Brown, J. S. (2005). Productive friction. *Harvard Business Review, 83*(2), 139–145.

Hart, S. L. (1992). An integrative framework for strategy-making processes. *Academy of Management Review, 17*(2), 327–351.

Haynie, J. M., Shepherd, D. A., & Patzelt, H. (2016). Cognitive adaptability and an entrepreneurial task: The role of metacognitive ability and feedback. In *Decision making in entrepreneurship* (pp. 237–265). Edward Elgar Publishing.

Helfat, C. E., & Peteraf, M. A. (2015). Managerial cognitive capabilities and the microfoundations of dynamic capabilities. *Strategic Management Journal, 36*(6), 831–850.

Helfat, C. E., & Winter, S. G. (2011). Untangling dynamic and operational capabilities: Strategy for the (N)ever-changing world. *Strategic Management Journal, 32*(11), 1243–1250.

Jobs, S. (1995). The lost interview. https://www.youtube.com/watch?v=TRZAJY23xio

Joseph, J., & Ocasio, W. (2012). Architecture, attention, and adaptation in the multibusiness firm: General electric from 1951 to 2001. *Strategic Management Journal, 33*(6), 633–660.

Kodama, M. (2001). Creating new business through strategic community management: Case study of a multimedia business. *International Journal of Human Resource Management, 12*(6), 1062–1084.

Kodama, M. (2002). Transforming an old economy company through strategic communities. *Long Range Planning, 35*(4), 349–365.

Kodama, M. (2003). Strategic innovation in traditional big business. *Organization Studies, 24*(2), 235–268.

Kodama, M. (2004). Strategic community-based theory of firms: Case study of dialectical management at NTT DoCoMo. *Systems Research and Behavioral Science: THe Official Journal of the International Federation for Systems Research, 21*(6), 603–634.

Kodama, M. (2007). *The strategic community-based firm*. Palgrave Macmillan.

Kodama, M. (2009). Boundaries innovation and knowledge integration in the Japanese firm. *Long Range Planning, 42*(4), 463–494.

Kodama, M. (2011a). *Interactive business communities*. Gower Publishing.

Kodama, M. (2011b). *Knowledge integration dynamics: Developing strategic innovation capability*. World Scientific Publishing.

Kodama, M. (2012). *Competing through ICT capability: Innovation in image communication*. Palgrave Macmillan.
Kodama, M. (2014). *Winning through boundaries innovation—Communities of boundaries generate convergence*. Peter Lang.
Kodama, M. (Ed.). (2015). *Collaborative innovation: Developing health support ecosystems*. Routledge.
Kodama, M. (2017). *Developing holistic leadership: A source of business innovation*. Emerald.
Kodama, M. (2018a). Boundaries innovation through knowledge convergence-developing triad strategic communities. *Technology Analysis & Strategic Management*, *30*(5), 609–624.
Kodama, M. (2018b) *Sustainable growth through strategic innovation: Driving congruence in capabilities*. Edward Elgar Publishing.
Kodama, M. (2019a). Boundaries knowledge (knowing)—A source of business innovation. *Knowledge and Process Management*, *26*(3), 210–228.
Kodama, M. (2019b). *Developing holistic strategic management in the advanced ICT era (Series on Technology Management, Vol. 35)*. World Scientific Publishing.
Kodama, M. (2020a). Developing knowledge communities through video-based information networks. *Knowledge and Process Management*, *27*(2), 103–122.
Kodama, M. (2020b). Digitally transforming work styles in an era of infectious disease. *International Journal of Information Management*, *55*, 102172.
Kodama, M. (Ed.). (2020c). *Developing Boundaries knowledge for innovation*. Edward Elgar Publishing.
Kodama, M. (2021a). Knowledge creation through collective phronesis. *Knowledge and Process Management*, *28*(3), 223–245.
Kodama, M. (2021b). *Managing IT for innovation: Dynamic capabilities and competitive advantage*. Routledge.
Kodama, M., & Hashimoto, K. (2024). Research on high-end disruptive innovations-Analysis and insights from the video conferencing systems market. *Technology in Society, 77*, Article 102576.
Kodama, M., & Shibata, T. (2014). Strategy transformation through strategic innovation capability—A case study of Fanuc. *R&D Management*, *44*(1), 75–103.
Kodama, M., & Shibata, T. (2016). Developing knowledge convergence through a boundaries vision—A case study of fujifilm in Japan. *Knowledge and Process Management, 23*(4), 274–292.
Leonard-Barton, D. (1992). Core capabilities and core rigidities: A paradox in managing new product development. *Strategic Management Journal, 13*(S1), 111–125.
Leonard-Barton, D. (1995). *Wellsprings of knowledge*. Harvard business school press.

Levitt, B., & March, J. G. (1988). Organizational learning. *Annual Review of Sociology*, 319–340.

March, J. (1991). Exploration and exploitation in organizational learning. *Organization Science, 2*(1), 71–87.

Markides, C. (1998). Strategic innovation in established companies. *Sloan Management Review, 39*(3), 31–42.

Markides, C. (1999). *All the right moves: A guide to crafting breakthrough strategy*. Harvard Business School Publishing.

Martins, L. L., & Kambil, A. (1999). Looking back and thinking ahead: Effects of prior success on managers' interpretations of new information technologies. *Academy of Management Journal, 42*(6), 652–661.

Marx, M., Gans, J. S., & Hsu, D. H. (2014). Dynamic commercialization strategies for disruptive technologies: Evidence from the speech recognition industry. *Management Science, 60*(10), 3103–3123.

McDonald, R., & Eisenhardt, K. (2017). *Parallel play: Startups, nascent markets, and the search for a viable business model* (Working Paper No. 14-088). Harvard Business School.

Nonaka, I., Hirose, A., & Takeda, Y. (2016). 'Meso'-foundations of dynamic capabilities: Team-level synthesis and distributed leadership as the source of dynamic creativity. *Global Strategy Journal, 6*(3), 168–182.

Nonaka, I., & Konno, N. (1998). The Concept of "Ba": Building a foundation for knowledge creation. *California Management Review, 40*(1), 40–54.

Nonaka, I., & Takeuchi, H. (2019). *The wise company: How companies create continuous innovation*. Oxford University Press.

Nonaka, I., Kodama, M., Hirose, A., & Kohlbacher, F. (2014). Dynamic fractal organizations for promoting knowledge-based transformation—A new paradigm for organizational theory. *European Management Journal, 32*(1), 137–146.

Nonaka, I., Toyama, R., & Hirata, T. (2008). *Managing flow: A process theory of the knowledge-based firm*. Palgrave Macmillan.

Nonaka, I., Toyama, R., & Konno, N. (2000). SECI, Ba and leadership: A unified model of dynamic knowledge creation. *Long Range Planning, 33*(1), 5–34.

Ocasio, W. (1997). Towards an attention-based view of the firm. *Strategic Management Journal, 18*(S1), 187–206.

Ocasio, W. (2011). Attention to attention. *Organization Science, 22*(5), 1286–1296.

Ocasio, W., & Joseph, J. (2018). The attention-based view of great strategies. *Strategy Science, 3*(1), 289–294.

Ocasio, W., Laamanen, T., & Vaara, E. (2017). Communication and attention dynamics: An attention-based view of strategic change. *Strategic Management Journal, 39*(1), 155–167.

O'Reilly, C. A., III., & Tushman, M. L. (2008). Ambidexterity as a dynamic capability: Resolving the innovator's dilemma. *Research in Organizational Behavior, 28*, 185–206.

O'Reilly, C. A., III., & Tushman, M. L. (2016). *Lead and disrupt: How to solve the innovator's dilemma*. Stanford University Press.

Perrow, C. B. (1994). *Accidents in high-risk systems*. National Emergency Training Center.

Raffaelli, R. (2019). Technology reemergence: Creating new value for old technologies in Swiss mechanical watchmaking, 1970–2008. *Administrative Science Quarterly, 64*(3), 576–618.

Rose, G. (2013). Generation kill: A conversation with Stanley McChrystal. *Foreign Affairs, 92*(4), 2–8.

Rosenbloom, N. (2000). Leadership, capabilities and technological change. *Strategic Management Journal, 21*, 1083–1103.

Schulze, A., & Brusoni, S. (2022). How dynamic capabilities change ordinary capabilities: Reconnecting attention control and problem-solving. *Strategic Management Journal., 43*(12), 2447–2477.

Shibata, T., & Kodama, M. (2008). Managing technological transition from old to new technology: Case of Fanuc's successful transition. *Business Strategy Series, 9*(4), 157–162.

Smith, S., & Tushman, M. (2005). Managing strategic contradictions: A top management model for managing innovation streams. *Organization Science, 16*(5), 522–536.

Spender, J. C. (1990). *Industry recipes: An enquiry into the nature and sources of managerial judgement*. Basil Blackwell.

Teece, D. J. (2007). Explicating dynamic capabilities: The nature and microfoundations of (sustainable) enterprise performance. *Strategic Management Journal, 28*(13), 1319–1350.

Teece, D. J. (2014). The foundations of enterprise performance: Dynamic and ordinary capabilities in an (economic) theory of firms. *Academy of Management Perspectives, 28*(4), 328–352.

Teece, D. J., Pisano, G., & Shuen, A. (1997). Dynamic capabilities and strategic management. *Strategic Management Journal, 18*(3), 509–533.

Tripsas, M., & Gavetti, G. (2000). Capabilities, cognition, and inertia: Evidence from digital imaging. *Strategic Management Journal*, 1147–1161.

van der Rhee, B., Schmidt, G. M., & Van Orden, J. (2012). High-end encroachment patterns of new products. *Journal of Product Innovation Management, 29*(5), 715–733.

Van Orden, J., Van der Rhee, B., & Schmidt, G. M. (2011). Encroachment patterns of the best products from the past decade. *Journal of Product Innovation Management, 28*(5), 726–743.

Weick, K., Sutcliffe, K., & Obstfeld, D. (1999). Organizing for high reliability: Processes of collective mindfulness. In B. Staw & R. Sutton (Eds.), *Research in organizational behavior* (pp. 81–117). JAI Press.

Welch, J., & Welch, S. (2005). *Winning*. HarperCollins.

Zahra, S. A., Neubaum, D. O., & Hayton, J. (2020). What do we know about knowledge integration: Fusing micro-and macro-organizational perspectives. *Academy of Management Annals, 14*(1), 160–194.

Zuckerman, E. W. (2016). Crossing the chasm to disruptive innovation. *MIT Sloan Management Review, 58*, 28–30.

CHAPTER 5

Creative New Product Development in Semiconductor Industry—Case Studies of Qualcomm, TSMC, and NVIDIA

5.1 Knowledge Creation for New Innovation

The importance of enhancing creativity across generations and contributing to various social activities is evident not only for corporate organizations but also for broader social organizations and individuals. Recently, the need for business strategies that address the fusion of different technologies and services, as well as the development of products and services and business models that span different industries, has been increasing. Conversely, companies are also strengthening the development and recruitment of creative thinkers. In the business field, the necessity for developing new products and services through "knowledge convergence" (or knowledge creation/knowledge integration) (Kodama, 2005; Nonaka & Takeuchi, 1995) is growing as a guideline for differentiating new product development and new business development in different fields. This is because many cases of innovative new products and services are realized through the fusion of knowledge from different fields (Kodama, 2007a).

Given this background, this chapter aims to explore a new theoretical model that accelerates the knowledge creation process by focusing on the thinking and actions of people and organizations for creative thinking and innovation. While Nonaka et al. have proposed the knowledge creation process through the "knowledge triad relationships" of "tacit knowledge, explicit knowledge, and phronesis" (Kodama, 2018;

M. Kodama, *Developing Knowledge Convergence Through Collective Phronesis*, https://doi.org/10.1007/978-981-96-4403-2_5

Nonaka et al., 2014), they have not deeply presented the details of the "creative practice process." Additionally, traditional academic research on innovation management has focused on industrial policy and R&D organization management, with few perspectives on the creative processes that focus on individuals and organizations at the micro level.

Although there is a wealth of research on creativity and innovation in the fields of management and psychology, the specific elements and practical processes that generate "creativity (novelty and usefulness)" (e.g., Amabile, 1996) remain unclear. In this academic context, this chapter aims to contribute to previous research by addressing the new concepts of "boundaries knowledge (knowing)" and "boundaries vision" (Kodama, 2019, 2024), which accelerate the knowledge creation framework and process of dynamic creativity at the micro level.

Previous research (Kodama, 2019) has focused on the new concept of "knowledge differences" (Kodama, 2006, 2007a, 2007b, 2019), which arise between people, organizations, and various different entities. This research reports that the new knowledge arising from the perspectives, awareness, and discoveries of people regarding such differences is called "boundaries knowledge" (or "boundaries knowing"). This boundaries knowledge (knowing) has been a theme that has rarely been discussed in the past, not only in the fields of knowledge management and business and management but also in other academic fields (other social sciences and humanities). The concept of "boundaries knowledge (knowing) through boundaries vision" is emphasized as influencing the creativity and innovation of people and organizations (Kodama, 2019).

Kodama (2019) conducted exploratory research on the characteristics of boundaries knowledge (knowing) as a core concept in the knowledge creation process and its relationship with the SECI model. This previous research reported that various "boundaries" elements exist in the boundary areas of the four phases of the SECI process (Nonaka & Takeuchi, 1995), namely, "knowledge integration" (Tacit → Tacit, Explicit → Explicit), and "knowledge transformation" (Tacit → Explicit, Explicit → Tacit). Practitioners sense knowledge differences from these various boundaries, activate "boundaries vision," and generate boundaries knowledge (boundaries knowing).

Therefore, incorporating the concept of boundaries knowledge (boundaries knowing) into the SECI model can provide a new framework and insights into the knowledge creation process, where boundaries knowledge generates "convergence knowledge (tacit knowledge and explicit knowledge)" (Kodama, 2018). However, the micro-processes of "knowledge creation (convergence) through boundaries knowledge" within and between organizations remain a black box and have not been deeply elucidated in previous research (Kodama, 2019).

This chapter points out through in-depth case study that boundaries knowledge, created between individuals, organizations, and various different entities, promotes the knowledge creation process through mechanisms of creation and sharing among practitioners and different organizations (referred to in this chapter as "boundaries knowledge synchronization"). Furthermore, for the realization of the creation and sharing of boundaries knowledge through boundaries knowledge synchronization, practitioners need to align knowledge boundaries among stakeholders and engage in an abductive synthesis process for knowledge creation activities. This requires that practitioners mutually learn and recognize different boundaries knowledge through the formation of "strategic communities" (e.g., Kodama, 2005) via abductive synthesis. As a result, the practical process of "boundaries knowledge synchronization" enables the creation and sharing of common boundaries knowledge among practitioners, including various stakeholders, and promotes the knowledge creation process.

5.2 Structure of This Chapter and Research Method

This chapter first elucidates the concept of "boundaries knowledge synchronization," which has not been discussed in academic research to date, based on previous studies. The mechanism of "boundaries knowledge synchronization" facilitates the creation, sharing, and empathy of "boundaries knowledge (boundaries knowing)" in the individual boundary areas of Socialization, Externalization, Combination, and Internalization within the SECI model among practitioners, thereby smoothly driving the SECI model. As an in-depth case study of knowledge creation through boundaries knowledge synchronization, this chapter examines the new product development process of Qualcomm, TSMC, and NVIDIA, global top players in the semiconductor industry.

This research has exploratory aspects of extracting details of certain people and organizations involved in corporate innovation activities, gathering data regarding the leadership processes of their activities, and carefully analyzing these. Therefore, the author has adopted a qualitative survey and case study analysis as their methodology. This research methodology provides for the rich gathering of data and rich analyses for introducing a new theoretical framework that cannot be found in previous research.

Many scholars have already pointed out the effectiveness of case studies (e.g., Eisenhardt, 1989; Pettigrew, 1990; Yin, 1994). Case studies are a very effective methodology for explaining the relationship between causes and results of phenomena and their appropriateness from multiple perspectives and interpretations through deep insights based on objective qualitative information and the researchers' subjective interpretation regarding individual cases, which cannot be obtained from statistical methods. Case studies are important not only in complementing generality through statistical methods but also in constructing novel, creative theories.

The case studies in this chapter focus on research questions relating to boundaries knowledge (knowing) in managing innovation in companies and provide an in-depth analysis and observations regarding how that boundaries knowledge (knowing) and boundaries knowledge synchronization achieved innovation activities.

In the creation and analysis of in-depth case studies of three enterprises, semi-structured interviews lasting 1–2 hours were conducted with executives (10), managers (14), staff (9), semiconductor manufacturing equipment vendors (managers: 9), and stakeholder companies (managers: 8). Additionally, publicly available external documents and press releases from three enterprises were utilized as secondary data. Based on the above research approach, this chapter first presents the conceptual model of "knowledge creation through boundaries knowledge synchronization," then analyzes and discusses this model through in-depth case studies of three enterprises. Finally, it presents new insights from the in-depth case studies, implications, and conclusions.

5.3 Conceptual Model of Boundaries Knowledge and Boundaries Knowledge Synchronization

5.3.1 Importance of Boundaries Knowledge (Knowing) and Boundaries Vision from Previous Research

Previous research has reported that the drivers accelerating knowledge creation are the concepts of "boundaries knowledge (knowing)" (Kodama, 2019) and "boundaries vision" (Kodama, 2024; Kodama & Shibata, 2016). In other words, to successfully achieve new innovations in knowledge creation across different specialized fields, the creation of boundaries knowledge (knowing) is crucial.

New innovations occur when the unique knowledge of different specialized fields is combined through various convergence processes (e.g., Hacklin et al., 2009; Kodama, 2005, 2009; Rafols & Meyer, 2010). This means that the knowledge creation process through boundaries vision is happening at a level that spans different specialized fields (Kodama, 2019). Convergence, by its nature, is based on the integration of knowledge that once belonged to separate technical fields. Therefore, to generate convergence, boundaries knowledge (knowing) that spans different specialized fields is necessary.

However, generally, there are knowledge boundaries (Carlile, 2002, 2004) between different types of knowledge. This means that there is always inherent heterogeneity or unique "knowledge differences" (Kodama, 2006, 2007a, 2019) between different types of knowledge. For example, corporate organizations are divided into various functional organizations and specialized fields, and between companies and industries, there are various types and forms of separation. These include many boundaries from macro to micro levels, and from visible to invisible ones (Kodama & Shibata, 2014).

Additionally, among practitioners within companies, there are not only organizational boundaries such as sectionalism but also knowledge boundaries at the micro level due to individual practitioners' values, backgrounds, and expertise. The knowledge differences created by these diverse boundaries can isolate the unique mental models and path-dependent knowledge that practitioners possess, becoming barriers to new innovations (e.g., Brown & Duguid, 2001; Carlile, 2002; Kogut & Zander, 1992; Leonard-Barton, 1995; Nonaka & Takeuchi,

1995; Spender, 1996). Therefore, how practitioners perceive, interpret, and act on these knowledge differences becomes a critical issue.

According to previous research, practitioners who share knowledge and create new knowledge discover (or create) diverse boundaries knowledge (knowing) within and outside the company (within and outside the organization, and even between individuals) and exhibit network thinking behavior patterns with boundaries vision to bridge these boundaries (Kodama, 2019, 2024; Kodama & Shibata, 2014). In the business context, boundaries vision refers to the practitioners' ideas and insights that recognize diverse boundaries, discover (or create) boundaries knowledge (knowing) at these boundaries, and design new business strategies and corporate strategies through the knowledge creation process that bridges these boundaries.

In other words, boundaries vision refers to the capabilities of practitioners to find boundaries knowledge (knowing) from the diverse discomforts and heterogeneities on boundaries, and to discover new hints, ideas, and insights from those. It also includes the ability to identify and connect various boundaries and stimulate new ways of seeing and understanding things, which constitutes new knowledge.

Boundaries vision is not static but a dynamic capability that constantly changes (Kodama, 2024). The demonstration and cultivation of such boundaries vision are essential for individual practitioners and organizations as the source of new knowledge creation. The process of "boundaries knowledge through boundaries vision" is the most fundamental element for converging different knowledge. For dynamic knowledge creation to be realized across multiple diverse boundaries, practitioners need to demonstrate boundaries vision and realize new products, services, and business models. Practically, managers and executives must focus on boundaries knowledge (knowing) and boundaries vision to create new innovations by integrating different knowledge.

According to many existing studies, the intersection and fusion of heterogeneous knowledge are sources of new innovations (e.g., Johansson, 2004; Kodama, 2007a). Therefore, whether practitioners can find relationships between multiple heterogeneous knowledge or between existing knowledge and heterogeneous knowledge, and derive new meanings and insights from these relationships, is a crucial point for realizing knowledge creation.

5.3.2 *Creation of Boundaries Knowledge (Knowing) Through Abductive Synthesis*

As previously mentioned, a crucial proposition for corporate strategy to adapt to or create within the worldview of knowledge convergence (or knowledge creation) lies in the creation of boundaries knowledge. Deep communication and collaboration processes between specialized fields significantly contribute to new innovations (Kodama, 2012; van Rijnsoever & Hessels, 2011). However, for such communication and collaboration to be promoted, it is essential to identify and effectively manage the knowledge boundaries perceived by individuals and organizations.

Capabilities are needed to understand whether boundaries knowledge, acquired from heterogeneity and knowledge differences on various boundaries, becomes the source of new knowledge creation. Generally, humans often feel discomfort at unfamiliar boundaries (boundaries with unfamiliar heterogeneous content), and the perceptual and cognitive abilities at such boundaries vary among individuals. In other words, boundaries knowledge lies in the knowledge that determines the differences in discomfort and heterogeneity between various boundaries (people, organizations, customers, environments) and between existing knowledge and heterogeneous knowledge.

Questions such as "Why do people avoid heterogeneous knowledge?", "Why do differences between goals and reality arise?", "How can contradictions in facing challenges be resolved or reconciled?", and "How can common goals be set among stakeholders in an environment full of uncertainty?" require practitioners to have the constructive ability to set hypotheses as true goals (objectives). The solution for this lies in the specific thinking and actions of practitioners, known as "abductive synthesis" (e.g., Anderson, 1986).

Abduction (e.g., Mitchell & Education, 2018; Samuels, 2000) is a method of thinking proposed by Charles Sanders Peirce (1839–1914), the founder of American "pragmatism." Peirce used the word "abduction" in contrast to the traditional methods of deduction and induction. This pragmatism, based on abduction, was utilized in American education by James (1912) and Dewey (1922). Abduction often employs transcendental hypotheses. Constructing transcendental hypotheses involves assuming unconfirmed or unknown matters, phenomena, laws, or theories. Three types of transcendental hypotheses are considered (e.g., Aliseda, 2005; Bertilsson, 2004; Kodama, 2007a): (1) hypotheses that have not been verified but can be verified if attempted, (2) hypotheses that are currently impossible to observe directly, and (3) hypotheses that assume the existence of things that are unavailable or nonexistent. In new product development in corporate activities, types 1 and 3 are often used, while type 2 is used in pure sciences such as archaeology, quantum mechanics, and particle theory. However, the correctness of such transcendental hypotheses is sometimes confirmed using deduction from the system of natural sciences.

In the actual new product development process, the realization of transcendental hypotheses itself becomes a challenge, and abduction is conducted to address this challenge. Through hypothesis testing, appropriate solutions are dialectically selected and integrated. Therefore, abduction leads practitioners' thinking to develop dialectically toward themselves and others infinitely. The transcendental hypotheses that are conceived one after another are narrowed down to only those with potential through verification.

The inspiration for excellent ideas, which are the source of innovation and creativity, largely depends on individual ideas and intuition (e.g., Kodama, 2016). Therefore, in the business world, it is challenging to create creativity through deductive methods that strictly apply existing theories while excluding individual experiential knowledge or inductive methods based on a large amount of data that everyone can agree on. In other words, the thinking method that enables creative problem-solving through exploration activities toward the unknown is effective through abduction (abductive synthesis) involving intense interaction through the formation of multilayer Ba among humans themselves and between humans (Kodama, 2007b).

Through such abductive synthesis, the knowledge difference that arises between the target hypothesis setting and the verification results induces new awareness and discoveries for practitioners through boundaries vision, enhancing the possibility of creating boundaries knowledge with new meanings (see Fig. 5.1). The process of abductive synthesis begins with the perception of facts, which requires practitioners to have a sense of purpose above all. By focusing based on their beliefs and thoughts, observing details (parts), and synthesizing them into the whole, new hypotheses are born. Abductive synthesis detects subtle signs and changes in individual real phenomena, synthesizes all related knowledge (existing and heterogeneous knowledge), creates leap hypotheses, and reaches new discoveries while refining and renewing hypotheses through trial and error. This process of abductive synthesis differs from the usual deductive and inductive methods.

Boundaries knowledge created through hypothesis setting and verification by abductive synthesis is not static but dynamic knowledge that constantly changes according to the situation. The dynamic creation of boundaries knowledge is indispensable for the source of new knowledge creation. Such boundaries knowledge is the most fundamental element for integrating and transforming different knowledge (tacit knowledge and explicit knowledge) in the SECI model to create new knowledge (see Fig. 5.1).

Dynamic boundaries knowledge (boundaries knowing), linked with boundaries vision, generates differences in discomfort and heterogeneity at boundaries in the dialectical fusion process between existing knowledge (empirical knowledge) and different kind of knowledge (heterogeneous knowledge) in Fig. 5.1. Furthermore, practitioners aim to find new

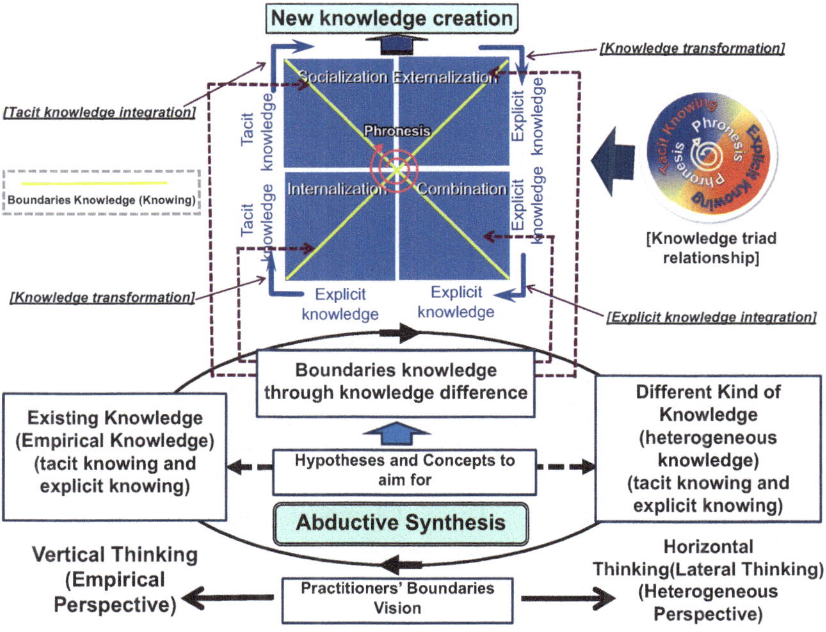

Fig. 5.1 Knowledge convergence process through SECI model

awareness, discoveries, and insights from there. The capabilities to identify various boundaries, connect them, and inspire new ways of seeing and understanding things correspond to the process of "boundaries knowledge through knowledge difference" (see Fig. 5.1). Practitioners need to use boundaries vision and broaden their thinking framework through "vertical thinking" based on past experiential knowledge in the same (similar) specialized fields and "horizontal thinking (lateral thinking)"(e.g., Bono, 2009) to widely pay attention to diverse heterogeneous knowledge in different fields. Therefore, practitioners need to find "boundaries knowledge" from "knowledge difference" through "abductive synthesis" between "target hypotheses or concepts" and "reality (existing experiential knowledge and heterogeneous knowledge)" (see Fig. 5.1).

This process of abductive synthesis accelerates the creation of "boundaries knowledge" in the boundary areas of each phase of the SECI process: "Socialization" (tacit knowledge → tacit knowledge: knowledge integration), "Externalization" (tacit knowledge → explicit knowledge: knowledge transformation), "Combination" (explicit knowledge → explicit knowledge: knowledge integration), and "Internalization" (explicit knowledge → tacit knowledge: knowledge transformation) (see Fig. 5.1). The existence of "boundaries knowledge (knowing)" leads to the realization of "knowledge integration" and "knowledge transformation" in the SECI process.

5.3.3 *Positioning of Boundaries Knowledge (Knowing) in the Knowledge Creation Process (SECI Model)*

In the SECI model, knowledge is created through the interaction that converts tacit knowledge (tacit knowing), rooted in individual experiences, into explicit knowledge (explicit knowing) that can be systematically shared. This spiral circulation becomes a dynamic process that enhances the quality and quantity of knowledge for both individuals and organizations (see Fig. 5.1). The SECI model consists of four phases, starting with "Socialization." For example, through direct experiences in interactions with external parties such as customers, business partners, and through various internal activities like sales, development, and manufacturing, practitioners sense diverse tacit knowledge embedded in environments of experiential and heterogeneous knowledge using their bodies and senses. However, to systematically share tacit knowledge that integrates experiential and heterogeneous knowledge, it must be verbalized. The next phase, "Externalization," involves transforming this tacit knowledge into explicit knowledge through analogies, metaphors, inference, and dialogue, converting it into language, concepts, and images.

To crystallize (concretize) the concept further, the "Combination" phase involves analyzing and systematizing it by combining it with other explicit knowledge (existing explicit knowledge or new unknown explicit knowledge) and processing it into forms accessible to everyone, such as documents, databases, and theoretical models. Specifically, this phase involves designing and manufacturing technologies, products, software, and services using IT/AI. In the final phase, "Internalization," actions are taken based on the new designs, manufacturing, and services, and they are introduced to the market as concrete products, services, and technologies. In this process, individuals acquire new tacit knowledge (tacit knowledge that integrates experiential and heterogeneous knowledge). Simultaneously, the value and new meanings mediated by products with customers and external partners are stimulated as tacit knowledge, leading back to "Socialization."

In relation to innovation, succinctly put, stakeholders such as customers who embody the living market share their tacit knowledge (Socialization), elevate tacit knowledge to concepts through essential dialogue beyond organizational boundaries (Externalization), systematize it across time and space using IT/AI (Combination), crystallize it into technologies, products, software, services, and business models, and internalize it as know-how (Internalization). At the same time, they stimulate new knowledge of stakeholders such as market customers, leading back to (Socialization).

In the knowledge creation theory (SECI model), knowledge has two dimensions: "tacit knowledge" and "explicit knowledge." These two dimensions are continuously and interactively converted, creating new knowledge. Knowledge creation activities are the process of mutual conversion between tacit knowledge derived from individuals' bodies, thoughts, and feelings, and explicit knowledge that verbalizes it. These two dimensions are contrasting but continuous. Individual tacit knowledge is shared with others and becomes explicit knowledge, combined with other explicit knowledge to create new explicit knowledge, which is then converted back into individual tacit knowledge, leading to the next conversion process. Innovation arises from this spiral-up process of conversion.

The third knowledge that promotes this spiral-up (synthesis and sublation of tacit knowledge and explicit knowledge) is phronesis (Nonaka et al., 2014). Phronesis is a concept proposed by the ancient Greek philosopher Aristotle in "Nicomachean Ethics," translated as "Prudence" or "Practical Wisdom" (Aristotle, 1980). Phronesis is a practical way of knowing that involves purpose, value, and action, with the value criterion of "Common Good," enabling the best judgment in each individual context with practical wisdom that involves embodiment. It is characterized by "Contemplation in Action," "contextual judgment," and "timely and exquisite balance."

According to Nonaka et al. (2014) in "Dynamic fractal organizations for promoting knowledge-based transformation—A new paradigm for organizational theory," in the SECI process of excellent companies and organizations, they present tacit knowledge as the first knowledge, explicit knowledge as the second knowledge, and practical knowledge (phronesis) as the third knowledge that drives the spiral loop. In Nonaka et al. (2014), they have considered the concepts of mutual conversion of tacit knowledge and explicit knowledge and phronesis separately in the past, but they position phronesis as the third knowledge that promotes the spiral-up of tacit knowledge and explicit knowledge, calling this form of synthesis of the three knowledges the "knowledge triad relationship" (see Fig. 5.1).

However, in a previous theory by Nonaka (Nonaka & Takeuchi, 1995; Nonaka et al., 2008), there has not been a deep discussion on the details of the processes of "knowledge integration" (Tacit → Tacit, Explicit → Explicit) and "knowledge transformation" (Tacit → Explicit, Explicit → Tacit) in the boundary areas of the four phases of the SECI process.

For example, the relationship between tacit knowledge and explicit knowledge is sometimes compared to the two sides of a coin, but the boundary is dynamic and cannot be clearly separated, with only gradations of difference. When expressing the relationship between tacit knowledge and explicit knowledge with the metaphor of an iceberg, the part visible above the water surface is explicit knowledge, and the much larger mass of ice hidden below the water surface is tacit knowledge, with the boundary between the two constantly changing with the movement of the iceberg and the waves (Nonaka, 2016). In other words, boundaries knowledge refers to the knowledge generated from the boundary between tacit knowledge and explicit knowledge, which is constantly changing with the movement of the iceberg and the waves (see Fig. 5.2).

Additionally, in "tacit knowledge integration (tacit knowledge → tacit knowledge)" mentioned by Polanyi (1962), which relates dispersed elements of tacit knowledge and inductively infers a consistent and comprehensive whole, creating new meanings comprehensively, there is also "boundaries knowledge" between different elements of tacit knowledge.

Nonaka (2016) mentions that the act and method of "knowing" by practitioners are generated by the capabilities of "tacit knowledge integration," and tacit knowledge integration can be said to be the skills of invention, discovery, and creation. For such "tacit knowledge integration," it is important to create new meanings through the creation of boundaries knowledge by recognizing knowledge differences. There, the creation of boundaries knowledge enables the integration of diverse tacit knowledge (tacit knowledge → tacit knowledge) and plays a role in creating new tacit knowledge.

Furthermore, as shown in Fig. 5.2, even in "explicit knowledge integration (explicit knowledge → explicit knowledge)" compared to tacit

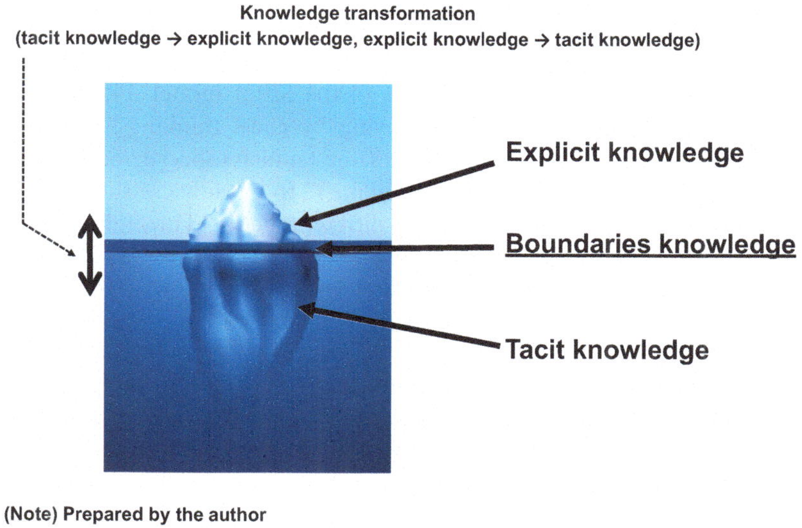

Fig. 5.2 Tacit knowledge, explicit knowledge and boundaries knowledge

knowledge, there is "boundaries knowledge" between different elements of explicit knowledge, which is evident from the perspective of science and engineering. The existence of such "boundaries knowledge (knowing)" leads to the realization of "tacit knowledge integration and explicit knowledge integration" and "knowledge transformation (tacit knowledge → explicit knowledge) and (explicit knowledge → tacit knowledge)."

Therefore, the boundary areas of knowledge integration and knowledge transformation in Socialization, Externalization, Combination, and Internalization in Fig. 5.1 are "boundaries knowledge (boundaries knowing)," and to appropriately drive the SECI model in groups and organizations, the creation, sharing, and empathy of boundaries knowledge among organizational members, including stakeholders, are indispensable. For this, the concept and actions of "boundaries knowledge synchronization" among stakeholders, explained in the following sections, are important.

5.3.4 Concept of Boundaries Knowledge Synchronization

As previously mentioned, prior research (Kodama, 2019, 2020) has reported the existence of "boundaries knowledge (knowing)" at the boundaries of knowledge integration (tacit knowledge to tacit knowledge and explicit knowledge to explicit knowledge) and knowledge transformation (tacit knowledge to explicit knowledge and explicit knowledge to tacit knowledge) in the four phases of the SECI model. Practitioners must utilize boundaries vision, employing "vertical thinking" rooted in past experiential knowledge within the same (similar) specialized fields, as well as "horizontal thinking(lateral thinking)" to broadly consider diverse and heterogeneous knowledge from different fields. Through "abductive synthesis" between "target hypotheses or concepts" and "reality (existing experiential knowledge and heterogeneous knowledge)," practitioners identify "boundaries knowledge" from "knowledge difference" (see Fig. 5.1).

From the perception and recognition process of knowledge difference through such abductive synthesis, boundaries knowledge is created in these four phases, enabling knowledge integration and knowledge transformation, dynamically driving the SECI model. However, such boundaries knowledge must be deeply shared and empathized with among different practitioners (e.g., between product planning sides like sales and marketing departments and technical sides like development and production departments in companies) for the SECI model to function as a whole within the organization (or project).

Individual practitioners have different experiential knowledge from various backgrounds and different perspectives on new knowledge (e.g., heterogeneous knowledge). Therefore, practitioners have different boundaries knowledge due to the perception and recognition of different knowledge differences. Driving the SECI model requires finding common knowledge (Kodama, 2007a, 2007b) from different boundaries knowledge and creating, sharing, and empathizing with common boundaries knowledge. This perspective has not been discussed in previous research (Kodama, 2019; Nonaka et al., 2014).

To creatively and productively resolve conflicts and frictions observed between different departments within an organization, it is necessary to create and share common boundaries knowledge among practitioners (stakeholders). Therefore, as mentioned next, it is crucial to embody the concept of "boundaries knowledge synchronization" to promote the creation, sharing, and empathy of boundaries knowledge among different practitioners (or stakeholders).

Practitioners create common boundaries knowledge through boundaries knowledge synchronization (creation, sharing, and empathy), driving the dynamic interaction of tacit knowledge and explicit knowledge for knowledge creation (SECI model). The creation of boundaries knowledge is not only required by top management but is particularly demanded of many middle managers and staff engaged in facing projects.

To achieve this, practitioners must demonstrate boundaries vision and construct strategic communities that synthesizes diverse dynamic contexts to create new boundaries knowledge (Kodama, 2019, 2024). Practitioners, based on the philosophy of phronesis, must know "what should be done" for the common good, have high aspirations, discern what is good for society as a whole, and build a knowledge creating company model (Kodama, 2021; Nonaka & Toyama, 2005) that organically links individual elements such as knowledge vision, driving objective, dialogue and practice, SECI, knowledge assets, and environment, creating new knowledge through the SECI model.

However, as previously mentioned, it is not clear at the micro level in prior research how the SECI process dynamically functions in strategic communities formed among multiple stakeholders (e.g., between product planning sides like sales and marketing departments and technical sides like development and production departments in companies). In each stage of the SECI process, the creation and sharing of boundaries knowledge trigger the process. However, as mentioned earlier, different stakeholders are likely to perceive and recognize different boundaries knowledge individually.

Regarding such issues, practitioners need to demonstrate boundaries vision, create boundaries knowledge through the formation of strategic communities, and strive to align the knowledge boundaries (pragmatic, semantic, and syntactic boundaries, which exist depending on the situation) that stakeholders face, as shown in Fig. 5.3 (Carlile, 2004; Kodama, 2019). Practitioners must practice thinking and actions to find common interests (e.g., Dalkir, 2013) and common knowledge from individual boundaries knowledge (boundaries knowledge generated in pragmatic boundaries faced in innovation tasks or problem-solving tasks).

To align knowledge boundaries (pragmatic boundaries) among stakeholders, it is necessary to alleviate tensions and integrate through abductive synthesis of extremes through creative confrontations or abrasion (Leonard-Barton, 1995), productive friction (Hagel & Brown, 2005),

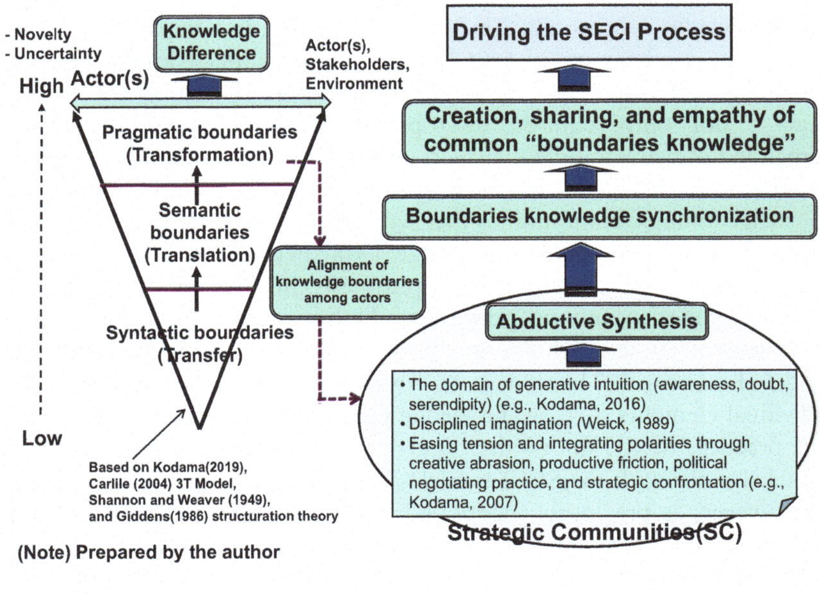

Fig. 5.3 Practice of boundaries knowledge synchronization to create, share, and empathize with boundaries knowledge

political negotiating practice (Brown & Duguid, 2001), and strategic contradictions (Smith & Tushman, 2005) (see Fig. 5.3).

For abductive synthesis, practitioners themselves and among practitioners must demonstrate new insights (Kodama, 2008), generative doubt (Weick, 2001), intuition such as sensitivity (Kodama, 2007a, 2016), and serendipity (e Cunha et al., 2015). Furthermore, through the formation of strategic communities, practitioners must mutually learn and recognize these different boundaries knowledge, demonstrate disciplined imagination (Weick, 1989), and create and share common boundaries knowledge among practitioners (see Figs. 5.3 and 5.4).

In other words, practitioners must understand, learn, and integrate different boundaries knowledge and share it among different stakeholders. As a result, the boundaries knowledge created through the formation of strategic communities will lead to shared and empathized boundaries knowledge among different stakeholders. This practical

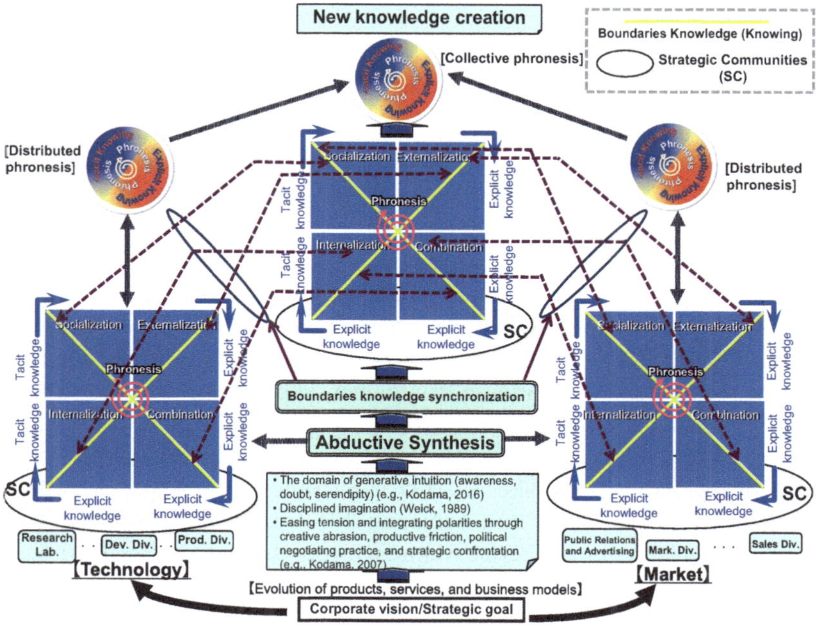

(Note) Prepared by the author

Fig. 5.4 Knowledge creation through boundaries knowledge synchronization

process is referred to as "boundaries knowledge synchronization" in this Chapter (see Figs. 5.3 and 5.4).

Furthermore, this practical process dynamically resonates the SECI process through the creation and sharing of common boundaries knowledge, generating collective phronesis (Kodama, 2021) for the entire practitioners (stakeholders). Simultaneously, the formation of collective phronesis triggers the creation of a dynamic fractal organization (Nonaka et al., 2014) with core knowledge (knowledge triad relationship) (Nonaka et al., 2014) based on the (distributed) phronesis possessed by individual practitioners. Thus, the concept of "boundaries knowledge synchronization" as a conceptual model in this chapter is considered a key element in forming collective phronesis (Kodama, 2021) and dynamic fractal organization (Nonaka et al., 2014) (see Fig. 5.4).

In this chapter, this conceptual model will be verified through in-depth case studies of Qualcomm, TSMC, and NVIDIA, global top players in the semiconductor industry.

5.4 Innovation in the Semiconductor Industry: Fabless and Foundry

Since the 1990s, the semiconductor industry has seen significant progress in horizontal specialization, leading to the emergence of companies focused exclusively on semiconductor design, manufacturing, and design tool development. For example, Qualcomm, which dominates the semiconductor market for smartphones, and NVIDIA, known globally for its graphics processing and AI development semiconductors, are called fabless companies. These specialized companies focus solely on semiconductor design and do not own semiconductor manufacturing facilities. On the other hand, Taiwanese companies like TSMC (Taiwan Semiconductor Manufacturing) and UMC (United Microelectronics Corp.) specialize in manufacturing semiconductors at staggeringly low costs. Additionally, companies like STMicroelectronics, Renesas Electronics, Intel, Texas Instruments, and Samsung Electronics are vertically integrated IDMs (Integrated Device Manufacturers) specializing in the design and manufacturing of specific semiconductors (SoCs, MPUs, DSPs, microcontrollers, DRAMs).

The background of this horizontal specialization includes the rapid advancement and specialization of semiconductor technology, the diversification and sophistication of user needs, and the demand for cost reduction, making it difficult for a single company to handle development alone. Specializing in specific areas to leverage economies of scale also played a significant role. This horizontal specialization has occurred simultaneously in digital industries such as software, hardware, semiconductors, and information and communications.

This section first explains the changes in the value chain of the semiconductor industry and highlights major global semiconductor companies in the fabless and foundry sectors, such as Qualcomm, NVIDIA, and TSMC, and demonstrates the process by which these companies have created "boundaries knowledge" from the fusion of existing and new knowledge, leading to the development of unique business models.

5.4.1 Changes in the Value Chain of the Semiconductor Industry

The business structure of the semiconductor industry has evolved due to technological innovations, shifting from a vertically integrated structure consisting of set development (system development), semiconductor design, semiconductor manufacturing (frontend/backend), semiconductor design tools, and semiconductor manufacturing equipment to an open and independent business structure for each of these business elements. Currently, the semiconductor industry sees various players participating in each business element, with "competition and cooperation" among these players (refer to the vertically disintegrated model in Fig. 5.5).

Meanwhile, companies like Intel and Samsung Electronics are vertically integrated semiconductor manufacturers (IDMs [Integrated Device Manufacturer]), possessing both the function of using semiconductors for their own systems (set products) and selling semiconductors to other companies. Besides comprehensive set manufacturers like Samsung, the semiconductor industry also includes specialized semiconductor manufacturers without their own set departments, such as Renesas Electronics (a joint venture of Hitachi, Mitsubishi, and NEC in Japan), Texas Instruments and Intel in the United States, and STMicroelectronics in Europe (refer to the vertically integrated model in Fig. 5.5).

There are also specialized semiconductor companies (fabless) focusing solely on the development, design, and sale of LSIs without having

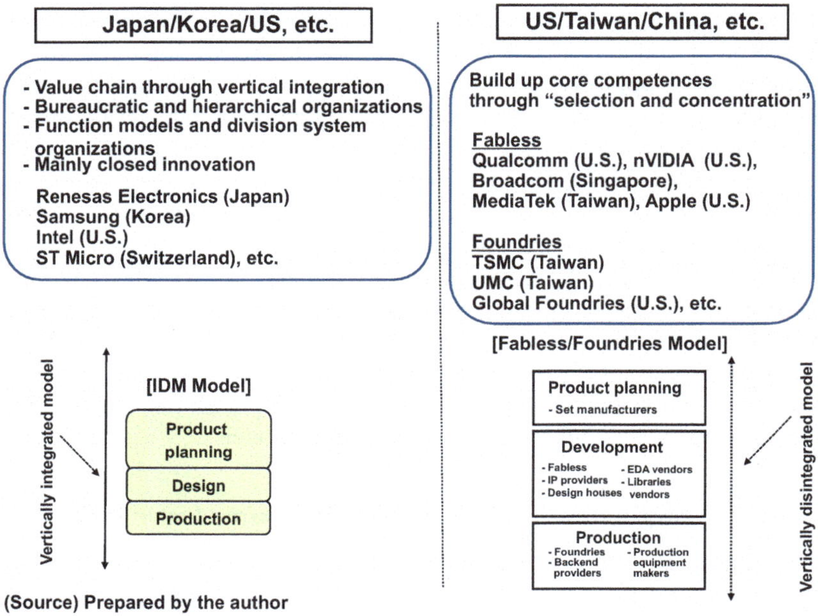

Fig. 5.5 Business models for semiconductors

production lines, and design houses specializing in development and design. Moreover, there are development vendors known as "IP providers," which focus on the intellectual property business of developing and selling semiconductor Intellectual Property (IP) such as CPU cores and function blocks (electronic circuits), instead of selling LSIs as products. Furthermore, specialized semiconductor vendors (foundries) that undertake LSI manufacturing tasks have emerged, especially in Taiwan. Representative companies of foundries include TSMC and UMC in Taiwan (refer to the Fabless/Foundries Model in Fig. 5.5).

In the 1990s, the demand for ASICs, dedicated LSIs for specific customers outside the PC market, increased. Meeting the needs of system manufacturer customers became a significant challenge for semiconductor manufacturers. To accurately and promptly develop and manufacture semiconductors as per customer requirements, semiconductor manufacturers provided toolkits for design methods at low costs to customers and made necessary design data readily available to them. This "sign-off" concept clearly delineated the responsibilities of customers and semiconductor manufacturers, establishing procedures to avoid design rework. This led to a new business model for efficiently designing and manufacturing dedicated LSIs.

During this period, semiconductor manufacturing also began to become independent. This refers to the separation of design and manufacturing in the semiconductor business. The technical background for the separation included, first, the modularization of design and manufacturing processes based on LSI design rules, and second, the existence of CAD, a design support tool. At that time, IDMs were developing their own CAD tool programs, but now, there are numerous companies specializing in design tool development (EDA vendors) in the United States. Additionally, "fabless manufacturers," mainly around Silicon Valley, emerged (companies that do not have production lines and outsource the production of circuit-designed products to foundries or IDMs, and sell completed products under their own brand, such as Qualcomm, Xilinx, and NVIDIA in the United States, and MegaChips in Japan). Furthermore, "design houses" specializing in circuit design contracting also emerged.

During this period, new players known as "IP providers" also appeared. IP providers license core technologies for large-scale circuit blocks, including microprocessors (MPUs), and specific design techniques. For example, ARM in the United Kingdom, which provides MPU cores used in many smartphone SoCs (System on Chip), and Rambus, which significantly influences PC architectures, are notable IP providers. The reuse of verified IP blocks is becoming increasingly important for quickly completing the design of complex and highly integrated SoCs.

IP providers have a distinct business model from design houses and fabless manufacturers, with customers ranging from IDMs, fabless companies, design houses, to foundries. This business model, like fabless and design houses, can be started with relatively small capital and carries low business risks but currently holds significant influence in the semiconductor industry.

In consumer electronics products, the importance of SoCs is increasing not only in smartphones but also in digital consumer electronics like digital TVs, network appliances, connected cars, IoT devices, and AI-based devices. Especially in products with short life cycles like home appliances, it is necessary to quickly develop and produce LSIs in large quantities. SoCs are widely adopted in consumer products like smartphones, and as the spread of consumer products with SoCs accelerates, the demands on SoC products are becoming more sophisticated, and the cycles are speeding up.

In designing these new SoC products, set manufacturers and fabless companies actively introduce IP provided by IP providers to avoid falling behind in time by designing everything in-house. With the increasing introduction of IP, the problem for SoC designers is having to start from scratch when a product that uses a specific IP adopts a different architecture in the next generation.

Therefore, TSMC's IP strategy promotes the reuse and distribution of IP in design by standardizing the design and manufacturing process through Open Innovation Platform (OIP), which will be described later, and providing IP that follows common design rules and electrical characteristics. Considering this background, for consumer electronics manufacturers, using foundries with high technology and large production capacity rather than producing semiconductors in-house enhances their competitiveness in both speed and cost, leading to increased production outsourcing to TSMC, resulting in positive feedback from network externalities (e.g., Katz & Shapiro, 1992; Kodama, 2009).

5.4.2 Qualcomm's New Business Model

Qualcomm Inc., an American semiconductor manufacturer, engages in R&D and licensing of wireless-related technologies. The company holds a substantial and significant intellectual property portfolio, particularly concerning core technologies for mobile phone systems. Most manufacturers of smartphones and tablets pay some fees (such as licensing fees or royalties) to Qualcomm. In January 2017, the Federal Trade Commission

(FTC) filed a lawsuit against Qualcomm, accusing it of engaging in anti-competitive practices by leveraging its dominant position in the sale and licensing of its baseband processors, potentially violating antitrust laws.

Qualcomm's main businesses include the R&D of wireless communication technologies such as Code Division Multiple Access (CDMA), development and sale of semiconductors and software, and licensing. The company does not provide final products like mobile phone terminals but instead focuses on being an R&D-oriented company, offering the results of its technological development, such as semiconductors, licenses, services, and applications (specifically, semiconductors for mobile devices utilizing the latest technology, system software, development tools, and network development products) to the wireless industry. Notably, Qualcomm holds a near-monopoly market share as a fabless company for mobile phone semiconductors.

Qualcomm was founded in July 1985 in San Diego, California, by seven communication engineers led by Irwin Jacobs. The company started by conducting contract research and development in the wireless communication field. The Federal Communications Commission (FCC) announced a concept for a mobile phone system using satellites, and the Hughes Group commissioned Qualcomm to develop the technology proposed to the FCC. Qualcomm proposed the CDMA system, which had the potential to significantly increase system capacity, and Hughes decided to accept this proposal. Originally, CDMA was used as military technology in the 1960s. However, the satellite-based wireless communication concept ultimately failed, and Hughes terminated the contract with Qualcomm. At this point, Qualcomm decided to abandon satellite system development and instead focus on developing CDMA for ground-based mobile phone systems.

The reasons for the company's strategic shift from the satellite communications business to the mobile phone business were mainly due to market demand and technological advancements, as outlined below.

(1) Market Demand: The mobile phone market was rapidly growing. By focusing on chipsets and technologies for mobile phones, Qualcomm could capture a larger market.

(2) Technological Evolution: Mobile phone technology was rapidly advancing, requiring high-performance processors and communication chipsets. Qualcomm chose to focus on the mobile phone business to meet these technological advancements.
(3) Maintaining Competitiveness: The mobile phone market was highly competitive, necessitating the rapid introduction of new technologies and products. By specializing in the mobile phone business, Qualcomm maintained its competitiveness.
(4) Profitability: The mobile phone business was highly profitable, leading Qualcomm to shift its strategy to maximize profits in this field.

In the early 1980s, the United States saw a rapid increase in subscribers to car phone services, prompting a shift from analog to digital. However, the standard digital technology at that time was Time Division Multiple Access (TDMA), and CDMA was not considered a candidate for standardization. In 1988, the Telecommunications Industry Association (TIA), the standardization body in the United States, adopted TDMA as the TIA standard. In Europe, GSM was standardized at the national and regional levels, with significant contributions from Ericsson and Nokia. Japan adopted the PDC system based on TDMA, later criticized as a Galapagos approach.

Despite the adoption of the TDMA standard, Qualcomm persistently advocated for CDMA's advantages. In 1988, they succeeded in a practical trial in San Diego and subsequently patented essential technologies for the 3G system, such as power control in 1991 and soft handoff in 1992. During this period, Qualcomm promoted external strategic alliances and experimental services driven by R&D as a venture company.

However, despite these new technologies, global mobile phone manufacturers remained cautious about standardizing CDMA. Consequently, in 1994, Qualcomm decided to enter the terminal manufacturing market by establishing a joint venture with Sony in Japan to create a new market for CDMA. This terminal manufacturing business continued until it was sold to Kyocera in 2000.

The mobile communication business comprises base stations, infrastructure equipment, and mobile phone terminals. To maintain influence in the communication infrastructure market, Qualcomm partnered with existing manufacturers. For example, after partnerships with Northern Telecom, Qualcomm sold its infrastructure manufacturing and sales business to Ericsson in 1999.

A significant turning point for Qualcomm's business expansion was the global launch of third-generation (3G) mobile phone services. NTT DoCoMo in Japan aimed to commercialize the world's first 3G mobile phone service and sought to standardize CDMA through W-CDMA in collaboration with the GSM camp led by Ericsson and Nokia. Qualcomm's CDMA2000, which evolved from cdmaOne (a 2G system led by Qualcomm), maintained compatibility with cdmaOne while developing. For Qualcomm, unifying the standards to W-CDMA would mean losing compatibility between the new 3G system and the existing 2G system (cdmaOne). Leveraging significant patents related to W-CDMA that it had accumulated and owned, Qualcomm resolved various complex stakeholder interests, ultimately selling its CDMA infrastructure business to Ericsson in 1999 and establishing a partnership with Ericsson, while granting non-exclusive licenses for CDMA infrastructure patents to Nokia. Although the long-standing patent disputes are not detailed here, eventually, both W-CDMA and CDMA2000 were established as global standards for 3G.

Qualcomm continued to promote R&D and commercialization of the new 3G system, CDMA2000, ensuring technical compatibility with the existing 2G infrastructure while advancing wireless network generations through cdmaOne (2G), CDMA2000 1x, CDMA1x EV-DO Rel.0, and CDMA1x EV-DO Rev. A in collaboration with global carriers. Concurrently, Qualcomm also licensed W-CDMA technology to global communications equipment manufacturers and supplied baseband chipsets, contributing to the evolution and development of the W-CDMA system in various forms.

The company shifted its strategy from a vertically integrated mobile phone business model to a horizontally specialized model focused on intellectual property and semiconductors. This shift was driven by the following four factors:

(1) Cost Reduction: In a vertically integrated model, all manufacturing processes are handled in-house, requiring significant capital investment. This increases costs and potentially reduced competitiveness.

By moving to a horizontally specialized model, the company was able to reduce capital investment and cut costs.

(2) Increased Specialization: The horizontal specialization model allows each company to focus on its area of expertise. Qualcomm specializes in managing intellectual property (patents) and semiconductor design, enhancing technical expertise by partnering with other companies for manufacturing.

(3) Adaptation to Market Changes: The semiconductor industry evolves rapidly, requiring the quick introduction of new technologies and products. The horizontal specialization model enables faster product development and market entry, which was crucial for maintaining competitiveness.

(4) Risk Diversification: In a vertically integrated model, managing all processes in-house concentrates risk. By shifting to a horizontal specialization model, Qualcomm was able to distribute risk across other companies, achieving more stable operations.

By adopting this strategy, Qualcomm aimed to establish itself as a leader in the industry, focusing on intellectual property and semiconductors.

This strategic shift led Qualcomm to provide a broad technology licensing program, as well as software and semiconductor chipsets to manufacturers (including suppliers of semiconductor chipsets, mobile terminals, infrastructure, and test equipment). Qualcomm's technology philosophy emphasizes continuous collaboration and complementary technological innovation in wireless technology, rather than competing technologies. By leading R&D and widely licensing its technological innovations, Qualcomm enables suppliers to bring infrastructure, test equipment, and mobile devices to market more quickly and at a lower cost. This business model allows manufacturers to commercialize mobile phone terminals like smartphones more quickly and at a lower cost than developing semiconductor chipsets and software solutions in-house.

For Qualcomm, revenue from technology licensing royalties accounts for about 30% of the company's total sales. The majority, about 60%, comes from semiconductor sales, including the baseband chipset series, and the remaining 10% from services. In other words, Qualcomm is a semiconductor company that also engages in technology licensing. Currently, around 180 companies worldwide have entered into licensing agreements with Qualcomm. Licensees have three options: (1) purchasing chipsets and software directly from Qualcomm, (2) purchasing chipsets from Qualcomm's licensees, or (3) designing and manufacturing chipsets in-house. Qualcomm's revenue structure consists of approximately 60% from baseband chipset sales and 30% from patent royalty revenue.

In recent years, Qualcomm's success has been fueled by strong partnerships with foundries. As fabless companies grow, so do foundries, creating win–win relationships. These relationships have evolved from the traditional horizontal specialization model to a collaboration model involving technical partnerships across all business processes, from planning and design to mass production. Qualcomm's technical strategy, known as Integrated Fabless Manufacturing (IFM) or virtual IDM (see Box 5.1), involves partnerships with major partners like foundries. The company employs the following strategies to strengthen its semiconductor business platform.

Qualcomm promotes the improvement of existing infrastructure technologies through external strategic alliances centered on existing organizations while simultaneously advancing R&D activities through external strategic alliances for new development projects aimed at realizing new systems such as 3.5G, 3.9G/4G, and 5G, 6G. The company also advances businesses to balance next-generation R&D with the improvement of existing technologies.

Qualcomm's new R&D areas focus on the semiconductor business and new business development investments in IoT, AI, and connected cars. Qualcomm's business strategy promotes growth by expanding the market through diverse applications of high-performance terminals and IoT, AI, and connected cars. Internally, the company forms a "Triad SC" consisting of "exploration SC," "exploitation SC," and "Synthesis SC," as mentioned in Chapter 2. Through strategic alliances (and sometimes acquisitions) with key stakeholders worldwide, the company achieves the coexistence of both old and new businesses. The background of business expansion through R&D success includes the existence of the "Triad SC (Knowledge Triad)" that realizes virtual IDM (IMF) shown in Box 5.1. This Triad SC (Knowledge Triad) dynamically involves intensive interaction between new and existing organizations and the SC. Such dynamic interactions contribute to the company's business ecosystem.

Additionally, Qualcomm engages in strategic alliances (forming exploration SC mentioned in Chapter 2) with external partners for advanced technologies like IoT, AI, and connected cars. The diversity of IoT spans applications from home installation equipment and security systems to traffic infrastructure control and horticulture. Devices such as speakers, glasses, watches, network cameras, signals, cars, vacuum cleaners, and soil monitors connect to the network through the internet. Mobile technology drives the evolution of IoT, integrating advancements into small devices like smartphones. Qualcomm's strategic perspective highlights the contribution of its technology to IoT evolution by implementing new technology in small devices like smartphones. An important step in the company's IoT proliferation strategy is applying 5G and 6G networks, progressing R&D through various exploration SC formations with diverse partners.

Qualcomm has a strategic cooperation relationship with South Korean IT giant NAVER in AI and IoT. Qualcomm supports NAVER and LINE's jointly developed AI solution "Clova" on its IoT platform. Meanwhile, NAVER adopts Qualcomm's SoC as the preferred system solution. The ultimate goal is for AI hardware manufacturers to use Qualcomm chips and Clova. Additionally, Qualcomm Technologies collaborates with Baidu to optimize Baidu's voice AI system "DuerOS," enhancing AI voice and smart assistant solutions for smartphones and IoT devices.

In the connected car sector, Qualcomm Technologies and Daimler announced a strategic partnership to develop advanced technologies like connected cars using 3G/4G communication technologies and wireless charging for electric vehicles. Qualcomm Technologies is also conducting joint evaluations of newly developed semiconductor products for the automotive sector. Furthermore, a strategic partnership with BlackBerry focuses on developing and producing in-car platforms for next-generation connected cars, optimizing specific hardware platforms of Qualcomm Technologies using BlackBerry's QNX software. Qualcomm aims to provide in-car platforms quickly and cost-effectively.

Qualcomm's success from a startup to a large corporation stems from early recognition of CDMA technology, persistent R&D efforts despite initial skepticism about its feasibility, and a consistent strategy to protect new technology with patents while aggressively investing in R&D for new businesses.

The Qualcomm Reference Design (QRD), a semi-finished kit combining Qualcomm's hardware and software, serves as a foundation for device manufacturers (Samsung, Huawei, Xiaomi, Lenovo, Asus, etc.)

to develop new products. This Customer as Innovator (CAI) kit reflects MediaTek's past strategy to secure semiconductor shares in China from Western manufacturers in the GSM world. QRD, particularly customized for specific applications or markets like smartphones, tablets, and wireless communication devices, allows terminal manufacturers to shorten development periods, reduce costs, and bring high-quality products to market. Specific advantages of using QRD include:

(1) Reduced Development Time: QRD's pre-tested design significantly shortens the time required for developing new products.
(2) Cost Reduction: Utilizing existing designs cuts additional costs arising from unique designs.
(3) Technical Support: Qualcomm offers technical support to manufacturers using QRD, providing problem-solving and optimization advice.
(4) Faster Market Entry: Using QRD enables quicker market entry, maintaining competitiveness.

Thus, QRD is a highly effective tool for product development, especially in emerging and rapidly growing markets. It allows mobile phone manufacturers to introduce more products to the market quickly, offering consumers diverse choices. Instead of selling chipsets individually, related components are integrated onto a printed circuit board, making it easy to produce smartphones by simply adding plastic covers.

Box 5.1. Qualcomm's "Triad SC (Triad System)" for Realizing Virtual IDM (IFM)

The Virtual IDM (IFM) combines the strengths of fabless companies and the advantages of manufacturers (IDMs). One of the features of Qualcomm's Virtual IDM strategy is the formation of SC and Networked SC as "exploitation SC" in the semiconductor development cycle of routine operations. This promotes close coordination and collaboration throughout the supply chain with fabless companies, EDA companies, IP and library companies, foundry companies, assembly (backend) companies, and test companies. This results in superior performance, efficiency, low cost, and shortened development periods for new semiconductor chipsets (refer to Fig. 5.6).

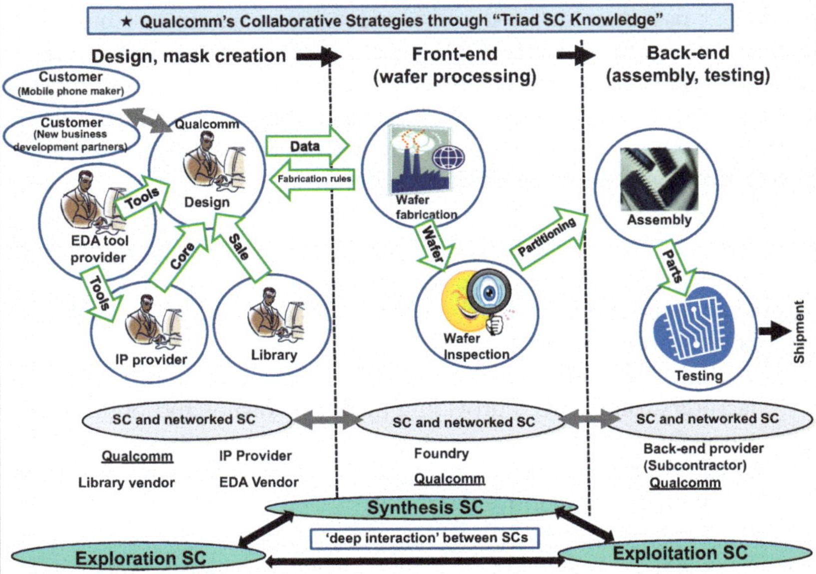

(Source) Prepared by the author

Fig. 5.6 Qualcomm's IFM (Virtual IDM) business model

The Virtual IDM shifts from the traditional turnkey method offered by foundries (where the foundry manages everything from wafer processing to packaging and Qualcomm receives only the finished product) to a method where Qualcomm intervenes and manages each major semiconductor process step. This allows for flexible manufacturing and shipping of semiconductor chipsets as finished products, adapting to actual demand and order situations. Therefore, close coordination and collaboration with partners are particularly required for Qualcomm.

The second feature of the Virtual IDM strategy is the establishment of a common platform for multiple foundry partners through process technology standardization. This increases the number of mass-production-capable foundries and suppliers (e.g., in the United States, Taiwan, South Korea, China, Singapore), ensuring stable supply and cost reduction. To promote these two features and secure medium- to long-term production line capacity, Qualcomm also cooperates with major suppliers in new process development through R&D investment. Therefore, coordination and collaboration with partners are critical factors for Qualcomm in realizing the Virtual IDM.

Moreover, forming and sustaining "strategic communities (SC)" (and networked SC) as "exploitation SC," which generates "dynamic capabilities (DC) and ordinary capabilities (OC)" (Teece, 2007, 2014) from upstream to downstream processes in the supply chain, are essential elements. This way, Qualcomm can ensure a reliable supply of semiconductor chipsets to mobile phone manufacturers and respond quickly to ever-changing customer needs. Qualcomm's Virtual IDM strategy not only coordinates the wireless semiconductor market value chain by evolving its semiconductor technology but also plays a role in coordinating the value chain of the mobile phone terminal market as finished products by having mobile phone manufacturers adopt Qualcomm's semiconductor chipsets.

The third feature of the Virtual IDM strategy is forming multilayered "exploration SC" with new business development partners (also customers) through intensive collaboration strategies in new business developments like IoT, AI, and connected cars. These new business development projects establish "exploitation SC" toward commercialization through coordination with existing organizations. The "Synthesis SC" centered on Qualcomm's leader teams (LT) is responsible for the series of resource allocation and final decision-making from R&D to business commercialization. At Qualcomm, forming a "Triad SC (Knowledge Triad)" achieves coexistence of the existing mobile communication business centered on the semiconductor business and new business developments like IoT, AI, and connected cars.

5.4.3 TSMC's New Business Model

TSMC was established in 1987 at the Hsinchu Science Park in Taiwan, aiming from the outset to be a dedicated foundry specializing in semiconductor manufacturing. The founder, Morris Chang, created a new business model in the semiconductor industry known as the "foundry." He encountered the emerging semiconductor industry and joined Texas Instruments (TI), then a venture company. TI was subcontracting the manufacturing of transistors for IBM's large computers but faced difficulties producing quality transistors. Through trial and error, Morris Chang succeeded in manufacturing high-quality transistors. During this process, he realized that mastering the subcontracting technology could allow him to stand on equal footing with major companies, which later became the foundational idea for establishing the foundry. This new realization aligns with the "sensing" element of "boundaries vision," as mentioned in Chapter 4.

A turning point for Chang came in 1985, at the age of 54, when Taiwanese authorities requested him to create a globally competitive semiconductor industry in Taiwan. He became the president of the Industrial Technology Research Institute (ITRI) in Taiwan. At that time, Japan was surpassing the United States and dominating the semiconductor industry. Taiwan only had small-town part manufacturers, and Taiwanese authorities hoped for the establishment of vertically integrated (IDM) semiconductor manufacturers like in Japan. However, lacking design technology, Chang's idea converged on a foundry dedicated solely to manufacturing.

Chang's experience at TI in the United States, where he succeeded in manufacturing transistors for IBM, influenced this decision. Despite facing opposition from Taiwanese authorities and industry stakeholders, who doubted the concept of investing heavily in semiconductor factories to manufacture semiconductors for other companies, Chang's entrepreneurial spirit drove the innovative idea of the foundry. This unusual thinking also reflects the "sensing" element of "boundaries vision."

Initially, large companies rejected Chang's investment requests for establishing the factory. Even Intel's founder, Gordon Moore, declined. Numerous proposals to major Japanese semiconductor companies (such as Toshiba, Mitsubishi, Sony, and Hitachi) were also met with disinterest. Despite these setbacks, Chang founded TSMC in 1987, with minimal sales for several years. However, in the early 1990s, Silicon Valley saw the rise of "fabless" companies specializing in semiconductor design. TSMC received many orders from Silicon Valley fabless companies (e.g., NVIDIA).

The reasons TSMC focused on contract manufacturing of semiconductors include the following:

(1) Specialization and Focus: By specializing in semiconductor manufacturing, TSMC could concentrate on optimizing production processes and technical expertise, achieving higher quality and efficiency than other companies.

(2) Risk Diversification: Semiconductor companies require significant investment to own manufacturing facilities. TSMC dispersed this risk by contracting manufacturing to other companies, effectively utilizing its own capital.
(3) Market Needs: The semiconductor industry rapidly evolves, continually demanding new technologies and products. TSMC responded swiftly to market needs by undertaking manufacturing processes, allowing other companies to focus on product development.
(4) Economies of Scale: TSMC's large-scale manufacturing capabilities enabled cost reduction and efficiency through mass production, offering economic options for other companies.

By specializing in semiconductor contract manufacturing, TSMC enhanced its competitiveness and succeeded in the industry. Since its inception, TSMC has created a business model leveraging the advantages of low cost and specialization in the foundry business. Initially lacking advanced process technology, the company faced no competition and expanded its production capacity through aggressive capital investment. This approach eventually led to the establishment of a new platform and business model.

Around the turn of the twenty-first century, while TSMC's process technology slightly lagged behind the cutting-edge technology held by other leading IDMs, the company gradually caught up through incremental innovation activities. It is no exaggeration to say that TSMC significantly transformed the semiconductor industry. Initially, TSMC only manufactured commissioned semiconductors. Gradually, it started developing cutting-edge semiconductor processes, offering IP, and providing customers with consistent design environments. As a result of its incremental innovation in manufacturing technology, TSMC's services expanded sequentially. The improvement in TSMC's manufacturing technology and design capabilities strengthened its relationship with customers and fostered collaboration.

Today, TSMC is the world's largest foundry and ranks among the top companies in the entire semiconductor industry, including IDMs. TSMC's platform solutions enable the manufacturing of semiconductor products tailored to various customers (fabless companies, design houses, IDM, etc.) through customization services and enhancement of special application specifications. This platform solution facilitates an easy-to-use environment for customers utilizing the foundry, offering the following three functions and services:

The first point is LSI design services. Specifically, through alliances with external partners (including small equity investments), TSMC provides comprehensive design services necessary for customers to design LSIs. These services include design and manufacturing information (such as circuit design libraries and verified IPs), as well as EDA services and LSI design contracting. For this reason, TSMC has established "Design Center Alliances (DCA)" with design houses and EDA vendors worldwide, offering superior design services to customers through close collaboration.

For example, using TSMC's process technology, library vendors can develop their own libraries and provide them to customers. IP vendors can use these libraries to develop their own IPs and offer them as a business to customers. Similarly, fabless companies and design houses can utilize these IPs and libraries to provide unique LSI design services. Additionally, TSMC validates its process technology using design tools and IP from EDA vendors, and conversely, EDA vendors can validate their design tools and IP using TSMC's process technology. The technologies of foundries, libraries, IPs, and EDA are complementary to each other. Each partner adds value to their technology and services through mutual collaboration.

The second point is LSI manufacturing and turnkey services. This includes prototype manufacturing services, quality assurance services, and semiconductor mask manufacturing services, referred to as the Cyber-Shuttle services by TSMC, offered to numerous customer companies and engineering universities. This business model significantly improves manufacturing yield and is much cheaper and more competitive than the manufacturing costs of major semiconductor manufacturers.

The third point is enhancing customer service. Through the internet, customers can always track the current stage of their ordered products, and TSMC currently has over 500 customers worldwide. To allow customers to use TSMC as if it were their own factory, TSMC not only provides face-to-face customer service but also maximizes the use of ICT to build a user-friendly virtual service. Customers can access the necessary information from anywhere in the world when needed. The ICT-integrated supply chain of TSMC, with excellent confidentiality, provides timely updates on fab yield management and progress to customers. This strong bond with customers forms "Strategic Communities (SCs)" (and networked SCs) that generate dynamic capabilities (DC) between TSMC and its customers, enabling the building of trust.

As such, the company has been consistently engaged in the foundry business since its establishment. The success of this business model led to the emergence of numerous fabless semiconductor companies, giving birth to the fabless industry. It is no exaggeration to say that TSMC has significantly transformed the semiconductor industry. Initially, TSMC focused solely on manufacturing commissioned semiconductors. Gradually, the company began developing cutting-edge semiconductor processes, providing IP, and offering a consistent design environment to customers. As a result of its incremental innovation, TSMC expanded its services sequentially. As TSMC's manufacturing technology and design capabilities improved, the company built closer relationships with its customers, fostering collaborative elements.

Entering the twenty-first century, Moore's Law indicated that further process miniaturization would make it increasingly difficult to clearly define design rules, as pointed out by semiconductor-related academic conferences and the industry. The industry transitioned from the "mass production era" of standard general-purpose semiconductor components like MPUs and DRAMs to the "small-lot production era" of SoCs (System on Chip, also known as system LSIs). As broadband and mobile phone services advanced, the fusion of communication and broadcasting and markets for automotive LSIs began to rise rapidly.

With this transition, the integration and microfabrication technology of LSIs developed rapidly, requiring stronger linkage between semiconductor design and manufacturing processes, which were separated in the 1990s. Not only did semiconductor logical design need to consider placement, routing, and manufacturing processes, but higher-level system design processes also had to account for logical design, placement, routing, and manufacturing processes. While TSMC established a business model of "design and manufacturing separation," the twenty-first-century SoC development required a shift to a business model emphasizing interdependency rather than simple interface separation.

Accompanying the miniaturization of SoCs, various technical issues emerged. First, as larger integrated LSIs were introduced to the market at low costs within short periods, design engineers faced a limit on the number of transistors they could design per man-month. Bridging the gap between Moore's Law (where the number of transistors in an LSI increases by 58% annually) and design productivity became a significant hurdle. To address this, the following were necessary:

(1) Improving productivity through the reuse of design assets like IP.
(2) Accelerating functional verification through emulation.
(3) Establishing new design flows with advanced EDA tools.

In the twenty-first century, the IP reuse rate needs to be increased to over 80%. While IP reuse is relatively easy for RISC processors, DSPs, and memory modules, the challenge lies in dedicated function circuits. Semiconductor design vendors must develop roadmaps and build platform architectures based on purpose-oriented IP design. Establishing LSI development roadmaps and platform architectures is necessary to promote purpose-oriented design organizationally, and requires a mindset shift among upstream system designers.

Secondly, with IP reuse allowing the construction of large design data in relatively short periods, the challenge becomes addressing the exponential increase in functional verification time. This solution involves using hundreds of FPGAs to perform real-time simulations of highly integrated LSIs, enhancing LSI completeness and enabling higher-quality design in shorter times using hardware emulators. Recently, emulators have enabled the reliable operation of large-scale LSIs.

Thirdly, after addressing logical layer issues through IP reuse and emulation acceleration, the next challenge is to address the increasingly severe physical layer issues. The primary problem is that wiring delays become more significant than transistor delays with higher integration. The wiring delay problem surfaces with miniaturization and scaling, causing timing errors after wiring that cannot be resolved, leading to deteriorated LSI performance. To address this, advanced EDA tools must be utilized, optimizing design iterations through concurrent interactive design flows involving simultaneous logic synthesis, placement, and routing.

On the other hand, with the miniaturization of LSIs to nano-size designs, it has become evident that merely feeding back and optimizing data between adjacent steps in the traditional semiconductor design and manufacturing process is insufficient. This is due to significant changes in the design and manufacturing rules of LSIs. Recently, issues have become more prominent, such as LSIs not functioning or having high failure rates in the market. For example, there have been cases where the cause of HDD (hard disk drive) malfunctions was traced back through the manufacturer to the LSI manufacturer, the assembly manufacturer, and the materials manufacturer. Excessive miniaturization is increasing the incidence of non-functional LSIs. The LSI process involves design upstream of the mask (a photomask with the semiconductor wiring pattern) creation step and manufacturing downstream, making it difficult to isolate problems in these processes. The concern is that extensive horizontal specialization in the semiconductor industry has made it unclear who is responsible when issues arise.

However, IDMs with competitive advantages in LSI inspection, analysis, and evaluation may find a vertically integrated business model advantageous for addressing the challenges of miniaturization. IDMs can enhance services like failure analysis and defect inspection, enabling a business model that integrates technology and brand.

Meanwhile, TSMC adopts a design method that feeds back and modifies manufacturing information at the design stage to improve manufacturing yield. This approach, known as Design for Manufacturing (DFM), involves optimizing design data from the start to facilitate manufacturing and testing. DFM means "design for manufacturability," where the manufacturing side creates "manufacturable processes" or modifies design data to be more manufacturable.

Specifically, with the miniaturization of semiconductor manufacturing technology, merely correcting for proximity effects in lithography on the mask is no longer sufficient in advanced semiconductor manufacturing. Identifying the causes of reduced manufacturing yields and feeding this information back into the design process is crucial. Additionally, optimizing design data from the design stage to facilitate manufacturing and testing is essential. This represents a tight virtual integration between semiconductor design and manufacturing processes, making the previously mentioned business model of simple "design and manufacturing separation" obsolete.

As Moore's Law continues to be pursued, addressing the various challenges arising in design and manufacturing due to the miniaturization of semiconductor processes becomes increasingly difficult. TSMC has strengthened its collaboration with customer and partner companies from design to manufacturing more than ever before, offering a service business aimed at shortening design cycles and providing a cost-efficient design environment. Consequently, TSMC has enhanced services in both the manufacturing sector, which is its strength, as well as in design and backend areas, effectively executing a virtual vertically integrated semiconductor business (solutions from design to manufacturing) similar to IDM.

TSMC, through its new coordination and collaboration business style with partner companies, can offer new products and services to customers such as fabless companies, design houses, IDMs, and set manufacturers. For example, development partners of IP cores and libraries become customers of TSMC's cutting-edge technology. They can validate their libraries and IP on the first semiconductor wafers developed for each new semiconductor manufacturing process. EDA vendors can support fabless companies and design houses in overcoming design issues and challenges using TSMC's technology. In return, EDA vendors can incorporate scripts and design guidelines into their EDA toolsets, improving yield in advanced semiconductor design. As a result, customers who adopt TSMC's advanced technology early can gain significant value and benefits from services provided by TSMC's third-party alliance members (TSM partners).

To enhance partnerships with customers, TSMC recognizes that advanced technology and production capacity alone are insufficient. The company integrates operations from semiconductor design services to backend services, providing customers with comprehensive solutions. This integration enables rapid product deployment, creating win–win relationships. TSMC extends its services in both forward (design) and backward (assembly and testing) directions, centering on contract manufacturing. This allows fabless semiconductor vendors to virtually acquire functions equivalent to vertically integrated semiconductor vendors (from design to manufacturing, assembly, and final testing, essentially an IDM) (see Fig. 5.7).

TSMC's overwhelming share in semiconductor manufacturing attracts companies possessing essential technologies for the realization of advanced logic LSIs, such as fabless companies, design houses, IP vendors, and manufacturing equipment manufacturers. These high-tech companies provide core technologies through their partnerships with TSMC, further enhancing TSMC's competitiveness. The key competitive advantage of TSMC lies in its focus on design support and semiconductor manufacturing, including web services, through virtual integration alliances with both TSMC group companies and external partners. This approach enables the execution of mask manufacturing, testing, packaging, and

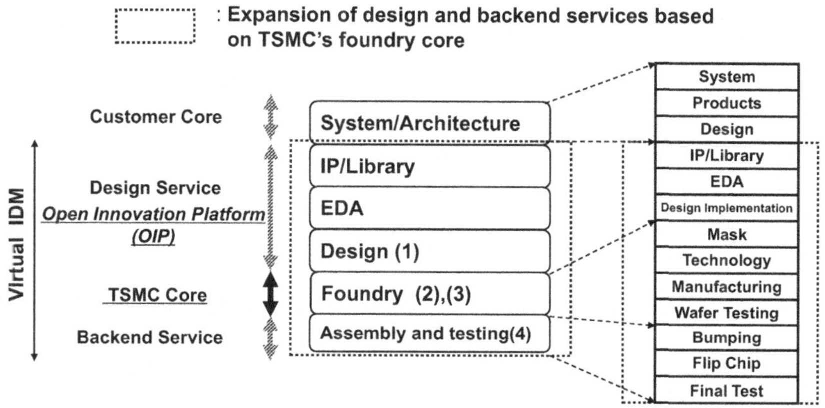

(Source) Prepared by the author

Fig. 5.7 TSMC's virtual IDM

inspection. TSMC coordinates these processes with the involved companies, while the actual execution of each step is carried out by TSMC's group companies or partner firms.

Additionally, TSMC has established a flat and flexible organizational structure, forming "strategic communities (SCs)" and networked SCs within and across management levels in the business strategy, R&D, manufacturing, and sales and marketing departments. These structures generate dynamic capabilities (DC) (Teece, 2007, 2014). As previously mentioned, TSMC creates high-quality SCs and Networked SCs with numerous partner companies, building a value chain that includes design support, prototyping services, mask manufacturing, wafer manufacturing, assembly, and final inspection.

For R&D projects related to next-generation semiconductor development, new R&D project organizations take the lead, promoting new knowledge creation activities through SCs and Networked SCs with external partners, including customers (e.g., Qualcomm, NVIDIA, Apple, fabless companies, and manufacturing equipment manufacturers). Additionally, the "Synthesis SC," centered around the company's leader teams (LT), is responsible for the entire resource allocation and final decision-making process from R&D to commercialization. At TSMC, the organizational form that achieves a balance and virtual vertical integration of "exploitation activities" related to existing businesses (primarily routine semiconductor manufacturing) and "exploration activities" related to new semiconductor R&D is known as the "Triad SC (Knowledge Triad)."

At the same time, the Triad SC (Knowledge Triad) for balancing R&D in next-generation semiconductor manufacturing technology and the improvement of existing technologies involves intensive interaction between new projects, existing organizations, and SC. This Triad SC (Knowledge Triad) generates "dynamic capabilities (DC)" and "ordinary capabilities (OC)" for TSMC's sustainable competitiveness through "knowledge convergence (or knowledge creation, knowledge integration, or asset orchestration)" (Kodama, 2005, 2009; Nonaka & Takeuchi, 1995; Teece, 2007) (see Fig. 5.8). Like Qualcomm, this Triad SC (Knowledge Triad) facilitates dynamic interactions between new and existing organizations and SC, creating a business ecosystem centered on the company.

TSMC attracts many fabless companies, design houses, IP vendors, library vendors, and EDA vendors, forming SC and Networked SC with

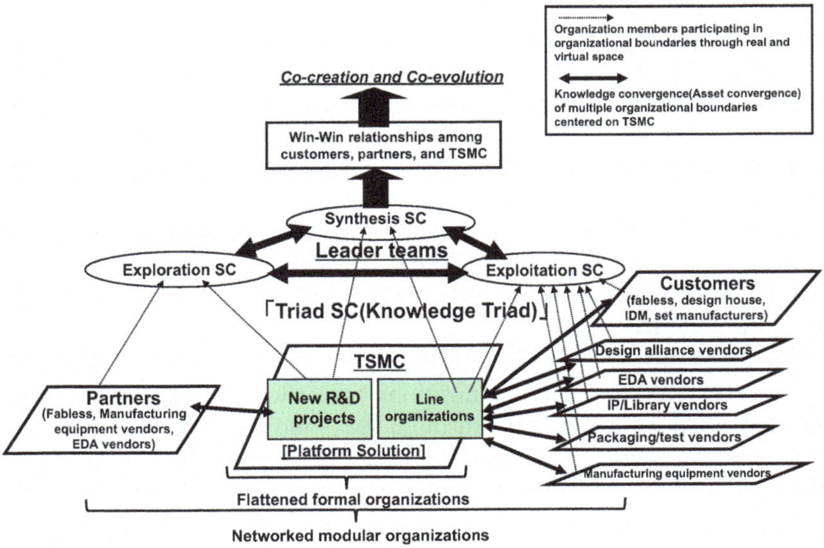

(Source) Prepared by the author

Fig. 5.8 Co-creation and co-evolution through TSMC's virtual IDM

these partner companies. This collaboration builds a high-value-added virtual factory value chain. Such win–win relationships allow TSMC to provide customers with fully customized diverse LSIs through coordination and collaboration with partners in various specialized fields.

The background behind foundries like TSMC advancing in manufacturing technology includes the strengthened collaboration between semiconductor manufacturing equipment manufacturers and foundries. By taking on manufacturing for numerous fabless companies, foundries increased the utilization rate of manufacturing equipment, reducing depreciation and generating profits. The rapid depreciation and profit generation allowed TSMC to acquire new manufacturing equipment, gradually gaining an advantage in manufacturing technology over other IDM companies. This phenomenon not only strengthened TSMC's collaboration with manufacturing equipment manufacturers but also fostered collaboration for developing new manufacturing equipment between TSMC and equipment manufacturers. Multiple manufacturing equipment manufacturers used TSMC's semiconductor production lines for prototype testing, validating new manufacturing equipment, and addressing technical issues such as connectivity with existing manufacturing equipment. For manufacturing equipment manufacturers, enhancing collaboration with TSMC, which has large-scale production lines, brought significant benefits, leading to long-term deep collaboration.

On the other hand, IDMs primarily focused on in-house development of manufacturing equipment, restricting the flow of information obtained from collaborative development of new equipment on their production lines to other IDMs or foundries. As a result, in the process of developing new manufacturing equipment, the production lines of foundries like TSMC were used more frequently than those of IDMs. Consequently, foundries like TSMC surpassed IDMs in manufacturing technology.

As a result, major foundries like TSMC have been able to develop new business ventures such as backend services and the "Open Innovation Platform (OIP) (see Box 5.2)" based on their core manufacturing technology. The OIP allows for the provision of technological innovations based on TSMC's manufacturing technology portfolio to many semiconductor design communities and ecosystem partners, including fabless companies and IDMs.

The OIP is a comprehensive design technology infrastructure aimed at streamlining the semiconductor design process and reducing design obstacles. It enables semiconductor design communities and their ecosystem partners to leverage TSMC's IP, design implementation, DFM capabilities, process technology, and backend services to implement innovations rapidly. Through various alliance programs, including Design Center Alliance, EDA Alliance, Cloud Alliance, and Value Chain Alliance, the OIP collaborates with market-leading EDA tools, libraries, IP, cloud, and design service partners. In this way, the OIP serves as a powerful platform to streamline the semiconductor design process and promote innovation.

For TSMC, technology alliances are the source of differentiation from other companies. In providing integrated solutions to customers from design to manufacturing, TSMC has moved away from past business models and executed a strategy transformation toward a new business model of a virtual IDM through the promotion of a "collaboration strategy."

In TSMC's definition, collaboration means moving from a traditional segregated model to an integrated model. In a traditional model (i.e., prior to 90 nm), very definitive roles and responsibilities were drawn between foundries and their customers. Foundries were 100% responsible for process technology and its definition, while customers were responsible for the design, including IP and Library selection.

However, in the new nanometer age, the responsibilities for integrated design for manufacturing, concurrent SPICE model development, advanced design flows, library, and IP optimization and production are shared, to varying extents, across relationships. Ultimately, this new definition of collaboration according to TSMC leads to shorter time-to-market, greater customer product differentiation, accelerated defect reduction, and faster yield ramp (see Fig. 5.9).

In the past, TSMC's strategy involved adopting technologically mature semiconductor process technologies from leading semiconductor manufacturers (IDMs) to manufacture semiconductor devices designed by its customers. However, TSMC now applies the "New Integrated Model" as a virtual IDM, closely collaborating with customers in process development, circuit design, and manufacturing (see Fig. 5.9).

The long-term "collaboration strategy" with Altera under this "New Integrated Model" is a success story for TSMC. Altera and TSMC have worked together in FPGA technology since 1993. From design through tape-out, they continuously refine the manufacturing process,

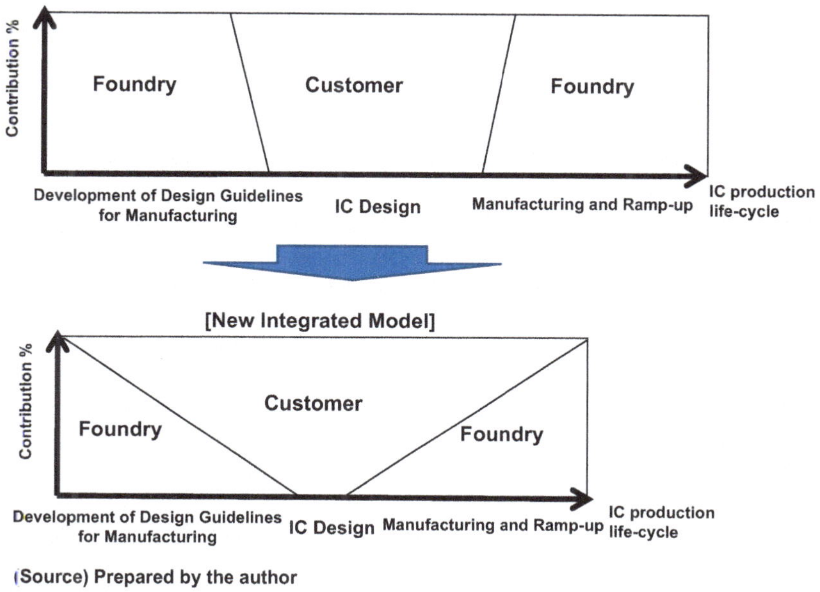

Fig. 5.9 New integrated model in TSMC

resulting in successfully produced chips from node to node. Traditionally, foundries and their IC customers operated somewhat autonomously in their respective areas—manufacturing process development and IC design—leading to longer times to market and higher costs. Through the new integrated foundry model shown in Fig. 5.9, Altera and TSMC engineers collaborate on both manufacturing process development and IC design, achieving better and faster results that are passed on to customers. TSMC often qualifies its manufacturing process with Altera test chips, addressing design issues upfront while validating circuit design and process characteristics. For Altera, a faster manufacturing ramp means a faster production cycle for the devices. TSMC's deep, broad collaboration with Altera ensures customer success from start to finish. This "collaboration strategy" quickly resolves design issues and challenges, enabling predictable product supply.

In a broader sense, the "New Integrated Model" business model through the "collaboration strategy" with such partners enables the provision of turnkey services, offering total solutions from design to manufacturing to customers. "Turnkey services" provide the advantage for end-users to deal with a single contractor for all orders, offering the entire process from LSI design to manufacturing (from (1) to (4) in Fig. 5.7). The rapid technological changes leading to the integration of design and manufacturing, coupled with strategies to enclose various customers and external partners, promote TSMC's evolution from a horizontal division of labor business model to a vertical direction.

To meet the demands for diverse SoC applications arising from rapid technological changes such as miniaturization and future broadband and ubiquitous (IoT: Internet of Things) as well as wireless communications, TSMC needs to shift from a business model specialized in certain functions of horizontal division of labor. This business model shift to the "New Integrated Model" for TSMC has a similar meaning to the previously mentioned Qualcomm's transition to a "virtual IDM" business model.

Thus, TSMC has examined both the vertically integrated model (IDM) and the horizontally specialized model focused on semiconductor manufacturing (foundry). From the knowledge differences between the new business model of building an ecosystem centered on their target foundry and the various challenges, TSMC identified the necessity of integrating the best of both IDM (existing knowledge) and foundry (different kind of knowledge) through interactive synthesis via abduction. As will be discussed later, this "boundary knowledge" for constructing such an ecosystem newly gave rise to the Virtual IDM and open innovation platform (see Table 5.2).

Box 5.2. TSMC's Open Innovation Platform (OIP)

As shown in Fig. 5.7, TSMC has expanded its core foundry capabilities into specialized fields such as design services and backend services. It promotes the utilization of its manufacturing platform by making its manufacturing information (such as IP) available to fabless companies worldwide. However, TSMC does not execute all design and backend services internally but maintains relationships with existing "modular organizations" like Design Center Alliances (DCA) and partners for backend services, adopting the "virtual IDM" model to change vertical boundaries intentionally based on factors like customer scale, technology, price, and delivery time.

Fabless companies like Qualcomm also adopt the "virtual IDM" business model through "networked modular organizations" (Kodama, 2009) for similar reasons. Fabless and foundries scan the surrounding areas of their business domains and enhance their peripheral vision (Day & Schoemaker, 2005) and boundaries vision (Kodama, 2018), flexibly adapting their value chains.

In 2008, TSMC announced the "Open Innovation Platform (OIP)" as an industry-wide initiative to enable design. The OIP includes interoperable ecosystem interfaces, co-developed components, and design flows across the supply chain, allowing for more efficient technological innovation and the sharing of newly created revenue and profits. The OIP provides technological innovations based on TSMC's technology portfolio to semiconductor design communities and ecosystem partners.

Foundries like TSMC open their platforms to semiconductor design communities and ecosystem partners. An attractive platform draws many fabless companies to TSMC. As more fabless companies (including IDMs) design according to TSMC's platform, it has become the de facto standard. A foundry with a proposed platform that becomes the de facto standard attracts customers, increasing equipment utilization, and enabling rapid depreciation. Consequently, TSMC can purchase new manufacturing equipment co-developed with equipment manufacturers using the profits generated. Over the years, this process advances TSMC's manufacturing technology ahead of others. This concentration of customers on TSMC's platform, facilitated by network externalities and a win–win structure, builds a business ecosystem through co-creation and co-evolution (see Fig. 5.8).

The OIP includes a suite of ecosystem interfaces and collaborative tools developed and supported by TSMC, promoting innovation effectively across the supply chain and sharing newly created revenue and profitability. The OIP strategy intensifies coordination and collaboration with external partners, fostering information sharing and co-development to deepen knowledge sharing. Simultaneously, it enhances internal design and backend capabilities, promoting knowledge integration (also asset orchestration) within its internal network. This approach shifts from combining capabilities of specialized "modular organizations" (open innovation) to incorporating highly interdependent elements (closed innovation) within the company, meaning a shift from "modular organizations" to more strongly integrated "networked modular organizations," or a "virtual IDM." This trend indicates a gradual shift from a horizontal division of labor business model to a vertical one.

Through open innovation strategies like the OIP, TSMC creates "dynamic capabilities (DC)" by integrating "cospecialized assets" for sustainable competitiveness. The company builds a vertically integrated value chain through the orchestration of cospecialized assets among customers (fabless, design houses, IDMs, set manufacturers), TSMC, and partners (design houses, EDA vendors, IP/library vendors, backend vendors), dynamically achieving congruence with the changing environment (Kodama, 2018). As a result, TSMC constructs a virtual vertically integrated value chain through a standardized production technology platform, simultaneously fostering win–win relationships among stakeholders, including customers, through value sharing and trust building with partners.

5.4.4 *NVIDIA's New Business Model*

NVIDIA was founded in 1993 by Jensen Huang, Chris Malachowsky, and Curtis Priem in Santa Clara, California. From its inception, the company focused on developing high-performance graphics processing units (GPUs). In 1995, NVIDIA introduced its first product, the NV1, which was featured in Sega's game console "Sega Saturn," but it did not achieve market success. However, the company continued to develop GPU technology and reached a significant turning point with the release of the GeForce 256 in 1999. The GeForce 256 was recognized as the "world's first GPU" and received high acclaim in the gaming market. NVIDIA continued to develop the GeForce series, expanding its market share not only in gaming but also in the professional graphics market. In the 2000s, the company's GPU technology was utilized in various fields, including film production and scientific research. Notably, NVIDIA's GPUs became indispensable tools in Hollywood special effects and animation production.

Entering the 2010s, NVIDIA further expanded the applications of its GPUs. The company began to play an important role in the fields of deep learning and artificial intelligence (AI). In 2012, NVIDIA released CUDA (Compute Unified Device Architecture), a deep learning framework that made it easier for researchers and developers to build AI models using GPUs. This marked the rapid proliferation of NVIDIA's GPUs in AI research.

In the field of autonomous driving technology, NVIDIA has also become a key player. The Drive PX platform, announced in 2015, garnered attention as an AI computing platform for autonomous vehicles. Many automakers adopted this technology, accelerating the development of autonomous vehicles. Furthermore, NVIDIA has focused on solutions for data centers. In 2016, the company introduced the Pascal architecture for data centers, gaining a significant share in the high-performance computing (HPC) and cloud computing fields. This led to a substantial increase in NVIDIA's revenue, solidifying its position as a leader in the GPU market.

NVIDIA's history is characterized by its ability to quickly respond to technological innovations and market needs. Since its founding, the company has continually worked on developing new technologies and applying them in various fields, leading to sustained growth. The realization that NVIDIA's GPUs were well-suited for AI development was driven by several key events related to the development and application of GPUs.

NVIDIA realized that GPUs were suited for AI development in 2006 when Professor Geoffrey Hinton, known as the father of deep learning, at the University of Toronto in Canada, used GPUs to run neural networks at high speed. He discovered that training neural networks could be done hundreds of times faster using GPUs. To elaborate, Alex Krizhevsky, who was in Professor Geoffrey Hinton's lab and later became a Nobel laureate, found that the numerous small arithmetic units integrated into GPUs were actually effective for AI. At that time, the term "AI" was not used. By participating in the world image recognition contest "ImageNet" held in September 2012 using a neural network model, they demonstrated that their image recognition error rate was significantly lower than that of other researchers. While other researchers had an error rate of about 25–30%, Alex Krizhevsky's recognition rate was only 16%. Subsequent tests conducted by companies like Baidu, Google, and Microsoft achieved even lower single-digit error rates.

This discovery led NVIDIA to focus on developing GPUs specialized for AI development. During this period, NVIDIA developed a programming model called Compute Unified Device Architecture (CUDA). CUDA is a software framework for using GPUs for general computing tasks, significantly improving performance in scientific computing and data processing. CUDA is designed to enable developers to fully leverage the computational power of GPUs, and the formation of this ecosystem is a key element in NVIDIA's strategy. The CUDA software development environment, which maximizes the computation speed of GPUs, saw widespread adoption by developers and researchers to accelerate their GPU usage. NVIDIA's strategy extended beyond semiconductor hardware to dominate in software as well (see Fig. 5.10). The following details how CUDA forms its ecosystem.

(1) Provision of Development Tools and Libraries: NVIDIA offers a wealth of development tools and libraries that support CUDA. This allows developers to efficiently create high-performance applications. Specifically, the CUDA Toolkit includes CUDA runtime libraries, compilers, debuggers, profilers, and other tools that support parallel computing on GPUs. Additionally, libraries such as CUDA Deep Neural Network Library (cuDNN) and TensorRT assist in optimizing deep learning.

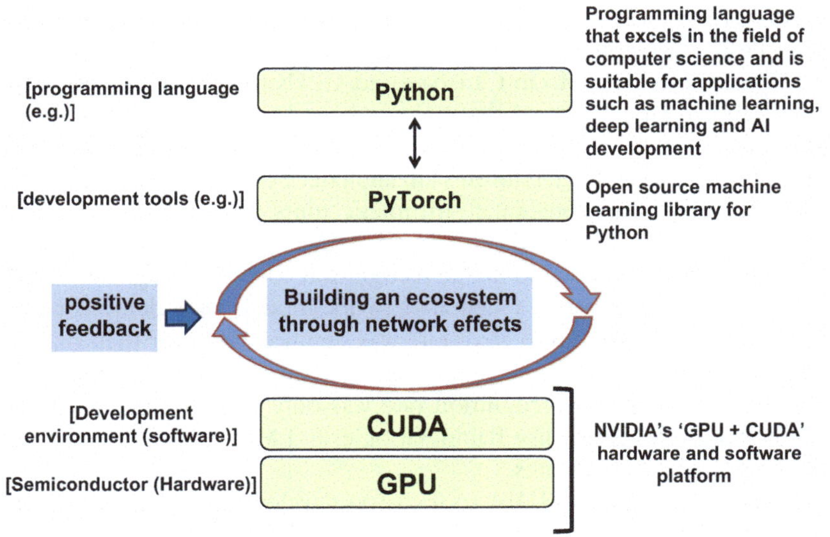

(Source) Prepared by the author

Fig. 5.10 AI developers' usage patterns on the "GPU + CUDA" platform (e.g.)

(2) Educational Programs and Community Support: To promote the adoption of CUDA, NVIDIA actively offers educational programs and community support. Collaborating with universities and research institutions, NVIDIA provides curriculums related to CUDA, as well as online courses and workshops for developers to learn the latest technologies. Furthermore, online communities like the NVIDIA Developer Zone provide environments for developers to exchange information and receive support.

For example, developers who use CUDA during their university days continue using the familiar CUDA after graduation. However, CUDA is a development environment specialized for NVIDIA GPUs and cannot operate other semiconductors. This raises the entry barrier for the GPU hardware. Even if competitors develop semiconductors with performance comparable to NVIDIA GPUs, developers might avoid them since they cannot run CUDA. By building a platform that integrates software and hardware, NVIDIA has established high entry barriers, solidifying its market evaluation in the GPU sector.

(3) Collaboration with Industries: NVIDIA promotes the use of CUDA by collaborating with various industries. For instance, solutions utilizing CUDA have been developed in diverse fields such as bioinformatics, financial engineering, oil exploration, and manufacturing. This promotes technological innovation tailored to the specific needs of each industry.

(4) Provision of Cloud Platforms: NVIDIA collaborates with major cloud service providers to offer CUDA-compatible GPU instances in the cloud. This enables companies and researchers to flexibly use high-performance computing resources. By utilizing CUDA-compatible GPUs on cloud platforms such as Google Cloud, Amazon Web Services (AWS), and Microsoft Azure, large-scale computations can be performed efficiently.

(5) Promotion of Open Standards: While CUDA is proprietary technology, NVIDIA also promotes open standards. By supporting standards compatible with other platforms, such as Open Accelerators (OpenACC) and Open Computing Language (OpenCL), NVIDIA aims to form a broader ecosystem. This provides developers with the flexibility to reuse code across multiple platforms.

(6) Research and Incubation Programs: NVIDIA supports research and incubation programs that utilize CUDA. NVIDIA Research

conducts advanced research on computing technologies and AI, with its outcomes fed back into the CUDA ecosystem. Additionally, the NVIDIA Inception program provides support to startup companies developing innovative solutions using CUDA.

Thus, the CUDA ecosystem, which is NVIDIA's hardware and software platform of "GPU + CUDA," is formed through the provision of development tools and libraries, educational programs and community support, collaboration with industries, provision of cloud platforms, promotion of open standards, and research and incubation programs. This has made CUDA a powerful platform widely used in fields such as scientific computing and AI. The introduction of this technology has led to GPUs playing a crucial role in AI and machine learning, establishing NVIDIA's position as a leader in AI development. The developments during this period have significantly influenced the advancement of current AI technology.

The expression "Destiny Meets Serendipity," mentioned by CEO Jensen Huang, is a metaphorical phrase used to explain NVIDIA's success. This expression means that success was the result of the overlap between destiny and serendipity. In other words, the processors designed by NVIDIA to achieve high throughput in data processing turned out to be extremely useful in the field of machine learning by chance. This combination led to NVIDIA's success. In this way, "Destiny Meets Serendipity" signifies how NVIDIA's technology brought about significant results in an unexpected manner.

At NVIDIA, the "Leaders Team," which has the nature of strategic communities, is composed of management layers that cross various departments, not just the top management. The organizational hierarchy is as follows: CEO: Jensen Huang, CFO: Colette Kress, and CTO: Michael Kagan, among others, form the top management. Each department, such as GPU engineering, AI development, data centers, autonomous vehicles, and research and development, has specialized heads. Jensen Huang, the CEO, has about 60 direct reports. He adopts a management style that avoids one-on-one meetings and emphasizes group meetings. Jensen Huang values sharing information with everyone and focuses on learning and growth as a team. Furthermore, there are teams temporarily organized according to specific projects or goals that have the characteristics of strategic communities. At NVIDIA, while each department is responsible for their specialized field, flexibility is maintained by organizing ad-hoc project teams for each project.

Executive leadership is exhibited at the top management level. The leader team, centered around the CEO and the executive management, demonstrates strategic direction and management. This includes the aforementioned CEO, CFO, CTO, and other executives who guide the company's overall vision and strategy. The executive management maintains channels for direct communication and collaboration with leaders of various departments, ensuring alignment with corporate goals and swift decision-making capabilities. While centralizing key functions, the company implements a framework that grants sufficient autonomy to each department for agile actions. Each leader maintains clear accountability and builds mechanisms for sharing resources and knowledge across departments, maintaining a balance between centralization and autonomy for the entire organization. As detailed in Chapter 8, the strength of NVIDIA's management lies in exhibiting "holistic leadership" that balances "centralized leadership," which maintains centralization, and "distributed leadership," which promotes autonomy.

Leaders at each management level facilitate the flow of information and knowledge across different divisional and functional organizations. Specifically, they utilize both formal and informal channels for communication and collaboration, establishing regular review processes between different organizations to ensure alignment and promote collaboration across various operations. For example, in GPU product development, strategic communities have been formed by integrating the software development and hardware development departments. Besides new product development, strategic communities are flexibly formed within NVIDIA for product upgrades and new network businesses utilizing GPUs. Within NVIDIA, diverse strategic communities are continually formed through organic collaboration between various formal organizations, adopting a type of networked organizational structure. This distinctive organizational form at NVIDIA can be referred to as a "Networked Collaborative Organization."

The fundamental structure of a networked collaborative organization lies in official organizations with a flat organizational structure and multi-layered strategic communities formed by practitioners from various official organizations (see Fig. 5.11). Each strategic community enables interactions through dialogue and practice, achieving a "balance between individual and organizational strength" and "knowledge creation from many viewpoints" via "exhaustive dialogue capability," creating a platform for new knowledge creation (Kodama, 2008, 2011, 2012).

Knowledge is deeply connected to context, including situations, scenarios, and spaces. To acquire, share, and create knowledge, practitioners must dynamically share context. Specific context cannot be shared unless practitioners participate in specific strategic communities at a certain time and space. Mediated by shared context, the SECI model's interaction becomes possible. At this time, exhaustive dialogue capability generates practitioners' "context architect capability" (Kodama, 2008, 2011, 2012), revealing hidden contexts, which are then shared among practitioners, forming new context. Such exhaustive dialogue capability induces the demonstration of boundaries vision (Kodama, 2019) in practitioners, triggering knowledge difference and boundaries knowledge.

Practitioners participate in multiple diverse strategic communities to generate higher-quality new knowledge, facilitating the flow of context

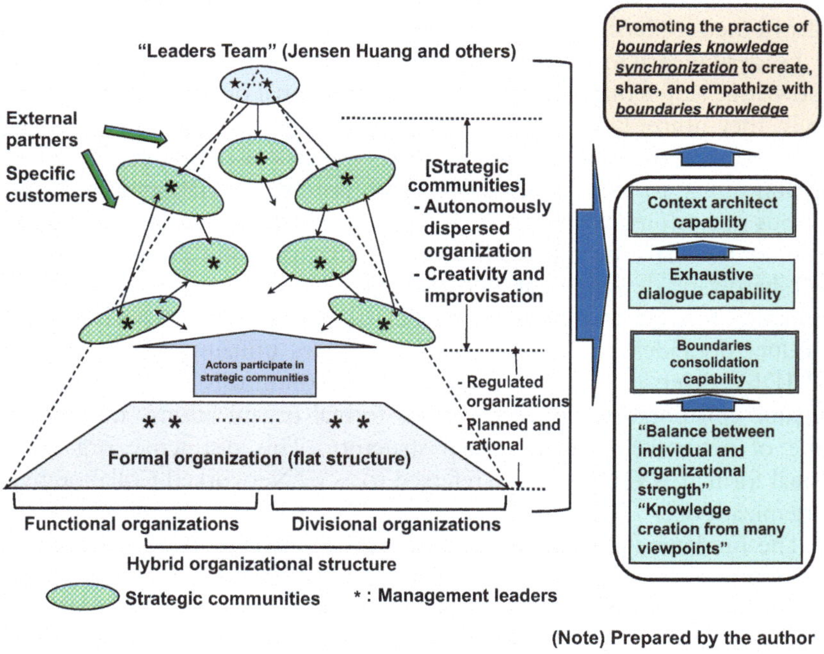

Fig. 5.11 Networked collaborative organization in NVIDIA

and knowledge between different strategic communities and sharing and inspiring this knowledge among practitioners in these communities. The "Balance between individual and organizational strength" and "knowledge creation from many viewpoints" within strategic communities generate the "boundaries consolidation capability" (Kodama, 2008, 2011, 2012) across organizations. Moreover, practitioners create new contexts through the networking of multiple different strategic communities, further enhancing the "context architect capability."

Such balance between individual and organizational strength and knowledge creation from many viewpoints embed the process of abductive synthesis within organizational members. Simultaneously, the boundaries consolidation capability promotes the practice of boundaries knowledge synchronization to create, share, and empathize with common boundaries knowledge among practitioners.

These strategic communities are not opposed to official organizations. Rather, strategic communities encompass management techniques for routine and daily tasks within official organizations, as well as management methods for problem-solving tasks and new product development tasks that are central to strategic communities. Practitioners not only adhere to decision-making processes based on basic discipline, planning, and rationality as official organizations, but also manage creative, autonomous, and challenging organizational behaviors within strategic communities. At the same time, they coordinate and further expand and develop multilayered strategic communities.

This organizational behavior of practitioners aligns with the concept of "disciplined imagination" mentioned by Weick (1989). By considering organizational management from the perspective of strategic communities, one is liberated from the traditional management model of official organizations, revealing an entirely new management model. In other words, depending on the context and environment, practitioners within official organizations create multilayered strategic communities across official organizations and flexibly reconstruct these strategic communities according to strategic goals.

In a networked collaborative organization, the term "official organization" does not imply the old-fashioned hierarchical bureaucratic organization (mechanical organization image). Instead, the networked collaborative organization features official organizations with a flat structure where delegation of authority and rapid decision-making are established (see Fig. 5.11). The flat official organization at NVIDIA adopts a hybrid organizational structure that combines elements of functional and divisional organizations. This structure allows the company to focus on product development while enabling innovation through inter-departmental collaboration, achieving both efficient operations and innovative development. In other words, it balances the activities of exploitation and exploration (March, 1981).

Specifically, the company organizes its business around major technology platforms, centralizing corporate functions that support all departments. It comprises multiple organizations, including functional organizations such as "R&D," "Engineering," "Marketing," "Finance," and "Human Resources," as well as divisional organizations like "GPU Division," "Data Center and AI Division," and "Automotive and Embedded Division." By hybridizing these functional and divisional organizations, NVIDIA achieves flexible and efficient operations.

For example, in new GPU development projects, the engineering, marketing, and finance departments collaborate to form project teams. In building an organization that promotes innovation, dedicated R&D teams are formed to establish a clear path for technology transfer between research and product development, embedding flexibility within the organization to quickly respond to market opportunities and overcome the so-called "valley of death." This approach enables each department to utilize its expertise while organizing temporary strategic communities for each project, allowing for rapid and effective development and market launch.

Examples of such projects include:

(1) AI Workbench Project: The NVIDIA AI Workbench is a platform that allows AI developers to easily build, train, and deploy AI models. Ad-hoc teams are organized to support various AI workflows in this project.
(2) Deep Learning Project: NVIDIA provides examples of deep learning utilizing Tensor Cores. Ad-hoc teams are organized to efficiently train and deploy the latest deep learning models in this project.
(3) Generative AI Example Project: NVIDIA provides reference workflows for generative AI. Ad-hoc teams are organized to accelerate generative AI systems in this project.

These projects aim to enable developers to efficiently build AI systems using NVIDIA's technology.

In this way, the leaders and managers of functional and divisional organizations collaborate with leaders and managers of other business units according to the context, forming autonomous strategic communities. As the complexity of the business model and the difficulty of challenges and issues increases, the decentralization and integration of strategic communities become simultaneously necessary.

In other words, the formation of networked strategic communities by practitioners enables the convergence of knowledge created in different strategic communities dispersed within and outside the company (Kodama, 2007a, 2007b). Strategic communities are organizational forms with mission-oriented and problem-solving tasks and include concepts of organizational forms such as projects and cross-functional teams (CFT). Multiple projects build a projects network (Kodama, 2007a, 2007b), where members of different projects collaborate to develop new business models, corresponding to networked strategic communities. The higher the degree of formation and networking of these strategic communities, the higher the degree of a networked collaborative organization. Moreover, external partners and specific customers are incorporated into strategic communities as needed.

Such a networked collaborative organization creates a "balance between individual and organizational strength" and "knowledge creation from many viewpoints" through "exhaustive dialogue capability," and simultaneously promotes the practice of "boundaries knowledge synchronization" to create, share, and empathize with common boundaries knowledge. Building such a networked collaborative organization requires a new management style for companies, like the organizational structure of NVIDIA under CEO Jensen Huang.

5.5 Boundaries Knowledge Through Knowledge Difference—From the Perspective of Abductive Synthesis

Initially, Qualcomm adopted a business model (I) as a finished product manufacturer (see Table 5.1), establishing its own value chain for the development, manufacturing, and sales of base stations and mobile devices. However, recognizing the significant risks of competing with set manufacturers adopting the GSM standard, Qualcomm decided to sell its base station business to Ericsson and its mobile device business to Kyocera. This decision stemmed from doubts and concerns about the vertically integrated business model.

Subsequently, Qualcomm strategically shifted to a business model (II), focusing on the R&D and intellectual property provision of semiconductors necessary for mobile devices and base stations—a part of the horizontal division of labor layer. The company recognized that competition with mobile device manufacturers developing their own semiconductors posed a barrier to ecosystem construction, and that customer migration from mobile device manufacturers to IDM posed a challenge to building its fabless ecosystem. Qualcomm understood the need to provide customers with complete semiconductor products, not just development and design services. This reflected concerns and doubts about simple horizontal division.

Table 5.1 New Business Model from Convergence between existing knowledge and different kind of knowledge (QUALCOMM case)

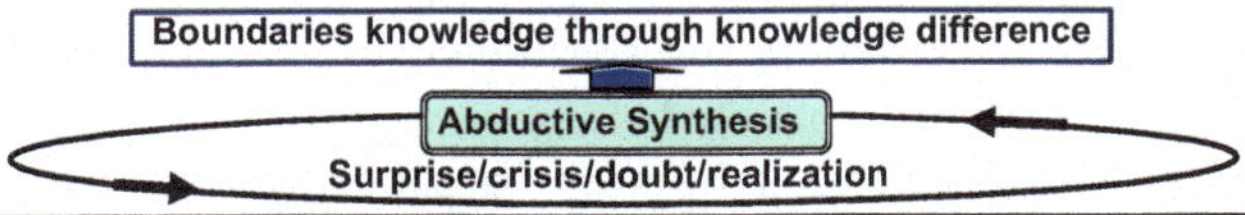

Knowledge	Existing Knowledge →	New Knowledge	← Different Kind of Knowledge
Business Model	[Business Model (I)] Mobile phone systems Vertical integration	[New Business Model] Fabless at the heart of the Ecosystem	[Business Model (II)] Mobile phone systems: Horizontal specialization (semiconductor fabless)
Knowledge difference and Boundaries knowledge	Awareness of the challenges as a Knowledge difference towards different KNOWLEDGE DIFFERENCES and ecosystem building - Business model as a manufacturer of finished products (builds its own value chain) - Competition with handset and base station manufacturers (Set manufacturers) is a barrier to building an ecosystem. - Eventually, the base station business was sold to Ericsson. -The decision to sell the mobile handset business to Kyocera. - Doubts and a sense of crisis about the current business model	[Boundaries knowledge for ecosystem building] How do we build an ecosystem by engaging our customers, the set manufacturers? (How to solve the knowledge gap between the two models?) → Need for integration with 2 business models (I and II) (how to integrate?) [Solution for new knowledge creation through SECI process] IFM (Integrated Fabless Manufacturing) → Virtual IDM CAI (Customer as innovators) user innovation for finished goods manufacturers → Qualcomm Reference Design (QRD) offering	Awareness of the challenges as a Knowledge difference towards different KNOWLEDGE DIFFERENCES and ecosystem building - Business Model of semiconductor R&D and intellectual property provision - The competition with the independent development of semiconductors by handset manufacturers is a barrier to the establishment of an ecosystem. - The problem of customer outflow from handset manufacturers to IDMs is a barrier to the creation of an ecosystem. - The need to provide customers with not only contracted development and design work, but also finished semiconductor products in an all-in-one package. - Doubt of the simple horizontal specialization and a sense of crisis.

(Note) Prepared by the author

Table 5.2 New business model from convergence between existing knowledge and different kind of knowledge (TSMC case)

Boundaries knowledge through knowledge difference

Abductive Synthesis

Surprise/crisis/doubt/realization

Knowledge	Existing Knowledge →	New Knowledge	← Different Kind of Knowledge
Business Model	[Business Model (I)] Vertically integrated semiconductor businesses (IDM)	[New Business Model] Foundry at the heart of the ecosystem	[Business Model (II)] Horizontal specialization in semiconductor manufacturing (foundry)
Knowledge difference and Boundaries knowledge	Awareness of the challenges as a Knowledge difference towards different KNOWLEDGE DIFFERENCES and ecosystem building - The problem of information leakage, such as intellectual capital for customers (e.g. fabless and set manufacturers), is a barrier to the creation of an ecosystem. - Doubts about the IDM business model - Morris-Chan's own experience at TI (semiconductor contract manufacturing from IBM)	[Boundaries knowledge for ecosystem building] How do we build an ecosystem by engaging our customers, fabless? (How to solve the knowledge gap between the two models?) → Need for integration with 2 business models (I and II) (how to integrate?) [Solution for new knowledge creation through SECI process] DFM (Design for Manufacturing) and New Integrated Model → Virtual IDM CAI (Customer as innovators) and open innovation platform for fabless user innovation	Awareness of the challenges as a Knowledge difference towards different KNOWLEDGE DIFFERENCES and ecosystem building -The competition with IDMs, which have an advantage in development design and manufacturing, is a barrier to the establishment of an ecosystem. - Lack of orders for advanced semiconductors is a barrier to building an ecosystem. Lack of orders for advanced semiconductors will be a barrier to the establishment of an ecosystem. (May specialize in manufacturing semiconductors that are a generation behind the competition). - The lack of customers with advanced development technology is a barrier to the establishment of an ecosystem. - The lack of customers with cutting-edge development technology is a barrier to the establishment of an eco-system.

(Note) Prepared by the author

Thus, Qualcomm questioned how to incorporate set manufacturers, their customers, and build an ecosystem centered around being fabless. How should they resolve the knowledge difference between the vertically integrated and horizontal division models? How could they discover boundaries knowledge for ecosystem construction? Through self-questioning, they ultimately identified the necessity of integrating these two business models (I and II) as the final boundaries knowledge.

As a solution for new knowledge creation through the SECI process, Qualcomm developed and provided the Qualcomm Reference Design (QRD), which promotes user innovation of finished product manufacturers through the IFM (Integrated Fabless Manufacturing) model and CAI (Customer as Innovators). By creating, sharing, and empathizing with boundaries knowledge within and between companies, Qualcomm drove the SECI process, built a fabless-centered ecosystem as a [New

Business Model], and successfully established trust and win–win relationships with stakeholders (see Table 5.1).

On the other hand, Morris Chang, the founder of TSMC, judged that implementing the IDM business model in Taiwan was too risky. He had doubts about the IDM business model (I), including issues such as intellectual capital and information leakage that could be barriers to ecosystem construction for customers like fabless and set manufacturers. Drawing on his past experience at Texas Instruments (TI) with semiconductor manufacturing contracted from IBM, Morris Chang chose a horizontal division of labor business model (II) focused on semiconductor manufacturing (foundry). Initially starting with simple manufacturing contracts, he later recognized that competition with IDMs, which excel in both development and manufacturing, could be a barrier to ecosystem construction, and the lack of orders for advanced semiconductors posed a risk of specializing in outdated semiconductor manufacturing. Consequently, he gradually realized the importance of design technology to support advanced technologies like miniaturization, beyond simple manufacturing contracts.

TSMC then questioned how to incorporate its fabless customers and build a foundry-centered ecosystem. How to resolve the knowledge difference between the vertically integrated and horizontal division models? How to discover boundaries knowledge for ecosystem construction? Through self-questioning, TSMC ultimately identified the necessity of integrating these two business models (I and II) as the final boundaries knowledge.

Ultimately, as a solution for new knowledge creation through the SECI process, TSMC promoted user innovation of fabless companies through DFM (Design for Manufacturing) and a new integrated model (Virtual IDM), as well as Customer as Innovators (CAI) and an open innovation platform. By creating, sharing, and empathizing with boundaries knowledge within and between companies, TSMC drove the SECI process, built a foundry-centered ecosystem as a [New Business Model], and successfully established trust and win–win relationships with stakeholders (see Table 5.2).

Initially, NVIDIA started its business with the business model (I) of developing and designing GPUs for the graphics market (fabless). However, recognizing the need to explore new markets and the future risks to company management, the executives felt an urgency. Subsequently, they sought a new business model (II) incorporating new markets for GPUs. At the beginning of the 2000s, the AI field was largely ignored, and they generally recognized the unlikelihood of applying GPUs to neural networks. However, noticing research activities at university institutions (like the University of Toronto) utilizing GPUs and CUDA for image recognition with neural networks, they realized the new potential demand for GPUs. Thus, the company prepared to embrace serendipitous opportunities in AI development.

Facing the question of how to build an ecosystem centered around GPUs and CUDA, NVIDIA, through the serendipitous realization of AI development as a new application, identified the necessity of integrating these two business models (I and II)—essentially, the need to integrate graphics technology with generative AI.

Ultimately, as a solution for new knowledge creation through the SECI process, NVIDIA built a platform using the QUDA (programming model) and promoted user innovation through Customer as Innovators (CAI) and an open innovation platform for AI developers. By creating, sharing, and empathizing with boundaries knowledge within and between companies, NVIDIA drove the SECI process, built a fabless-centered ecosystem for GPU development as a [New Business Model], and successfully established trust and win–win relationships with stakeholders (see Table 5.3).

Based on the common insights from the knowledge convergence processes (new knowledge creation) at Qualcomm, TSMC, and NVIDIA, the following points can be considered. Elements such as doubts, concerns, and realizations among the management and executive layers of these companies produced dynamic capabilities that promoted the integration (synthesis) of existing knowledge and different kinds of knowledge, preventing the rigidity and entrapment of the organizations' core competencies. Additionally, these elements, through the trial-and-error processes of business model abduction, as seen in the cases of Qualcomm and TSMC, generated higher-quality (higher-dimensional) knowledge through the convergence of different types of knowledge. Furthermore, in the case of NVIDIA, they played a crucial role as an actionable process for serendipitous business opportunities.

Moreover, appropriate knowledge differences act as triggers for creating appropriate boundaries knowledge (see Fig. 5.12). Abduction refers to the cognitive logic of new discovery, such as the brain's process of linking previously unconnected existing knowledge and different kinds of knowledge, intellectual and creative acts, and mental leaps (Reichertz,

Table 5.3 New business model from convergence between existing knowledge and different kind of knowledge (NVIDIA case)

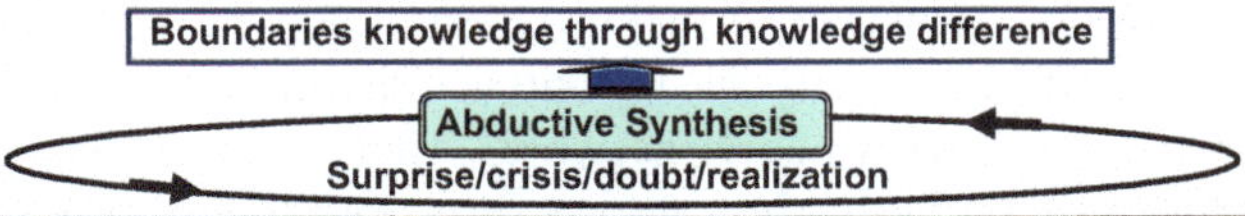

Knowledge	Existing Knowledge →	New Knowledge	← Different Kind of Knowledge
Business Model	[Business Model (I)] Development and design of GPUs for the graphics market (Fabless)	[New Business Model] Ecosystem centered around the 'GPU + CUDA' hardware and software platform	[Business Model (II)] Explore business models that incorporate new markets for GPUs
Knowledge difference and Boundaries knowledge	Awareness of the challenges as a Knowledge difference towards different KNOWLEDGE DIFFERENCES and ecosystem building Acknowledgement of the need to develop new markets due to the limited number of customers. Sense of future threat to company management.	[Boundaries knowledge for ecosystem building] Awareness of Serendipity → Need for integration of graphics technology with Generative AI (resolving the KNOWLEDGE DIFFERENCE between the two models) [Solution for new knowledge creation through SECI process] - Build a platform through QUDA (programming model) - Promote user innovation through CAI (customer as innovators) and open innovation platform for AI developers	Awareness of the challenges as a Knowledge difference towards different KNOWLEDGE DIFFERENCES and ecosystem building - In the early 2000s, the AI field was a neglected entity. - Perceptions of its application to neural networks were negative. - Research activities using GPUs and CUDA at a university research institute (University of Toronto) (image recognition using neural networks) - Awareness of new potential needs for GPUs - Openness to contingent opportunities (Serendipity)

(Note) Prepared by the author

2007). Abduction also means an inferential process where ongoing observation and contemplation lead to some surprise, crisis, doubt, or realization, guiding new hypotheses and theories, and ultimately providing a direction for optimal ideas (which, in this case, correspond to new business models) (Agar, 2010; Alvesson & Karreman, 2007; Locke et al., 2008; Reichertz, 2007). Such abductive discovery-oriented business processes combine inductive and deductive steps, which are iterative and recursive.

Surprise, doubt, and realization challenge existing strategies and motivate the willingness to transform existing strategic schemes, enhancing the possibility of refreshing the organization's past memories and routines. Additionally, surprises, doubts, and realizations stemming from new information and events update the embedded memories within the organization, offering the potential to understand possible strategic shifts. These

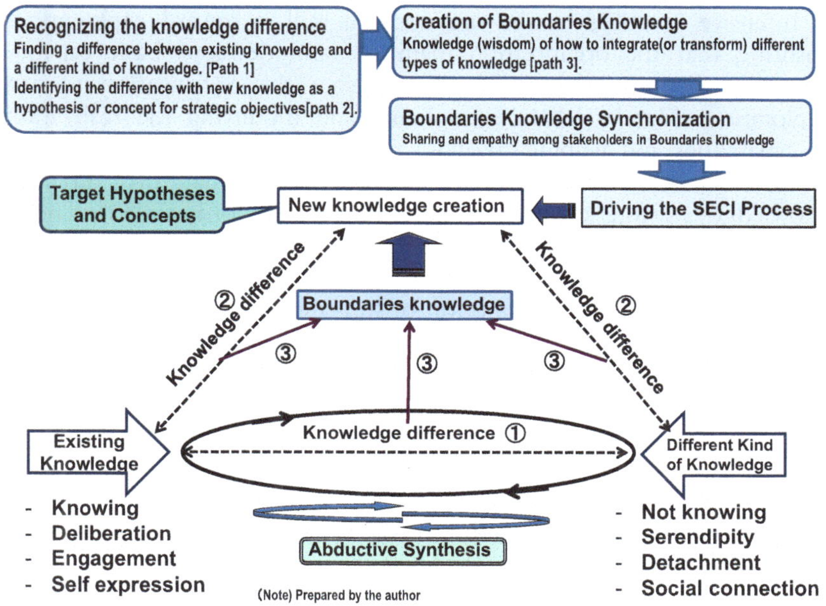

Fig. 5.12 Please replace Fig. 5.12 to attached file. Knowledge integration (transformation) process through dialectical synthesis

processes drive the organization to recognize and embrace unexpected outcomes as new opportunities.

Klag and Langley (2013) presented opposing elements such as Not Knowing, Serendipity, Detachment, and Social Connection for each element of Knowing, Deliberation, Engagement, and Self-expression. They introduced a theoretical process where these opposing elements (forces) are integrated (synthesized) in a generative space through dialectics (abductive synthesis) (see Fig. 5.7). Through dialectics, the forces of these differing elements (in other words, the differing knowledge of existing knowledge and different kinds of knowledge) can be integrated (synthesized). While what the organization knows is considered a reliable foundation for strategic action, the space for unknown challenges is also accepted by recognizing and utilizing surprises, doubts, and realizations to understand the complex and uncertain changing management environment.

Intensive practices in the organization pull it toward exploitation, ensuring that the organization maintains and develops basic capabilities. On the other hand, flexibility pushes the organization toward exploration (March, 1991), stimulating and modifying the realization of capabilities and helping to avoid the rigidity of existing capabilities (Leonard-Barton, 1992). In other words, the combination of differing knowledge (existing knowledge and different kinds of knowledge) helps in dynamically updating capabilities, thereby preventing the progression of capability rigidity and stagnation (Leonard-Barton, 1992; Miller, 2022). Additionally, the promotion of surprises, crisis, doubts, and realizations in the state of rational organization plays a crucial role in a process that allows for serendipitous work (Vogus et al., 2014; Weick, 2001).

From this perspective, NVIDIA's serendipitous strategic actions and their judgment that their GPUs are suitable for AI development can be seen as a dialectical process. While relentlessly advancing their GPU strategy in the graphics field, NVIDIA executed strategic actions under a dialectical framework, maintaining the ability to explore the novel possibilities of AI development as serendipity. Therefore, creating "optimality" under a dialectical viewpoint can be considered an effective management option. In other words, by emphasizing serendipity, there is a potential opportunity to achieve optimality under paradox. This also suggests the crucial importance of optimal decision-making in the face of inherently contradictory demands and the realization of new business models for CEOs at Qualcomm and TSMC.

However, the critical element driving such dialectical synthesis (abductive synthesis) is the ability to recognize differences between existing knowledge and different kinds of knowledge and to clearly grasp the direction the organization should aim for (e.g., the optimal idea: in this case, a new business model). From the knowledge differences between differing knowledge (existing knowledge and different kinds of knowledge), one can recognize "missing knowledge" necessary to achieve synergistic effects and optimal ideas through the integration of their merits. As shown in Fig. 5.12, recognizing knowledge difference involves identifying the difference between existing knowledge and different kinds of knowledge [Path ①] and identifying the difference with new knowledge as a hypothesis or concept for strategic objectives [Path ②].

Therefore, the creation of boundaries knowledge, which is the knowledge (wisdom) of how to integrate (or transform) different kinds of knowledge [Path ③], requires the understanding of knowledge differences among diverse knowledge through the process of abductive synthesis. In this case, the necessity of integrating (or transforming) different business models (I and II) corresponds to boundaries knowledge. The horizontal division model, business model II, generally promotes management efficiency (e.g., Kodama, 2011). On the other hand, the vertical integration model, business model I, tends to promote management creativity (so-called innovation activities) (e.g., Kodama, 2009). Consequently, pursuing synergies through the integration (or transformation) of these two different business models becomes an important element of boundaries knowledge. Furthermore, this boundaries knowledge, when shared and empathized among stakeholders within and between companies, drives the SECI process (see Fig. 5.12).

As previously mentioned, in the SECI model, boundaries knowledge (knowing) exists at the boundaries of knowledge integration (tacit knowledge to tacit knowledge and explicit knowledge to explicit knowledge) and knowledge transformation (tacit knowledge to explicit knowledge and explicit knowledge to tacit knowledge) in its four phases. Through the perceptual and recognition process of knowledge difference (Paths ① to ③) via abductive synthesis, boundaries knowledge in these four phases is created, achieving knowledge integration and knowledge transformation, and dynamically driving the SECI process.

In Figure 5.13, the boundary areas in knowledge integration and knowledge transformation of Socialization, Externalization, Combination, and Internalization represent "boundaries knowledge (boundaries knowing)." To effectively drive the SECI model in groups or organizations, creating, sharing, and empathizing with boundaries knowledge among organizational members, including stakeholders, is essential. To creatively and productively resolve conflicts and friction observed between different departments within the organization, common boundaries knowledge must be created and shared among practitioners (stakeholders). Therefore, the concept and practice of "boundaries knowledge synchronization" are vital to promote the creation, sharing, and empathy of boundaries knowledge among different practitioners (or stakeholders).

Practitioners, through boundaries knowledge synchronization, create common boundaries knowledge (creation, sharing, and empathy), which drives the dynamic circulation of tacit and explicit knowledge (SECI model) for knowledge creation. Creating boundaries knowledge is not only necessary for top management but is especially required for many middle managers and staff engaged in facing projects. Furthermore,

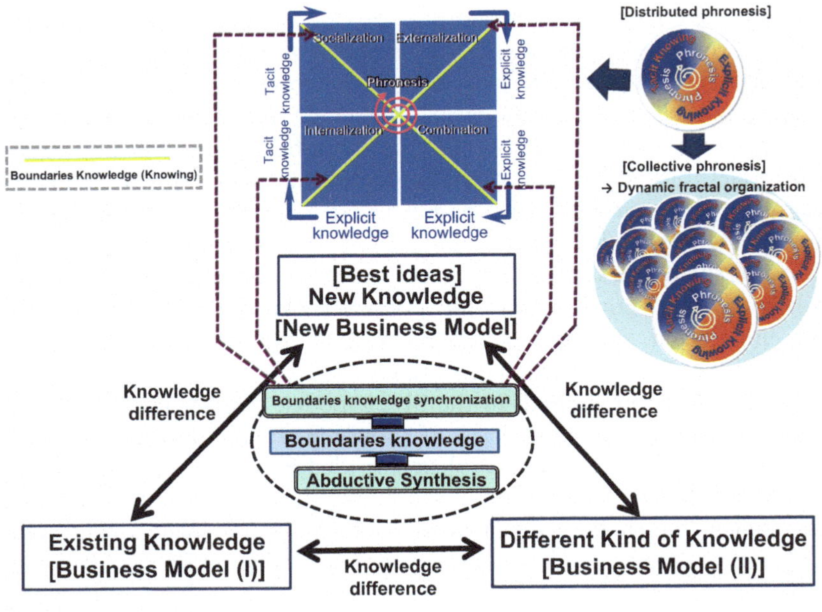

Fig. 5.13 Boundaries knowledge through knowledge difference

the concept of "boundaries knowledge synchronization" is also a key element in forming collective phronesis (Kodama, 2012) and dynamic fractal organization (Nonaka et al., 2014) as mentioned in Chapter 3 (see Figure 5.13).

5.6 Implications and Conclusion

This chapter has introduced a new theoretical model called "boundaries knowledge synchronization," which addresses boundaries knowledge created between humans, organizations, and various entities, a topic rarely discussed in academic research. The study analyzed and considered how "boundaries knowledge synchronization" facilitates the creation, sharing, and empathy of "boundaries knowledge (boundaries knowing)" in the SECI model by Nonaka and Takeuchi (1995) through in-depth case studies of new product development.

In realizing the creation, sharing, and empathy of boundaries knowledge through the practice process of boundaries knowledge synchronization, practitioners need to align boundaries knowledge among stakeholders and engage in the process of abductive synthesis related to knowledge creation activities. This requires practitioners to mutually learn and recognize different boundaries knowledge through the formation of "strategic communities" and abductive synthesis. In summary, this chapter has contributed to the existing knowledge creation theory by introducing the concepts and frameworks of "knowledge creation through boundaries knowledge" and "boundaries knowledge synchronization" within the SECI model by Nonaka and Takeuchi (1995).

In today's knowledge society, it is crucial for individuals living in the corporate world to not only recognize the necessity of knowledge creation through the convergence of diverse knowledge across different values and fields within organizations but also to build a global network of outstanding individuals and organizations worldwide. The most important task is to acquire "creativity" by integrating (converging) the excellent knowledge dispersed globally with individual and organizational knowledge.

The first academic contribution of this chapter lies in providing a new micro perspective on "creativity development." The process of dynamic creativity development at the micro level involves the creation of "boundaries knowledge through boundaries knowledge synchronization." The acquisition of "creativity" through the framework of "knowledge creation through boundaries knowledge" becomes a source of valuable products, services, and business models that generate new competitiveness in the knowledge economy. The fusion of diverse technologies and different industries leads to the creation of new products, services, and business models that transcend various boundaries, forming a value chain that becomes a new strategic model. Therefore, companies need to recognize the management that transcends the boundaries of knowledge possessed by individuals, groups, and organizations to create new businesses through knowledge creation.

On the other hand, traditional organizational learning theories (e.g., Cyert & March, 1963) have referred to the development of human and organizational capabilities and practice processes. However, learning and creation are different; creation involves generating something that did not exist in the past. Creation is not born from nothing but from new combinations (convergence) of existing knowledge and things (e.g., Zhou &

Shalley, 2007). In cognitive science terms, learning is the process of enriching existing knowledge networks by incorporating new information, while creation is the process of bridging new links between existing networks, especially heterogeneous networks (e.g., Fauconnier & Turner, 1998). The trigger for such link-bridging lies in "boundaries knowledge through boundaries vision."

Both learning and creation enrich knowledge networks, but the processes leading to them differ. Learning involves information provided externally, while creation is an internally driven process of self-realization and new combinations of knowledge. Although the trigger may come from outside, the process of discovering the solution is spontaneous and generative. It is necessary to activate boundaries vision from various boundaries and create new boundaries knowledge through the practice process of boundaries knowledge synchronization.

The second academic contribution of this chapter lies in providing new insights into the field of knowledge management. Polanyi (1962) clarified the dimension of tacit knowledge but did not elucidate the interaction with explicit knowledge. Nonaka (2016) mentioned that Polanyi's (1962) theory of knowledge alone could not clarify the principles of knowledge creation. On the other hand, Nonaka and Takeuchi (1995) revealed the knowledge creation process where two types of knowledge, tacit and explicit, synergize through mutual transformation (knowledge transformation). Furthermore, Nonaka et al. (2014) introduced "practical knowledge (phronesis)" as the third type of knowledge driving the spiral loop of tacit and explicit knowledge. Building on these prior studies, this chapter incorporated the concept of "boundaries knowledge (boundaries knowing)" within the boundary areas of the four phases of the SECI process (Nonaka & Takeuchi, 1995; Nonaka et al., 2014) and presented insights into how the practice process of "boundaries knowledge synchronization" promotes the knowledge creation process among different stakeholders.

Future research perspectives of this chapter include expanding research on "creativity development and innovation" across different research fields such as management, economics, psychology, arts, science, and engineering. Practically, it is expected to contribute significantly to society by fostering "creative human resources" while envisioning interdisciplinary development of "knowledge creation theory" across different research fields (management, economics, psychology, arts, science, engineering, etc.).

References

Agar, M. (2010). On the ethnographic part of the mix: A multi-genre tale of the field. *Organizational Research Methods, 13*(2), 286–303.

Aliseda, A. (2005). The logic of abduction in the light of Peirce's pragmatism. *Semiotica, 2005*(153), 363–374.

Alvesson, M., & Karreman, D. (2007). Constructing mystery: Empirical matters in theory development. *Academy of Management Review, 32*, 1265–1281.

Amabile, T. M. (1996). *Creativity in context: Update to the social psychology of creativity*. Hachette UK.

Anderson, D. R. (1986). The evolution of Peirce's concept of abduction. *Transactions of the Charles S. Peirce Society, 22*(2), 145–164.

Aristotle. (350BCE/1980). *The Nicomachean Ethics*. (David Ross, trans.). Oxford: Oxford University Press.

Bertilsson, T. M. (2004). The elementary forms of pragmatism: On different types of abduction. *European Journal of Social Theory, 7*(3), 371–389.

Brown, J. S., & Duguid, P. (2001). Knowledge and organization: A social-practice perspective. *Organization Science, 12*(2), 198–213.

Bono, E. (2009). *Lateral thinking: A textbook of creativity*. Penguin UK.

Carlile, P. (2002). A pragmatic view of knowledge and boundaries: Boundary objects in new product development. *Organization Science, 13*(4), 442–455.

Carlile, P. (2004). Transferring, translating, and transforming: An integrative framework for managing knowledge across boundaries. *Organization Science, 15*(5), 555–568.

Cyert, R. M., & March, J. G. (1963). *A behavioral theory of the firm* (pp. 169–187). Prentice-Hall

Dalkir, K. (2013). *Knowledge management in theory and practice*. Routledge.

Dewey, J. (1922). An analysis of reflective thought. *The Journal of Philosophy*, 29–38.

Day, G., & Schoemaker, J. (2005). Scanning the Periphery. *Harvard Business Review*, 135–148.

e Cunha, M. P., Rego, A., Clegg, S., & Lindsay, G. (2015). The dialectics of serendipity.

Eisenhardt, K. (1989). Building theories from case study research. *Academy of Management Review, 14*, 532–550.

Fauconnier, G., & Turner, M. (1998). Conceptual integration networks. *Cognitive Science, 22*(2), 133–187.

Hacklin, F., Marxt, C., & Fahrni, F. (2009). Coevolutionary cycles of convergence: An extrapolation from the ICT industry. *Technological Forecasting and Social Change, 76*(6), 723–736.

Hagel, J., III., & Brown, J. S. (2005). Productive friction: How difficult business partnerships can accelerate innovation. *Harvard Business Review, 83*, 82–91.

James, G. O. (1912). The problem of mechanical flight. *Science, 36*(924), 336–340.

Johansson, F. (2004). *The medici effect*. Harvard Business School Press.

Katz, M. L., & Shapiro, C. (1992). Product introduction with network externalities. *The Journal of Industrial Economics*, 55–83.

Klag, M., & Langley, A. (2013). Approaching the conceptual leap in qualitative research. *International Journal of Management Reviews, 15*(2), 149–166.

Kodama, M. (2005). Knowledge creation through networked strategic communities: Case studies in new product development. *Long Range Planning, 38*(1), 27–49.

Kodama, M. (2006). Knowledge-based view of corporate strategy. *Technovation, 26*(12), 1390–1406.

Kodama, M. (2007a). *The strategic community-based firm*. Palgrave Macmillan.

Kodama, M. (2007b). *Project-based organization in the knowledge-based society* (Vol. 12). Imperial College Press.

Kodama, M. (2008). *New knowledge creation through ICT dynamic capability: Creating knowledge communities using broadband*. IAP.

Kodama, M. (2009). Boundaries innovation and knowledge integration in the Japanese firm. *Long Range Planning, 42*(4), 463–494.

Kodama, M. (2011). *Knowledge integration dynamics: Developing strategic innovation capability*. World Scientific.

Kodama, M. (2012). *Competing through ICT Capability: Innovation in Image Communication*. Springer.

Kodama, M. (2016). *Interactive business communities: Accelerating corporate innovation through boundary networks*. Routledge.

Kodama, M. (2018). Boundaries innovation through knowledge convergence-developing triad strategic communities. *Technology Analysis & Strategic Management, 30*(5), 609–624.

Kodama, M. (2019). Boundaries knowledge (knowing)—A source of business innovation. *Knowledge and Process Management, 26*(3), 210–228.

Kodama, M. (Ed.). (2020). *Developing Boundaries Knowledge for Innovation*. Edward Elgar Publishing.

Kodama, M. (2021). Knowledge creation through collective phronesis. *Knowledge and Process Management, 28*(3), 223–245.

Kodama, M. (2024). Dynamic capabilities and asset orchestration. *Knowledge and Process Management, 31*(2), 101–127.

Kodama, M., & Shibata, T. (2014). Strategy transformation through strategic innovation capability—A case study of Fanuc. *R&D Management, 44*(1), 75–103.

Kodama, M., & Shibata, T. (2016). Developing knowledge convergence through a boundaries vision—A case study of fujifilm in Japan. *Knowledge and Process Management, 23*(4), 274–292.

Kogut, B., & Zander, U. (1992). Knowledge of the firm, combinative capabilities, and the replication of technology. *Organization Science, 3*(3), 383–397.

Locke, H. S., & Braver, T. S. (2008). Motivational influences on cognitive control: Behavior, brain activation, and individual differences. *Cognitive, Affective, & Behavioral Neuroscience, 8*(1), 99–112.

Leonard-Barton, D. (1992). Core capabilities and core rigidities: A paradox in managing new product development. *Strategic Management Journal, 13*(S1), 111–125.

Leonard-Barton, D. (1995). *Wellsprings of knowledge: Building and sustaining the sources of innovation.* Harvard Business School Press.

March, J. G. (1981). Footnotes to organizational change. *Administrative Science Quarterly*, 563–577.

March, J. (1991). Exploration and exploitation in organizational learning. *Organization Science*, *2*(1), 71–87.

Miller, C. (2022). *Chip war: The fight for the world's most critical technology.* Simon and Schuster.

Mitchell, A., & Education, A. E. (2018). A review of mixed methods, pragmatism and abduction techniques. In *Proceedings of the European conference on research methods for business & management studies* (pp. 269–277).

Nonaka, I. (2016). Cultivating organizational knowledge maneuverability—Tacit knowing, intersubjectivity, distributed leadership (in Japanese). *Hitotsubashi Business Review, 64*(3), 68–85.

Nonaka, I., & Takeuchi, H. (1995). *The knowledge-creating company.* Oxford University Press.

Nonaka, I., & Toyama, R. (2005). The theory of the knowledge-creating firm: Subjectivity, objectivity and synthesis. *Industrial and Corporate Change, 14*(3), 419–436.

Nonaka, I., Kodama, M., Hirose, A., & Kohlbacher, F. (2014). Dynamic fractal organizations for promoting knowledge-based transformation—A new paradigm for organizational theory. *European Management Journal, 32*(1), 137–146.

Nonaka, I., Toyama, R., & Hirata, T. (2008). *Managing flow: A process theory of the knowledge-based firm.* Palgrave Macmillan.

Pettigrew, A. M. (1990). Longitudinal field research on change: Theory and practice. *Organization Science, 1*(1), 267–292.

Polanyi, M. (1962). *Personal knowledge: Towards a post-critical philosophy.* University of Chicago Press.

Rafols, I., & Meyer, M. (2010). Diversity and network coherence as indicators of interdisciplinarity: Case studies in bionanoscience. *Scientometrics, 82*(2), 263–287.

Reichertz, J. (2007). Abduction: The logic of discovery of grounded theory. In A. Bryant & K. Charmaz (Eds.), *The Sage handbook of grounded theory* (pp. 214–228). Sage Publications.

Samuels, W. J. (2000). Signs, pragmatism, and abduction: The tragedy, irony, and promise of Charles Sanders Peirce. *Journal of Economic Issues, 34*(1), 207–217.

Smith, W. K., & Tushman, M. L. (2005). Managing strategic contradictions: A top management model for managing innovation streams. *Organization Science, 16*(5), 522–536.

Spender, J. C. (1996). Making knowledge the basis of a dynamic theory of the firm. *Strategic Management Journal, 17*(S2), 45–62.

Teece, D. J. (2007). Explicating dynamic capabilities: The nature and micro-foundations of (sustainable) enterprise performance. *Strategic Management Journal, 28*(13), 1319–1350.

Teece, D. J. (2014). The foundations of enterprise performance: Dynamic and ordinary capabilities in an (economic) theory of firms. *Academy of Management Perspectives, 28*(4), 328–352.

Van Rijnsoever, F. J., & Hessels, L. K. (2011). Factors associated with disciplinary and interdisciplinary research collaboration. *Research Policy, 40*(3), 463–472.

Vogus, T. J., Rothman, N. B., Sutcliffe, K. M., & Weick, K. E. (2014). The affective foundations of high-reliability organizing. *Journal of Organizational Behavior, 35*(4), 592–596.

Weick, K. E. (1989). Theory construction as disciplined imagination. *Academy of Management Review, 14*(4), 516–531.

Weick, K. E. (2001). Leadership as the legitimation of doubt. In *The future of leadership: Today's top leadership thinkers speak to tomorrow's leaders* (pp. 91–102).

Yin, R. K. (1994). *Case study research: Design and methods* (2nd ed.). Sage.

Zhou, J., & Shalley, C. E. (2007). *Handbook of organizational creativity*. Psychology Press.

CHAPTER 6

New Knowledge Creation Through Technology Convergence Case Studies of Toyota and Panasonic

6.1 IT Innovation Through Convergence

In cutting-edge fields such as IT, energy, automotive, electronics, semiconductors, biotechnology, pharmaceuticals, and materials science, superior core technologies are dispersed among companies, organizations, and individuals worldwide. The integration of these advanced core technologies serves as a source of innovation, leading to new products and services (e.g., Kodama, 2007).

IT innovation broadly transforms work styles, lifestyles, and production activities across various sectors of society. It changes how products are made and how resources are utilized, contributing directly and indirectly to CO_2 reduction by incorporating IT technologies into various advanced devices. IT innovation promotes energy-efficient manufacturing by advancing energy-saving investments and measures. This kind of IT innovation fosters "convergence," which involves the fusion and integration of different technologies and services, as well as the creation of business models that span different industries (see Fig. 6.1).

On the other hand, following the adoption of the new international framework for reducing greenhouse gas emissions, the Paris Agreement, from 2020 onwards, all participating countries, including developed, emerging, and developing nations, are strongly required to tackle global warming under this Paris Agreement. Specifically, in recent years, Cyber-Physical Systems (CPS) and Internet of Things (IoT) have become

M. Kodama, *Developing Knowledge Convergence Through Collective Phronesis*, https://doi.org/10.1007/978-981-96-4403-2_6

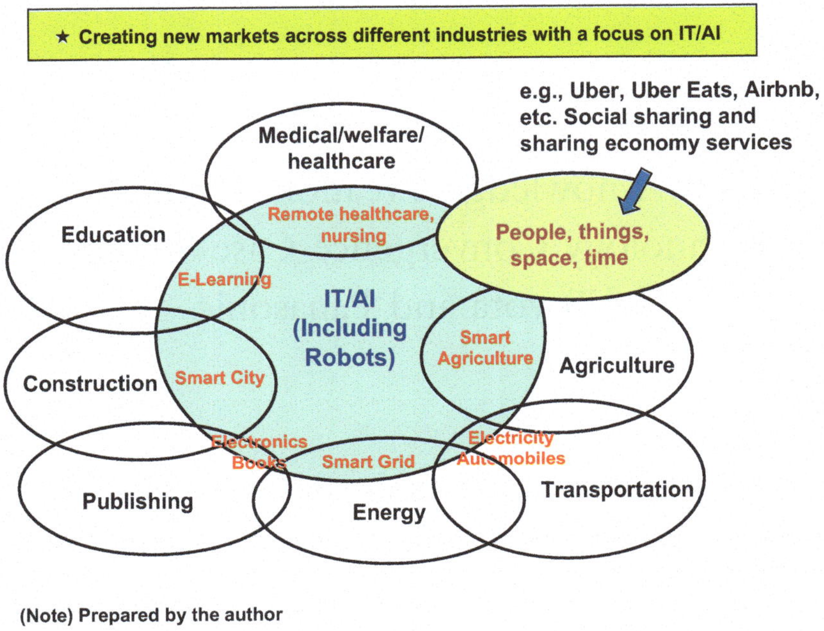

Fig. 6.1 The era of convergence—Examples of technology integration (knowledge integration) centered around IT

global trends, and the collaboration and integration of the IT industry with various other industrial sectors are transforming people's lives, social activities, and various businesses. The evolution of these innovative technologies is underpinned by the convergence of IT and electronics technologies, including sensing technology, location information technology, energy management systems (such as HEMS, BEMS, FEMS), energy-saving devices, and data utilization.

Furthermore, the smart communities, such as smart towns and smart cities, which are currently being emphasized in various countries, are attracting attention as next-generation social systems that connect homes, buildings, and transportation systems through IT networks to efficiently utilize energy within regions. In smart communities, the use of IT solutions such as energy management systems (HEMS, BEMS, FEMS) to optimize the operation of smart meters, renewable energy, and EVs, as well as CEMS to integrate these systems, and ITS for transportation systems, is indispensable. The development of these innovative technologies significantly contributes to reducing CO_2 emissions and dramatically increasing energy-saving effects. Moreover, the future-anticipated XR technology is expected to minimize the physical resources generated, utilized, and consumed in various processes of social, economic, and business activities, thereby directly and indirectly contributing to addressing global environmental issues. In Japan, specific services focusing on smart cities and smart towns have been initiated, primarily by companies like Toyota and Panasonic.

To this end, the IT industries of various countries need to understand their environmental contributions, such as measures against global warming, and further strengthen technical and business partnerships with various industries, supply chains, and venture companies. By doing so, they can promote new technologies and businesses through convergence strategies that open up the future and contribute to the global society (Kodama, 2014).

So far, the evolution of IT has shortened the time and space of business processes and supply chains in all industries, improved management efficiency, and accelerated decision-making. At the same time, it has created new business models that cross and integrate different industries (Kodama, 2020, 2021). IT innovation promotes the "co-creation and co-evolution" of the entire industry toward improving the global environment, enhancing the potential to form a dynamic "global ecosystem" as a new value chain.

To create new business models through the convergence of different technologies and cross-industry IT innovation, companies, public organizations, government bodies, and even entire nations must consider what strategic actions and organizational reforms they should undertake. Questions such as what kind of leadership and management are required for this purpose are practical challenges faced by many stakeholders worldwide, including academic research.

Convergence, a key driver of recent innovation, is considered an essential element in creating new knowledge. In the past, high-tech companies have aimed to evolve and develop products through incremental innovation of individual specialized technologies (e.g., Christensen, 1997). However, in recent years, the need for developing new products and services through the convergence of different technologies has increased (e.g., Kodama, 2007, 2014, 2015, 2016).

Furthermore, the evolution of IT has shortened the time and space of business processes and supply chains across various industries, enhancing management efficiency and accelerating decision-making. At the same time, it has created new business models that span different industries. This phenomenon is often driven by the fusion of technologies from different fields, leading to innovative new products and services (e.g., Kodama, 2007, 2014, 2015, 2016).

For example, the convergence of IT with other industries is creating new markets in areas such as smart grids, smart cities, smart towns, smart agriculture, telemedicine, and various sharing services. This convergence of different technologies and industries is rapidly progressing in many high-tech fields, including smartphones, IoT, Big Data, AI, robotics, and environmentally friendly vehicles. The advancement and diversification of technology, along with the rapid evolution of IT, are making the business models that companies need to provide more complex.

Therefore, in the twenty-first century, the necessity for strategies that address the convergence of different technologies and services, such as IT, and the development of products, services, and business models that span various industries is increasingly important (e.g., Kodama, 2011, 2014, 2015). These enable companies and organizations to offer new value creation to their customers. To this end, it is essential not only to integrate different areas of expertise within the company (organization) but also to integrate diverse knowledge across companies (organizations) as a core strategy (Kodama, 2011, 2015; Nonaka et al., 2008).

The element that achieves innovation in response to such convergence lies in "co-creation among stakeholders" (e.g., Kodama, 2015, 2018). However, there are various boundaries among the actors, such as individual stakeholders. There are also knowledge boundaries between individual areas of expertise. These boundaries may involve heterogeneous content or inherent differences, referred to as "knowledge differences" (Kodama, 2006, 2007, 2019). The wisdom to identify such heterogeneity and differences is known as "boundaries knowledge" (Kodama, 2018, 2019, 2020). Additionally, the wisdom to identify these boundaries and further connect them to inspire new knowledge also corresponds to boundaries knowledge.

On the other hand, the SECI model, based on the knowledge creation theory (Nonaka & Takeuchi, 1995, 2019), promotes the construction of a multilayered network of spaces that cross both internal and external boundaries of companies, including customers, thereby accelerating the creation of new knowledge to achieve innovation in response to convergence (Nonaka et al., 2014). For this purpose, it is also important for practitioners to create boundaries knowledge (Kodama, 2019) by forming or discovering various Ba and bridging these different Ba. Additionally, it has been reported that practitioners' phronesis (and collective phronesis) (Kodama, 2021) generates boundaries knowledge and accelerates the dynamic interaction between tacit and explicit knowledge (the so-called SECI model) for convergence.

The creation of boundaries knowledge (tacit knowledge and explicit knowledge that identify the heterogeneity and differences of boundaries) serves as a factor that promotes knowledge integration and knowledge transformation at each stage of the SECI process: socialization, externalization, combination, and internalization (Kodama, 2019) (see Fig. 6.2). The creation of boundaries knowledge is not only required by top management but also demanded of many middle managers and staff. In this chapter, the actors who play a central role in the creation of such knowledge are referred to as "Boundary Architects."

As previously mentioned, prior research (Kodama, 2019) has focused on the new concept of "knowledge differences" (Kodama, 2006, 2007, 2019), which arises between individuals, organizations, and various disparate entities. It reports that the capabilities of human perception, awareness, and discovery of such differences are termed "Boundaries Vision." Furthermore, the "new knowledge" that emerges from boundaries vision is referred to as "boundaries knowledge" (or "boundaries knowing"). These concepts of boundaries vision and boundaries knowledge (knowing) have rarely been discussed in the fields of knowledge management, business and management, or even in other academic disciplines (other social sciences and humanities). The concept of "boundaries knowledge (knowing) through boundaries vision" is emphasized as influencing the creativity and innovation possessed by individuals and organizations (Kodama, 2019).

Kodama (2019) conducted exploratory research on the characteristics of boundaries knowledge (knowing), a core concept in the knowledge creation process, and its relationship with the SECI model. This prior research reported that within the four phases of the SECI process (Nonaka & Takeuchi, 1995)—namely, "knowledge integration" (Tacit → Tacit, Explicit → Explicit) and "knowledge transformation" (Tacit → Explicit, Explicit → Tacit)—there exist various elements of "boundaries."

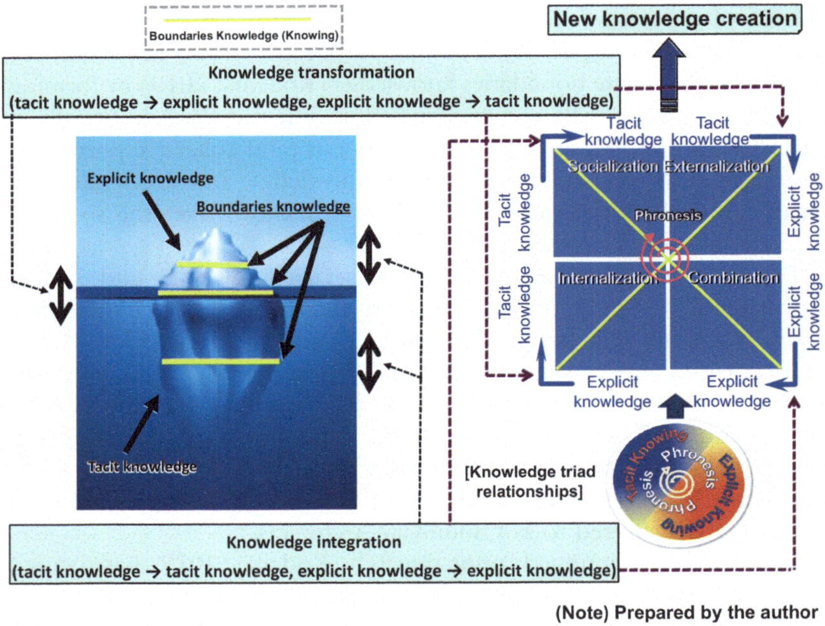

Fig. 6.2 Boundaries knowledge and SECI model

Practitioners perceive "knowledge difference" from these diverse "boundaries," further activating "boundaries vision" and generating "boundaries knowledge (boundaries knowing)."

Therefore, by incorporating the concept of boundaries knowledge (boundaries knowing) into the SECI model, it becomes possible to provide a new framework and insights for the knowledge creation process, where boundaries knowledge generates "convergence knowledge (tacit knowledge and explicit knowledge)" (Kodama, 2018). However, the micro-processes of "knowledge creation (convergence) through boundaries knowledge" within and between organizations remain a black box and have not been deeply elucidated in prior research (Kodama, 2019).

This chapter points out that boundaries knowledge, created between individuals, organizations, and various different entities, promotes the knowledge creation process through a mechanism called "boundaries knowledge synchronization," where this knowledge is created, shared, and empathized among different stakeholders. This is demonstrated through in-depth case studies of Toyota and Panasonic. Furthermore, achieving the creation, sharing, and empathy of boundaries knowledge through boundaries knowledge synchronization requires aligning boundaries knowledge among different stakeholders and an abductive synthesis process related to knowledge creation activities. For this purpose, stakeholders need to mutually learn and recognize different boundaries knowledge through the formation of "multi-layered Ba" (e.g., Kodama, 2021) via abductive synthesis. As a result, the practical process of "boundaries knowledge synchronization" can facilitate the creation, sharing, and empathy of common boundaries knowledge among stakeholders, thereby promoting the knowledge creation process.

6.2 Structure of This Chapter and Research Method

This chapter first elucidates the concept of "boundaries knowledge synchronization," which has not been previously discussed in academic research. The mechanism of "boundaries knowledge synchronization" facilitates the creation, sharing, and empathy of "boundaries knowledge (boundaries knowing)" in the SECI model's individual boundary areas of Socialization, Externalization, Combination, and Internalization among practitioners, thereby driving the SECI model smoothly. As in-depth case studies of knowledge creation through boundaries knowledge synchronization, this chapter examines the cases of Toyota's smart city and Panasonic's smart town.

This research has exploratory aspects of extracting details of certain people and organizations involved in corporate innovation activities, gathering data regarding the leadership processes of their activities, and carefully analyzing these. Therefore, the author has adopted a qualitative survey and case study analysis as their methodology. This research methodology provides for the rich gathering of data and rich analyses for introducing a new theoretical framework that cannot be found in previous research.

Many scholars have already pointed out the effectiveness of case studies (e.g., Eisenhardt, 1989; Pettigrew, 1990; Yin, 1994). Case studies are a highly effective methodology for explaining the relationship between causes and results of phenomena and their appropriateness from multiple perspectives and interpretations through deep insights based on objective qualitative information and the researchers' subjective interpretation regarding individual cases, which cannot be obtained from statistical methods. Case studies are important not only in complementing generality through statistical methods but also in constructing novel, creative theories.

The case study in this article focuses on research questions relating to boundaries knowledge (knowing) in managing innovation in companies and provides an in-depth analysis and observations regarding how that boundaries knowledge (knowing) achieved innovation activities. In creating and analyzing the in-depth case studies of Toyota and Panasonic, semi-structured interviews of 1–2 hours were conducted with Toyota's executives (2), managers (4), staff (2), stakeholder companies (managers: 3), local governments (managers: 2), and Panasonic's executives (2), managers (5), staff (3), stakeholder companies (managers: 4), local governments (managers: 2), and residents (2). Additionally, publicly available external materials and press releases from Toyota and Panasonic were also utilized as secondary data.

Based on the above research approach, this chapter first outlines the prior research on knowledge creation theory (SECI model) and boundaries knowledge. Next, it presents the conceptual model of "knowledge creation through boundaries knowledge synchronization," followed by an analysis and discussion of this model based on the in-depth case studies of Toyota's smart city and Panasonic's smart town. Finally, new insights from the in-depth case studies, implications, and conclusions are presented.

6.3 Prior Research on Knowledge Creation Theory (SECI Model) and Boundaries Knowledge

6.3.1 SECI Model Promoting Knowledge Creation Through Convergence

The SECI model posits that knowledge is created through interactions that convert tacit knowledge, rooted in individual experiences, into explicit knowledge that can be systematically shared. This spiral process enhances the quality and quantity of knowledge for both individuals and organizations (see Fig. 6.2). The SECI model consists of four phases, beginning with "Socialization." For example, through direct experiences in interactions with customers, business partners, and various internal departments such as sales, development, and manufacturing, practitioners perceive diverse tacit knowledge embedded in the environment, including experiential and heterogeneous knowledge. However, to systematically share this tacit knowledge, which is a fusion of experiential and heterogeneous knowledge, it must be verbalized. The next phase, "Externalization," involves transforming this tacit knowledge into explicit knowledge through analogies, metaphors, inferences, and dialogues, converting it into language, concepts, and images.

To crystallize the concept further, it is essential to analyze and systematize it by combining it with other explicit knowledge (existing explicit knowledge or newly discovered explicit knowledge) through "Combination." This involves processing it into forms accessible to everyone, such as documents, databases, and theoretical models. Specifically, this phase involves designing and manufacturing concrete technologies, products, software, and services using IT/AI from the concept. In the final phase, "Internalization," actions are taken based on the new designs, manufacturing, and services, and these are introduced to the market as concrete products, services, and technologies. Through this process, individuals acquire new tacit knowledge (tacit knowledge that integrates experiential knowledge and heterogeneous knowledge). Simultaneously, the value and new meanings mediated by the products stimulate tacit knowledge in customers and external partners, leading back to "Socialization."

In relation to innovation, succinctly put, stakeholders such as customers who embody the living market share their tacit knowledge (Socialization). This tacit knowledge is then elevated into concepts through essential dialogues that transcend organizational boundaries (Externalization). Utilizing IT/AI, this knowledge is systematized across time and space (Combination), crystallizing into technologies, products, software, services, and business models, and internalized as know-how (Internalization). Simultaneously, the knowledge stimulates new knowledge among market stakeholders, leading back to (Socialization).

In the knowledge creation theory (SECI model), knowledge has two dimensions: "tacit knowledge" and "explicit knowledge." These two dimensions continuously convert into each other, creating new knowledge. Knowledge creation activities involve the mutual conversion process between tacit knowledge, derived from an individual's body, thoughts, and feelings, and explicit knowledge, which is verbalized. Although these two dimensions are contrasting, they are continuous. An individual's tacit knowledge is shared with others and becomes explicit knowledge, which is then combined with other explicit knowledge to create new explicit knowledge. This new explicit knowledge is converted back into an individual's tacit knowledge, leading to the next conversion process. Innovation arises from this spiral-up of the conversion process.

The promotion of this spiral-up (synthesis and sublation of tacit knowledge and explicit knowledge) is driven by the third type of knowledge, phronesis (Nonaka et al., 2014). Phronesis, a concept proposed by the ancient Greek philosopher Aristotle in "Nicomachean Ethics," is translated as "Prudence" or "Practical Wisdom" (Aristotle, 1980). Phronesis is a practical way of knowing that involves purpose, value, and action, characterized by the value criterion of the "Common Good." It is practical knowledge with embodiment that allows for the best judgment in each specific context. It features "Contemplation in Action," "contextual judgment," and "timely and exquisite balance."

According to Nonaka et al. (2014) in "Dynamic Fractal Organizations for Promoting Knowledge-Based Transformation—A New Paradigm for Organizational Theory," the SECI process in excellent companies and organizations presents tacit knowledge as the first type of knowledge, explicit knowledge as the second, and practical knowledge (phronesis) as the third type that drives the spiral loop. In Nonaka et al. (2014), the concepts of mutual conversion between tacit knowledge and explicit knowledge and phronesis were previously considered separately. However, phronesis is now positioned as the third type of knowledge that promotes the spiral-up of tacit and explicit knowledge, referred to as the "knowledge triad relationship" (see Fig. 6.2).

However, in Nonaka's Theory (Nonaka & Takeuchi, 1995; Nonaka et al., 2008), there has not been a deep discussion on the processes of "knowledge integration" (Tacit → Tacit, Explicit → Explicit) and "knowledge transformation" (Tacit → Explicit, Explicit → Tacit) in the boundary areas of the four phases of the SECI process.

For example, the relationship between tacit knowledge and explicit knowledge is sometimes compared to the two sides of a coin, but their boundary is dynamic and cannot be clearly separated, resembling a gradient with varying shades. When using the iceberg metaphor to describe the relationship between tacit knowledge and explicit knowledge, the visible part above the water represents explicit knowledge, while the much larger mass hidden below the surface represents tacit knowledge. The boundary between the two is constantly changing due to the movement of the iceberg and the waves (Nonaka, 2016). In other words, "boundaries knowledge" refers to the knowledge generated from the constantly shifting boundary between tacit and explicit knowledge, as mentioned by Nonaka (2016) (see Fig. 6.2).

Additionally, Polanyi (1962) mentions that in the process of "tacit knowledge integration" (tacit knowledge → tacit knowledge), which involves relating dispersed elements of tacit knowledge to inductively infer a consistent and comprehensive whole and generate new meanings, "boundaries knowledge" exists between different elements of tacit knowledge.

Nonaka (2016) states that practitioners' acts and methods of "knowing" are all produced by the capabilities of "tacit knowledge integration," which can be considered skills of invention, discovery, and creation. For such "tacit knowledge integration," it is crucial to create new meanings through the recognition of knowledge differences and the creation of boundaries knowledge. In this context, the creation of boundaries knowledge enables the integration of diverse tacit knowledge (tacit knowledge → tacit knowledge) and plays a role in generating new tacit knowledge.

Furthermore, as illustrated by the iceberg metaphor in Fig. 6.2, it is evident from a science and engineering perspective that "boundaries knowledge" exists between different elements of explicit knowledge, even in the context of explicit knowledge integration (explicit knowledge → explicit knowledge). The presence of such "boundaries knowledge (knowing)" facilitates the realization of "tacit knowledge integration and explicit knowledge integration" and "knowledge transformation (tacit knowledge → explicit knowledge) and (explicit knowledge → explicit knowledge)."

Therefore, the boundary areas in the knowledge integration and knowledge transformation processes of Socialization, Externalization, Combination, and Internalization in Fig. 6.2 lie in "boundaries knowledge (boundaries knowing)." To effectively drive the SECI model within groups and organizations, it is essential for organizational members, including stakeholders to create, share, and empathize with boundaries knowledge. For this purpose, the concept and practice of "boundaries knowledge synchronization" among stakeholders, as explained in the following sections, become crucial.

6.3.2 Overview of Previous Research on Boundaries Knowledge

According to previous studies (Kodama, 2018, 2019, 2020), "boundaries knowledge (knowing)" and "boundaries vision" are crucial elements driving the spiral loop of the SECI model (see Fig. 6.3). As mentioned earlier, practitioners recognize various boundaries in their daily business activities. These boundaries are composed of actors with different backgrounds and knowledge, as well as stakeholders, including the environment.

Carlile (2004) refers to three characteristics of knowledge at these boundaries: deference, dependency, and novelty (Carlile & Rebentisch, 2003). He mentions that these correlated characteristics of knowledge can be represented by imagining boundaries as vectors between two or more actors. This vector starts from a point where deference and dependency are known, and as novelty increases, the knowledge difference expands.

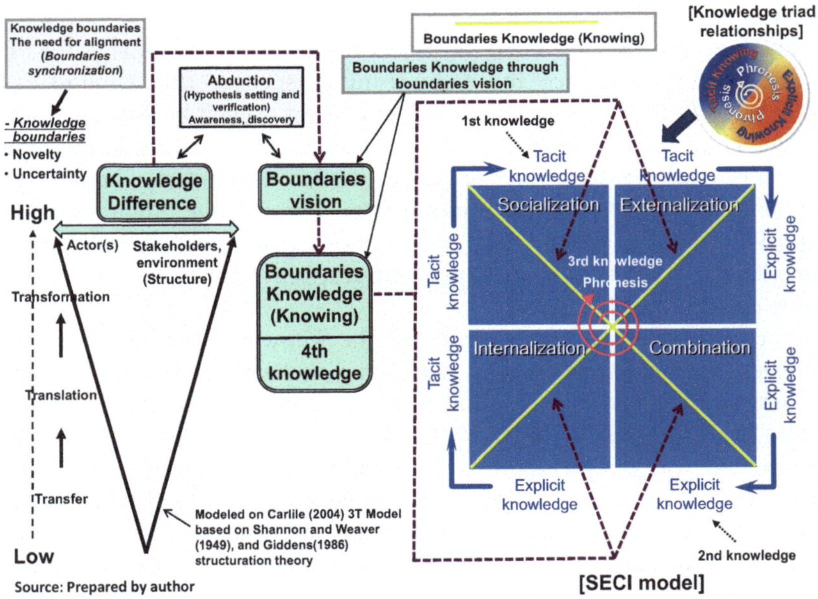

Fig. 6.3 Knowledge difference, Boundaries vision, Boundaries knowledge, SECI model

This signifies an increasing degree of effort in knowledge creation activities aimed at achieving greater complexity and innovation. As Kodama (2019, 2020) mentions, this vector model can be extended not only to the relationships between actors (stakeholders) but also to the interactions between actors and the environments they face (such as markets and technologies) (see Fig. 6.3).

The background of this vector model extension lies in Giddens' (1984) structuration theory. He raised the issue of how the dialectical interaction between the actions of actors and social forces shapes society. His argument is that actors continuously reproduce social structures (environments) as agents of change. In other words, actors are closely intertwined with social structures (environments), and humans, while influenced by the environment, also have the agency to change it. Therefore, as novelty increases, the degree of interaction between actors and the environment (structure) and knowledge differences increase, leading to a greater degree of effort in knowledge creation activities aimed at innovation in the environment (structure).

Carlile (2004) applied Shannon and Weaver's (1949) communication theory to this vector model by incorporating three levels of boundaries, developing the 3 T (Transfer [Syntactic boundary] → Translation [Semantic boundary] → Transformation [Pragmatic boundary]) model, also known as the 3 T model. When considering Giddens' (1984) structuration theory, this model is illustrated as shown in Fig. 6.3 (Kodama, 2019).

In environments where individuals, organizations, and companies face the necessity of innovation and significant challenging tasks, novelty and uncertainty increase rapidly. This means that the knowledge difference, which is the vector spread in knowledge boundaries between actors and the environment (structure), as well as among actors including stakeholders, expands both qualitatively and quantitatively. In such high-novelty situations (Transformation level [Pragmatic boundary]), actors and stakeholders can achieve new knowledge creation by transforming existing knowledge. In the words of A. Giddens, actors actively transform the environment through practices based on their "knowledgeability" (Carlile, 2004).

On the other hand, it has been shown that new knowledge creation through many innovations occurs at the boundaries between specialized fields (Leonard-Barton, 1995). This proposition suggests that the thinking and organizational behavior of individuals spanning different specialized fields are key factors in successfully achieving innovation and contributing to competitive advantage. Furthermore, previous research has clarified why it is difficult to create and sustain innovation (Carlile, 2004). It has also been reported that the thinking and organizational behavior of individuals spanning different specialized fields are constrained by path dependency of knowledge (March, 1972; Rosenkopf & Nerkar, 2001). For example, it has traditionally been recognized that it is easier to concentrate exploratory activities in closely related specialized fields.

In response to emerging novelties (for example, technological evolution and potential market changes in the form of new product Architectures and business models), existing organizations face not only the learning costs of such novelties, but also the cost of transforming their "current" knowledge in use (sector-specific knowledge core capabilities). These costs will negatively affect the motivation of the parties of existing companies to perform such knowledge transformation. This tends to make them path-dependent, leveraging the core capabilities they have accumulated in the past, even though the presence of novelty (which requires the acquisition of new knowledge to address) is important for existing companies (Carlile, 2004).

As novelty increases, common knowledge (or mutual knowledge) (e.g., Carlile, 2002; Cramton, 2001; Star & Griesemer, 1989) used in the past among members of an organization (Cramton, 2001) may not have the capacity to represent the new novelty faced (Carlile & Rebentisch, 2003), suggesting that path dependency of knowledge (March, 1972) has a negative effect (Hargadon & Sutton, 1997). In particular, Carlile (2004) notes that problematic scenarios often occur when path-dependent knowledge that constrains new knowledge representing the novelty faced or required capabilities is reused by parties with power in existing organizations. Therefore, if the novelty faced is not recognized, and if there is no development of new and sufficient knowledge to address the novelty and the ability of the parties to utilize knowledge and resolve the novelty, the long-term consequences for existing organizations will be the generation of potential and costly problems or, as in this case, the downsizing or withdrawal of existing business. On the other hand, it has been reported that deep communication and collaboration processes between specialized fields significantly contribute to new innovations (Kodama, 2012; van Rijnsoever & Hessels, 2011).

However, to promote such communication and collaboration, it is crucial to identify and effectively manage the knowledge boundaries perceived by individuals and organizations. Additionally, it is necessary to have the capabilities to understand how boundary knowledge, acquired from the heterogeneity and knowledge differences at various boundaries, can become the source of new knowledge creation.

Generally, people often feel discomfort at unfamiliar boundaries (boundaries with unfamiliar and heterogeneous content), and the perceptual and cognitive abilities at such boundaries vary from person to person. In other words, the cognitive ability of "explicit knowing" and the non-cognitive ability of "tacit knowing" differ among individuals. The creation of "boundary knowledge" requires aligning the knowledge boundaries among actors (different stakeholders). Especially when actors face unknown challenges or difficult problems, convergence toward pragmatic boundaries is necessary. This alignment of boundaries is referred to in this chapter as "boundary synchronization" (see Fig. 6.3).

To reiterate, "boundaries knowledge" refers to the capabilities of practitioners to identify and understand the differences and heterogeneity at various boundaries (people, organizations, customers, environments). It also encompasses the practitioners' abilities to derive new insights from these differences. Additionally, the capabilities to identify various boundaries, connect them, and inspire new perspectives and ways of understanding also fall under "boundaries knowledge." This involves questions such as "Why do differences arise?", "How can contradictions be resolved or reconciled?", and "How can common goals among stakeholders be identified and set?" Practitioners are required to have the constructive ability to set hypotheses that aim for true goals (objectives). For this, practitioners' specific thinking and actions are rooted in "abduction" (e.g., Anderson, 1986).

According to previous studies (Kodama, 2019, 2020), the knowledge differences that arise between the hypothesis setting aimed at goals through such abduction and the verification results can induce awareness and discoveries through "boundaries vision." This enhances the possibility of generating "boundaries knowledge (knowing)," which is the "fourth knowledge" with new meaning (see Fig. 6.3).

Abduction begins with the detection of facts, but it requires practitioners to have a strong sense of purpose. By focusing based on their beliefs and thoughts, observing details (parts), and synthesizing them into a whole, new hypotheses are born. Abduction involves detecting subtle signs and changes in individual real-world events, synthesizing all relevant knowledge, and creating bold hypotheses. Through trial and error, these hypotheses are tested, refined, and renewed, leading to new discoveries. This process of abduction differs from traditional deductive and inductive methods.

The "boundaries knowledge" generated from hypothesis setting and verification through abduction is not static but dynamic. The creation of such "boundaries knowledge" is essential for the source of new knowledge creation. This "boundaries knowledge" integrates and transforms different knowledge in the SECI model, becoming the most fundamental element for creating new knowledge (see Fig. 6.3).

Dynamic "boundaries knowledge (boundaries knowing)" works in conjunction with "boundaries vision" (Kodama & Shibata, 2016), producing differences in discomfort and heterogeneity at boundaries. For practitioners, this leads to new insights, discoveries, and knowledge. The capabilities to identify various boundaries, connect them, and inspire new perspectives and ways of understanding also correspond to the process of "boundaries knowledge through boundaries vision" (see Fig. 6.3).

6.4 Driving the SECI Model Through Boundaries Knowledge Synchronization Centered on Boundary Architects—Theoretical Conceptual Model

Kodama (2021) mentions that practitioners' phronesis generates boundaries knowledge, driving the dynamic exchange of tacit and explicit knowledge for convergence (the so-called SECI model). The creation of boundaries knowledge (tacit knowledge or explicit knowledge that identifies heterogeneity and differences at boundaries) promotes knowledge integration and knowledge transformation at each stage of the SECI process: socialization, externalization, combination, and internalization (see Figs. 6.2 and 6.3). The creation of boundaries knowledge is not only required by top management but also by many middle managers and staff. This chapter refers to the central actors in this knowledge creation process as "Boundary Architects."

Boundary Architects and other actors demonstrate boundaries vision and create new boundaries knowledge. Furthermore, these actors build multilayered Ba by synthesizing various dynamic contexts. Based on the philosophy of phronesis, these actors understand what should be done for the common good, possess high aspirations, determine what is good for society as a whole, and construct a knowledge creating company model that organically links individual elements such as knowledge vision, driving objectives, dialogue and practice, SECI, knowledge assets, and environment (Kodama, 2021; Nonaka & Toyama, 2005). Through this model, they create new knowledge via the SECI model.

However, it is not clear at the micro level how the SECI process dynamically functions within a multilayered Ba formed among multiple stakeholders. It is hypothesized that the creation and sharing of boundaries knowledge trigger each stage of the SECI process. However, different stakeholders are likely to perceive and recognize different boundaries knowledge individually.

Each stakeholder has different experiences from various backgrounds and holds different perspectives on new knowledge (e.g., heterogeneous knowledge). Therefore, stakeholders will have different boundaries knowledge due to their perception and recognition of knowledge differences. Thus, to drive the SECI process, it is necessary to find common knowledge (Kodama, 2007) from different boundaries knowledge and create, share, and empathize with common boundaries knowledge. This perspective has not been discussed in previous studies (Kodama, 2019; Nonaka et al., 2014).

In particular, to creatively and productively resolve conflicts and frictions observed between different departments within an organization, it is necessary to create and share common boundaries knowledge among stakeholders. Therefore, as mentioned next, it is important to embody the concept of "boundaries knowledge synchronization" to promote the creation, sharing, and empathy of boundaries knowledge among different stakeholders.

However, as mentioned earlier, how the SECI process dynamically functions within the multilayered Ba formed among multiple stakeholders has not been clarified at the micro level in previous studies. In each stage of the SECI process, the creation and sharing of boundaries knowledge act as triggers. However, as previously mentioned, different stakeholders are likely to perceive and recognize different boundaries knowledge individually.

Regarding such issues, stakeholders need to demonstrate boundaries vision, create boundaries knowledge, and attempt to align the knowledge boundaries (pragmatic, semantic, and syntactic boundaries, which exist depending on the situation) that stakeholders face, as shown in Fig. 6.4, through the formation of multilayered Ba (Carlile, 2004; Kodama, 2019). Stakeholders should practice thinking and acting to find common interest (e.g., Dalkir, 2013) and common knowledge from the individual boundaries knowledge that different stakeholders possess (boundaries knowledge generated by pragmatic boundaries faced in innovation tasks or problem-solving tasks).

For the alignment of knowledge boundaries (pragmatic boundaries) among stakeholders, it is necessary to alleviate tensions through creative confrontations or abrasion (Leonard-Barton, 1995), productive friction (Hagel & Brown, 2005), political negotiating practice (Brown & Duguid, 2001), and strategic contradictions (Smith & Tushman, 2005), and to integrate through abductive synthesis of the extremes (e.g., Kodama, 2007) (see Fig. 6.4).

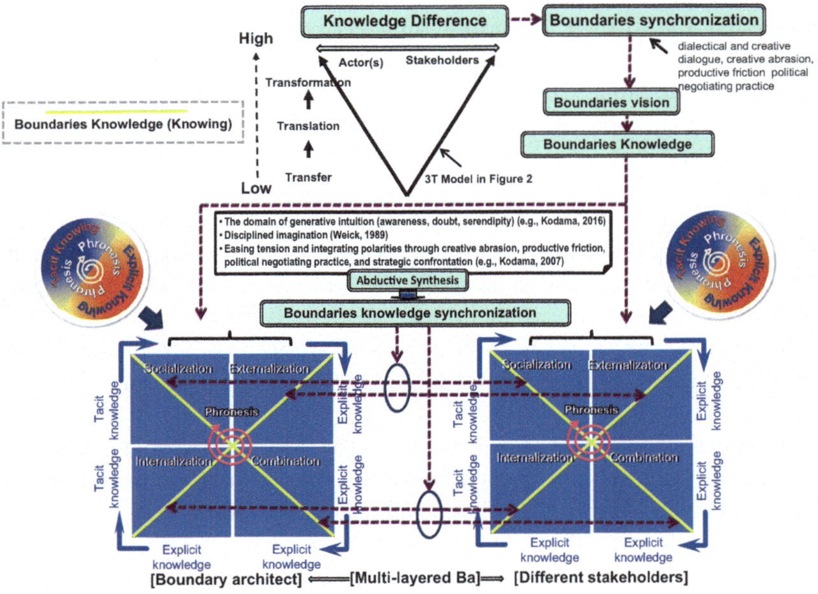

(Note) Prepared by the author

Fig. 6.4 Boundaries synchronization, boundaries knowledge synchronization in SECI model

To achieve abductive synthesis, stakeholders must exhibit new insights, generative doubt (Weick, 2001), intuitive abilities such as sensitivity (Kodama, 2007, 2016), and serendipity (e Cunha et al., 2015). Additionally, through the formation of multilayered Ba, stakeholders need to mutually learn and recognize these different boundaries of knowledge, exercise disciplined imagination (Weick, 1989), and create and share common boundaries of knowledge among stakeholders (see Fig. 6.4).

In other words, stakeholders must understand, learn, and integrate different boundaries of knowledge through the process of abductive synthesis and share them among different stakeholders. As a result, the boundaries of knowledge created through the formation of multilayered Ba will be shared and empathized among different stakeholders. This practical process is referred to as "boundaries knowledge synchronization" (see Fig. 6.4).

Boundary architects play a central role in creating boundaries knowledge through the formation of multilayered Ba, while also striving to align the knowledge boundaries held by stakeholders (corresponding to the aforementioned "boundaries synchronization"). They practice thinking and actions to find common interests (e.g., Dalkir, 2013) and common knowledge from the individual boundaries of knowledge held by different stakeholders. Through this, stakeholders will mutually learn and recognize these different boundaries of knowledge through the formation of multilayered Ba, creating and sharing common boundaries of knowledge among stakeholders.

In other words, boundary architects are responsible for integrating and sharing different boundaries of knowledge among different stakeholders. As a result, the boundaries of knowledge created by boundary architects will be shared and empathized among different stakeholders. This practical process is referred to as "boundaries knowledge synchronization" in this chapter (see Fig. 6.4).

Furthermore, this practical process allows the SECI process to dynamically resonate through the creation and sharing of common boundaries knowledge by stakeholders, who are individual actors possessing distributed phronesis. This resonance generates collective phronesis for the entire group of actors (or stakeholders). Simultaneously, the formation of collective phronesis triggers the creation of a dynamic fractal organization, with the core knowledge (previously mentioned as the "knowledge triad relationship") being the distributed phronesis held

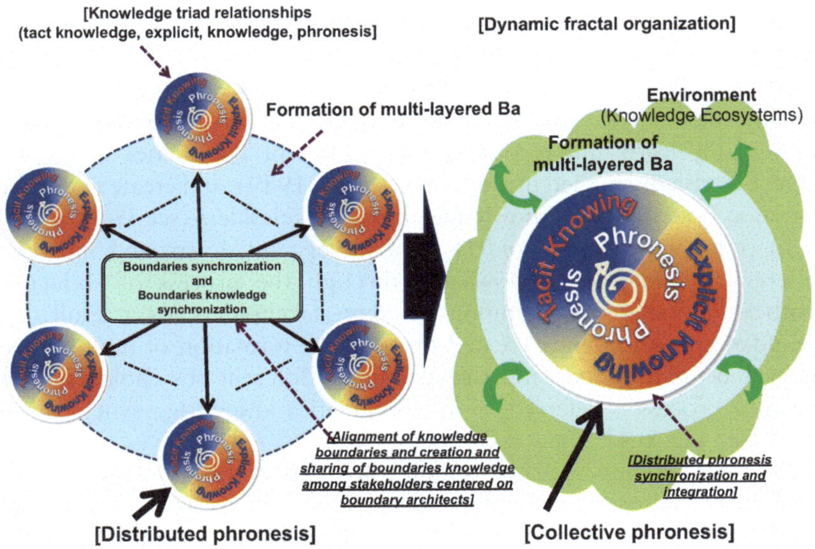

(Note) Prepared by the author

Fig. 6.5 Formation of collective phronesis and dynamic fractal organizations through boundaries knowledge synchronization—a conceptual model

by individual actors. Thus, in this chapter, the concepts of "boundaries synchronization" and "boundaries knowledge synchronization" are considered key elements in forming collective phronesis and dynamic fractal organization (see Fig. 6.5).

In this chapter, we will verify this conceptual model through in-depth case studies.

6.5 In-depth Cases Analysis

As global concern over the issue of global warming intensifies, there is a growing momentum to address this problem through the development of new technologies and the creation of innovations. The construction of smart cities and smart towns is seen as one such initiative. A smart city is an environmentally conscious urban area that aims to optimize social infrastructure, such as electricity, water, communication, and transportation systems, by utilizing ICT to reduce energy consumption and carbon dioxide emissions. Furthermore, the construction of such cities is expected to solve various urban issues, including population growth, aging, traffic congestion, and security.

In this chapter, as previously mentioned, we analyze case studies of smart cities centered around Toyota and smart towns centered around Panasonic. We find that the success of these projects requires a knowledge creation process (SECI model) that realizes technological integration (knowledge integration). Our analysis shows that the drivers promoting this SECI process lie in the boundaries knowledge created, shared, and empathized among different stakeholders. We consider that the elements promoting the creation, sharing, and empathy of such boundaries knowledge are the practical processes of "boundaries knowledge synchronization."

6.5.1 Toyota Case (Woven City)

The concept of Toyota's Woven City began with the idea of utilizing the site of Toyota Motor East Japan's Higashi-Fuji Plant. Former President Akio Toyoda announced the project at CES 2020 in January 2020, and construction began in February 2021. Woven City is based on the concepts of a "human-centered city," a "living laboratory," and an "ever-evolving city," aiming to "mass-produce happiness" through continuous improvement (see Fig. 6.6). This project focuses on the evolution of mobility (autonomous vehicles, micromobility, and a road network for pedestrians with different speeds), sustainable energy (utilizing solar energy, geothermal energy, and hydrogen fuel cell technology to achieve a carbon–neutral society), smart homes (practical application of robot technology to support daily life using AI technology and sensors), and the development of autonomy, connectivity, hydrogen energy infrastructure, and industrial cooperation. It also serves as a testing ground for Toyota's autonomous driving technology and smart logistics.

Several challenges existed in realizing Toyota's Woven City. Technically, infrastructure development was necessary to demonstrate new technologies such as autonomous driving and smart logistics. The first challenge was the demonstration of autonomous driving technology, requiring tests in real-life environments to ensure the safety and reliability of autonomous vehicles. The second challenge was smart logistics, necessitating the construction of an efficient logistics system, including the development of new logistics models using autonomous vehicles and robots. The

[Toyota's Smart City]

Philosophy:
•**Human-Centered:** Woven City prioritizes people's happiness and well-being.
•**Co-Creation:** Residents and inventors collaborate to generate new ideas and technologies.
•**Sustainability:** The city aims for a sustainable future by utilizing environmentally friendly technologies and energy sources.
Goals:
•**Expanded Mobility:** Providing efficient and enjoyable movement for people, goods, information, and energy, offering inspiring mobility experiences.
•**Accelerated Technological Innovation:** Promoting the development of new technologies and services, redefining future mobility.
•**Engagement with Society:** Residents and visitors experience new technologies firsthand, providing real-time feedback and fostering co-creation.

[Panasonic's Smart Town]

Philosophy:
•**Multi-Generational Coexistence:** Creating a community where people of all ages, from children to the elderly, live together and support one another.
•**Health Promotion:** Supporting residents' health to achieve vibrant and healthy lives.
•**Sustainability:** Promoting environmentally friendly city development by utilizing renewable energy.
Goals:
•**Energy Sustainability:** Covering the entire city's electricity consumption with renewable energy, aiming for carbon neutrality.
•**Safe and Secure Living:** Ensuring residents' safety through high-performance town cameras and AI technology.
•**Healthy Lifestyle:** Providing health promotion programs based on residents' physical constitution and vital data.

(Note) Photo publication has been approved by the copyright side.

(Note) Prepared by the author

Fig. 6.6 Toyota's Smart City and Panasonic's Smart Town

third challenge was the establishment of next-generation communication technology, requiring the development of high-speed and stable communication infrastructure, particularly important for IoT devices and autonomous vehicles. The fourth challenge was energy management, involving the use of renewable energy and the introduction of efficient energy management systems. The fifth challenge was data security, requiring security measures to safely manage and utilize large amounts of data. To overcome these challenges, Toyota has conducted extensive technological development and demonstration experiments.

Socially, cooperation with local residents and municipalities was essential, particularly affecting the finances and employment in Susono City. The first social challenge was the anxiety of local residents, who were concerned about the project's impact and lack of information, particularly regarding traffic congestion and security issues. The second challenge was the revitalization of the local economy, requiring the activation of the local economy and job creation associated with the utilization of the Higashi-Fuji Plant site. The third challenge was addressing the needs of the elderly, requiring the provision of mobility and care to accommodate the increasing elderly population. The fourth challenge was the diversity of residents, necessitating the creation of an environment where diverse residents, including the elderly, families with children, and inventors, could coexist. To address these challenges, Toyota deepened understanding through dialogue and briefings with local residents and proceeded with the project.

In terms of economic challenges, securing project funding and managing costs were crucial, especially for large-scale urban development projects that required significant investment. The realization of Toyota's Woven City faced the following economic challenges:

(1) **Revitalizing the Local Economy**: Utilizing the site of the former Higashi-Fuji Plant required efforts to revitalize the local economy and create jobs.
(2) **Investment Costs**: Building a massive futuristic city required substantial investment, making funding and cost management critical issues.
(3) **Attracting Companies**: It was important to clearly define the benefits for companies entering Woven City and to successfully attract them.
(4) **Technological Development and Demonstration**: Creating an environment for technological development and demonstration, such as autonomous driving and smart logistics, was necessary. To address these challenges, Toyota actively promoted cooperation with local residents and companies.

In addition to project management within Toyota, collaboration with external partners was required to achieve various technological innovations. The realization of Toyota's Woven City faced the following organizational challenges:

(1) **Collaboration with Local Residents**: It was necessary to explain and gain understanding of the concerns and questions of local residents.

(2) **Integration of Diverse Technologies**: Organizational coordination was needed to integrate and conduct demonstration experiments with various technologies, such as autonomous driving, AI, and robotics.
(3) **Cooperation Among Companies**: Coordination was required to smoothly advance collaboration with many companies and research institutions.
(4) **Project Management**: Managing the progress and schedule of an unprecedented large-scale project was a challenge.

To overcome these challenges, Toyota actively promoted cooperation with local residents and companies.

As a distinctive measure in organizational strategy, open innovation played an important role in realizing Toyota's Woven City. Toyota worked with companies like ENEOS and NTT to build energy management systems and smart city platforms.

(1) **Collaboration with ENEOS**: Toyota and ENEOS jointly promoted the production and use of CO_2-free hydrogen in Woven City. Specifically, they built and operated hydrogen stations and produced and supplied hydrogen derived from renewable energy.
(2) **Collaboration with Woven Planet Holdings**: Toyota's subsidiary, Woven Planet Holdings, worked on building a hydrogen supply and demand management system and supplying hydrogen to fuel cell vehicles (FCEVs).
(3) **Collaboration with Other Partner Companies**: Toyota also collaborated with companies like Nissin Foods and Rinnai to conduct demonstration experiments on smart logistics and next-generation remote communication products.

Furthermore, Toyota and NTT, Japan's largest telecommunications carrier, have established the following collaborations to realize Woven City:

(1) **Joint Construction of a Smart City Platform**: Both companies are jointly building and operating a "Smart City Platform" responsible for data management and information distribution in the smart city.

(2) **Utilization of Next-Generation Communication Technologies**: NTT plans to experiment with and implement next-generation communication technologies such as "Beyond 5G" and "IOWN" in Woven City.
(3) **Capital and Business Alliance**: To commercialize the smart city business and build a long-term, continuous cooperative relationship, both companies have entered into a capital and business alliance. This aims to realize Woven City as a smart city utilizing advanced IT technologies.

Additionally, Toyota is promoting the participation of various inventors, including startups, developers from other companies, and residents, to jointly develop future technologies. As part of the Global Open Innovation Program, Toyota Research Institute-Advanced Development (TRI-AD) collaborates with partners worldwide to demonstrate new technologies. These collaborations make Woven City a "multi-layered Ba" where diverse technologies and ideas converge.

The challenges of a project composed of diverse stakeholders, such as Woven City, lie in the implementation of concrete incubation through trial and error of the constructed services and platforms, as well as the devised products and services, and the realization of a reliable commercialization process. To promote these incubations and commercialization, Toyota's leaders, known as boundary architects, act as central figures in project promotion, executing incubation planning and scheduling. This allows them to extract the necessary issues for incubation using their valuable core knowledge.

An important point in this incubation process is to incorporate specific strategies and tactics, such as the content and implementation methods of customer monitoring in the actual field. Numerous experiments were conducted in the actual field through knowledge creation activities (SECI process) among collaborative partners within the multilayered Ba, centered around the boundary architects. Through surveys and interviews with many customers, the project aimed to verify the validity of new systems and business models while enhancing the quality of products and services for commercialization.

In such incubation, the execution of a dynamic SECI process, which involves learning and creation processes among diverse stakeholders, including residents and municipalities within the multilayered Ba, was crucial for knowledge innovation. Specifically, existing knowledge held by each member, including boundary architects, was shared and mutually inspired and proliferated, recognizing mutual knowledge differences, creating boundary knowledge to achieve strategic goals, and sharing and empathizing with this knowledge among members (stakeholders).

As boundary architects, Toyota's leaders played a crucial role in integrating and sharing diverse boundaries knowledge among different stakeholders. This process, known as "boundaries knowledge synchronization," facilitated the sharing of boundaries knowledge created by the boundary architects among various stakeholders. The synchronization of boundaries knowledge creation and sharing aligned the dynamic SECI processes of each stakeholder, fostering the creation of new knowledge to achieve strategic goals and promoting the organizational sharing and accumulation of this knowledge. Simultaneously, this practical process allowed the distributed phronesis of individual actors (stakeholders) to dynamically resonate through the SECI process, leading to the emergence of collective phronesis among all actors (stakeholders).

However, as mentioned earlier, several challenges and issues arose in the conceptualization of Toyota's Woven City. The introduction of advanced technologies brought about friction and potential delays in implementation. Additionally, there were economic and employment issues related to the utilization of the site after the factory's withdrawal. A significant lack of information about the specific plans and impacts of Woven City was also noted among local residents and stakeholders. Concerns about traffic congestion and security issues were particularly prominent among the local community. Consequently, Woven Planet (a Toyota subsidiary) and Susono City held multiple explanatory meetings for local residents to address their concerns and questions. Based on the feedback, Toyota planned a phased move-in, initially accommodating about 360 residents. Efforts were made to attract companies related to autonomous driving technology and energy to revitalize the local economy. Furthermore, open demonstration experiments were promoted, creating an environment where various companies and researchers could conduct experiments. By addressing these challenges, Toyota overcame obstacles and advanced the Woven City project in collaboration with the local community.

Additionally, Toyota's Woven City project faced several challenges and criticisms from external parties. Positioned as an "experimental city," there was internal pressure within the Toyota Group to avoid failure. Consequently, the project relied on consulting firms with urban development experience. Despite advocating for agile development, external critiques pointed out that this philosophy was not fully practiced. In Susono City, Shizuoka Prefecture, where Woven City is being constructed, issues arose related to reduced tax revenue and job losses following the closure of Toyota's factory, complicating relations with the local community. To address these diverse challenges and issues, Toyota promoted flexibility and deep dialogue with the local community, facilitating the four phases of the knowledge creation process.

As shown in Figure 6.4, "boundaries knowledge synchronization" through "boundaries synchronization" among different stakeholders synchronized the dynamic SECI processes of each stakeholder. Stakeholders created new knowledge to achieve strategic goals and promoted the organizational sharing and accumulation of this knowledge (see Figure 6.4). For example, the SECI process through the creation, sharing, and empathy of boundaries knowledge via "boundaries knowledge synchronization" can be explained as follows (see Figure 6.7).

(1) **Socialization (S) Stage (Tacit knowledge → Tacit Knowledge: Tacit Knowledge Integration Process)**

To achieve the desired tacit knowledge, Toyota and various stakeholders needed to integrate diverse tacit knowledge based on accumulated experiences and know-how through the "knowledge integration process" (tacit knowledge → tacit knowledge). Recognizing "knowledge differences" and generating "boundaries knowledge" from them became crucial. In other words, "boundaries knowledge" drove the new "(Tacit) knowledge integration process." These newly generated "boundaries knowledge" was incorporated into new hypotheses, leading to the discovery and creation of new tacit knowledge through the reconstruction and reintegration of diverse tacit knowledge, aiming for a significant refinement/renewal of hypotheses (see Fig. 6.4).

As mentioned earlier, Polanyi (1962) referred to the process of relating dispersed elements of tacit knowledge to infer a consistent, comprehensive whole inductively and create new meanings as "tacit knowledge integration." On the other hand, Nonaka (2016) mentioned that practitioners' acts and methods of "knowing" are all generated by the capabilities of "tacit knowledge integration," which can be considered skills of invention, discovery, and creation. For such "tacit knowledge integration," it

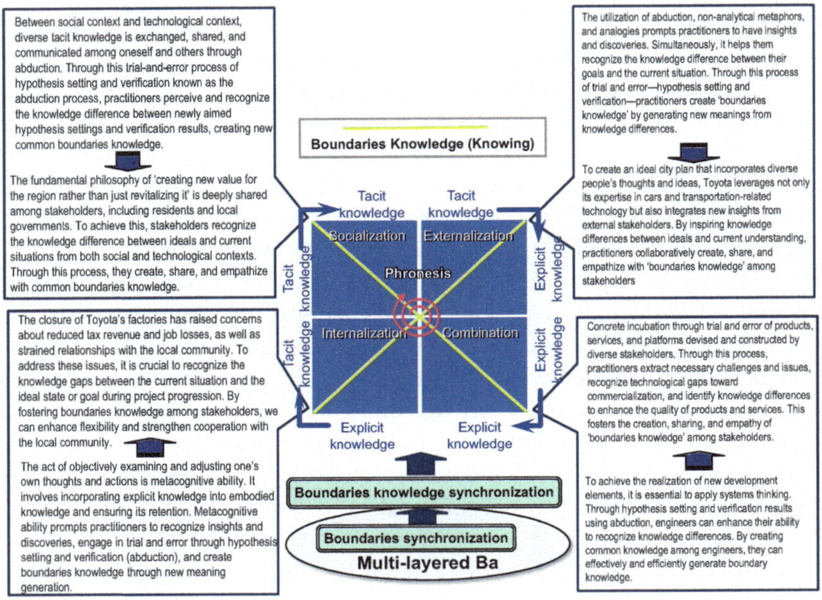

(Note) Prepared by the author

Fig. 6.7 The creation, sharing, and empathy of boundaries knowledge in the Woven City project

is essential to create new meanings through the generation of "boundaries knowledge" by recognizing the previous "knowledge differences." Here, the generation of "boundaries knowledge" enables the integration of diverse tacit knowledge (tacit knowledge → tacit knowledge) and plays a role in creating new tacit knowledge (see "Socialization" in Fig. 6.4).

From this perspective, Toyota and various stakeholders demonstrated the capabilities of "boundaries vision" (Kodama & Shibata, 2016) to discover, perceive, recognize, and create new "boundaries knowledge" through abductive spiral interactions between social and technical contexts (and between these macro and micro-level contexts) for realizing Woven City (see Figs. 6.2 and 6.3). Creative dialectical dialogues (Kodama, 2007) such as "Is this the image of the products and services that residents truly want?", "The initial impression is quite different from the reality!", and "Wouldn't it work if we did this here?" were conducted between Toyota and various stakeholders (sometimes including residents) through direct experiences in the abstract space (living world domain). In this abstracted time and space of the images, the beliefs and thoughts of Toyota and various stakeholders clashed. Toyota and stakeholders achieved "boundaries synchronization," converging on pragmatic boundaries.

Specifically, the fundamental philosophy of "creating new regional value rather than regional regeneration" was deeply shared among stakeholders, including residents and local governments. To realize this, Toyota and various stakeholders recognized the knowledge differences between ideals and the current situation from social and technical contexts and promoted the creation, sharing, and empathy of common boundaries knowledge among diverse stakeholders through "boundaries knowledge synchronization."

(2) **Externalization (E) Stage (Tacit Knowledge → Explicit Knowledge: Knowledge Transformation Process)**

The use of metaphors and analogies prompted awareness and discoveries for Toyota and various stakeholders, simultaneously making them recognize "knowledge differences." Through the generation of new meanings from these "knowledge differences," Toyota and various stakeholders, through an abductive process of hypothesis setting and testing, created "boundaries knowledge" via "boundaries synchronization" aimed at convergence on pragmatic boundaries.

To achieve the desired explicit knowledge, it was crucial for Toyota and various stakeholders to appropriately recognize the "knowledge differences" based on their accumulated experiences and know-how, and further generate "boundaries knowledge" through the "knowledge transformation process" (tacit knowledge → explicit knowledge). In other words, the "boundaries knowledge" generated from the interpretation of technical possibilities (e.g., differences from the product and service development processes previously realized by Toyota and stakeholders, which are also "knowledge differences") drove the new "knowledge transformation process" (see "Externalization" in Fig. 6.4).

Specifically, in creating an ideal city plan incorporating various people's thoughts and ideas, not only Toyota's expertise in car and transportation-related technologies but also new insights from external stakeholders' products and services were integrated. The "boundaries knowledge" inspired by the knowledge gap (knowledge difference) between the ideal and reality was created, shared, and empathized through "boundaries synchronization" and "boundaries knowledge synchronization" aimed at convergence on pragmatic boundaries among Toyota and various stakeholders.

(3) Combination (C) Stage (Explicit Knowledge → Explicit Knowledge: Explicit Knowledge Integration Process)

To realize new development elements, it is necessary to discover and create boundaries knowledge from the knowledge differences between different explicit knowledge. Identifying such new development elements requires a systems thinking approach (e.g., Kodama, 2019) and an abductive process of hypothesis setting and testing, where the knowledge differences between hypotheses and test results are stimulated. As a result of this process, Toyota and various stakeholders can create boundaries knowledge based on formalized knowledge differences and drive the "(explicit) knowledge integration process" (explicit knowledge → explicit knowledge) (see "Combination" in Fig. 6.4).

The ability to accurately identify new development elements in the Combination domain and the creativity to generate boundaries knowledge are related to the "common knowledge" (e.g., Carlile, 2002; Cramton, 2001; Star & Griesemer, 1989) of Toyota and various stakeholders. The presence of common knowledge is necessary for Toyota and various stakeholders to acquire domain-specific knowledge required for the development of new products and services. Common knowledge promotes knowledge sharing and knowledge inspiration (Kodama, 2007) among Toyota and various stakeholders with different expertise. At the same time, Toyota and various stakeholders enhance their ability to recognize knowledge differences and effectively and efficiently create boundaries knowledge through "boundaries synchronization" and "boundaries knowledge synchronization" aimed at convergence on pragmatic boundaries.

Thus, the discovery and creation of boundaries knowledge enabled the integration of diverse explicit knowledge. By incorporating boundaries knowledge into the integration process of accumulated diverse explicit knowledge, combination is achieved. The integration of explicit knowledge not only forms a cohesive knowledge system but also leads to the creation of new knowledge and concepts, such as the smart platform for Woven City, by combining diverse explicit knowledge.

Specifically, the concrete incubation of product and service platforms conceived and constructed by Toyota and various stakeholders was carried out through trial and error. Through this process, necessary issues and problems were identified, and technical gaps for commercialization were recognized. Furthermore, boundaries knowledge derived from knowledge differences to improve the quality of products and services was discovered, and boundaries knowledge was created, shared, and empathized through "boundaries synchronization" and "boundaries knowledge synchronization" aimed at convergence on pragmatic boundaries among Toyota and various stakeholders.

(4) **Internalization (I) (Explicit Knowledge → Tacit Knowledge: Knowledge Transformation Process)**

To accumulate high-quality tacit knowledge within individuals and organizations, the process of abduction through "reflective practice" (Nonaka & Takeuchi, 1995; Schon, 1987) is crucial. Ichiro Suzuki, a renowned Major League Baseball player, mentioned that he feels as if there is another self watching his batting and bunting form. This suggests that he continuously improves by logically and objectively assessing his actual movements, imagining his ideal form and body movements, and feeding back boundaries knowledge through the differences (also known as "knowledge differences").

The act of objectively observing and correcting one's thoughts and actions is known as "metacognitive ability" (e.g., Haynie et al., 2012). This ability allows practitioners to internalize theoretically considered explicit knowledge as bodily knowledge. Such metacognitive ability encourages new insights and discoveries among practitioners, simultaneously making them aware of "knowledge differences." Through the new meaning generated from these "knowledge differences," Toyota and various stakeholders, via the abduction process of hypothesis setting and testing through trial and error, created "boundaries knowledge" through "boundaries synchronization" and "boundaries knowledge synchronization" aimed at convergence on pragmatic boundaries. The knowledge differences and boundaries knowledge generated through reflective practice in the "Internalization" phase drive the "knowledge transformation process," leading to the accumulation of high-quality tacit knowledge, which is a source of differentiation, among Toyota and various stakeholders as practitioners (see "Internalization" in Fig. 6.4). Thus, boundaries knowledge generated from new meanings derived from "knowledge differences" is an element that produces high-quality tacit knowledge, a source of differentiation.

On the other hand, issues such as reduced tax revenue and job losses due to the closure of Toyota's factories have surfaced, and the relationship with the local community has also become a challenge. In response to these issues and challenges, Toyota and various stakeholders recognized the knowledge gaps between the current state and the ideal form or goals during the project's progress and promoted "boundaries synchronization" among stakeholders to converge on pragmatic boundaries to deepen cooperation with the local community. Through "boundaries knowledge synchronization," boundaries knowledge was created, shared, and empathized.

6.6 Panasonic Case (Suita Sustainable Smart Town)

The Suita Sustainable Smart Town (Suita SST) is a sustainable smart town project utilizing former factory sites based on Panasonic's Corporate Real Estate (CRE) strategy (see Fig. 6.6). Following the Fujisawa SST in Fujisawa City and the Tsunashima SST in Yokohama City, this project is being promoted in partnership with Suita City, Osaka Prefecture, to create a next-generation smart town and disseminate it widely both domestically and internationally. The stakeholders, including local governments and Panasonic, aim to achieve decarbonization and address the challenges of a super-aging society. Instead of focusing solely on traditional infrastructure design, the project proposes a sustainable smart life centered around people, enhancing the value of living spaces and time.

Specifically, the project aims to achieve carbon neutrality by powering the town with renewable energy. By continuously capturing the ever-changing needs of individuals and providing optimal services, it seeks to create a healthy and vibrant future. In the Sustainable Smart Town, stakeholders centered around Panasonic aim to solve social and regional issues by introducing a co-creation mechanism involving partner companies, residents, local governments, and universities. They develop and trial next-generation solutions in energy, security, mobility, wellness, and community, contributing to regional value enhancement and proposing various town development initiatives.

At the time, there were several challenges and issues in realizing the Suita Sustainable Smart Town. Achieving multi-generational living was a challenge, as limiting it to only permanent residents could fix the population dynamics and potentially reduce regional vitality. To address this, family condominiums, senior condominiums, and shared housing for single individuals were established, creating an environment where diverse generations could coexist. Achieving carbon neutrality was also a significant challenge. Balancing the supply and consumption of renewable energy and ensuring stable energy supply was difficult. To address this, solar power generation was introduced, and renewable energy was supplied from Kansai Electric Power, aiming to realize a 100% renewable energy town. Furthermore, promoting regional coexistence was an important issue, requiring the enhancement of regional value and the formation of resident communities. To address this, the project collaborated with health and medical town development, establishing interaction parks and wellness complexes to promote interaction among residents and enhance regional unity.

In addressing the challenges toward realizing Suita SST, Panasonic's first initiative was to coordinate and collaborate with diverse stakeholders, including local residents and government bodies. Specifically, they facilitated coordination among 15 cross-industry companies and the city of Suita. Achieving consensus and shared goals among companies from different sectors was challenging, and the coordination of their specialized expertise and visions was crucial. Additionally, streamlining administrative procedures and regulations with the local government in Suita was necessary and sometimes impacted the project's progress. Furthermore, effective coordination was required to understand the needs of the diverse residents and provide services and infrastructure accordingly.

The redevelopment of the former Panasonic-owned factory site required changes and adjustments to the land use plan. This occasionally caused temporary delays in the project's progress. Additionally, during the design and construction of new buildings and facilities, adjustments were necessary to ensure compliance with building codes and other relevant regulations. Environmental considerations also played a role, necessitating compliance with regulations related to renewable energy adoption and energy efficiency improvements. As a result, additional investment in facilities and technical adjustments were required.

Furthermore, community engagement and explanatory meetings were required, including addressing various challenges. As a result, there were temporary delays in the project timeline. However, through understanding and cooperation with local residents, Panasonic and other stakeholders contributed to the long-term success of the project. These adjustments and collaborations laid the foundation for smooth project progress, closely coordinated between Suita City, Panasonic, and various stakeholders.

Additionally, there were technical and operational challenges related to achieving technology convergence (knowledge convergence). As a prerequisite for advancing the project, there was a need to meet the condition of powering the entire city with 100% renewable energy—a concept known as the "Renewable 100 Town." Specific technical challenges included ensuring energy resilience, designing systems to secure power even during outages, and implementing area-wide power reception systems to mitigate blackout risks across the entire city. Another critical aspect was the implementation of security systems. To achieve an accurate and efficient town security system, collaboration with security camera image analysis technology and security services was essential.

In order to promote the health and well-being of residents, it was challenging to introduce new technologies and solutions for health enhancement and early detection of cognitive decline. Furthermore, efforts were required to achieve sustainable urban development, aiming for carbon neutrality and a well-being of society.

To address the underlying conditions, stakeholders from various companies worked on the technical challenges necessary to integrate the technologies and solutions they provided, enabling the entire smart town to function. Panasonic, along with other cross-industry companies, tackled the technical challenges required to make various technologies and solutions work together seamlessly for the smart town as a whole. In this way, Panasonic collaborated closely with each company and Suita City to drive the project forward through co-creation, overcoming numerous issues and challenges.

The first characteristic of the co-creation project is the diverse partnerships mentioned earlier. Fifteen advanced companies collaborate with Suita City, and cross-industry enterprises work together to drive the project. Secondly, the project aims to address social and regional challenges by developing and trialing solutions in next-generation energy, security, mobility, wellness, and community domains. Thirdly, it emphasizes community-based urban development, with residents, local government, administration, and universities cooperating to enhance local value. Fourthly, the project focuses on sustainable energy use, achieving a "100% Renewable Energy Town" by maximizing the utilization of renewable energy sources to cover the entire city's electricity consumption. Lastly, Suita SST promotes health and well-being, supporting residents' health improvement and early detection of cognitive decline. Through diverse partnerships and community-driven co-creation, Suita SST strives for a sustainable and healthy urban environment.

The role of the Suita Sustainable Smart Town (SST) is to actively seek solutions to surrounding social issues and environmental changes without turning a blind eye, and to implement those solutions into daily life. For example, being a pioneer in achieving carbon neutrality is one such endeavor. The SST project members believe that the true start comes not from groundbreaking ceremonies but from continuous "co-creation," where the city evolves sustainably, enhancing local value. In Suita SST, all members involved in community development work together with the shared goal of ongoing evolution.

The central role in promoting co-creation projects like this lies with the "Suita Sustainable Smart Town Council." This council, which includes 15 organizations and the city of Suita, collaborates with a wide range of stakeholders, including businesses from various fields (real estate, gas, electricity, health, railways, telecommunications, finance, security, construction, etc.), residents, local government, universities, and partner companies. Together, they develop and trial next-generation technologies and solutions related to energy, security, mobility, wellness, and community.

At Suita SST, the intention is to enhance the overall value of the city by creating diverse value through such collaboration. While this aligns with Panasonic's strategy, value creation is not solely the work of Panasonic alone. Through collaboration between Panasonic and its 15 partner companies, co-creation will lead to the generation of diverse value, facilitated by the formation of a "multi-layered Ba."

The generation of a "multi-layered Ba," achieved through co-creation among diverse entities similar to the form of a council, corresponds to the formation of an organizational platform for realizing new knowledge creation. The concept of "Ba" is crucial when considering processes where different entities intersect and give rise to value creation and innovation. The concept of "Ba" was originally proposed by the Japanese philosopher Kitaro Nishida in 1965. Additionally, Nonaka and Takeuchi (1995) positioned "Ba" as one of the essential elements for generating new knowledge within their knowledge creation theory, introducing the concept of "Ba" into the field of management for the first time.

In the case of Suita Sustainable Smart Town (SST), various multi-layered "Ba" were formed during the process of city generation and construction, involving participation from Panasonic, partner companies, the city of Suita, and residents. Each participant in the Ba brought different knowledge, values, and interests. By aligning knowledge boundaries (converging toward pragmatic boundaries) among stakeholders (equivalent to "boundaries synchronization" in Fig. 6.4), common boundaries knowledge was discovered across diverse pragmatic boundaries. This synchronization of knowledge boundaries accelerated the SECI process, leading to the creation of new ideas and knowledge (see Fig. 6.8).

In Suita SST, companies participating in the project become members of the council and drive the project with this organization at its core. The council is led by Panasonic, the project leader, serving as the representative secretariat and overseeing the organization's operations. While Panasonic takes on a leading role in driving the Suita SST project based on its strategic vision, it is not involved in every aspect of the project. Due to its background as an electronics manufacturer, Panasonic does not possess extensive expertise in urban development like Suita SST. The project is led by Panasonic, but it also serves as a space for value co-creation among participating project members.

Panasonic recognizes that it cannot create value for Suita SST on its own, and it expects value co-creation to occur among other participating members. To achieve this, the role of the Suita SST Council, to which all project participants belong, is crucial. The Suita SST Council serves as a "multi-layered Ba" where the intellectual resources—such as technology and know-how—of project participants collide, interact, and merge. The concept of "Ba" is extremely important when examining the processes of knowledge creation and value co-creation. It goes beyond a mere physical location; it also encompasses the mental aspects shared by people, such as values, intentions, and bonds.

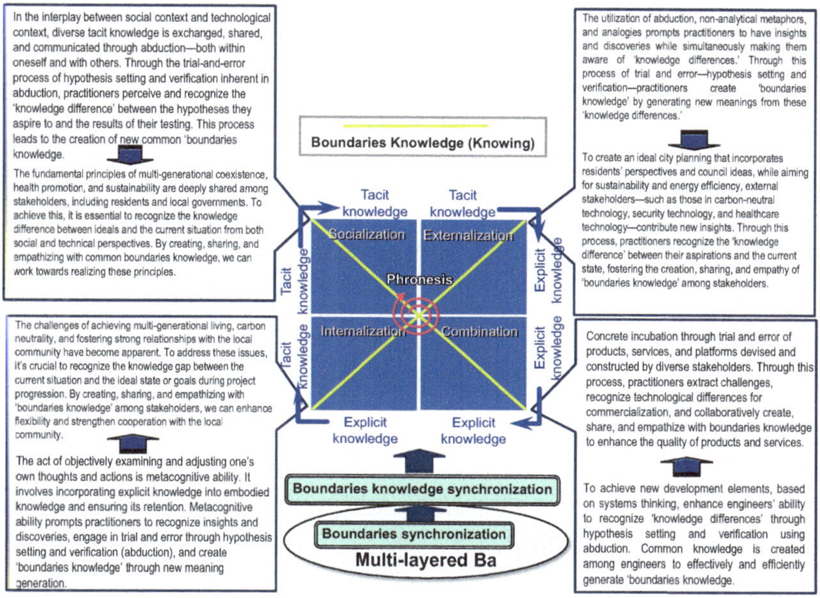

(Note) Prepared by the author

Fig. 6.8 The creation, sharing, and empathy of boundaries knowledge in the Suita SST Project

If there is no shared purpose among the members gathered in a meeting room, even conducting a lengthy meeting there won't yield meaningful value. On the other hand, when individuals are connected by shared values and intentions, even if they are physically distant, meaningful value can emerge through communication channels. In other words, the concept of a "place" extends beyond mere physical locations like meeting rooms; it encompasses a broad range of relational connections based on shared meaning (Tokoro, 2015, 2018, 2020).

In order for a "Ba" to come alive and for vibrant interactions to occur among its participants, certain requirements must be present within that "Ba." These requirements include respecting the autonomy of participating members and having a leader who steers the "Ba." The leader referred to here corresponds to what was previously mentioned as "Boundary Architects." It is crucial that the autonomy of participating members is respected, and that those engaged in the "Ba" have the right to freely express their opinions and take action.

At first glance, it may seem entirely natural, but in reality, there are often various reasons why such rights are not guaranteed. One common scenario is when a few influential members take charge of a "Ba" and compel other members to comply. If project planning and management are determined solely by the preferences of specific members, and dissenting opinions are not allowed, free exchange among members becomes difficult, ultimately hindering meaningful value creation. Additionally, situations where power dynamics in business relationships—such as capital ties or transactional dependencies—prevent open communication among members can also have a negative impact on value creation.

In the context of the previously mentioned actors (stakeholders), "boundaries synchronization" is crucial. For instance, even when pragmatic convergence among stakeholders is necessary, there can be instances of "knowledge boundary mismatch" when specific influential individuals emphasize semantic or syntactic boundaries. Achieving "boundaries synchronization" requires ensuring the autonomy of participating members. To achieve this, Panasonic, as the leading company in the project, encourages open and free discussions and exchanges among stakeholders. While providing overall guidelines, Panasonic also adopts an attitude that relies on the intellectual resources of other members for specific domains, fully understanding that exchanging intellectual resources among stakeholders leads to the creation of new value. Consequently, Panasonic provides ample opportunities for each stakeholder to contribute fully.

What kind of existence are the "Boundary Architects," who are leaders? As mentioned earlier, the "Ba" should not constrain the statements or actions of participating members; it is necessary to ensure the autonomy of the participating members. However, on the other hand, this also carries the risk of disorder or discussions without clear direction within the "Ba," which could lead not to value creation but rather serious conflicts of interest. To avoid such situations, there is a need for entities that appropriately steer the process of intellectual resource exchange among members and guide it toward value creation rather than conflict of interests. The "Boundary Architects," as leaders, fulfill precisely this role.

6.7 New Insights from Case Studies

6.7.1 Collective Phronesis and Dynamic Fractal Organization

To provide new products and services to customers, especially in the context of technologies like ICT, companies must consider both product/service/business model marketing and development from the customer's perspective. Additionally, it's crucial for companies to absorb various feedback, opinions, requests, and criticisms related to their relevant products and services.

One particularly important perspective involves forming a "multi-layered Ba" through active dialogue and collaboration within boundary architects. These boundary architects include not only corporate leaders from companies like Toyota and Panasonic but also stakeholders such as vendor leaders. Together, they have built technology platforms for new smart cities and smart towns. The outcomes of such activities centered around Ba have become essential elements in co-creation efforts.

For residents, local governments, and stakeholders including Toyota and Panasonic, the initial challenge lies not only in mutual communication among stakeholders but also in actively engaging with local communities and residents through project participation and dialogues. Rather than unilaterally establishing products or business models as was common in the era of mass production and sales, the focus now is on conceptualizing new business models and products/services through dialogue among stakeholders.

In other words, boundary architects consider each partner company, local government, and resident as integral members of the corporate team. Together, they collaboratively construct the concepts for business models and products/services. An essential perspective here is to resonate the visions and values—whether related to achieving new product concepts or realizing innovative business models—between boundary architects and development project leaders from both the corporate side and the local community, including residents.

In particular, in the cases of Toyota and Panasonic, achieving smooth progression through each stage of the SECI model required recognition of "knowledge differences," as depicted in Figure 6.4. Additionally, alignment of knowledge boundaries among different stakeholders, including boundary architects within the 3T model, was crucial. Here, various dialogues and actions—such as dialectical and creative dialogue, creative confrontations or abrasion (Leonard-Barton, 1995), productive friction (Hagel & Brown, 2005), and political negotiating practice (Brown & Duguid, 2001)—played a significant role. These interactions helped synchronize knowledge boundaries among stakeholders within the 3T model, ultimately fostering empathy and resonance across diverse stakeholders (refer to Figure 6.4).

However, as mentioned in Figure 6.4, boundary architects such as Toyota and Panasonic primarily play a role in creating "boundaries knowledge" through "boundaries vision." The creation and sharing of "boundaries knowledge" among stakeholders become essential drivers of the SECI process. In this case, during each stage of the SECI model by various stakeholders, the formation of a multilayered Ba among team members facilitated the sharing of boundaries knowledge. This synchronization of SECI processes at the same speed and pace allowed for knowledge integration and transformation (from tacit knowledge to tacit knowledge, tacit knowledge to explicit knowledge, explicit knowledge to explicit knowledge, and explicit knowledge to tacit knowledge), corresponding to what we can term "boundaries knowledge synchronization."

Furthermore, this "boundaries knowledge synchronization" not only aligned distributed phronesis among boundary architects and different stakeholders through the formation of multilayered Ba but also generated integrated collective phronesis across all organizational members. Simultaneously, the "knowledge triad relationships" model—comprising tacit knowledge, explicit knowledge, and phronesis—expanded to encompass the entire organization, leading to the establishment of a dynamic fractal organization (refer to Fig. 6.9).

6.7.2 Entrepreneurship Process of Social Innovation

In the context of social innovations such as Toyota's Woven City and Panasonic's Suita SST, which aim for sustainable economic development in urban planning (e.g., Van der Have & Rubalcaba, 2016), the process of new business creation (commercialization) involves multiple diverse stakeholders. Key to this process is the dynamic nature of the SECI model. Leaders (Boundary Architects) from Toyota and Panasonic, driving these projects, exhibit "social intrapreneurship" (e.g., Aparicio et al., 2020) and take on roles related to corporate social responsibility (CSR). However, when faced with environmental changes, mismatches in knowledge boundaries often arise among stakeholders due to differences

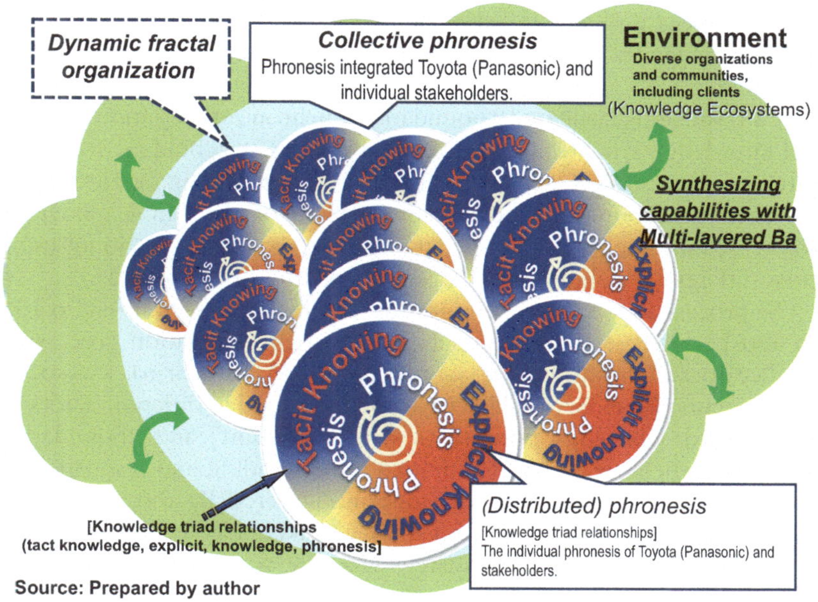

Fig. 6.9 Phronesis, collective phronesis and dynamic fractal organization

in perception and recognition. This can make the process of transforming existing knowledge into new knowledge challenging.

In these two cases, boundary architects at the core of projects within Toyota and Panasonic played a crucial role. Faced with complex environmental changes, they exhibited "boundaries vision" that transcended diverse boundaries. Their vision was rooted in the idea and vision that people worldwide should benefit from smart cities and smart towns. These boundary architects appropriately identified the "knowledge differences" perceived and recognized by various stakeholders, inspiring and creating new "boundaries knowledge" based on their own perceptions.

Furthermore, acting as integral members of the knowledge ecosystem, these actors—representing different stakeholders—worked toward forming a multilayered Ba. Through repeated dialogues and practical interactions, they discovered "common knowledge" and "common interest" across different stakeholders. As a result, this shared "boundaries knowledge" was created, shared, and resonated among the actors (stakeholders).

As a result, this facilitated "boundaries synchronization" and "boundaries knowledge synchronization" among various stakeholders, fostering mutual understanding and resonance of values among actors. Such a process contributes to the dynamic nature of the SECI model in project advancement, ultimately accelerating collaborative innovation across different stakeholders (e.g., as described by Kodama, 2015).

The process aimed at new business development (as seen in Fig. 6.10) can also be interpreted as a model explaining the realization process of so-called social innovation (e.g., Voorberg, 2015). In their roles as social entrepreneurs, boundary architects—those who bridge different actors—work toward achieving "boundaries synchronization" and "boundaries knowledge synchronization" for mutual understanding and resonance of values. To do this, they form dynamic multilayered Ba through which the SECI process is synchronized among stakeholders. By integrating distributed phronesis, they ultimately give rise to collective phronesis, enabling the realization of a dynamic fractal organization (refer to Fig. 6.10).

6.8 Implications and Conclusion

In this chapter, we presented a novel theoretical model called "boundaries knowledge synchronization" and delve into in-depth case studies of smart cities centered around Toyota in Japan and smart towns centered around Panasonic. These urban planning initiatives aim for sustainable economic development. The importance of fostering creativity across generations—whether within profit-oriented or non-profit organizations, corporate entities, broader social organizations, or even individual people—is self-evident.

Especially in recent years, collaboration activities with diverse stakeholders, including social endeavors, have been encouraged in the business domain (e.g., Kodama, 2015, 2018). Within this context, there is heightened interest in different areas: creating new products and services that differentiate from competitors, developing novel businesses across various fields, and aligning with Sustainable Development Goals (SDGs). The focus lies on "knowledge convergence" (Kodama, 2014) and "knowledge transformation" (Nonaka et al., 2014), where innovative ideas

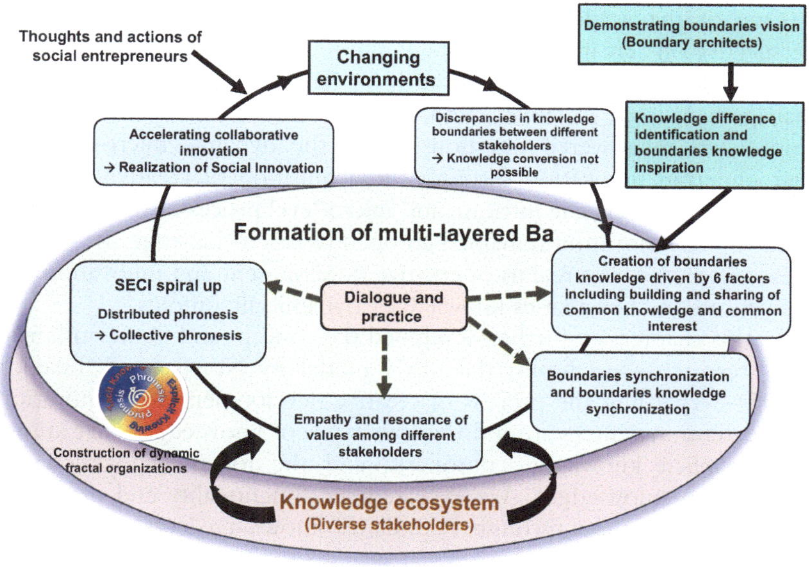

(Note) Prepared by the author

Fig. 6.10 Entrepreneurial process model for new business development

for new products, services, and business models emerge through the fusion of knowledge from disparate domains. Consequently, organizations promoting social business, not just corporations, are emphasizing talent development with a creative mindset (e.g., Kodama, 2021).

In this chapter, we focus on the concept of "knowledge difference" that arises among diverse "different things or concepts" within interactions between individuals, organizations, and various stakeholders. Through observing collaboration processes among different stakeholders, we analyze and discuss the mechanisms behind the creation and sharing of "boundaries vision" and "boundaries knowledge" (or "boundaries knowing"). These emerge from how humans perceive, notice, and discover things. Furthermore, we explore in-depth case studies to reveal that "boundaries knowledge," generated across human interactions, organizations, and diverse contexts, involves a mechanism known as "boundaries knowledge synchronization." This synchronization process facilitates knowledge creation across different stakeholders.

One of the academic contributions of this chapter lies in a fresh perspective on "creative development and innovation." Research on "creativity" has accumulated significantly in fields such as psychology and management (e.g., Amabile, 1988, 1995). However, many of these prior studies left unanswered questions about the dynamic micro-processes that underpin innovation through the acquisition of creativity. Specifically, understanding the intricate and micro-level processes that lead from creativity to innovation remained an open research challenge. It is within these micro-dynamic realms of creative development and innovation that the process of "boundaries knowledge" dynamically unfolds.

In this chapter, we further developed the concept and framework from prior research—specifically, the SECI model by Nonaka and Takeuchi (1995)—regarding the process of creative development and innovation. This extension centers around the four types of knowledge: tacit knowledge, explicit knowledge, phronesis, and the fourth type known as "boundaries knowledge." We explored the functionality and process of "knowledge creation through boundaries knowledge" (as proposed by Kodama, 2019, 2020).

In particular, our in-depth case studies reveal that successful collaboration processes among different stakeholders require the practical process of "boundaries knowledge synchronization." This process involves creating "boundaries knowledge" and facilitating its sharing and resonance among stakeholders. Ultimately, this contributes to promoting knowledge creation activities.

As a second theoretical contribution, this chapter has shed light on the formation mechanisms of "collective phronesis" (Kodama, 2021) and "dynamic fractal organization" (Nonaka et al., 2014)—concepts previously not fully explored in existing research. By introducing novel concepts related to the fourth type of knowledge, namely "boundaries knowledge," specifically "boundaries synchronization" and "boundaries knowledge synchronization," we revealed these mechanisms.

The backdrop for this theoretical contribution lies in the pivotal role played by Boundary Architects—those central to knowledge creation activities. They facilitate the creation of "boundaries knowledge" through "boundaries vision" and promote the sharing of this knowledge among various stakeholders. In doing so, they become essential drivers of the SECI process.

Through in-depth case studies, multilayered Ba was formed among team members at each stage of the SECI model for various stakeholders. This facilitated "boundaries synchronization" between stakeholders, resulting in the sharing of "boundaries knowledge." Furthermore, stakeholders, driven by "boundaries knowledge synchronization," synchronized the SECI process at the same speed and pace. This, in turn, promoted creativity and innovation through knowledge integration and transformation (from tacit knowledge to tacit knowledge, tacit knowledge to explicit knowledge, explicit knowledge to explicit knowledge, and explicit knowledge to tacit knowledge).

Boundaries knowledge synchronization, as described, emerged through the collaborative efforts of boundary architects and diverse stakeholders. By leveraging their distributed phronesis within the formation of multilayered Ba, they achieved synchronization. This process integrated all organizational members into a collective phronesis. Simultaneously, the "knowledge triad relationships" model—comprising tacit knowledge, explicit knowledge, and phronesis—expanded across the entire organization, leading to the establishment of a dynamic fractal organization. In this way, our chapter presents a novel theoretical model by extending a series of concepts and frameworks centered around boundaries knowledge, shedding light on the mechanisms behind collective phronesis and dynamic fractal organization.

In this chapter, we extended the concept and framework related to "boundaries knowledge," which serves as the basis for micro-dynamic creative development and innovation. Through in-depth case studies, we explored the mechanisms behind "collective phronesis" (as proposed by Kodama, 2021) and "dynamic fractal organization" (following Nonaka et al., 2014). Specifically, we introduce novel concepts such as "boundaries knowledge through boundaries vision," "boundaries synchronization," and "boundaries knowledge synchronization."

As we navigate the knowledge society of today and the future corporate landscape, the necessity for these activities extends beyond creative knowledge creation through convergence of diverse knowledge across different values and specialized domains within an organization. They also involve building a global network that connects exceptional individuals and organizations worldwide. By integrating dispersed knowledge from these sources into individual and organizational knowledge, we address the critical challenge of acquiring creativity.

Acquiring creativity serves as a wellspring for valuable products, services, and business models that enhance competitiveness in the knowledge economy. Within this context, human knowledge—of which technology is a crucial element—is a source for generating novel offerings. By merging diverse technologies and transcending various boundaries, new products, services, and business models emerge, often leading to innovative strategic models such as value chains and business ecosystems (e.g., Kodama, 2019, 2021).

On the other hand, when considering human and organizational capacity development and practical processes, traditional organizational learning theory (e.g., Cyert & March, 1963) comes into play. However, it's essential to recognize that learning and creativity are distinct. Learning involves external information that builds new connections, whereas creativity involves the spontaneous exploration and novel associations of previously nonexistent elements. While external stimuli can trigger creative processes, the discovery of solutions remains inherently self-driven and generative. In this context, actors like boundary architects play a crucial role by activating "boundaries vision" from diverse boundaries, thereby creating new "boundaries knowledge."

From a cognitive science perspective, learning involves incorporating new information (and even knowledge) into existing knowledge networks, enriching the network. In contrast, creativity bridges new links between existing networks, especially across heterogeneous networks (e.g., Fauconnier & Turner, 1998). In other words, while learning builds upon existing knowledge, creativity draws from novel combinations—akin to convergence—across diverse elements (e.g., Zhou & Shalley, 2007). These triggers for linking and bridging reside within the elements of "boundaries knowledge through boundaries vision." Moreover, achieving innovation through organizational creative processes, especially across different stakeholders, necessitates thoughtful practice related to "boundaries synchronization" and "boundaries knowledge synchronization" for actors.

Looking ahead, expanding research on "creative development and innovation" should cut across various fields such as management, economics, sociology, psychology, arts, natural sciences, engineering, and medicine. Theoretical and practical efforts should focus on nurturing "creative talent" capable of significantly contributing to society (by realizing innovation). Simultaneously, interdisciplinary research is essential for achieving "knowledge convergence (knowledge creation)" across different research domains (humanities, social sciences, natural sciences, etc.) and enabling "creative-oriented development and innovation" that spans diverse stakeholders and industries (e.g., collaborative innovation, as discussed by Kodama, 2015).

References

Amabile, T. M. (1988). A model of creativity and innovation in organizations. *Research in Organizational Behavior, 10*(1), 123–167.

Amabile, T. M. (1995). Attributions of creativity: What are the consequences? *Creativity Research Journal, 8*(4), 423–426.

Anderson, D. R. (1986). The evolution of Peirce's concept of abduction. *Transactions of the Charles S. Peirce Society, 22*(2), 145–164.

Aparicio, S., Turro, A., & Noguera, M. (2020). Entrepreneurship and intrapreneurship in social, sustainable, and economic development: Opportunities and challenges for future research. *Sustainability, 12*(21), 8958.

Aristotle. (350BCE/1980). *The Nicomachean Ethics*. (David Ross, trans.). Oxford University Press.

Brown, J. S., & Duguid, P. (2001). Knowledge and organization: A social-practice perspective. *Organization Science, 12*(2), 198–213.

Carlile, P. (2002). A pragmatic view of knowledge and boundaries: Boundary objects in new product development. *Organization Science, 13*(4), 442–455.

Carlile, P. (2004). Transferring, translating, and transforming: An integrative framework for managing knowledge across boundaries. *Organization Science, 15*(5), 555–568.

Carlile, P. R., & Rebentisch, E. S. (2003). Into the black box: The knowledge transformation cycle. *Management Science, 49*(9), 1180–1195.

Christensen, C. M. (1997). *The innovator's dilemma: When new technologies cause great firms to fail*. Harvard Business School Press.

Cramton, C. D. (2001). The mutual knowledge problem and its consequences for dispersed collaboration. *Organization Science, 12*(3), 346–371.

Cyert, R. M., & March, J. G. (1963). *A behavioral theory of the firm* (pp. 169–187). Prentice-Hall.

Dalkir, K. (2013). *Knowledge management in theory and practice*. Routledge.

e Cunha, M. P., Rego, A., Clegg, S., & Lindsay, G. (2015). The dialectics of serendipity. *European Management Journal, 33*(1), 9–18.

Eisenhardt, K. (1989). Building theories from case study research. *Academy of Management Review, 14*, 532–550.

Fauconnier, G., & Turner, M. (1998). Conceptual integration networks. *Cognitive Science, 22*(2), 133–187.

Giddens, A. (1984). *The constitution of society*. Polity Press.

Hagel, J., III., & Brown, J. S. (2005). Productive friction: How difficult business partnerships can accelerate innovation. *Harvard Business Review, 83*, 82–91.

Hargadon, A., & Sutton, R. I. (1997). Technology brokering and innovation in a product development firm. *Administrative Science Quarterly*, 716–749.

Haynie, J. M., Shepherd, D. A., & Patzelt, H. (2012). Cognitive adaptability and an entrepreneurial task: The role of metacognitive ability and feedback. *Entrepreneurship Theory and Practice, 36*(2), 237–265.

Kodama, M. (2006). Knowledge-based view of corporate strategy. *Technovation, 26*(12), 1390–1406.

Kodama, M. (2007). *The strategic community-based firm*. Palgrave Macmillan.

Kodama, M. (2011). *Knowledge integration dynamics—Developing strategic innovation capability*. World Scientific Publishing.

Kodama, M. (2012). *Competing through ICT capability: Innovation in image communication*. Springer.

Kodama, M. (2014). *Winning through boundaries innovation: Communities of boundaries generate convergence*. Peter Lang.

Kodama, M. (Ed.). (2015). *Collaborative innovation: Developing health support ecosystems*. Routledge.

Kodama, M. (2016). *Interactive business communities: Accelerating corporate innovation through boundary networks*. Routledge

Kodama, M. (2018). Boundaries innovation through knowledge convergence-developing triad strategic communities. *Technology Analysis & Strategic Management, 30*(5), 609–624.

Kodama, M. (2019). Boundaries knowledge (knowing)—A source of business innovation. *Knowledge and Process Management, 26*(3), 210–228.

Kodama, M. (2020). Developing knowledge communities through video-based information networks. *Knowledge and Process Management, 27*(2), 103–122.

Kodama, M. (2021). Knowledge creation through collective phronesis. *Knowledge and Process Management, 28*(3), 223–245.

Kodama, M., & Shibata, T. (2016). Developing knowledge convergence through a boundaries vision—A case study of Fujifilm in Japan. *Knowledge and Process Management, 23*(4), 274–292.

Leonard-Barton, D. (1995). *Wellsprings of knowledge: Building and sustaining the sources of innovation*. Harvard Business School Press.

March, J. (1972). Model bias in social action. *Review of Educational Research, 42*(4), 413–429.

Nonaka, I. (2016). Cultivating organizational knowledge maneuverability—Tacit knowing, intersubjectivity, distributed leadership (in Japanese). *Hitotsubashi Business Review, 64*(3), 68–85.

Nonaka, I., & Takeuchi, H. (1995). *The knowledge-creating company*. Oxford University Press.

Nonaka, I., & Takeuchi, H. (2019). *The wise company: How companies create continuous innovation*. Oxford University Press.

Nonaka, I., & Toyama, R. (2005). The theory of the knowledge-creating firm: Subjectivity, objectivity and synthesis. *Industrial and Corporate Change, 14*(3), 419–436.

Nonaka, I., Kodama, M., Hirose, A., & Kohlbacher, F. (2014). Dynamic fractal organizations for promoting knowledge-based transformation—A new paradigm for organizational theory. *European Management Journal, 32*(1), 137–146.

Nonaka, I., Toyama, R., & Hirata, T. (2008). *Managing flow: A process theory of the knowledge-based firm*. Palgrave Macmillan.

Pettigrew, A. M. (1990). Longitudinal field research on change: Theory and practice. *Organization Science, 1*(1), 267–292.

Polanyi, M. (1962). *Personal knowledge: Towards a post-critical philosophy*. University of Chicago Press.

Rosenkopf, L., & Nerkar, A. (2001). Beyond local search: Boundary-spanning, exploration, and impact in the optical disk industry. *Strategic Management Journal, 22*(4), 287–306.

Schon, A. (1987). *Educating the reflective practitioner*. Jossey-Bass.

Shannon, C., & Weaver, W. (1949). *The mathematical theory of communications*. University of Illinois Press.

Star, S. L., & Griesemer, J. R. (1989). Institutional ecology, translations' and boundary objects: Amateurs and professionals in Berkeley's Museum of Vertebrate Zoology, 1907-39. *Social Studies of Science, 19*(3), 387–420.

Smith, W., & Tushman, M. (2005). Managing strategic contradictions: A top management model for managing innovation streams. *Organization Science, 16*(5), 522–536.

Tokoro, N. (2015). *The smart city and the co-creation of value: A source of new competitiveness in a low-carbon society*. Springer.

Tokoro, N. (2018). Realization of a health support ecosystem through a smart city concept: A collaborative dynamic capabilities perspective. In *Collaborative dynamic capabilities for service innovation: Creating a new healthcare ecosystem* (pp. 135–151).

Tokoro, N. (2020). The process of creating knowledge between different actors in co-creation ba: A case study of the Panasonic smart city project. In *Developing boundaries knowledge for innovation* (pp. 119–132). Edward Elgar Publishing.

Van der Have, R. P., & Rubalcaba, L. (2016). Social innovation research: An emerging area of innovation studies? *Research Policy, 45*(9), 1923–1935.

Van Rijnsoever, F. J., & Hessels, L. K. (2011). Factors associated with disciplinary and interdisciplinary research collaboration. *Research Policy, 40*(3), 463–472.

Voorberg, W. H., Bekkers, V. J., & Tummers, L. G. (2015). A systematic review of co-creation and co-production: Embarking on the social innovation journey. *Public management review*, *17*(9), 1333–1357.
Weick, K. E. (1989). Theory construction as disciplined imagination. *Academy of Management Review, 14*(4), 516–531.
Weick, K. E. (2001). Leadership as the legitimation of doubt. In *The future of leadership: Today's top leadership thinkers speak to tomorrow's leaders* (pp. 91–102).
Yin, R. K. (1994). *Case study research: Design and methods* (2nd ed.) Sage.
Zhou, J., & Shalley, C. E. (2007). *Handbook of organizational creativity.* Psychology Press.

CHAPTER 7

Holistic Leadership and Dynamic Fractal Organizations to Bring About Collective Phronesis—Comparative Case Studies

7.1 Adaptation Process to Technology Convergence (Knowledge Convergence)

In the twenty-first century, the business environment surrounding companies is undergoing significant changes. Business globalization, rapid technological innovation, the penetration of the internet society, market maturation, price competition, and environmental issues are among the many challenges that business executives and managers face. It goes without saying that companies need to continuously create new products, services, and business models to maintain sustainable competitive advantage and growth over the long term. In particular, the creation of new business models that fundamentally renew existing products and services or transform existing business rules induces significant shifts in corporate strategy. For example, Apple's iPod and iTunes and iPhone, which brought about significant changes in the music distribution business and smartphones, respectively, have formed new value chains in the ICT industry.

To quickly adapt to environmental changes, it is necessary to continuously refine the company's existing core competencies and strengthen its main businesses. This requires incremental innovation through the evolution of capabilities accumulated through daily continuous improvement activities. On the other hand, acquiring the capabilities to promote business development aimed at creating new environments (markets) through

M. Kodama, *Developing Knowledge Convergence Through Collective Phronesis*, https://doi.org/10.1007/978-981-96-4403-2_7

technology convergence (knowledge convergence) requires radical innovation, which involves integrating different knowledge to acquire new core competencies that did not exist before (e.g., Grant, 1996; Kodama, 2005). In particular, "radical innovation" (e.g., Leifer et al., 2000) has provided theoretical and practical guidelines for companies to strategically shift toward new market development and technology creation. The important implication of these innovation strategies is not only to quickly adapt to environmental changes but also to acquire the capabilities to promote business development aimed at creating new environments (markets).

However, while Kodak declined in the photographic film business due to the impact of digitalization, Japan's Fujifilm, which was in the same industry and faced similar circumstances, successfully made a strategic shift to digital business. Kodak recognized the threat posed by market changes due to digitalization early on, but it clung to its existing business in pursuit of maximizing shareholder value and profits. Kodak consistently adopted rigid strategies, such as buying back large amounts of its own stock with abundant funds and taking measures to support its stock price. Moreover, Kodak's top management (including middle management) at the time did not consider challenging new knowledge creation activities in response to environmental changes brought about by digitalization.

Through multiple case studies, this chapter analyzes and examines why superior existing companies' products and business models are encroached upon by new products and business models created by "technology convergence (knowledge convergence)," forcing existing companies to withdraw from the market. The purpose of this chapter is to clarify the theoretical concepts and frameworks that explain the mechanisms by which existing companies cannot adapt to technology convergence (knowledge convergence).

This chapter is structured as follows: First, the research method is discussed. Second, case studies of successes and failures in knowledge convergence are described. Third, the theoretical concepts and frameworks explaining why existing companies cannot respond to technology convergence (knowledge convergence) are clarified from the perspectives of existing research, such as knowledge creation theory (Nonaka & Takeuchi, 1995, 2019) and boundaries knowledge theory (Kodama, 2019). Fourth, new insights obtained from multiple case studies are provided. Finally, managerial implications and conclusions for practitioners are offered.

7.2 Research Method

This research has exploratory aspects of extracting details of certain people and organizations involved in corporate innovation activities, gathering data regarding the leadership processes of their activities, and carefully analyzing these. Therefore, the author has adopted a qualitative survey and case study analysis as their methodology. This research methodology provides for the rich gathering of data and rich analyses for introducing a new theoretical framework that cannot be found in previous research.

Many scholars have already pointed out the effectiveness of case studies (e.g., Eisenhardt, 1989; Pettigrew, 1990; Yin, 1994). Case studies are a highly effective methodology for explaining the relationship between causes and results of phenomena and their appropriateness from multiple perspectives and interpretations through deep insights based on objective qualitative information and the researchers' subjective interpretation regarding individual cases, which cannot be obtained from statistical methods. Case studies are important not only in complementing generality through statistical methods but also in constructing novel, creative theories.

The case study in this article focuses on research questions relating to boundaries knowledge (knowing) in managing innovation in companies and provides in-depth analysis and observations regarding how that boundaries knowledge (knowing) achieved innovation activities. In creating and analyzing the in-depth case studies, semi-structured interviews of 1–2 hours were conducted with Kodak, Fujifilm, Panasonic, Nokia, Nissan Motor Company, Apple, Motorola. Additionally, publicly available external materials and press releases from these companies were also utilized as secondary data.

Based on the above research approach, this paper first outlines the prior research on knowledge creation theory (SECI model) and boundaries knowledge. Next, it presents the conceptual model of "knowledge creation through boundaries knowledge synchronization," followed by an analysis and discussion of this model based on the in-depth case studies of these companies. Finally, new insights from the in-depth case studies, implications, and conclusions are presented.

7.3 Case Studies of Successes and Failures in Knowledge Convergence

7.3.1 Kodak and Fujifilm

While Kodak declined in the photographic film business due to the impact of digitalization, Japan's Fujifilm, which was in the same industry and faced similar circumstances, successfully made a strategic shift to digital business. Kodak recognized the threat posed by market changes due to digitalization early on, but clung to its existing business in pursuit of maximizing shareholder value and profits. Kodak consistently adopted rigid strategies, such as buying back large amounts of its own stock with abundant funds and taking measures to support its stock price. Moreover, Kodak's top management (including middle management) at the time did not consider challenging new knowledge creation activities in response to environmental changes brought about by digitalization.

On the other hand, Fujifilm utilized its advanced photographic film technology already possessed within the company to develop and commercialize special protective film technology for LCDs (applying film technology to LCD TVs). Additionally, as an example of technology convergence (knowledge convergence) of different existing technologies, Fujifilm applied its collagen technology, originally used to prevent the drying of photographic film, to develop new cosmetics, which have become hit products. Fujifilm has successfully entered and thrived in the cosmetics industry, which was previously an unrelated field. Furthermore, the company has ventured into the development of pharmaceuticals, including a drug that has recently gained attention as a potential treatment for Ebola hemorrhagic fever.

Unlike Kodak, Fujifilm succeeded not by maximizing shareholder value and profits but by avoiding zero profit to ensure its survival. It achieved this through the convergence of advanced and diverse knowledge possessed and accumulated by itself and other companies (Kodama, 2018; Kodama & Shibata, 2016). This success was underpinned by the formation and organizational integration of strategic communities (SC) with the characteristics of multiple pragmatic boundaries within and outside Fujifilm's organizational boundaries.

7.3.2 Nokia

Nokia, which once reigned as the top mobile phone manufacturer in the world, sold 461.31 million units in 2010, capturing 28.9% of the global market share. Symbian, its smartphone OS, also led the market, accounting for 37.6% of the 296.64 million smartphones sold worldwide in 2010. Nokia's rapid success in the mobile phone sector had led it to become the world's best-selling mobile phone brand by 1998. In 2011, to address the intensifying competition from iOS and Android operating systems, Nokia entered into a strategic partnership with Microsoft. In 2014, Nokia sold its mobile and devices division to Microsoft.

The reason Nokia failed in the smartphone business was that the architecture of traditional mobile phones was entirely different from that of smartphones. Unlike traditional mobile phones, which were hardware-centric, smartphones required the integration of hardware and software technologies, as well as advanced software capabilities. Nokia's management failed to recognize the need for a shift in core competencies from traditional mobile phones to smartphones. Additionally, the market was overly segmented, leading to a significant increase in the number of models, which required time-consuming OS modifications and caused architectural issues in software development. Meanwhile, the management reduced R&D investments, causing Nokia to lag behind the iPhone. Although strategic goals were set, there were no leaders with software expertise, as the management team primarily consisted of individuals with backgrounds in finance and law. Consequently, they failed to understand that the core issue Nokia faced was related to software.

Furthermore, organizational issues arose as the emotions shared between top and middle managers during the smartphone innovation process triggered a cycle of behaviors that harmed both the process and its outcomes (Vuori & Huy, 2016). The dispersed attention structure among top and middle managers affected shared emotions, hindering the integration of attention. This situation ultimately hindered the necessary shift in core competencies toward smartphones and significantly influenced the innovation process and outcomes in software development.

7.3.3 Panasonic

For nearly 20 years, Panasonic has not produced a hit product that could serve as a pillar of revenue. Although sales have increased since the 1970s, operating profits have steadily declined since the 1980s, eventually leading to a deficit. However, until the company fell into the red, Panasonic was unable to undertake fundamental reforms. The reason Panasonic could not produce hit products is ingrained in its corporate culture. The long-standing success of the "mass production and mass sales" business model became a burden, preventing employees from generating new hit products and driving transformation.

Panasonic's successful model in the twentieth century was the "mass production and mass sales" business model established by its founder, Konosuke Matsushita, supported by a divisional system. Each time Panasonic launched a new product, it created a division responsible for that product (e.g., TV division, video division, refrigerator division, iron division), with up to 127 divisions at its peak. These divisions competed to increase sales, driving Panasonic's growth. Each division was an independent organization with functions ranging from sales to manufacturing and R&D.

The products developed and produced by each division were sold through Panasonic's extensive network of affiliated stores, which numbered up to 27,000 at its peak. However, the business model of producing more products to sell more distanced the company from its customers. Since the 1980s, the emergence of large-scale retailers took customers away from Panasonic's affiliated stores, leading to a rapid decline and closure of these stores. Consequently, Panasonic's operating profits continued to decline, and the "mass production and mass sales" business model quickly collapsed with changing times.

One pillar of reform was the dismantling of the divisional system, enabling the selection and concentration of management resources and business domains. The introduction of the domain system aimed to develop products that responded to changing customer needs and integrate internal resources in response to technological changes. For example, as shown in Fig. 7.1, there is the convergence of video, music, and PC media. During the era of the divisional system, many products were based on analog technology, and single-item products like video and audio equipment sufficed. However, as technology shifted from analog to digital and with technology convergence, the new usage pattern of connecting individual products via networks necessitated organizational transformation.

In the audio-visual (AV) sector, for instance, the integration of video, audio, and data information through media like DVDs and SD cards

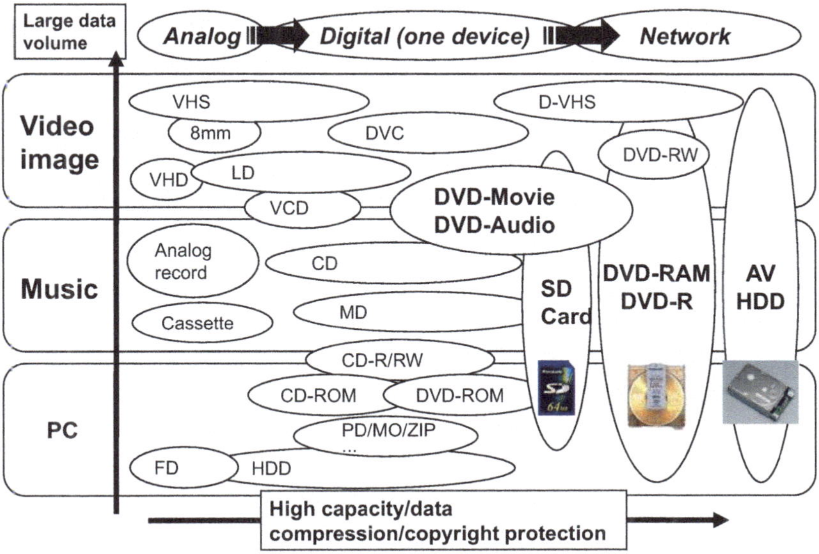

(Note) Constructed by the author based on the author's interview with Panasonic (Matsushita Electric)

Fig. 7.1 Technology convergence of video, music and PC media

across various devices (digital TVs, digital videos, digital cameras, mobile information terminals) required integration of previously separate technologies. Therefore, having separate development teams for each product division became highly inefficient due to overlapping development efforts. Thus, the dispersed development teams needed to be integrated into the AV Technology Center (see Fig. 7.2).

Additionally, product divisions (e.g., video division, digital AV network division, electronic musical instrument division) needed to be reorganized into domains based on customer usage patterns (home use, personal use, and media or devices for these AV products). Figure 7.2 illustrates the organizational reform of Panasonic AVC Networks Company (PAVC), responsible for planning, developing, and manufacturing digital home appliances (e.g., DVD recorders, digital cameras, digital TVs). PAVC is an organization that handles the planning, development, and manufacturing of AV products, including those for overseas markets, centered on digital home appliances. Under the fundamental structural reforms within

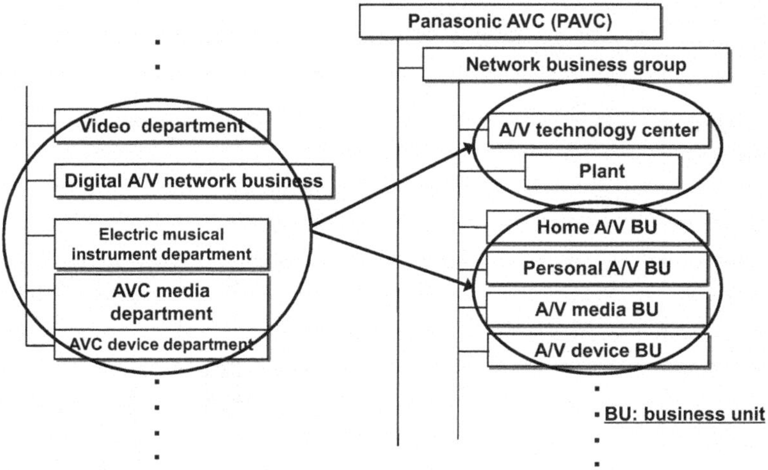

(Note) Constructed by the author based on the author's interview with Panasonic (Matsushita Electric)

Fig. 7.2 Organizational reforms to respond to technology convergence

Panasonic to respond to such technological convergence, the company's performance rapidly made a "V-shaped" recovery.

The source of capability for the strategic shift from technology-driven to customer-driven product development and fundamental organizational reform lies in the formation and organizational integration of strategic communities (SC) characterized by multiple pragmatic boundaries within and outside Panasonic's organizational boundaries. This study shows that Panasonic succeeded in its convergence strategy in the digital field by balancing the integration of vertically integrated SCs and horizontally integrated SCs (Kodama, 2007a).

7.3.4 Nissan Motor Company

In the latter half of the twentieth century, Nissan Motor Company struggled with high costs and excessive interest-bearing debt, which put pressure on its management. The company experienced ongoing management turmoil from the early 1990s, and in 1998, it fell back into the red. In terms of business strategy, Nissan's competitiveness against rivals like Toyota and Honda declined, leading to a loss of market share. Additionally, delays in management reforms and restructuring prevented fundamental improvements in the company's corporate structure. These factors culminated in a massive deficit of 684.3 billion yen for the fiscal year ending March 2000.

In response to this management crisis, Renault, a French automobile manufacturer, provided financial support to Nissan. Carlos Ghosn was sent from Renault to serve as Nissan's CEO. Ghosn emphasized the importance of identifying Nissan's problems, establishing priorities, promoting two-way communication at all management levels, and discovering innovative solutions to issues. The foundation of Ghosn's management approach was the Cross-Functional Team (CFT), where employees from various fields gathered beyond departmental and job boundaries to engage in active discussions and analyze issues from multiple angles. CFTs correspond to the aforementioned strategic communities (SC). As part of Nissan's revival plan, nine CFTs were established within the company (see Fig. 7.3). This approach is a "knowledge convergence" method of organizational reform.

The themes addressed by these CFTs included: (1) business development, (2) purchasing, (3) manufacturing and logistics, (4) research and development, (5) marketing and sales, (6) general administrative

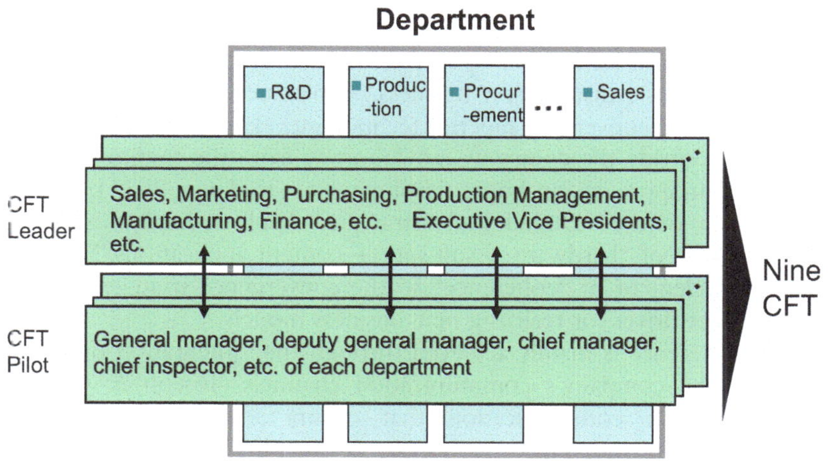

(Note) Constructed by the author based on the author's interviews with Nissan

Fig. 7.3 Nissan's revival—9 CFTs as knowledge convergence

expenses, (7) financial costs, (8) reduction of vehicle models, and (9) organizational and decision-making processes. Each CFT consisted of about 10 members and was not a decision-making body but a group that proposed measures to reduce production costs, improve design and quality, and enhance profitability across departmental boundaries. The actual decisions were made by the executive committee, including Ghosn. The CFTs worked tirelessly for three months, holding numerous meetings to create the revival plan. Although 200 people were directly involved in the CFTs, hundreds of other employees contributed to the planning, and a total of 2000 ideas were considered by the CFTs. Ghosn stated, "The top must have the determination to fight against ingrained old ideas," and he successfully implemented a new knowledge creation process by fostering "creative friction" and "productive tension" through the formation of pragmatic Ba like the CFTs within the company.

Thus, the different strategic context of corporate transformation at Nissan created a new "pragmatic Ba." The change agent (Ghosn) discovered and provided different knowledge assets within each Ba, transforming the pragmatic Ba into a SECI process adapted to different strategic contexts and executing the strategy, as noted by Kodama (2017).

7.3.5 *Apple and Motorola*

This was a radical innovation by Apple: transitioning from the PC business to the music distribution business. Apple succeeded in creating a new business by converging superior technologies (knowledge) from both inside and outside the company, moving away from the traditional Mac development approach (in-house development) (Kodama, 2021). Under the concept of the "Digital Hub Strategy," Apple refined its convergence strategy of "hardware + software + content applications." Within Apple, the element of "coherence" in the convergence strategy became an important driver for realizing new business models.

This coherence is mainly achieved through the "integration of attention" via the company's communication channels (Joseph & Ocasio, 2012) and the communication that occurs among organizational members within these channels (Ocasio & Joseph, 2018; Ocasio et al., 2017). The coherence across the organization's channels enhances the likelihood of providing organizational members with a consistent understanding of how business solutions should appear in addressing management challenges and problem-solving, avoiding ambiguity in interpreting strategic opportunities and threats.

On the other hand, Ocasio and Joseph (2018) compare the new product development of Apple and Motorola from the perspective of capabilities to maintain attention over the long term. Despite starting from similar strategic ideas regarding smartphones, the performance levels achieved by these two companies were significantly different. This indicates a clear mechanism by which the process of "strategic action," including the conversion and framing of ideas into concrete and successful strategic agendas and solutions, is enabled by dynamic capabilities (e.g., Teece, 2007, 2014).

Furthermore, a superior strategy allows a company to utilize its identity, thereby continuously focusing attention on driving organizational processes aligned with strategic goals (Ocasio & Joseph, 2018). Identity brings commonality to the focus of attention among organizational members, becoming a crucial determinant of the company's perspective of attention (Ocasio, 2011). Such identity is the source of the company's unique capabilities, materializing as institutional commitments and repeated patterns of decision-making.

Although Apple and Motorola shared a common identity as leading companies in high-tech products, their identities were quite different in many other respects. Apple's strong organizational identity was based on designing and developing superior products aimed at changing the world. The focus on digital design, obsession with enhancing customer experience, and not just meeting but delighting and surprising customers are also part of Apple's organizational identity.

On the other hand, Motorola, which had a more traditional organizational identity as an engineering company, did not share the same organizational identity as Apple (Ocasio & Joseph, 2018). At that time, Motorola reorganized into four business units—mobile devices, networks, connected home, and business enterprise—with a clear intention to concentrate resources across multiple divisions and pursue a seamless mobility strategy. However, the company maintained conflicting customer bases, technologies, and value standards across different business units, hindering seamlessness in its overall vision. This lack of focus and attention on developing unique ideas across the organization led to strategic failures.

The differences between Apple and Motorola stem from their organizational structures. The presence of Jobs and Apple's functional organization creatively and efficiently achieved consistent agendas and issues that promoted collaboration. In contrast, Motorola's multi-division structure made it difficult to agree on common agenda items and integrate attention, leading to a breakdown in collaboration.

Thus, Apple had an organizational identity focused on achieving superior smartphones through a consistent convergence strategy, concentrating on the convergence strategy, and focusing on creating customer value, continuously drawing the attention of organizational members. A company's identity shapes and reflects its product concepts, the scope of product offerings, differentiation from other companies offering similar products, and the rules of competition. To realize a superior strategy that determines a business model, a company can utilize its identity to focus on the strategic agenda and continuously draw the attention of actors within the company. This structured interaction of the two elements—"attentional control and strategic action (framing and solving of the strategic agenda)"—through the "Attention-based view" (Ocasio, 1997, 2011) enables the modification of existing knowledge and drives new knowledge within and between organizations.

7.3.6 *Analysis from Seven Case Studies—Evaluation of Corporate Actions on Knowledge Convergence Strategy*

Companies like Kodak, Nokia, and Motorola failed to adapt to knowledge convergence amid technological changes, resulting in their inability to create new knowledge (such as new products, services, and business models) driven by the SECI process. On the other hand, Fujifilm and Apple generated significant technological changes themselves, creating new markets through knowledge convergence. Additionally, companies like Panasonic and Nissan initially struggled to respond to major technological and market changes but achieved knowledge convergence by driving the SECI process through organizational reforms. Therefore, to successfully achieve knowledge convergence driven by the SECI process, insights from prior research such as the "Attention-Based View" and the "Boundaries-Based View" are necessary.

Firstly, for organizational members, including top management, to recognize the necessity of knowledge convergence, elements of the Attention-Based View such as coherence and integration of attention, as mentioned by Ocasio and Joseph (2018), are required in the cases of Nokia, Apple, and Motorola. Secondly, to achieve knowledge convergence like Fujifilm and Apple, it is necessary to enhance the quality of collaboration among organizational members, share a common identity, and intensively share strategic goals and challenges. To this end, it is necessary to synchronize various boundaries among members, including stakeholders, into pragmatic boundaries, as elements of the Boundaries-Based View by Carlile (2004) and Kodama (2007a, 2019).

Such synchronization into pragmatic boundaries mutually influences coherence and integration of attention concerning the aforementioned strategic context. Furthermore, this synchronization into pragmatic boundaries leads to the generation of "boundaries knowledge" necessary to drive the SECI process, as indicated by prior research by Kodama (2025). When driving the SECI process, the creation of new tacit knowledge in the initial "Socialization" phase is necessary. In this phase, it is essential to create, share, and empathize with boundaries knowledge necessary for tacit knowledge integration from diverse tacit knowledge among actors.

Specifically, it is important to share identity and vision and create and share common tacit knowledge about "what, why, and for what purpose" to execute as an organization. Without the creation and sharing of such new tacit knowledge, it is impossible to transform a company strategically and culturally. Companies that cannot generate new tacit knowledge (in other words, cannot transform existing tacit knowledge) will be unable to achieve new knowledge convergence, as seen in Kodak, Motorola, and pre-transformation Panasonic and Nissan, which clung to existing businesses and routines.

Judging from these lessons, companies that adapt to (or create) knowledge convergence (technology convergence) succeed in creating new knowledge, while those that don't adapt are destined to lose their existing markets and decline. In other words, failing companies cling to the tacit knowledge accumulated from past successes in existing businesses and fail to appropriately respond to changes in the environment (technological innovations and new business models), and are thus unable to drive the spiral of new knowledge creation (SECI model).

When these cases are organized according to the evaluation criteria of the Attention-Based View and the Boundaries-Based View, the presence or absence of new tacit knowledge creation, and the presence or absence of the SECI process, they appear as shown in Table 7.1. Based on these analytical results, a theoretical model of corporate behavior to adapt to (or create) knowledge convergence and generate new knowledge creation processes is derived from the perspectives of "Attention-Based View," "Boundaries-Based View," and the SECI process.

7.4 Theoretical Concepts and Framework of This Chapter

7.4.1 *Attentional Control (Engagement) and Problem Solving to Achieve Synchronization at Pragmatic Boundaries—Attention-Based View (ABV)*

The core element of the SECI process is orchestrating new knowledge arising from various pragmatic boundaries within and outside the company (in other words, synchronizing pragmatic boundaries existing within and outside the company to integrate or transform knowledge), which becomes the source of innovation. At pragmatic boundaries, various problems and challenges are raised, and actors need to tackle these challenges and create new knowledge. Therefore, the key is how to achieve the synchronization (convergence) of thoughts and activities among actors at pragmatic boundaries. This synchronization at pragmatic boundaries leads to the generation of boundaries knowledge necessary to drive the SECI process.

Maintaining thoughts and activities among actors at pragmatic boundaries under environments of novelty and uncertainty forces individual actors to focus their attention and willpower on the challenges and problems they face. This is because, at pragmatic boundaries, existing knowledge and experience cannot be easily applied by the actors. As Schulze and Brusoni (2022) mention, keeping actors' attention focused over long periods toward organizational and corporate transformation imposes stress on both individuals (e.g., Laureiro-Martinez, 2014) and organizations (e.g., Ocasio, 1997, 2011).

According to Ocasio (1997), the attention process is a structured cognitive process that involves selecting the "answers" to solve the "issues" that organizations should focus on. "Attentional Control (Engagement)" promotes new interpretations and intentionally and sustainably allocates cognitive resources to decision-making in response to specific stimuli (e.g., strategic goals) (Ocasio, 2011). This process enables organizational actors to concentrate their time, energy, and effort on

Table 7.1 Analysis and insights from case studies on knowledge convergence

Company (References)	*Organizational issues*	*[Attention-Based View]*	*[Boundaries-Based View]*	*Creation of new tacit knowledge*	*New SECI process*
Kodak (Kodama, 2018)	- Stockholder supremacy - Obsession with Existing Businesses	Lack of coherence and integration of attention	Asynchronous to pragmatic boundaries	Stagnation	Stagnation
Fujifilm (Kodama, 2018; Kodama & Shibata, 2016)	- Promoting understanding of technology convergence - Fostering a sense of urgency among executives and management	Realization of coherence and integration of attention	Formation of SC through synchronization to pragmatic boundaries	Generation	driving force
Nokia	- Promoting understanding of technology convergence - Fostering a sense of urgency among executives and management	Lack of coherence and integration of attention	Asynchronous to pragmatic boundaries	Stagnation	Stagnation

(continued)

Table 7.1 (continued)

Company (References)	*Organizational issues*	*[Attention-Based View]*	*[Boundaries-Based View]*	*Creation of new tacit knowledge*	*New SECI process*
Panasonic (Kodama, 2007a)	- Lack of understanding of technology convergence - Damage of divisional structure → Implementing Structural Reforms	Lack of Coherence and integration of attention → realization	Asynchronous to pragmatic boundaries → SC formation through synchronization	Stagnation → generation	Stagnation → driving force
Nissan (Kodama, 2017)	- Damage of stove-piped organization - Lack of creativity and efficiency → Implementing Structural Reforms	Lack of Coherence and integration of attention → realization	Asynchronous to pragmatic boundaries → SC(CFT) formation through synchronization	Stagnation → generation	Stagnation → driving force

Company (References)	*Organizational issues*	*[Attention-Based View]*	*[Boundaries-Based View]*	*Creation of new tacit knowledge*	*New SECI process*
Apple (Kodama, 2017; Ocasio & Joseph, 2018)	- Promoting understanding of technology convergence - Pursuit of Vision-Identity sharing-Creative Destruction (iPod → iPhone)	Realization of coherence and integration of attention	Formation of SC through synchronization to pragmatic boundaries	Generation	Driving force
Motorola (Ocasio & Joseph, 2018)	- Damage of stove-piped organizations - Lack of vision and knowledge sharing between organizations - Lack of consistent identity	Lack of coherence and integration of attention	Asynchronous to pragmatic boundaries	Stagnation	Stagnation

driving organizational processes toward solving problems and achieving goals aligned with strategic objectives ([A] in Fig. 7.4).

Attentional engagement is based on two distinct but interconnected complementary processes: "executive attention" and "attentional vigilance (or sustained attention)" (Ocasio, 2011). Executive attention allows people to switch their focus from one stimulus to another, while attentional vigilance enables people to maintain their focus on something over a long period. Effective decision-making within organizations is impossible without either of these two forces (Ocasio, 2011). The executive attention process allows organizational actors to shift their focus from operational tasks driven by routine capabilities to adaptive tasks driven by new knowledge creation. The attentional vigilance process helps actors maintain their focus on the transformation process over a long period while performing routine capabilities daily (Schulze & Brusoni, 2022).

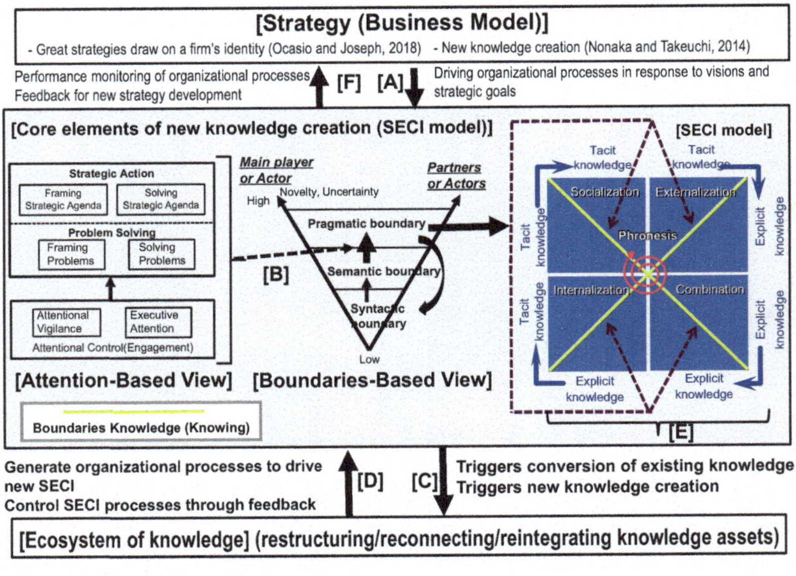

(Note) Prepared by the author

Fig. 7.4 Attention-based and boundaries-based views driving the knowledge creation process (SECI)

Schulze and Brusoni (2022), building on Ocasio's (2011) views, suggest that maintaining "attentional vigilance" can explain what companies can achieve. They also point out that some companies are better at switching gears in response to environmental changes occurring at different speeds through behavioral changes enabled by "executive attention" (see Fig. 7.4). In other words, "Attentional Control (Engagement)" as a control mechanism can be interpreted as a management tool for directing the attention of companies (organizations) and their actors over the long term (Ocasio & Wohlgezogen, 2010).

To explore how dynamic capabilities (Teece, 2007, 2014) transform ordinary capabilities (Teece, 2014), Schulze and Brusoni (2022) utilized the "Attention-based view (ABV)" of firms (Ocasio, 1997). The significance of this study lies in the fact that previous literature has scarcely explained how dynamic capabilities modify ordinary capabilities. The model presented by Schulze and Brusoni (2022) empirically demonstrates, through structured interaction of two elements—"attention control and problem-solving"—that dynamic capabilities can reconfigure resources (knowledge) and consequently transform ordinary capabilities.

In the "problem-solving" process depicted in Fig. 7.4, which includes "framing problems" and "solving problems," problems are accurately described to discover meaningful solutions, and directions are executed to achieve the reconfiguration, recombination, and reintegration of knowledge (resources). This process impacts existing knowledge. The study by Schulze and Brusoni (2022) contributes to understanding the micro-processes by which dynamic capabilities modify ordinary capabilities.

Based on the insights from Schulze and Brusoni (2022), the author proposes a new theoretical process model that links the previously mentioned Boundaries-based view (BBV) with the Attention-based view (ABV) elements of attention control and problem-solving to achieve "synchronization (convergence) at pragmatic boundaries" (Fig. 7.5 shows the relationship between the main elements of BBV and ABV). This theoretical model points out that the structured interaction of the two elements—attention control and problem-solving—presented by Schulze and Brusoni (2022) shifts the nature of boundaries among actors from "semantic boundaries to pragmatic boundaries," synchronizing (converging) actors at pragmatic boundaries.

According to Carlile (2002, 2004), in environments with syntactic boundaries (information processing model) or semantic boundaries (organizational learning model), there is no significant forced transformation

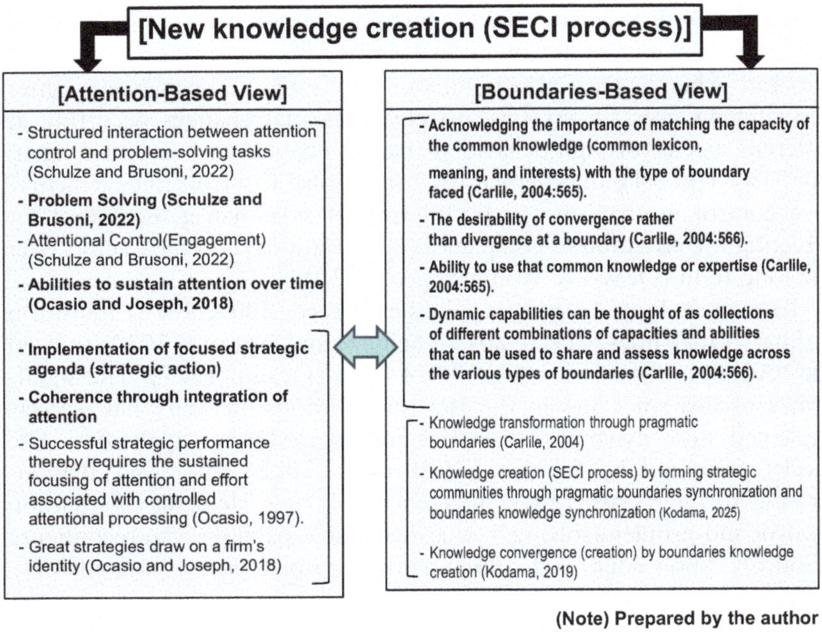

Fig. 7.5 Relationship between attention-based and boundaries-based views in the SECI process

of past accumulated knowledge, such as reuse, utilization, improvement, and enhancement of existing knowledge. Therefore, companies (organizations) can perform their usual routines (ordinary capabilities). However, in companies (organizations) facing uncertainty and novelty in their business environment, it is necessary to synchronize (converge) the nature of boundaries among actors to pragmatic boundaries, and actors need to address current challenges and problem-solving. Synchronization to pragmatic boundaries leads to the generation of boundaries knowledge necessary to drive the SECI process. This organizational process drives the SECI process (closely related to dynamic capabilities) of actors and triggers the transformation (reconfiguration, recombination, reintegration, etc.) of existing knowledge (equivalent to ordinary capabilities) within the ecosystem (including the company itself and various stakeholders) (see Fig. 7.5).

The structured interaction of the two elements, "attention control and problem-solving," promotes the thought and action processes of actors synchronized (converged) at pragmatic boundaries, driving new dynamic capabilities within and between organizations. Specifically, the structured interaction between attention control and problem-solving tasks synchronizes (converges) the boundaries faced by actors, generating, sharing, and utilizing common knowledge (common lexicon, meaning, and interests) among actors, and promoting the generation of boundaries knowledge. This facilitates communication and collaboration among actors at pragmatic boundaries, enabling the transformation of individual existing knowledge (expertise) held by actors (see Fig. 7.5). Figure 7.5 outlines the conceptual relationship and connectivity between the Boundaries-based view (BBV) and the Attention-based view (ABV).

The "attention control" process, which includes high-level attention processes and attentional vigilance processes, shifts semantic boundaries to pragmatic boundaries. Furthermore, the problem-solving process synchronizes actors to pragmatic boundaries, allowing organizational actors to switch their focus from operational tasks driven by routine capabilities to adaptive and creative tasks driven by the new knowledge creation process ([B] in Fig. 7.4). As a result, existing routine capabilities (or ordinary capabilities) are transformed, inducing new knowledge creation ([C] in Fig. 7.4), and driving and controlling organizational processes to generate new boundaries knowledge in the four phases of the SECI process ([D] in Fig. 7.4). These adaptive and creative tasks, driven by the SECI process, form the aforementioned strategic communities (SC) and achieve the reconfiguration, recombination, and reintegration of knowledge through the ecosystem. In other words, strategic communities (and networked strategic communities) are formed within and between companies, and the SECI process drives the reconfiguration, recombination, and reintegration of knowledge ([E] in Fig. 7.4). Additionally, over time, the performance of organizational processes born from new knowledge creation is monitored within the company (organization), and feedback for new strategy formulation is also executed ([F] in Fig. 7.4).

7.4.2 Attentional Control (Engagement) and Strategic Action to Achieve Synchronization at Pragmatic Boundaries—Attention-Based View (ABV)

The case study on agile development presented by Schulze and Brusoni (2022) analyzes the process of generating dynamic capabilities from the structured interaction of two elements—attention control and problem-solving—in the product development process within R&D organizations. The authors further consider these concepts of the Attention-Based View (ABV) and Boundaries-Based View (BBV) from the perspective of corporate strategy (including product strategy).

Ocasio (1997) points out that successful strategic performance requires sustained attention and effort associated with controlled attentional processing. For accurate planning and execution (including the speed of execution) of strategic actions within a company, decision-makers at both individual and team levels need to concentrate their energy, efforts, and attention on a limited number of issues and tasks. To achieve successful strategic performance, sustained attention and effort related to "controlled attentional processing" is necessary for actors (Ocasio & Joseph, 2018).

When defining strategy as a pattern of attention, from the perspective of the Attention-Based View (ABV), it is not the original ideas, plans, or intentions that produce the realized strategy, but rather the focused "strategic agenda" characterized by the consistency that ultimately emerges (Ocasio & Joseph, 2018). The strategic agenda of a company prioritizes specific sets of actions that shape the selection of markets and customer segments, driving the formulation and realization of the target business model (key elements constituting the value chain and business ecosystems: the range of product and service offerings; the firm's value propositions; firm pricing and cost structure; the development, acquisition, and deployment of knowledge and capabilities; the development of alliances and partnerships and responsiveness to competitors, etc.). The scope of a company's strategic agenda is inherently broad, complex, dynamic, and continuously evolving. The resulting strategy reflects not only the composition of previous strategic choices but also a consistent strategic agenda for the ongoing development and refinement of new strategies (Ocasio & Joseph, 2018).

In the trial-and-error process (strategic action) aimed at "framing strategic agenda" and "solving strategic agenda" for realizing a business model, the element of coherence becomes particularly important within the company (organization). This coherence is primarily achieved through the integration of attention via the company's communication channels (Joseph & Ocasio, 2012) and the communication occurring among organizational members within these channels (Ocasio & Joseph, 2018; Ocasio et al., 2017). Coherence across the organization's channels enhances the likelihood of providing organizational members (actors) with a consistent understanding of what business solutions should look like for addressing management issues and problem-solving, thereby avoiding ambiguity in interpreting strategic opportunities and threats. Consequently, companies can focus on value creation and sustain attention toward the realization of superior strategies. To achieve this, structured interactions between the two elements of "attentional control and strategic action" and organizational processes for synchronizing (converging) on pragmatic boundaries among actors are necessary ([B] in Fig. 7.4) (see Figs. 7.4 and 7.5).

The organizational process of "strategic action" consists of the elements of framing strategic agenda and solving strategic agenda, which require an interactive and trial-and-error process among actors at pragmatic boundaries. This process of framing strategic agenda and solving strategic agenda corresponds to the "framing problems" and "solving problems" presented by Schulze and Brusoni (2022). The interaction of attention and strategic action (framing and solving strategic agenda) influences knowledge within and outside the company, leading to the transformation of existing routine capabilities (ordinary capabilities) ([C] in Fig. 7.4).

This leads to driving and controlling organizational processes for new knowledge creation (SECI process) ([D] in Fig. 7.4) (see Figs. 7.4 and 7.5). Such adaptive and creative strategic actions drive the SECI process, forming the aforementioned "strategic communities (SC)" and achieving the reconfiguration, recombination, and reintegration of knowledge. In other words, strategic communities (and further networked strategic communities) are formed within (and between) companies, and the SECI process drives the reconfiguration, recombination, and reintegration of knowledge ([E] in Fig. 7.4). As the strategy is executed over time, the performance of organizational processes born from new knowledge creation is monitored, and feedback for new strategy construction is also implemented ([F] in Fig. 7.4).

Schulze and Brusoni (2022) mention that while the distinction between framing problems and solving problems is not particularly new in past literature, traditionally, more attention has been paid to problem-solving in both practice and education. They point out that humans tend to jump straight to the solution phase. This tendency is because actors are inclined to adopt predefined solutions, especially those that seem close to their area of expertise.

From the perspective of the boundaries-based view (BBV), this tendency occurs because actors, even when facing pragmatic boundaries, are likely to interpret them as syntactic and semantic boundaries and thus tend to reuse or leverage existing knowledge. It is necessary to expend effort on framing problems among actors based on actual root causes at pragmatic boundaries and then develop countermeasures.

Ocasio and Joseph (2018) compare the new product development of Apple and Motorola from the perspective of capabilities to maintain attention over the long term. Despite starting from similar strategic ideas regarding smartphones, the performance levels achieved by these two companies were significantly different.

Moreover, an excellent strategy enables a company to utilize its identity, thereby continuously focusing attention on the strategic agenda and driving organizational processes aligned with strategic goals ([A] in Fig. 7.4) (Ocasio & Joseph, 2018). Identity brings commonality to the focal points of attention among organizational members, which becomes a crucial determinant of the company's attentional perspective (Ocasio, 2011). Such identity has the effect of synchronizing (converging) the nature of boundaries among actors (their thoughts and actions) into pragmatic boundaries. Simultaneously, identity is the source of the company's unique capabilities, materializing as institutional commitments and repeated patterns of decision-making (see Fig. 7.5).

To reiterate, although Apple and Motorola shared a common identity as leading companies in high-tech products, their identities were quite different in many other respects. Apple's strong organizational identity was based on designing and developing superior products aimed at changing the world. The focus on digital design, obsession with enhancing customer experience, and not just meeting but delighting and surprising customers are part of Apple's organizational identity. On the other hand, Motorola, while also focusing on superior products, had a more traditional organizational identity as an engineering company and did not share the same organizational identity as Apple (Ocasio & Joseph, 2018).

A company's identity shapes and reflects its product concepts, the scope of its product offerings, differentiation from other companies offering similar products, and the rules of competition. Therefore, as shown in Fig. 7.4, by leveraging identity, a company can focus on the strategic agenda and continuously direct attention toward actors within the company to realize an excellent strategy that determines the business model. In other words, the structured interaction of the two elements, "attentional control and strategic action (framing and solving the strategic agenda)," promotes the thought and action processes of actors synchronized (converged) into pragmatic boundaries, altering the knowledge that constitutes existing routine capabilities (ordinary capabilities). Simultaneously, through the reconfiguration, recombination, and reintegration of knowledge within and outside the company ecosystem, it becomes possible to drive a new SECI process within and between companies (organizations). Thus, Fig. 7.4 corresponds to a theoretical model of corporate behavior that adapts to (or creates) knowledge convergence and generates new knowledge creation processes.

7.5 Holistic Leadership, Phronetic Leadership, Dynamic Fractal Organization, Collective Phronesis

7.5.1 *Driving the SECI Process with Centralized Leadership, Distributed Leadership, and Dialectical Leadership*

The knowledge creation theory by Nonaka and Takeuchi (1995) is a principle that synthesizes subjective and interpretive approaches with objective and analytical approaches, viewing them as a dialectical dynamic of tacit and explicit knowledge, subjectivity and objectivity, and micro and macro perspectives. Nonaka and Toyama (2007) incorporated the concept of phronesis into their knowledge creation theory, emphasizing that leaders who drive knowledge creation activities as a strategy must exhibit "Phronetic leadership." Phronetic leadership is the process of synthesizing the components of knowledge creation activities toward an ideal and practicing them consistently. They highlight the importance of the concept of phronesis as a crucial factor required for such knowledge-based leadership.

According to Nonaka, Phronetic leadership is defined as "the ability to make decisions and act in the best possible manner for the greater good in specific situations." In other words, it involves phronesis (high-quality tacit knowledge), which allows for the best judgment and actions in each context and situation, with prudence regarding values and ethics. Wisdom is high-quality tacit knowledge acquired in specific contexts. By repeatedly engaging in the SECI process in daily specific situations, knowledge becomes wisdom, and promoting this practice is what "Phronetic leadership" entails.

Nonaka et al. (2008) identify six elements of "Phronetic leadership":

(1) The ability to judge goodness,
(2) The ability to share contexts with others to create Ba,
(3) The ability to grasp the essence of particular situations/things,
(4) The ability to reconstruct the particulars into universals and vice versa using language/concepts/narrative,
(5) The political power to realize concepts for the common good,
(6) The ability to foster phronesis in others to build a resilient organization.

Excellent leaders possess these six abilities and, through trial and error in daily practice, repeatedly formulate and execute the best and optimal strategies. Additionally, Nonaka et al. (2014) refer to phronesis as the third type of knowledge that spirally converts tacit knowledge and explicit knowledge. In other words, phronesis is the very engine that drives the SECI process and encompasses the six elements mentioned above by Nonaka. These six elements of phronesis are also crucial for driving distributed leadership, centralized leadership, and dialectical leadership. Based on the insights from previous research on phronesis, The author would like to examine the elements of phronesis to drive "holistic leadership," which encompasses centralized leadership, distributed leadership, and dialectical leadership.

The first ability, "the ability to judge goodness," involves establishing a firm set of personal values and philosophy, envisioning ideals based on superior values (truth, goodness, and beauty), and promoting practices toward their realization. The excellent values and philosophy of leaders form the fundamental requirements for creating the "platform for resonating values" as the foundation for value creation mentioned earlier. Furthermore, this ability triggers the construction of solid "principles" and "creeds" shared among employees within the formal organization, establishing the company's vision and strategic goals, and driving centralized leadership centered on top management. Simultaneously, firm personal values and philosophy act as a trigger for driving distributed leadership among members practicing in the informal organization, which is the local site of knowledge creation, toward the development of good products. In this way, the ability to judge goodness influences both centralized leadership and distributed leadership.

The second ability, "the ability to share contexts with others to create Ba," promotes the creation of Ba, which directly shares contexts such as tacit knowledge that becomes the source of new knowledge. Ba is a "shared dynamic context," a dynamic state of mind and body where participants in Ba share and create knowledge. The establishment of Ba, by connecting individuals beyond themselves with others, generates intellectual capital such as care, love, and trust, efficiently linking multiple Ba layers and forming the basic requirements for the creation of new communities. This ability acts as a trigger for driving distributed leadership among leaders and members in the informal organization toward the process of converting Ba into SECI. Simultaneously, in the formal organization, it acts as a trigger for driving centralized leadership among top management and senior managers to construct Ba that generates social capital across the company and beyond, and to promote the multilayered connection of multiple Ba using small-world networks. In this way, the ability to share contexts with others to create Ba influences both centralized leadership and distributed leadership.

The third ability, "the ability to grasp the essence of particular situations," promotes leaders' ability to see through the background of various events, intuitively sense the essence of things, and accurately design the future. This ability enables leaders, whether in top or middle management, to shift their perspective from the macro formal organization to the micro informal organization where localized knowledge creation activities are carried out by members with distributed leadership, using their insight to discern the essence of matters. Furthermore, they drive centralized leadership by constructing and sharing new visions and strategic goals based on the essence of new events fed back from the informal organization, in collaboration with members who possess centralized leadership within the formal organization. Additionally, members engaged in knowledge creation activities within the informal organization refine and realize the nature of products and services that truly contribute to society and their company through a process of trial and error in practice, demonstrating distributed leadership among themselves. In this way, the ability to grasp the essence of particular situations influences both centralized leadership and distributed leadership.

The fourth ability, "the ability to reconstruct the particulars into universals and vice versa," promotes the process of visualizing and conceptualizing micro-level intuitions through dialogue, relating them to macro-level conceptual abilities (historical imagination, vision, scenarios), and explaining and persuading members. This ability is crucial for leaders to drive the SECI process within informal organizations and, at the same time, dynamically interchange diverse contexts between macro formal organizations, where visions and strategic goals are shared, and micro informal organizations, where localized knowledge creation activities are executed, thereby realizing ideals. In this way, the ability to reconstruct the particulars into universals and vice versa influences both centralized leadership and distributed leadership.

The fifth ability, "the political power to realize concepts for the common good," involves mobilizing others toward goals, consolidating power, and promoting the construction of a "platform for resonating values." The strategy formulation and execution process is dynamic, chaotic, and full of contradictions. The leadership that is crucial for smoothly advancing the knowledge creation process must be particularly demonstrated in the "boundaries knowledge layer."

The boundaries knowledge layer refers to the boundary areas in the SECI process depicted in Fig. 7.4, where Socialization (tacit knowledge to tacit knowledge: knowledge integration), Externalization (tacit knowledge to explicit knowledge: knowledge transformation), Combination (explicit knowledge to explicit knowledge: knowledge integration), and Internalization (explicit knowledge to tacit knowledge: knowledge transformation) phases occur. The existence of boundaries knowledge (knowing) leads to the realization of knowledge integration and knowledge transformation in the SECI process.

Part of the methodology required in the "boundaries knowledge layer" involves not merely adapting passively or compromising with logical dichotomies, but rather extracting a dynamic order that nullifies dichotomies with commitment, and practically resolving contradictions through dialectical leadership. This process is, in reality, a political process that achieves objectives through social interactions with others, fundamentally based on political judgment. Political judgment is exercised through understanding and empathizing with others' feelings and emotions, detecting nuances, and considering the timing and limits of mutual interventions in everyday verbal and non-verbal communication (Steinberger, 1993). Leaders, through such political abilities, must exercise dialectical leadership in the boundaries knowledge layer, where friction and conflict from boundary negotiations between distributed leadership and centralized leadership are most intense. They must select and combine appropriate means according to the situation, using political power improvisationally to achieve the desired knowledge creation activities.

The sixth ability, "the ability to cultivate and distribute phronesis," is embedded within the organization and forms the basis for various individuals to execute distributed leadership according to the situation. This ability represents the on-site capability of employees to respond flexibly and creatively to environmental changes and serves as the driving force for daily knowledge creation activities within the informal organization. Moreover, strategies such as phronesis are not devised and implemented by a few leaders or members of the organization. To promote excellent knowledge creation activities company-wide, many leaders and managers with the ability to cultivate and distribute phronesis are needed. It is necessary to establish a system where top management, at the center, transmits, cultivates, and supports phronesis embedded in the whole personality of individuals through practice. For this purpose, an educational system to cultivate and distribute phronesis must be promoted within the company, centered on top management, through centralized leadership in formal organizations.

As described above, the six elements of phronesis promote the formation of the platform for resonating values, which is the foundation of value creation, and drive leaders' centralized leadership, distributed leadership, and dialectical leadership. Excellent phronesis forms excellent visions and strategic goals, constructing a platform for resonating values for the company's value creation foundation. Simultaneously, through the construction of such a platform for resonating values, organizational leaders demonstrate holistic leadership across the organization and beyond, realizing new knowledge creation through community creation starting from excellent Ba (see Fig. 7.6).

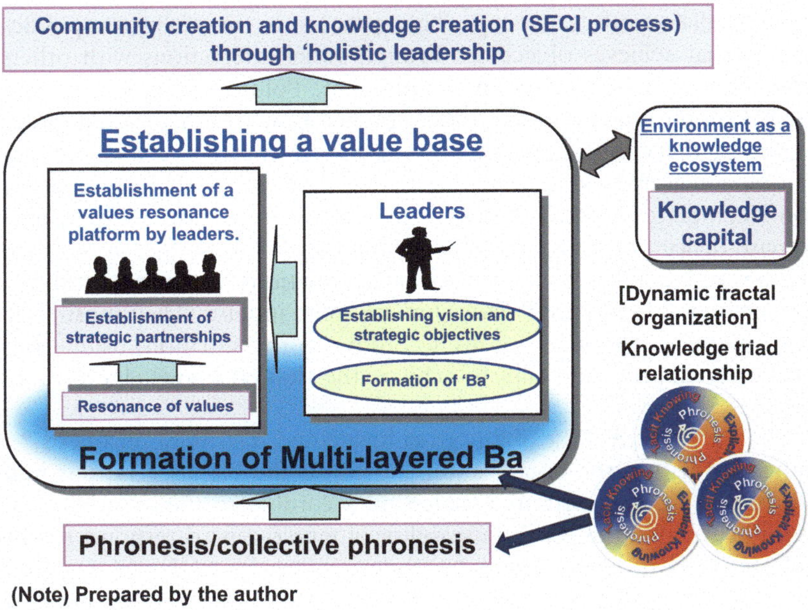

Fig. 7.6 Establishment of value base

7.5.2 *Driving Holistic Leadership with Phronesis and Collective Phronesis—Building the Foundation for Value Creation and Community Creation*

From the comparative analysis of case studies, it is evident that companies where organizational culture and values (identity) are widely shared among employees (such as Fujifilm and Apple in Table 7.1) can effectively share tacit knowledge among employees, thereby promoting the company's knowledge creation (SECI process). In fact, based on the founder's philosophy, companies with excellent performance, like Toyota, have invested significant energy in permeating their unique corporate culture and values throughout their organizations. The sharing of organizational culture and values creates unique systems and rules within companies, which instill unique ways of thinking, perspectives, and behavior patterns in employees. The top leaders of organizations (CEOs and executives) play a crucial role in building a unique corporate culture and promoting the sharing of values among employees, particularly through their centralized leadership (Kodama, 2018).

Schein (1985) argues that the essence of top management leadership is not management leadership for achieving goals, but the creation, management, and destruction of organizational culture. Furthermore, Selznick (1957) emphasizes the importance of the leader's myth-making power. To share culture and values within an organization, it is effective to boost employee morale and communicate unique visions and strategic goals through myths and stories. Myths and stories not only promote the construction and sharing of corporate vision but also play a role in converging decision-making related to strategy formulation and execution in daily corporate activities. As mentioned earlier, the element of coherence is mainly achieved through the integration of attention via the company's communication channels (Joseph & Ocasio, 2012) and the communication occurring among organizational members within these channels (Ocasio & Joseph, 2018; Ocasio et al., 2017). The overall coherence of the organization's channels enhances the possibility of providing organizational members with a consistent understanding of how business solutions should appear in addressing management issues and problem-solving, avoiding ambiguity in interpreting strategic opportunities and threats. So, what is the centralized leadership that excellent companies use to infuse myths and stories within the company and create, establish, and reform unique organizational culture?

To deeply infuse a unique corporate culture, leaders need to achieve "resonance of values" and "trust building" (Kodama, 2007b). Resonance of values and trust building are gradually formed as employees clash their subjective views and values through "dialectical dialogue" and "creative dialogue" while discussing visions and goals. Deep dialectical dialogue enables the sharing of strategic visions and goals among employees, including top management. However, in reality, individual employees' interpretations of visions and strategic goals vary greatly. For example, like Honda, it is necessary for leaders to repeatedly ask fundamental questions such as "Why?" and "For what purpose are we doing this?" and to share and establish this style among employees. By understanding each other's differences in interpretation and sharing and resonating values, employees can achieve synchronization through pragmatic boundaries based on the boundaries-based view, creating a sense of unity in strategy formulation and execution. Such behavior simultaneously realizes coherence and integration of attention through the attention-based view (see Figs. 7.4 and 7.5).

To create new value through resonance of values and trust building among employees, it is necessary for leaders and employees to deeply share the "six strategic contexts" (Kodama, 2017) of "Who," "What," "Why," "With whom," "When," and "How" among members, and to provide leadership to concretely implement these contexts. This involves sharing phronesis, a high-quality tacit knowledge, among employees, including leaders, enabling employees to practice the best decision-making and processes, discover and acquire new value both inside and outside the organization, and create new knowledge.

The concept of phronesis means prudence, practical reason, and practical wisdom. In other words, phronesis can be described as "the ability of leaders to form resonance of values and mutual trust, make appropriate decisions, and find the best actions to execute specific strategies and create new knowledge." Such phronesis forms the foundation of the holistic leadership discussed so far.

7.5.3 Establishing the Foundation for Value Creation and Community Creation

Leaders who belong to an organization and are part of it (whether in top management, middle management, or as independent entrepreneurs with entrepreneurship) must quickly and interactively capture the external environment, technological changes, market structure, and customer needs surrounding their organization. They need the ability to always set a vision and clarify concepts for what they should do and what they want to achieve to establish their organization's competitive advantage. For the vision and strategic goals they set (which may be filled with their own thoughts and beliefs), leaders need leadership that can create human networks both inside and outside the company, including customers, based on clarified strategic concepts through interaction with the knowledge ecosystem (see Fig. 7.4). An important perspective is that building human networks by changing specific networks promotes dialogue and collaboration with core leaders inside and outside the company, creating new knowledge.

For new knowledge creation, it is important to form a place of empathy and resonance of values for visions and strategic goals through constructive and creative dialogue with leaders inside and outside the company. This forms a platform of resonance of value among multiple leaders and establishes strategic partnerships with leaders. The engine for constructing this new value creation foundation through these series of strategic thoughts and actions by leaders lies in phronesis and collective phronesis, which integrates the phronesis of all members (see Fig. 7.6).

However, sharing the vision and strategic goals for a new business with others and building a platform for resonating values is not an easy task. This requires conceptualizing complex business models, challenges, and processes, and clearly articulating them to engage others' interest and motivation. For leaders, it is crucial to establish a win–win relationship for the future of the business. This means forming communities based on Ba, creating synergies from each other's core competencies, and building relationships that reinforce each other's weaknesses. It is important to view others as part of the value chain or value network, not merely as functions to be controlled by one's own power, but as partners in exploring business models that influence both businesses.

Phronesis and collective phronesis serves as engines for forming communities that continuously generate new knowledge. Practically, leaders must form a platform for resonating values at the organizational level, and include many members from both inside and outside the company. With a solid platform of resonance based on phronesis and collective phronesis, leaders can further demonstrate holistic leadership and initiate the SECI spiral. Through the execution of the SECI process by leaders demonstrating phronesis and collective phronesis, and holistic leadership, new products and services are developed and sold, and quality improvements and new product developments are repeatedly spiraled.

As shown in Fig. 7.6, the network of multilayered Ba that realizes "knowledge triad relationships" of phronesis, which spirally converts tacit knowledge and explicit knowledge, is ultimately an "invisible organization" that is difficult to describe like an organizational chart. This invisible organization dynamically expands the multilayered Ba while maintaining the metaphor of a sphere with minimal effective diversity and knowledge triad relationships. Within the Ba, the knowledge triad relationships of "tacit knowledge, explicit knowledge, and phronesis are established, and exploration (creation of knowledge), exploitation (utilization of knowledge), and synthesis (formation of phronesis) are dialectically sublated.

The Ba connects as the smallest unit of this knowledge triad relationship, dynamically expanding and constructing through interactions between humans and organizations, within various organizations within the company, between organizations, and into the environment as a knowledge ecosystem. In other words, knowledge triad relationships are common from the individual to the whole through a fractal structure. This is the concept of the new organizational theory called the "dynamic fractal organization" (Nonaka et al., 2014).

"Fractal" is a term used in complex adaptive systems theory, meaning that parts are formed in a shape similar to the whole, or when these parts are assembled, they form the same shape again. In a company, by having fractal properties where any part of the organization, when expanded, becomes the same shape as the whole, decision-making and knowledge creation levels can be the same at any level. Thus, knowledge triad relationships are observed across various individual organizations within the company, between organizations, and even between companies. In other words, the fractal nature of the organization can be found in project organizations, line organizations, indirect department organizations, various management layers (top, middle management, lower layers), each specialized and functional layer, and beyond the walls between companies.

Companies with dynamic fractal organizations possess knowledge triad relationships as the smallest unit, enabling environmental adaptation and creation through the mutual conversion of tacit and explicit knowledge, and simultaneously allowing the sustainable evolution of new and existing knowledge assets, as innovation is realized through practical wisdom.

7.6 Implications and Conclusion

This chapter explores through case studies why existing companies are forced to withdraw from existing markets due to new products and business models created by "technology convergence (knowledge convergence)." During this exploratory research, field surveys revealed that existing companies cannot appropriately transform the high-quality tacit knowledge accumulated in the past in response to changes in the environment (technological innovation and new business models) and cannot drive the new knowledge creation spiral (SECI model).

This chapter clarifies why existing companies cannot respond to technology convergence from the perspective of existing research on knowledge creation theory and boundaries knowledge. It also mentions the core elements of holistic leadership, dynamic fractal organization, and collective phronesis required for companies and individual practitioners to respond to various knowledge convergences, including technological innovation.

From the perspective of the "Boundaries-based view (BBV)," the core element of the SECI process is to create, share, and empathize with new boundaries knowledge arising from various pragmatic boundaries within and outside the company (in other words, to synchronize pragmatic boundaries among actors within and outside the company and achieve boundaries knowledge synchronization), which becomes the source of innovation. Pragmatic boundaries raise various issues and challenges, and actors need to tackle these challenges and create new boundaries knowledge. Therefore, the key is how to achieve synchronization (convergence) of thoughts and activities among actors on pragmatic boundaries.

To drive the SECI process, which is the core element of new knowledge creation, it is necessary to transform existing tacit knowledge and create new tacit knowledge (tacit knowledge integration). For this, it is important to achieve boundaries knowledge synchronization among actors. This chapter presents the need for an integrated model of the organization's (company's) Boundaries-based view (BBV) and Attention-based view (ABV), as well as the SECI model.

This chapter presents a new theoretical model that realizes synchronization (convergence) at pragmatic boundaries by linking the Boundaries-based view (BBV) with attention control and problem-solving from the Attention-based view (ABV). This model points out that the structured interaction of the two elements, attention control and problem-solving, shifts the nature of boundaries among actors from semantic boundaries to pragmatic boundaries and synchronizes (converges) actors at pragmatic boundaries.

In companies (organizations) facing the uncertainty and novelty of the current management environment, it is necessary to synchronize (converge) the nature of boundaries among actors to pragmatic boundaries, and actors need to address current issues and problem-solving. This organizational process realizes boundaries knowledge synchronization among actors, transforms existing tacit knowledge, and triggers the SECI process. This chapter shows that such an integrated framework of the Boundaries-based view (BBV), Attention-based view (ABV), and SECI model is a key management element that determines the execution performance of corporate strategies (including product strategies) and realizes new knowledge creation in companies (organizations).

References

Carlile, P. (2002). A pragmatic view of knowledge and boundaries: Boundary objects in new product development. *Organization Science, 13*(4), 442–455.

Carlile, P. (2004). Transferring, translating, and transforming: An integrative framework for managing knowledge across boundaries. *Organization Science, 15*(5), 555–568.

Eisenhardt, K. (1989). Building theories from case study research. *Academy of Management Review, 14*, 532–550.

Grant, R. M. (1996). Toward a knowledge-based theory of the firm. *Strategic Management Journal, 17*(S2), 109–122.

Joseph, J., & Ocasio, W. (2012). Architecture, attention, and adaptation in the multibusiness firm: General electric from 1951 to 2001. *Strategic Management Journal, 33*(6), 633–660.

Kodama, M. (2005). Knowledge creation through networked strategic communities: Case studies in new product development. *Long Range Planning, 38*(1), 27–49.

Kodama, M. (2007a). *The strategic community-based firm*. Palgrave Macmillan.

Kodama, M. (2007b). *Knowledge innovation—strategic management as practice*. Edward Elgar Publishing.

Kodama, M. (2007c). *Project-based organization in the knowledge-based society*. Imperial College Press.

Kodama, M. (2007d). Innovation and knowledge creation through leadership-based strategic community: Case study on high-tech company in Japan. *Technovation, 27*(3), 115–132.

Kodama, M. (2017). Developing strategic innovation in large corporations—The dynamic capability view of the firm. *Knowledge and Process Management, 24*(4), 221–246.

Kodama, M. (2018). *Sustainable growth through strategic innovation—Developing congruence in capabilities*. Edward Elgar Publishing.

Kodama, M. (2019). Business innovation through holistic leadership-developing organizational adaptability. *Systems Research and Behavioral Science, 36*(4), 365–394.

Kodama, M. (2021). *Managing IT for innovation: Dynamic capabilities and competitive advantage*. Routledge.

Kodama, M., & Shibata, T. (2016). Developing knowledge convergence through a boundaries vision—A case study of fujifilm in Japan. *Knowledge and Process Management*, *23*(4), 274–292.

Laureiro-Martinez, D. (2014). Cognitive control capabilities, routinization propensity, and decision-making performance. *Organization Science, 25*(4), 1111–1133.

Leifer, R. (2000). *Radical innovation: How mature companies can outsmart upstarts*. Harvard Business Press.

Nonaka, I., Hirata, T., Kohlbacher, F., & Toyama, R. (2008). *Managing flow. Basingstoke*. Palgrave macmillan

Nonaka, I., Kodama, M., Hirose, A., & Kohlbacher, F. (2014). Dynamic fractal organizations for promoting knowledge-based transformation–A new paradigm for organizational theory. *European Management Journal*, *32*(1), 137–146.

Nonaka, I., & Takeuchi, H. (1995). *The knowledge-creating company: How Japanese companies create the dynamics of innovation*. Oxford University Press.

Nonaka, I., & Takeuchi, H. (2019). *The wise company: How companies create continuous innovation*. Oxford University Press.

Nonaka, I., & Toyama, R. (2007). Strategic management as distributed practical wisdom (phronesis). *Industrial and Corporate Change*, *16*(3), 371–394.

Ocasio, W. (1997). Towards an attention-based view of the firm. *Strategic Management Journal, 18*(S1), 187–206.

Ocasio, W. (2011). Attention to attention. *Organization Science, 22*(5), 1286–1296.

Ocasio, W., & Joseph, J. (2018). The attention-based view of great strategies. *Strategy Science, 3*(1), 289–294.

Ocasio, W., Laamanen, T., & Vaara, E. (2017). Communication and attention dynamics: An attention-based view of strategic change. *Strategic Management Journal*.

Ocasio, W., & Wohlgezogen, F. (2010). Attention and control. In *Organizational control* (pp. 191–221). Cambridge University Press.

Pettigrew, A. M. (1990). Longitudinal field research on change: Theory and practice. *Organization Science, 1*(1), 267–292.

Schein, H. (1985). *Organizational culture & leadership*. Jossey-Bass.

Schulze, A., & Brusoni, S. (2022). How dynamic capabilities change ordinary capabilities: Reconnecting attention control and problem-solving. *Strategic Management Journal*, Epub-ahead.

Selznick, P. (1957). *Leadership in administration*. Harper & Row.

Teece, D. J. (2007). Explicating dynamic capabilities: The nature and microfoundations of (sustainable) enterprise performance. *Strategic Management Journal, 28*(13), 1319–1350.

Teece, D. J. (2014). The foundations of enterprise performance: Dynamic and ordinary capabilities in an (economic) theory of firms. *The Academy of Management Perspectives, 28*(4), 328–352.

Vuori, T. O., & Huy, Q. N. (2016). Distributed attention and shared emotions in the innovation process: How Nokia lost the smartphone battle. *Administrative Science Quarterly*, *61*(1), 9–51.

Yin, R. K. (1994). *Case study research: Design and methods* (2nd ed.). Sage.

CHAPTER 8

Building Communities Through Holistic Leadership for Sustainable Innovation

8.1 Introduction—The Era of Knowledge Creation and Leadership

The rapid expansion of ICT/AI and the development of environmentally conscious systems are accelerating transformations in various fields such as industry, economy, and society. ICT/AI continues to evolve as a platform that interactively networks people around the world, enabling the dissemination, sharing, inspiration, creation, and accumulation of diverse data, information, and knowledge. Meanwhile, environmentally conscious systems are becoming essential infrastructure as core technologies for circular socio-economic systems.

For example, new business models driven by ICT/AI platforms, represented by innovative products like the iPhone and ChatGPT, and the emergence of new technological systems such as smart grids and electric vehicles aimed at realizing circular socio-economic systems, are poised to significantly shift strategic models that traditionally focused on inter-company competition within industries.

The phenomenon of "convergence," which underlies the development of new technologies through the fusion of different technologies, including ICT/AI, and the creation of new business models that span different industries, is making traditional inter-company competition increasingly complex. Convergence rapidly accelerates strategic alliances, joint ventures, strategic outsourcing, and M&A among companies,

M. Kodama, *Developing Knowledge Convergence Through Collective Phronesis*, https://doi.org/10.1007/978-981-96-4403-2_8

includes customers, and can significantly alter existing corporate boundaries. In this context, "collaboration strategies" through inter-industry cooperation beyond mere inter-industry competition, are becoming increasingly important as core drivers of corporate strategy. In other words, for modern innovative companies, it is urgent to shift from strategies that emphasize inter-company competition within industries and inter-industry competition to collaboration strategies with various industries (companies), including customers.

In recent years, companies have faced the urgent task of promoting global business expansion, including in emerging markets, through collaboration strategies with partners worldwide and the leadership to execute these strategies. Additionally, in the knowledge economy of the twenty-first century, individual values and attitudes toward life and work have significantly changed, and the nature and concept of "communities," including corporate organizations and non-profit organizations, are also evolving.

Particularly within corporate organizations, the rapid expansion of ICT has led to the proactive adoption of knowledge management methods aimed at accumulating and utilizing knowledge within individuals and organizations, driving corporate transformation at a global level. However, the critical perspective is that no matter how much ICT/AI is integrated to transform operations, the foundation of a company's strategic actions lies in the innovation of individual values, knowledge, and core competencies accumulated by individuals.

Furthermore, to promote ICT/AI businesses and circular businesses that span different industries, as mentioned earlier, companies must strategically incorporate external knowledge and core competencies that they do not possess internally. Companies need leadership that can generate continuous business innovation through collaboration strategies that emphasize relationships with others.[1]

Therefore, corporate leaders must actively create communities based on the formation of diverse multilayered Ba with internal and external partners, including customers, to build organizational platforms for promoting collaboration strategies. This involves innovating their own core competencies while absorbing the core competencies of excellent external partners and promoting the fusion and integration of these competencies with their own. The strategic actions of corporate leaders toward community creation based on the formation of Ba ultimately lead to the continuous creation of new value for customers.[2]

Such dense collaboration strategies through community creation promote knowledge creation activities among various organizations both within and outside the company. Community creation within the company enhances its organizational capabilities, while community creation among companies, including customers, can trigger the synergy of core competencies between companies.

Furthermore, the fundamental idea behind collaboration strategies through inter-industry cooperation lies in promoting "co-creation and co-evolution" through community creation. Co-creation means creating new businesses, economies, and societies together with customers and partners, while co-evolution is based on the idea of evolving not only the community but also broader economic and social communities with customers and partners to achieve sustainable innovation.

Therefore, the most important challenge for companies (organizations) in promoting collaboration strategies is how to create communities that generate co-creation and co-evolution both within and outside the company, including customers. To this end, community leaders must demonstrate leadership that creates communities based on the formation of diverse Ba within companies, while also transcending the narrow strategic views of inter-industry competition and competition within industries. It is crucial to acquire leadership oriented toward collaboration with diverse partners and customers worldwide. Thus, today, the way leadership is exercised to promote knowledge creation activities through collaboration strategies that span across and within companies (organizations) at a global level is being strongly questioned.

8.2 ICT Innovation Through Convergence

In cutting-edge technology fields such as ICT, energy, automotive, electronics, semiconductors, biotechnology, pharmaceuticals, and materials science, excellent core technologies are distributed among companies, organizations, and even individuals worldwide. The integration of these superior core technologies is the source of innovation, leading to new products and services (e.g., Kodama, 2007).

ICT innovation broadly changes work styles, lifestyles, and production activities across various sectors of society. It alters the way products are made and resources are utilized, and by embedding ICT technology into various advanced devices, it directly and indirectly contributes to CO_2 reduction. ICT innovation promotes energy-saving investments and measures, advancing energy-efficient manufacturing. Such ICT innovation fosters "convergence," which involves the fusion and integration of different technologies and services, as well as the creation of business models that span different industries.

Meanwhile, in the context of the adoption of the new international framework for reducing greenhouse gas emissions, the Paris Agreement, all participating countries, including developed, emerging, and developing nations, are strongly required to tackle global warming. Specifically, in recent years, Cyber-Physical Systems (CPS) and the Internet of Things (IoT) have become global trends. The collaboration and integration of the ICT industry with various other industrial sectors are transforming people's lives, social activities, and various businesses. The evolution of these innovative technologies is underpinned by the convergence of ICT and electronics technologies, including sensing technology, location information technology, energy management systems (HEMS, BEMS, FEMS, etc.), energy-saving devices, and data utilization.

Furthermore, the smart communities such as startup towns and smart cities, which are currently becoming prominent in various countries, are attracting attention as next-generation social systems that connect homes, buildings, and transportation systems through ICT networks to efficiently utilize energy within the region. In smart communities, the use of ICT solutions such as energy management systems (HEMS, BEMS, FEMS) to optimally operate smart meters, renewable energy, EVs, and CEMS for integrated management, as well as ITS for transportation systems, is indispensable. The development of these innovative technologies significantly contributes to reducing CO_2 emissions and dramatically increases energy-saving effects. Moreover, the XR technology expected in the future will minimize the physical resources generated, utilized, and consumed in various processes of social, economic, and business activities, directly and indirectly contributing to addressing global environmental issues.

Therefore, to achieve this, ICT/AI industries in various countries need to understand their environmental contributions, such as measures against global warming, and further strengthen technical and ethical business partnerships with various industries. By promoting new technologies and businesses through convergence strategies that open up the future, these industries can contribute to the global society. The impacts of climate change, such as extreme weather, rising sea levels, and loss of biodiversity, are now unavoidable major issues. Solving these problems requires new styles of collaboration involving companies, industries, communities, governments, and individuals. By promoting new technologies and businesses through convergence strategies that open up the future, they must contribute to the global society.

So far, the evolution of ICT/AI has shortened the time and space of business processes and supply chains in all industries, enhancing management efficiency and speeding up decision-making, while also creating new business models that cross and integrate different industries (Kodama, 2020, 2021). ICT innovation promotes the co-creation and co-evolution of entire industries toward improving the global environment, forming a dynamic "global ecosystem" as a new value chain, and increases the potential for achieving sustainable innovation (see Fig. 8.1).

To create new business models that generate ICT innovation through the convergence of different technologies and industries, what strategic actions and organizational reforms should companies, public organizations, government bodies, and even entire nations take? What should leadership and management be for this purpose? These practical

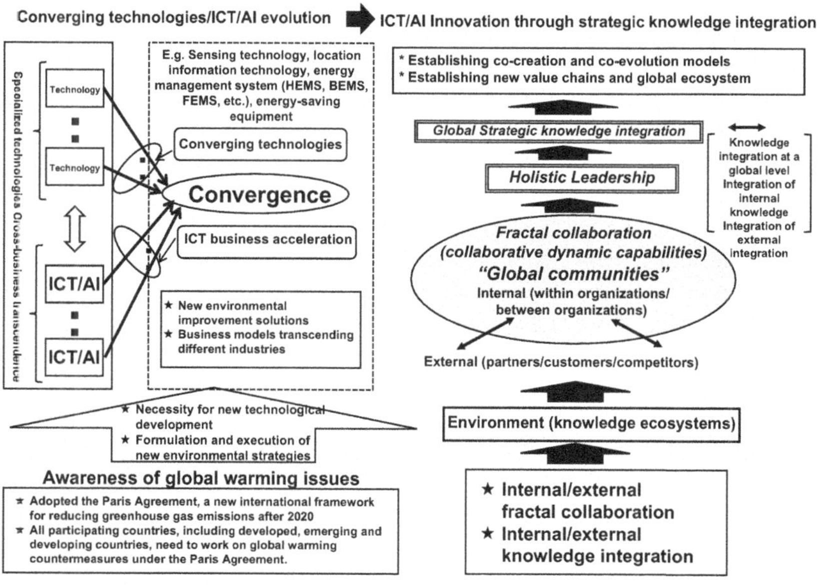

(Note) Prepared by the author

Fig. 8.1 Global ICT/AI innovation through holistic leadership

challenges, given to many stakeholders worldwide, include numerous academic research topics.

Although the details of strategies in individual industries, companies, and government organizations in each country vary, the key concept of organizational behavior to adapt to (or create) this worldview of convergence lies in the new "strategic knowledge integration" at the global level. The organizational platform that supports such global strategic knowledge integration is the formation of "global communities." Global communities are important organizational platforms that evolve core knowledge within a country while actively exploring excellent knowledge worldwide and integrating it with domestic core knowledge (see Fig. 8.1).

In promoting global strategic knowledge integration, it is crucial not only to integrate knowledge within diverse organizations but also to form global communities consisting of excellent stakeholders worldwide, including customers. The most important task is to integrate superior knowledge from the external environment, an ecosystem of dispersed knowledge worldwide, with the knowledge within organizations. The keyword to accelerate such global knowledge integration within and outside the organization is "fractal collaboration."

The formation of global communities across various countries involves appropriately generating and evaluating "common knowledge (i.e., lexicon, meaning, and interests)" (Carlile, 2004) among diverse stakeholders and utilizing these collaborative dynamic capabilities (Kodama, 2018) to trigger fractal collaboration.

Furthermore, the leadership of leaders from various countries is essential to accelerate new strategic knowledge integration through "ICT collaboration" formed by global communities across diverse nations. For this purpose, "holistic leadership" (Kodama, 2017), which involves holistic thinking and actions, becomes a particularly important management element for global leaders.

8.3 Inevitable Global Environmental Issues

Recently, more companies are embarking on accelerating digital transformation (DX), cloud, and AI. The importance of various cloud services, which are central to these technological innovations, as well as the data centers necessary for AI development and applications, is increasing. This is driven by advancements in ICT/AI technology aimed at expanding new markets, such as improved processing speeds and higher capacities.

Specifically, worldwide demand for more data centers, which are expected to consume more electricity, is anticipated. This raises concerns about the impact on global environmental issues, making data center measures urgent.

By 2025, the ICT industry is expected to use 20% of the world's electricity and emit up to 5.5% of the world's carbon dioxide emissions. Additionally, data centers themselves are projected to account for more than half of the industry's emissions, releasing 1.9 billion tons of carbon dioxide (2025 forecast), equivalent to 3.2% of the world's total carbon dioxide emissions. To reduce such carbon dioxide emissions, the latest cooling technologies for data centers include: (1) Immersion cooling: a method of cooling ICT equipment by immersing it in an insulating liquid (such as fluorinated inert liquid or silicone oil). (2) Cooling systems using new refrigerants: cooling systems that use new non-fluorocarbon refrigerants. (3) Utilization of power semiconductor (gallium nitride) technologies: using advanced power semiconductors to improve the energy efficiency of data centers.

Furthermore, as medium- to long-term measures for data centers, the use of low-orbit satellites and the moon is being considered. Firstly, the American company LyteLoop plans to launch dozens of small satellites to establish data centers in low orbit. Secondly, by placing data centers in space rather than on the ground, the low temperatures in space and the advantage of solar power generation, as well as physical security, can be ensured. Thirdly, in the distant future, data centers may be constructed on the moon, and interplanetary internet (via satellites) between the Earth and the moon may be realized.

Moreover, there is a significant demand for reducing power consumption in network equipment that connects data centers. For example, in the IWON concept proposed by NTT, Japan's largest telecommunications carrier, the plan is to replace the transmission and processing of information from electrical signals to optical signals. This aims to eliminate waste such as electrical resistance, improve power efficiency by 100 times (reducing power consumption to 1/100), increase transmission capacity by 125 times, and reduce latency to 1/200. Significant energy-saving effects are expected, with full-scale implementation targeted around 2030.

Thus, the impacts of climate change, such as extreme weather, sea level rise, and loss of biodiversity due to global warming, have become unavoidable major issues. To solve these problems, new styles of collaborative activities involving companies, industries, communities, governments, and individuals are necessary. This chapter discusses the following two frameworks:

1. Co-creation model for decarbonization management: "Integration of Mind, Skill, and Body"
2. Management of co-creation through fractal collaboration

8.4 Concept for Decarbonized Management

8.4.1 Holistic Leadership Framework from Previous Research

The keyword "Holistic leadership" has been discussed in the academic research field, particularly in the context of "Spiritual leadership" (e.g., Dhiman, 2017) and "School leadership" (e.g., Shaked & Schechter, 2017). Managers of organizations and teachers in schools are not only expected to have management techniques and skills but also to possess high awareness, humanity, and morality, embodying spirituality. Such leaders can foster dedicated collaboration among organizational members and lead organizations to success. Fry (2003) mentions that spiritual leaders must develop courageous visions and mission statements that promote cooperation, trust, and mutual spiritual development, embracing credibility, education, trust, and inspiration. They must be competent in four areas to acquire knowledge about group activities. Furthermore, Fry (2003) states that "Spiritual leadership" requires "holistic leadership" that integrates the four fundamental areas defining human existence: body (physical), mind (logical/rational thinking), heart (emotions, feelings), and spirit.

Although these previous studies are important literature for organizational management, they hardly mention the leadership elements necessary for companies to continuously grow sustainably over the long term toward knowledge creation through continuous innovation. This chapter reviews major literature from extensive previous research on leadership using the keywords "organizational adaptability," "knowledge creation," "corporate innovation," and "new product development (NPD)." Specifically, it refers to the "holistic leadership" framework that integrates four areas from approaches deeply related to these keywords from previous research: (1) leadership corresponding to Complex Adaptive System (CAS), (2) leadership in the knowledge creation process, (3) approaches from corporate innovation literature, and (4) approaches from new product development literature.

(1) Approach from Complex Adaptive System (CAS) Literature

One of the greatest challenges faced by corporate leaders is how to enhance organizational adaptability, allowing individual practitioners and organizations to not only develop existing businesses but also innovate in ever-changing and highly competitive environments. Organizational adaptability in developing existing businesses means "exploitation," while innovation signifies "exploration" (March, 1991). March (1991) expressed this conflicting necessity in the two aspects of organizational learning as this exploration and exploitation. Exploration involves creating new knowledge, skills, and processes through investigation, diversity, risk-taking, experimentation, play, flexibility, innovation, and discovery to maintain the future viability of the corporation (organization). Exploitation, on the other hand, uses existing knowledge, skills, and processes through selection, refinement, efficiency, implementation, and execution to achieve current corporate (organizational) success.

Leadership for organizational adaptability, which balances exploitation and exploration, differs from traditional leadership theory. The traits of leadership for organizational adaptability newly derived from this research differ from the traits of "style leadership" theory, which, like conventional leadership theory, are attributes of only top management and certain leaders. Style leadership theory has been criticized for not sufficiently considering contingencies (Gill, 2006). This is due to the existence of style leadership independent of a strategy context or organizational context that changes dynamically, and thus, the leadership style and behavior remain static. Therefore, it can be said that static leadership of this type is unsuitable as a leadership theory for achieving business innovation in dynamically changing management environments.

As Uhl-Bien and Arena (2018) also pointed out, leadership for organizational adaptability is different from transformational leadership. Instead of emphasizing top-down transformational promotion by leaders, such as visions and inspiration (e.g., Baur et al., 2016), the focus is on how leaders enable adaptability within the organization and its people when faced with complex and challenging tasks such as realizing new innovations. This means that leaders and managers at each level of management promote communication and collaboration among members within their organizations, while providing flexibility, agility, and adaptability to the rapid and often unpredictable changes in the world (e.g., Keister, 2014; Uhl-Bien et al., 2007).

Uhl-Bien and Arena (2018) derived an integrated framework for leadership for organizational adaptability by reviewing major theories from the literature on ambidexterity and dynamic capabilities, organization theory, entrepreneurship, innovation, networks, and complexity theory. They clarify the implications of the approach to leadership for organizational adaptability.

In the integrated framework by Uhl-Bien and Arena (2018) (see Fig. 8.2), the leadership necessary for organizational adaptability includes three types of leadership: (a) "entrepreneurial leadership" (e.g., endogenous entrepreneurship), (b) "enabling leadership" that enables adaptive processes through adaptive space, and (c) "operational leadership" that incorporates novelty into the core of business operations as an adaptive new order, and deals with novelty (e.g., reintegration). These three types of leadership are not hierarchical processes; rather, they can be exercised at any management level, whether in informal or formal organizations.

"Entrepreneurial leadership," focuses on innovation, and is mainly exercised in autonomous and decentralized networks of new organizations, which are informal organizations. In contrast, "operational leadership," centered on core business operations, is mainly exercised in centralized and existing organizations, which are formal organizations. "Enabling leadership" is exercised in the middle ground between "decentralization and centralization," that is, between informal organizations (networks) and formal organizations (structures).

"Entrepreneurial leadership" does not presuppose a bottom-up approach. In fact, this leadership often originates from the top (such as CEOs like Steve Jobs mentioned in Chapter 3). Whether initiated by top leaders or not, business challenges remain the same at any management level. Leaders must advance entrepreneurial ideas to commercialization (practical application), and such processes are conducted in "adaptive spaces" (see Fig. 8.2).

Complex adaptive systems realize adaptive spaces (Arena et al., 2017; Uhl-Bien & Arena, 2017) where the adaptability arises at the junction of the conflicting needs of exploration (entrepreneurial activities) and

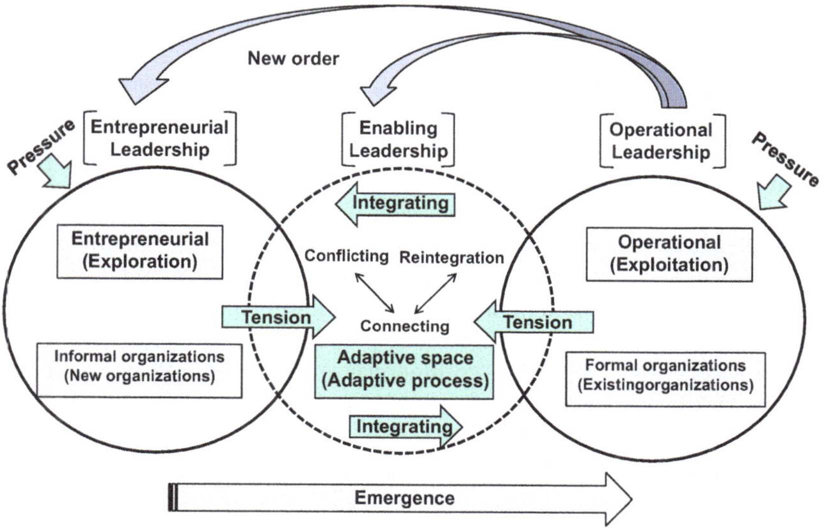

Source: Created by the author based on Figures 4 and 5 in Uhl-Bien, et al. (2018)

Fig. 8.2 Framework of leadership from complex adaptive theory

exploitation (activities of existing core businesses), overcoming conflicts and tensions. These adaptive spaces deal with the tensions caused by these pressures and use integration mechanisms (e.g., connecting) to generate adaptive responses (such as innovations through learning and knowledge creation) that can be implemented as a new adaptive order in the core of business operations as new businesses.

Integration mechanisms (e.g., connecting) involve linking ideas, knowledge, human resources, and technologies to expand novelty and innovation, forming new orders favorable to the existing management systems. Leaders create adaptive spaces by building informal organizations (network structures such as strategic communities) that activate and amplify the emergence of novelty and innovation, achieving connections (Arena et al., 2017; Uhl-Bien & Arena, 2017). Leaders effectively engage with conflicts (i.e., tension) and connections (i.e., integration), triggering and amplifying idea creation (knowledge creation and adaptive responses toward innovation) and enabling the realization of structures and processes for new adaptive orders in organizations (i.e., reintegration).

This core "adaptive process" involves addressing the tension between the necessity of innovation and the promotion of existing core businesses (March, 1991). Adaptive processes by leaders manifest in the following behaviors: Entrepreneurial leaders advance new ideas that conflict with the existing core business management systems (ideas that are difficult to implement, too costly, require resources not currently present in the organization, oppose dominant organizational identities, or are disruptive technologies). Entrepreneurial leaders reconfigure these ideas into more feasible, superior ones (new products, processes, services, technologies, market directions) and realize commercialization as official management systems (business operation systems) through the operational leadership of leaders in existing organizations.

In the middle of the process from idea creation to commercialization, enabling leaders create conditions (adaptive spaces) that allow conflicting and connecting through the exercise of enabling leadership, triggering, activating, and further amplifying ideas, expanding them into new orders (emergence) that fit the adaptive needs of organizations and their environments. Enabling leaders support this process from idea creation to commercialization (see Fig. 8.2).

As shown in Fig. 8.2, when positioning the three types of leadership—"entrepreneurial leadership," "enabling leadership," and "operational leadership"—within categories such as organizational management levels, informal organizations, formal organizations, new organizations, and existing organizations, as well as adaptive spaces, an important perspective is that these three types of leadership are not hierarchical processes. Rather, they are appropriately positioned and exercised at any management level (top management, middle management, lower management), organizational form (formal and informal organizations), and in adaptive spaces that enable conflict and connection.

On the other hand, these three types of leadership can be described as "ambidextrous leadership" (O'Reilly & Tushman, 2004), which is centered on enabling leadership and encompasses the two different elements of entrepreneurial leadership and operational leadership. Ambidextrous leadership is a trait not only appearing at the top of an organization but also present in all members within the organization (Birkinshaw & Gibson, 2004). Employees with ambidextrous leadership consciously choose their targets and methods to focus their energy, without seeking permission or support from their superiors. They are sufficiently motivated to act on their own initiative and recognize the need to take strategically aligned actions while aiming for adaptation by creating collaborative situations between different organizations (Birkinshaw & Gibson, 2004).

As will be discussed later, "entrepreneurial leadership," "enabling leadership," and "operational leadership" correspond to "distributed leadership," "dialectical leadership (the coexistence of distributed leadership and centralized leadership)," and "centralized leadership," respectively.

8.5 (2) Approach from Knowledge Creation Theory Literature

Von Krogh et al. (2012) conducted a detailed review of leadership research within knowledge creation theory and drew the following two conclusions. Firstly, previous research has primarily focused on "centralized leadership." Generally, the knowledge creation process needs to be realized within its context. Therefore, it is unrealistic to expect knowledge creation in organizations to be the duty of exceptional leaders, reminiscent of the traditional "great man" theory of leadership. The theories of "strategic leadership" (e.g., Bollinger & Smith, 2001; Bontis & Fitzenz, 2002; Fedor et al., 2003; Ho, 2009; Inkpen, 1998; Lakshman, 2005, 2007; Skyrme & Amidon, 1997), "style leadership" (e.g., Bell DeTienne et al., 2004; Huang et al., 2008; Ribière & Sitar, 2003; Singh, 2008; Yang, 2007), and "transformational leadership" (e.g., Gagné, 2009) each exhibit an excessive bias toward centralized leadership and present practical issues within the knowledge creation process. This is because, realistically, it is the leaders on the ground who implement knowledge creation.

Secondly, while organizational knowledge creation theory (organizational knowledge creation theory) has recognized the individual contributions to knowledge creation, it has not explicitly considered the synergy or tension between distributed leadership (Kodama, 2003; Nonaka & Toyama, 2002) and centralized leadership. Autonomy, empowerment, and the need for distributed leadership, although addressed in many previous studies, have nonetheless been discussed in relation to centralized leadership. However, the nature of distributed leadership in knowledge creation has hardly been presented (e.g., Couillard & Lapierre, 2003). Even in studies explicitly combining centralized leadership and distributed leadership (Robertson & Swan, 2003), the interrelationship of these leadership activities within specific organizational contexts has been weakly addressed.

From this perspective, von Krogh et al. (2012) found crucial insights in advancing a new theoretical framework for leadership in organizational knowledge creation based on these critiques. Furthermore, they highlighted that previous research has not explicitly examined the relationships between SECI, Ba, and knowledge assets, but rather analyzed specific parts of the model.

In response to previous criticisms, von Krogh et al. (2012) have presented a new theoretical framework for leadership that aims to demonstrate how to integrate distributed leadership and centralized leadership, involving leaders and members in the SECI process within organizations. Nonaka et al. (2014) referred to leadership that facilitates the SECI process—a spiral mutual conversion of tacit and explicit knowledge—and balances exploration and exploitation as “phronetic leadership.” This interpretation aligns with the previously mentioned “leadership for organizational adaptability.”

They emphasized the importance of the presence of three layers (structural layer, conditional layer, core active layer) that constitute a corporate organization and the forms of leadership within each layer (centralized leadership, centralized& distributed leadership, and distributed leadership) to promote knowledge creation activities (see Fig. 8.3). The formal organization, as the “structural layer,” is characterized by a formal structure, managerial responsibility, management, and division of labor, whereas the informal organization, as the “core active layer,” features autonomous and voluntary groups with authority and responsibility (e.g., Bernard, 1988; Scott, 1961; Wren, 1987).

From the perspective of organizational theory, von Krogh et al. (2012) pointed out that the intersection of autonomous decentralized actions within informal organizations and routine processes within formal organizations creates various frictions and conflicts. These elements are critical for observing and analyzing innovations known as knowledge creation activities and suggest the expansion of future research domains.

Informal organizations are essential for organizational knowledge creation, creativity, and innovation. The knowledge creation activities that occur within informal organizations are extremely dynamic and depend on elements such as individual efforts, contributions, and luck (Nonaka & von Krogh, 2009). Therefore, von Krogh et al. (2012) state that in

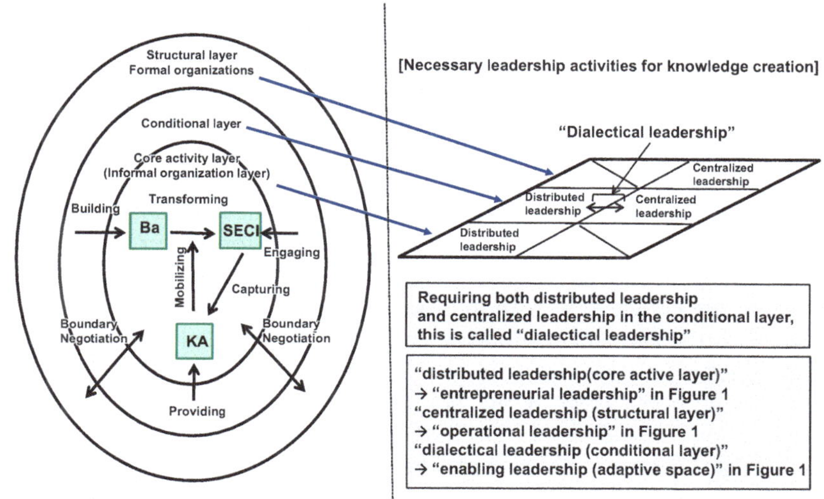

Source: von Krogh, Nonaka and Rechsteiner (2012), Figure 1

Source: Created by the author based on von Krogh, Nonaka and Rechsteiner (2012), Table 3

Fig. 8.3 Framework of leadership from knowledge creation theory

considering leadership in organizational knowledge creation, attention should be paid to the intersection of activities related to distributed leadership, which is strongly associated with informal organizations (so-called informal human networks) (Kodama, 2003; Nonaka & Toyama, 2002), and centralized leadership, which is more strongly associated with formal organizations (Kodama, 2003). This intersecting part corresponds to the adaptive spaces and adaptive processes of the CAS approach mentioned in the previous section by Uhl-Bien and Arena (2018).

To deepen the understanding of leadership for organizational adaptability, similar to the assertions of von Krogh et al. (2012), research must focus on how leaders promote adaptive processes through feasible adaptive spaces (Uhl-Bien & Marion, 2009; Uhl-Bien et al., 2007). Von Krogh et al. (2012) clarified this intersecting characteristic by introducing activities in the third layer (conditional layer) as an "intersection" connected to both the formal organization (structural layer) and the informal organization (core active layer). In the "conditional layer," distributed leadership and centralized leadership activities shape the conditions necessary for interactions between micro-strategies, Ba, knowledge assets, and the SECI process. Moreover, in the conditional layer, leaders are required to balance distributed leadership and centralized leadership (see Fig. 8.3).

In this conditional layer, as indicated by organizational knowledge creation theory (Nonaka & Takeuchi, 1995), top-level and middle-level managers mediate crucial resources and make them accessible, enabling interactions among members or groups engaged in knowledge creation activities. Leadership and management in the conditional layer hold significant importance for the organization by linking informal organizations, in which the knowledge creation process occurs, known as the core active layer, with the formal organization that overlays it, called the "structural layer." According to von Krogh et al., (2012, p. 263), the functions of the conditional layer at the boundary between formal and informal organizations include: "(1) facilitate the integration of Ba, SECI, and knowledge assets; and (2) provide the flow of resources, people, connections, and information for knowledge creation." They propose three leadership activities to accomplish this: building, providing, and engaging (see Fig. 8.3).

To succeed in innovation through knowledge creation activities, practitioners need to engage in various boundary negotiations centered around the conditional layer among these three layers. The three leadership activities in the conditional layer as mentioned by von Krogh et al., (2012, Table III in p. 268)—"Building Ba," "Providing knowledge assets," and "Motivating participants to engage"—along with the boundary negotiations among the three layers are interpreted as the adaptive processes in the adaptive spaces approach of CAS mentioned earlier. This involves addressing the conflicts and tensions between the necessity of innovation and the needs of existing core businesses (March, 1991).

In essence, leaders engage in conflict (addressing and negotiating pressures for innovation and core business) and connection (linking ideas and resources to expand novelty and innovation into a favorable new order for business operation systems). By realizing adaptive spaces, they advance ideas and create business operation systems that lead to new adaptive orders (see Fig. 8.3). Practitioners synthesize contradictions and undergo dynamic transitions by engaging in practical activities within conditional layers and adaptive spaces between formal and informal organizations. In such conditional layers, leaders need to demonstrate dialectical leadership that balances distributed leadership and centralized leadership.

The practical activities of practitioners in the formal structural layer and the informal core active layer have an interactive relationship over time. Practitioners share new contexts and knowledge, inspire, and create new knowledge through practical activities in informal organizations. They then transform the newly inspired and created contexts and knowledge in informal organizations into new outcomes (solutions to problems and challenges, development of prototypes, and completion of commercial products) through practical actions across entire formal organizations, creating new knowledge.

Informal organizations do not oppose formal organizations. Practitioners complement the dual nature of these organizational forms through practical actions aimed at realizing knowledge creation. Leadership and management that integrate the bureaucratic nature of formal organizations with the network characteristics of informal organizations are crucial for innovation. One such concept is the existence of conditional layers or adaptive spaces (see Figs. 8.2 and 8.3).

Additionally, as shown in Figs. 8.2 and 8.3, the three forms of leadership proposed in the CAS approach by Uhl-Bien and Arena (2018)—entrepreneurial leadership, operational leadership, and enabling leadership (adaptive space)—correspond to the distributed leadership (core active layer), centralized leadership (structural layer), and dialectical leadership (conditional layer) presented by von Krogh et al. (2012).

Next, let's explain the relationship between the SECI model and these three forms of leadership. In knowledge creation theory, there are two dimensions of knowledge: "tacit knowledge" and "explicit knowledge," which are mutually converted and continuously create new knowledge (Nonaka & Takeuchi, 1995). Knowledge creation activities involve the mutual conversion process of tacit knowledge derived from an individual's body, thoughts, and feelings, and explicit knowledge that has been verbalized. These two dimensions are contrasting but continuous. An individual's tacit knowledge is shared with others to become explicit knowledge, which combines with other explicit knowledge to create new explicit knowledge, which is then converted back into tacit knowledge, leading to the next conversion process. Innovation arises from the spiraling up of this conversion process (the SECI model).

The third dimension of knowledge that facilitates this spiraling up (sublation of tacit and explicit knowledge) is practical wisdom (Phronesis). Phronesis is a concept proposed by the ancient Greek philosopher Aristotle in his "Nicomachean Ethics" and is translated as prudence or practical wisdom. Phronesis is practical knowledge that allows for the best judgment in each specific context, based on the value standard of the common good. It is characterized by "contemplation in action," "contextual judgment," and "timely balancing."

Thus, positioning phronesis as the third type of knowledge that promotes the spiraling up of tacit and explicit knowledge, this model that synthesizes the three types of knowledge is called the "Knowledge Triad Relationship" (Nonaka et al., 2014) (see Fig. 8.4). As previously mentioned, informal organizations are essential for organizational knowledge creation, creativity, and innovation. The knowledge creation activities occurring within informal organizations are highly dynamic and influenced by elements of tacit knowledge (tacit knowing), such as personal beliefs, thoughts, creativity, and practical ability (e.g., Kodama, 2017).

Therefore, considering leadership in organizational knowledge creation, it is closely related to the "tacit knowing domain." In this domain, distributed leadership (core active layer) of members active in informal organizations is mainly exercised (Kodama, 2003; Nonaka & Toyama, 2002) (see Fig. 8.4). On the other hand, in formal organizations, the leaders play a role in exercising centralized leadership, formulating visions and strategic goals, and initiating these visions and strategies in the overall direction of various organizational units.

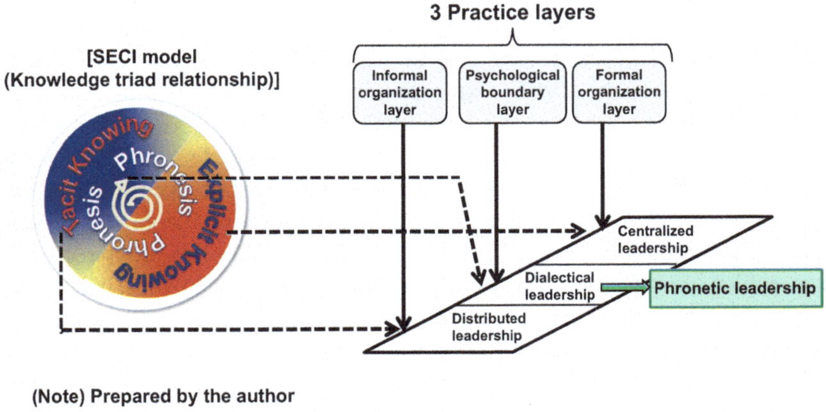

Fig. 8.4 Relationship between three types of leadership and the SECI model

A vision clarifies existing knowledge areas within the organization and links these to the areas where new knowledge should be pursued. Furthermore, the vision serves as an important means of justifying the involvement of organizational members in tasks related to knowledge creation, providing an overview of various challenges and issues to be addressed. Such a knowledge vision motivates employees toward higher driving goals.

Therefore, as an element that promotes organizational knowledge creation by organizational members, it is closely related to the "explicit knowing domain." In this domain, the centralized leadership (structural layer) of organizational members is mainly exercised (Kodama, 2003; Nonaka & Toyama, 2002) (see Fig. 8.4).

Furthermore, as mentioned earlier, in the conditional layer, which serves as an "intersection" connecting both formal organizations (structural layer) and informal organizations (core active layer), distributed leadership and centralized leadership form the necessary conditions for the interactions between strategy, Ba, knowledge assets, and the SECI process. In the conditional layer, leaders are required to balance distributed leadership, which promotes "tacit knowing," and centralized leadership, which promotes "explicit knowing." Nonaka et al. (2014) refer to the leadership that facilitates the SECI process—a spiral mutual conversion of tacit and explicit knowledge—and balances exploration and exploitation as phronetic leadership, corresponding to the previously mentioned leadership for organizational adaptability.

Phronesis promotes the spiral-up of the SECI process (synthesis of tacit and explicit knowledge) and forms the Knowledge Triad Relationship (see Fig. 8.4). Practitioners drive the SECI process through dynamic transitions, synthesizing contradictions, and addressing various frictions and conflicts that arise in practical activities within the conditional layer or adaptive space. Therefore, in the conditional layer, leaders need to demonstrate dialectical leadership that balances distributed leadership and centralized leadership. Dialectical leadership is also phronetic leadership, which involves the practice of phronesis to promote the synthesis of tacit and explicit knowledge.

8.6 (3) Approach from Corporate Innovation Literature

In literature on corporate innovation through the construction of an "ambidextrous organization," balancing the tension between the necessity for innovation and the necessity for production by existing businesses is crucial for companies (organizations) to maintain adaptability and viability over the long term (Tushman & O'Reilly, 1996). An ambidextrous organization leverages current capabilities (exploitation) while exploring entirely new capabilities (exploration) (Levinthal & March, 1993).

In other words, to achieve renewal (innovation) and adapt to the future through new product development and breakthrough innovation, change, flexibility, creativity, and entrepreneurship are necessary, along with visionary, all-inclusive leadership centered on new organizations. At the same time, efficiency and profit through existing core businesses require order, control, and stability, demanding authoritative and top-down leadership centered on existing organizations (Cegarra-Navarro & Dewhurst, 2007; O'Reilly & Tushman, 2004). These different types of leadership correspond to entrepreneurial leadership and operational leadership in Fig. 8.2, and distributed leadership and centralized leadership in Fig. 8.3.

Because exploration and exploitation have fundamentally different logics and very different structures, the core of ambidexterity involves a tension that is central to the long-term survival of the company. Organizations gain adaptability through this tension, but reconciling this tension is very difficult and must be well managed (Tushman & O'Reilly, 1996). If not, the company may eventually face difficulties (He & Wong, 2004). Leaders who successfully manage the duality of creativity for innovation and efficiency for existing business promotion require adaptability precisely because conflicting forces exist simultaneously in the core tension of ambidexterity (Smith & Tushman, 2005).

There is a psychological space–time where tensions and conflicts arise between new organizations (exploratory businesses) and existing organizations (exploitative businesses). This corresponds to the adaptive space or conditional layer mentioned in Figs. 8.2 and 8.3, requiring the exercise of enabling leadership and dialectical leadership by leaders.

The ambidextrous organization (O'Reilly & Tushman, 2004) is a successful pattern for new businesses in American companies. In American companies, "ambidextrous leadership" is exercised, with new organizations and existing organizations each setting different business goals and simultaneously achieving short-term and long-term innovations under shared visions and values. Fujitsu, a leading Japanese telecommunications equipment company, has created an independent new business (NC: Numerical Computing) within the company by constructing an ambidextrous organization, growing it as an in-house venture organization (later Fanuc) (Kodama & Shibata, 2014). Furthermore, even after separating from Fujitsu as Fanuc, they achieved technological transitions in products through the construction of an ambidextrous organization that balanced existing organizations with new organizations responsible for new technologies (Shibata & Kodama, 2008).

However, while the organizational pattern of constructing a separate new organization different from the main body, as seen in an ambidextrous organization, is very efficient for new strategic innovations, it is not without problems. There are challenges regarding the long-term integration and harmony of "new organizational culture" and "old organizational culture" (Markides, 1997). Additionally, by contrast, other research has indicated that general managers are a source of friction so that interchange between the organizations in the form of a mutual general manager should be limited while interaction at a practical level should be increased (Govindarajan & Trimble, 2005).

On the other hand, companies like Apple and Japan's DOCOMO aimed for strategy transformation through new business creation. Apple launched the music distribution business with iPod and iTunes music store (Kodama, 2011b), and DOCOMO launched the world's first service to connect mobile phones to the internet, i-mode (Kodama, 2002, 2003, 2004). They created new businesses through a "collaboration strategy" between new project-based organizations and existing organizations within the same company. The case of DOCOMO, as an "integrated organization," succeeded in innovation by coexisting different corporate cultures within the same company and managing the interference and friction between organizations and individuals.

Although an integrated organization like DOCOMO involves significant friction in creating new businesses, it is considered advantageous for the integration of corporate cultures and the formation of new identities. Even in such an integrated organization, similar to an ambidextrous organization, there exists a psychological space–time of tension and conflict between new organizations (promoting exploratory business with "distributed leadership") and existing organizations (promoting exploitative business with "centralized leadership"). This corresponds to the adaptive space or conditional layer mentioned in Figs. 8.2 and 8.3, requiring leaders to exercise enabling leadership and dialectical leadership (see Fig. 8.5).

From the corporate innovation cases of Apple and DOCOMO, a common perspective on organizational behavior within companies is the need for "integrative capability" to connect multiple organizations within the company (existing organizations, new organizations, projects, etc.) and between companies (external partners and customers). Integrative capability forms adaptive space and generates the adaptive process (conflicting/connecting/reintegrating). Organizations and companies that produce new innovations rely on a close collaboration strategy (Kodama, 2015) with existing organizations, external partners,

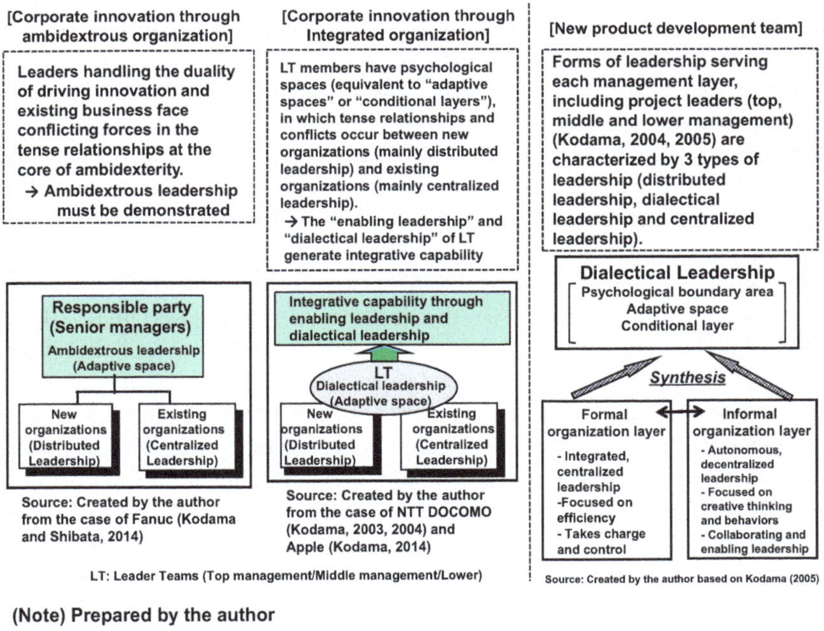

Fig. 8.5 A framework of leadership from corporate innovation and new product development

customers, and other stakeholders, making the presence of integrative capability essential to link various organizations and companies.

The basis of this integrative capability is the group of practitioners at each management level of the company, known as leader teams (LT), who play the role of exercising integrative capability. The leadership that generates this integrative capability corresponds to enabling leadership or dialectical leadership in the adaptive space or conditional layer (see Fig. 8.5).

8.7 (4) Approach from New Product Development Literature

In previous literature on leadership research in NPD (New Product Development) (e.g., Dougherty, 1996; McDonough & Barczak, 1991), not only elements of a participative leadership style and a flexible approach have been discussed, but also the balance between creativity and efficiency, and the balance between participative control and directive control (e.g., Eisenhard & Tabrizi, 1995; Shenhar & Dvir, 1996) are necessary. The behavior and dialectical management of such leaders themselves and among leaders have not been extensively discussed in past project management or CFT (Cross-Functional Team) research in NPD. However, Lewis et al. (2002) argue that successful product development requires balancing numerous paradoxes. They clarify the frequent but ambiguous calls for subtle control: effective managers provide strong leadership to keep teams focused and on schedule, while empowering team members to foster motivation and creativity. This means that leaders need to create adaptive space and execute the adaptive process to manage various paradoxes.

On the other hand, in literature on the leadership structure of new product development in high-tech companies by Kodama (2004, 2005), it is noted that the forms of leadership exercised by practitioners at various management levels (top management, middle management, lower management), including project leaders, have the following three types of leadership traits:

The first type of leadership is "centralized leadership" (integrated, centralized leadership, and directive control [strategic leadership and forceful leadership]) as the foundation for rules and discipline in formal organizations and leadership traits required for achieving the vision and executing strategic planning. As mentioned earlier, centralized leadership involves positions, processes, or activities controlled by some central authority, mainly within formal organizations. Centralized leadership plays the role of formulating the corporate vision and official strategic goals and initiating these in the overall direction of various organizational units.

The second type of leadership is distributed leadership (autonomous, decentralized leadership and participative control [creative leadership and servant leadership]), which emerges particularly from the formation of informal networks and is both independent and distributed with creative and supportive elements. The role of leadership in distributed leadership (Kodama, 2003; Nonaka & Toyama, 2003) is decentralized in various forms mainly within informal organizations. In distributed leadership, more than one individual in each team shares the roles, responsibilities, activities, and functions of leadership. Leadership lies in the quality of the group, and the concept of distributed leadership encompasses the series of roles that the group must fulfill.

The third aspect is leadership arising in the psychological boundary area between the formal organization and informal organization, with elements of dialectical leadership (Kodama, 2004, 2005) demonstrated in areas where practitioners psychologically perceive and recognize paradoxes. Essentially, this means that practitioners exist in a three-layered structure comprised of the formal organization layer, the informal organization layer, and the psychological boundary layer (hereafter, this three-layered structure will be referred to as the "practice layers") and respectively demonstrate the above three types of leadership (see Fig. 8.5). This is similar to the three-layered model of leadership by von Krogh et al. (2012) shown in Fig. 8.2.

Practitioners repeatedly undergo dynamic transitions, synthesizing contradictions and resolving the various frictions and conflicts that arise from practical activities between formal and informal organizations. This space–time created by transitions to resolve contradictions is the third area, the "psychological boundary layer" as an intersection, which corresponds to the adaptive space by Uhl-Bien and Arena (2018) and the conditional layer by von Krogh et al. (2012) (see Fig. 8.5).

Networks (informal organizations) ensure creativity and flexibility when expressing the corporate vision in specific tasks, whereas the formal organization as a bureaucracy ensures efficiency and speed in executing tasks. To adapt to environmental uncertainty, the key is how to flexibly and improvisationally change organizational structures by appropriately using bureaucracy and networks depending on the situation. Therefore, by coexisting networks and bureaucracies within the same company, creating the adaptive space, which is key to CAS construction, the conditional layer, which is key to knowledge creation realization, and the "psychological boundary layer," which is key to successful new product development, companies integrate formal organizations and informal organizations, maximizing synergy and balancing exploration and exploitation (March, 1991). This is leadership for organizational adaptability and forms the core framework of holistic leadership.

Based on the four approaches reviewed above, the next section will discuss the integrated framework of holistic leadership.

(2) **Integrated Leadership Framework**

By integrating the four research approaches mentioned previously, holistic leadership means integrating the leadership within the three practice layers that practitioners constantly face in their daily practice processes (see Fig. 8.6).

The first of the three practice layers is the formal organization layer, where practitioners exercise centralized leadership through operational leadership to promote efficient strategic management. The element of centralized leadership, known as "strategic leadership" (e.g., Bollinger & Smith, 2001; Bontis & Fitz-enz, 2002; Fedor et al., 2003; Ho, 2009; Inkpen, 1998; Lakshman, 2005, 2007; Skyrme & Amidon, 1997), demonstrates how leaders and managers at various management levels influence organizational effectiveness by formulating strategies, visions, and missions, thereby promoting the development of organizational culture. Strategic leadership includes elements such as the process of making strategic decisions, the behavior of top management within the organization, and the composition of the executive team (e.g., House & Aditya, 1997; Reinmoeller, 2004).

These strategic leadership elements involve leaders and managers at various management levels setting policies, providing guidance, and giving instructions to their teams to achieve strategic goals (Fedor et al., 2003). Leaders and managers emphasize tasks and issues essential for planning knowledge creation processes (Ho, 2009) and demonstrate initiative in setting the path for knowledge sharing (Inkpen, 1998).

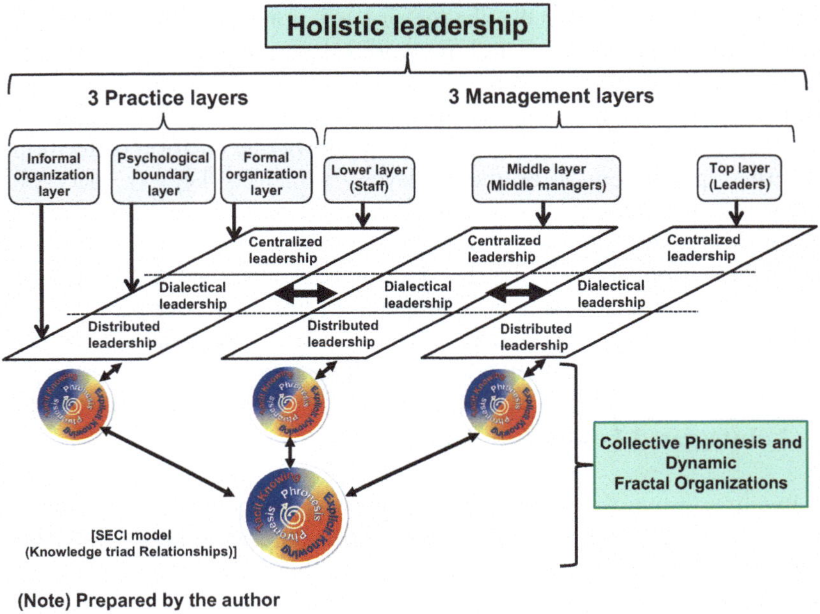

Fig. 8.6 The framework of holistic leadership and dynamic fractal organizations

Additionally, strategic leadership combines management elements focused on sharing and integrating explicit knowledge and leadership elements focused on communication and sharing tacit knowledge for vision (Rowe, 2001).

Secondly, in the informal organization layer, practitioners exercise distributed leadership through entrepreneurial leadership to promote creative knowledge creation activities. Elements of distributed leadership include roles such as "innovator," "mentor," "facilitator," "catalyst," "coordinator," "controller," and "evaluator" that leaders and managers at various management levels within the organization undertake.

Distributed leadership fosters "collaborative leadership" (Bryson & Crosby, 1992; Chrislip & Larson, 1994; Osterlof & Frey, 2000) and "creative leadership" (Lewis et al., 2002), encouraging members within departments, projects, and teams to think and act autonomously, collaboratively, creatively (and imaginatively), and entrepreneurially.

Furthermore, "transformational leadership," as an element of distributed leadership, motivates and creatively stimulates subordinates to do their best for the organization, empowers them, generates strong commitment to the organization, and cultivates a culture of knowledge creation (Goh, 1998). Additionally, distributed leadership includes elements of "servant leadership" (Greenleaf, 1979), where leaders and managers act as supporters ("followers") in helping subordinates achieve their vision and goals.

In this way, centralized leadership exercised in the formal organization layer is planned, directive, analytical, rational, and also possesses managerial elements. On the other hand, distributed leadership exercised in the informal organization layer has autonomous, spontaneous, intuitive, creative, entrepreneurial, collaborative, and supportive elements.

Furthermore, a new theoretical perspective in this book is the "psychological boundary layer" (adaptive space in Fig. 8.2 or conditional layer in Fig. 8.3) that exists at the boundary between these two layers of formal and informal organizations. Various contradictory elements arise at the boundary between formal and informal organizations, such as the aforementioned "tug-of-war between efficiency and creativity." In this psychological boundary layer, practitioners often face various psychological pressures and frictions such as "diverse human relationships," "internal political power," "new business and core business," "differences in expertise (deference)," "honesty vs. façade," "heterogeneous cultures," and "discipline and autonomy."

We refer to this unseen domain where practitioners perceive and recognize such diverse and contradictory psychological situations as the psychological boundary layer. In this psychological boundary layer, leaders view the organization not as over-structured (mechanistic) or under-structured (e.g., organic), but as "semi-structured." Leaders maintain the organization in a state of dynamic equilibrium by balancing at the edge of chaos that exists between order and disorder. They constantly act cautiously to avoid slipping into pure chaos or pure structure (Brown & Eisenhardt, 1997, 1998).

By creating a semi-structure (Eisenhardt & Tabrizi, 1995) that promotes interaction, intuition, and improvisation, leaders can achieve complex adaptive systems. Complex adaptive systems (Axelrod & Cohen, 1999) are systems that adapt and evolve in response to environmental pressures, which trigger complexity (Stacey, 1995). As a response to this pressure, leaders build informal organizations that support and sustain the innovation process and nurture network-type interactions, giving the system adaptability and generating adaptive responses (Perry-Smith & Mannucci, 2017).

As discussed in this book, companies, organizations, and individuals with "improvisation," like Apple, P&G, Microsoft, Zoom, TSMC, Qualcomm, NVIDIA, and DOCOMO, balance on the edge of chaos. In complexity theory terms, "improvisation" is a "dissipative equilibrium," an unstable edge between two attractors (i.e., structure and chaos) that tend to pull the system away from the edge of chaos toward the rigidity of too much structure or the confusion of too little structure. When systems (individuals, organizations, companies, economies, etc.) balance between loose structures and fixed structures (the "edge of chaos"), they "self-organize" and exhibit consistent complex adaptive behavior.

This psychological boundary layer exists for practitioners at all management levels. Particularly crucial for new knowledge creation processes and business innovation is the construction of a psychological boundary layer that balances the centralized leadership in the formal organization layer and the distributed leadership in the informal organization layer. In this layer, practitioners need dialectical leadership (balancing enabling leadership from Fig. 8.2 or both centralized and distributed leadership from Fig. 8.3).

In other words, holistic leadership means that practitioners dynamically balance and integrate centralized leadership, distributed leadership, and dialectical leadership across the three practice layers of the formal organization layer, the psychological boundary layer, and the informal organization layer, with practitioners (top management, middle management, and staff at various management levels) using these forms of leadership dynamically according to the situation (see Fig. 8.6).

Furthermore, such holistic leadership possesses the "fractal nature of leadership." This means that practitioners at each management level have a three-layer structure (three practice layers) of leadership forms: centralized leadership, distributed leadership, and dialectical leadership. Additionally, the overall leadership of the entire corporate organization, integrating top, middle, and lower management, also has a similar three-layer structure of leadership forms. The term "fractal" (Mandelbrot, 1983) is used in complex adaptive theory (e.g., Morel & Ramanujam, 1999; Stacey, 1995) and refers to the idea that parts are shaped similarly to the whole, or that assembling these parts creates the same shape as the whole once again.

In other words, holistic leadership implies that the leadership forms exhibited by practitioners (top, middle, lower) within the organization have a fractal nature, meaning that even if any part is extracted and enlarged, it retains the same structure as the whole. This fractal nature of leadership ensures that the level and quality of leadership needed to implement decision-making and knowledge creation processes regarding strategy formulation and execution within the organization are consistent at all management levels. Therefore, holistic leadership can also be referred to as "fractal leadership."

Moreover, to achieve the simultaneous pursuit and balance of efficiency and creativity in corporate strategy, intense interaction between the different forms of leadership (centralized leadership, distributed leadership, and dialectical leadership) among the top management, middle management, and staff is necessary. This importance of "leadership interaction" reveals the leadership needed for the practical knowledge creation activities and daily efficiency improvement processes at the lower staff level, which have been underestimated by traditional leadership theories. Additionally, it emphasizes the need to thoroughly analyze and consider the elements of leadership exhibited by top leaders not only in the formal organization layer but also in the informal organization layer and the psychological boundary layer (see Fig. 8.6).

As mentioned in Chapter 3, collective phronesis is the aggregation of excellent autonomous distributed phronesis (practical knowledge or practical wisdom) possessed by individuals. It is a comprehensive phronesis for collective management, bringing together the collective wisdom across organizations (Kodama, 2021; Nonaka & Takeuchi, 2019; Nonaka et al., 2008). Phronesis promotes the driving force of the spiral SECI model between tacit knowing and explicit knowing. In other words, collective phronesis refers to the quality wisdom and practical ability mobilized from autonomous distributed phronesis within an ecosystem of knowledge that includes individuals, organizations, companies, communities, and industries.

Furthermore, the collective phronesis, as an aggregation of practical knowledge, operates not only within closed corporate boundaries (project organizations, line organizations, overhead organizations, various management levels such as top, middle, and lower management) but also in multilayered Ba across diverse organizations and communities, including customers in the environment. These interconnected layers (multilayered networks of Ba) interact interdependently with the environment, people, organizations, and companies, creating and evolving an ecosystem of knowledge (Nonaka et al., 2008). This is a crucial element in forming a dynamic fractal organization (Nonaka et al., 2014) that integrates the three types of leadership: centralized leadership, distributed leadership, and dialectical leadership (see Fig. 8.6).

Additionally, as mentioned in Chapter 3, the spiral practical process between tacit and explicit knowledge involves the dynamic resonance of the SECI process through the creation and sharing of common boundary knowledge by distributed phronesis possessed by individual actors. This generates collective phronesis for all actors (or stakeholders). Simultaneously, the formation of collective phronesis triggers the creation of dynamic fractal organizations, with the distributed phronesis of individual actors as core knowledge (previously described as the "knowledge triad relationship") (see Fig. 8.6).

8.7.1 Co-creation Model for Decarbonized Management: Fusion of Mind, Skill, and Body

To promote decarbonized management, it is necessary to encourage societal awareness and behavioral change through cross-organizational and inter-organizational collaboration, including different stakeholders. By assembling multiple companies and organizations and forming a "self-reliant, decentralized, and collaborative synergy group," a foundation for new co-creation can be established, enhancing the potential to accelerate decarbonized management.

The basic organizational strategy based on the concept of a self-reliant, decentralized, and collaborative synergy group lies in the "fusion of mind, skill, and body." The "fusion of body" refers to the integration of workplaces and the fusion of various systems, including the strategy-making process and implementation. The "fusion of skill" involves the integration of different skills and knowledge from various organizations. Rather than considering one's own organization's skills as the best or one's own knowledge as the only correct one, superior skills and knowledge should be mutually adopted and integrated to achieve decarbonized management.

Such "fusion of body" enables the creation of Ba (shared context-in-motion) (Nonaka & Takeuchi, 1995) through the dynamic sharing of space and time among people. The creation of Ba generates (1) common sense, (2) self-transcendence, and (3) self-organization. As tacit knowledge (tacit knowledge) emerging from the common sense created in the shared Ba of space and time, the unique energy knowledge (sense of presence, enthusiasm, tension, etc.), rhythm knowledge (improvisation, groove, etc.), and historical knowledge (background, stories, etc.) of organizational members are born and shared among members. In organizations where all members face decarbonized management together, the existence of such Ba as common sense is always necessary.

Specifically, these are (1) cross-organizational projects, (2) stakeholder involvement, (3) strengthening community engagement, and (4) promoting public–private partnership projects, and the formation of Ba (multilayered Ba) is crucial for this.

In Ba aimed at decarbonized management, it is necessary to operate not with a structure where a specific authority is at the top, but through a decision-making process where all members equally express their opinions, correctly understand decarbonized management, and aim to realize proper management. Members should fully utilize their abilities, leading to the emergence of high creativity and numerous ideas for decarbonized management. To achieve decarbonized management, intense discussions and dialogues among members in open relationships foster an improvised meaning space that transcends self. Through the process of self-transcendence, where members gain an external perspective, they can think from a higher perspective by sharing contexts beyond their limited viewpoints.

Moreover, a self-organizing Ba dynamically balances creativity and efficiency, enabling agile responses to any environmental changes and inducing autonomous decentralization among members. This, in turn, triggers the fusion of skills for the creation of new knowledge. The generation of Ba forms an autonomous decentralized "business community" among members. This promotes the fusion of skills among different members, leading to processes such as (1) knowledge integration, (2) knowledge convergence (Kodama, 2014), and (3) knowledge creation (Nonaka & Takeuchi, 1995). In other words, the "fusion of skills" is a core activity element for members across formal organizations within the informal organization layer for knowledge integration (knowledge convergence/knowledge creation).

Specifically, it involves (1) constructing environmentally conscious business models (wisdom and technology), (2) integrating different technologies, and (3) utilizing data and technology to achieve innovation. Such fusion of body and fusion of skills promote autonomous decentralized thinking and actions among members, inducing distributed leadership to realize "self-reliant, decentralized, and collaborative" aspects as an entire organization (see Figure 8.7).

Finally, "fusion of mind" aims to unify the hearts of all members across different organizations toward a shared vision and strategic objectives for decarbonized management. This fusion of mind promotes the sharing of knowledge vision and driving objectives mentioned in Chapter 3. Each organization, united as one, works toward the vision of sustainable social growth through decarbonized management. Specifically, it involves (1) thorough decarbonization awareness, (2) internal permeation and behavioral change, (3) transforming routines centered on decarbonized management, and (4) education and human resource development toward a new mindset.

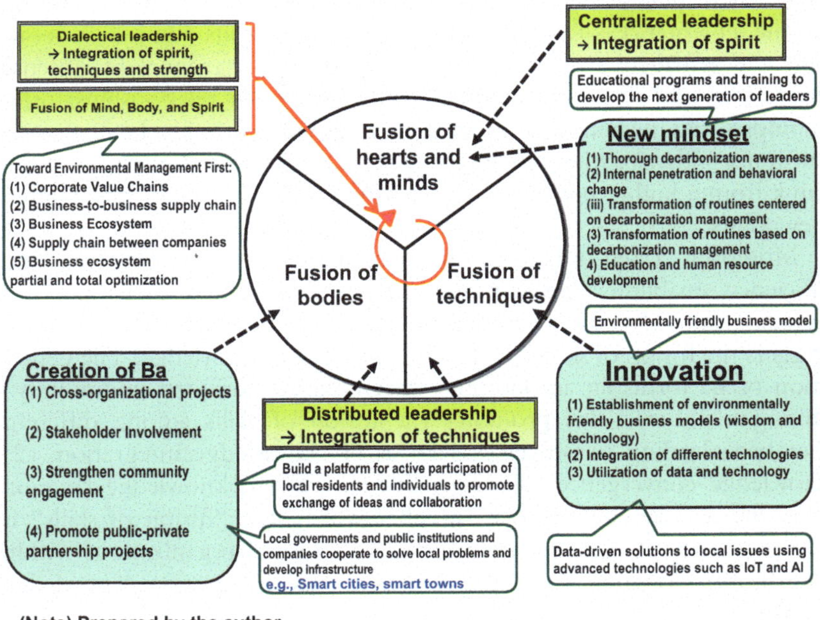

(Note) Prepared by the author

Fig. 8.7 Holistic leadership for decarbonized management—"fusion of mind, body, and spirit"

Such fusion of mind drives centralized leadership based on a unified strategic perspective of the company, promoting actions toward achieving strategic synergies with all members sharing strategic goals, integrating organizations, companies, and stakeholders (see Figure 8.7). Additionally, the fusion of mind, skill, and body functions company-wide, integrating centralized leadership that promotes thought and action based on shared strategic perspectives with autonomous decentralized and collaborative distributed leadership through dialectical leadership (see Figure 8.7).

Specifically, it aims to achieve (1) the corporate value chain, (2) the supply chain between companies, and (3) the coexistence of partial and overall optimization of the business ecosystem for environmental management first. These elements of fusion of mind, fusion of skill, and fusion of body, and further the fusion of mind, skill, and body, form self-reliant, decentralized, and collaborative synergy groups through holistic leadership. Observing such holistic leadership at the organizational scale level, it implies that the "leadership triad relationship" of fusion of mind inducing centralized leadership, fusion of skill and body inducing distributed leadership, and fusion of mind, skill, and body promoting dialectical leadership is formed at all management levels and at the organizational, corporate, and stakeholder levels. This constructs a dynamic fractal organization characterized by the leadership triad relationship.

4.3 Co-creation Management Through Fractal Collaboration—Formation of Leadership Triad Relationship and Dynamic Fractal Organizations

Insights from new leadership theory derived from "complex adaptive theory" suggest a new form of collaboration for decarbonized management. Axelrod and Cohen (1999) perceive the issue of how numerous people should act while mutually adapting in an unpredictable world as a complex adaptive system. They argue that through intricate mutual interactions among participants, the entire system (i.e., the organization) continuously changes.

Complex adaptive systems, such as living organisms, evolve toward the "edge of chaos," a boundary between order and disorder, stability and chaos, and adapt to the environment near the edge of chaos. Systems that are too ordered become frozen and unable to exhibit complex movements, while overly chaotic systems are unmanageable. Systems on the edge of chaos show complex movements and can quickly adapt to the environment. Similarly, organizations and practitioners that possess autonomy, flexibility, and creativity, like those mentioned in this book

(Apple, Cisco, Microsoft, Zoom, TSMC, Qualcomm, NVIDIA), are more likely to generate continuous corporate innovation (Obolensky, 2010).

To realize decarbonized management and adapt to (or create) new environmental changes, as previously mentioned, merely relying on existing transformational leadership or style leadership is insufficient. Adapting to (or creating) new environments cannot be achieved by the leadership of only top management or middle management within a corporate organization. Dense linkages and interactions involving top, middle, and lower management in a trinity are essential.

The reason for applying such a complex systems approach is that it is challenging to develop these discussions within the paradigm of traditional leadership theory. Concepts of "emergence" and "fluctuation" from the expanded self-organization paradigm provide elements of "emergent and fluctuating leadership," which are crucial for practitioners at all management levels within corporate organizations. For explaining and interpreting dynamic organizational phenomena such as mindset reform and organizational transformation toward decarbonized management, this complex adaptive systems theory offers new perspectives that traditional transformational leadership and style leadership, which often focus on linear process models, cannot provide.

In companies promoting decarbonized management, members adeptly manage the "tug-of-war between control and decentralization" and the "balance between efficiency and creativity" through holistic leadership in response to changes in situational (strategic context and organizational context). Members exhibit centralized leadership through "directive control (strategic leadership & forceful leadership)" to achieve "speed and efficiency," while simultaneously exercising distributed leadership through "participative control (creative leadership & collaborative leadership)" to pursue "autonomous decentralization and creativity."

They skillfully use these different leadership elements according to the situation and balance them through dialectical leadership. Moreover, all employees (top leaders, middle managers, lower staff) possess the elements of such holistic leadership (see Fig. 8.8).

To reiterate, holistic leadership means that members dynamically balance and integrate centralized leadership, distributed leadership, and dialectical leadership across the three practice layers of the formal organization layer, the psychological boundary layer, and the informal organization layer, with members (top management, middle management,

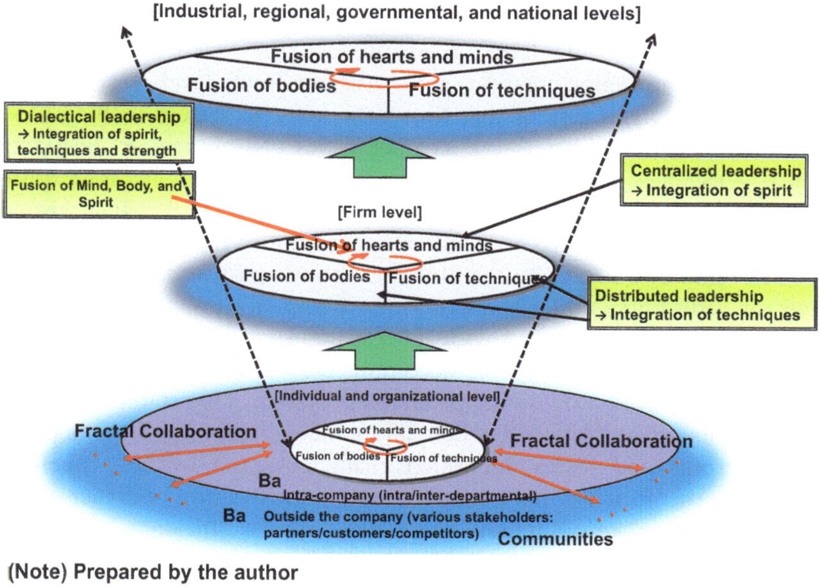

Fig. 8.8 Fractal collaboration through fractality in leadership

and staff at various management levels) using these forms of leadership dynamically according to the situation.

Such holistic leadership possesses the "fractal nature of leadership." This means that practitioners at each management level have a three-layer structure (three practice layers) of leadership forms: centralized leadership promoting the fusion of mind, distributed leadership promoting the fusion of skill and body, and dialectical leadership promoting the fusion of mind, skill, and body. Additionally, the overall leadership at the organizational, corporate, and group levels, integrating top, middle, and lower management, also has a similar three-layer structure of leadership forms.

Holistic leadership with this fractal nature of leadership leads to promoting "fractal collaboration" at all management levels. The term "fractal" (Mandelbrot, 1983) is used in complex adaptive theory (e.g., Morel & Ramanjam, 1999; Stacey, 1995) and means that parts are shaped similarly to the whole, or assembling these parts creates the same shape as the whole once again. In companies, possessing this fractal nature, where any part of the organization, when extracted and expanded, retains the same shape as the whole, ensures that the speed and efficiency of decision-making and the quality level of creative activities such as knowledge integration (knowledge creation) are consistent at any level.[3]。

The supply chain system that forms the keiretsu system in the automotive industry also has fractal characteristics (Nishiguchi & Beaudet, 2000). Organizational structures that balance exploitation and exploration at companies like Apple and P&G also exhibit fractal characteristics (Kodama, 2014). More recently, the restructuring of Japan Airlines (JAL) has been noted. JAL, hit by the global economic crisis of the late 2000s, filed for bankruptcy under the Corporate Reorganization Act in January 2010. The person entrusted with its restructuring was Kazuo Inamori, the founder of Kyocera. Upon becoming chairman in February 2010, Inamori introduced a divisional profitability system. He established small departments called "Ameba," where all members understood the department's profits and losses, identified challenges, and worked together to resolve them, achieving efficiency and rationalization. Furthermore, multiple Amebas were integrated to achieve similar efficiency and rationalization at the super-Ameba level. Then, super-Amebas were integrated to strategically achieve efficiency and rationalization at the company-wide level. The fractal structure, where the same structure and role of the smallest unit, the Ameba, is seen at the super-Ameba and company-wide levels, was adopted. In other words, at any level—Ameba, super-Ameba, or company-wide—the structure similar to the smallest unit, the Ameba, can be seen. It was Inamori and other leaders who expanded the relationships inside and outside the Amebas and moved each Ameba.

Thus, to achieve decarbonized management, the leadership triad relationship through the fusion of mind, skill, and body, i.e., holistic leadership, creates dynamic fractal organizations across various organizations and companies at the organizational, corporate, and group levels, promoting fractal collaboration. This allows for the identification of fractal nature of leadership and fractal collaboration across project organizations, line organizations, indirect department organizations, various management levels (top management, middle management, lower management), different specialties and professional levels, and even beyond inter-company barriers (see Fig. 8.8).

8.8 Implications and Conclusion

In addressing global warming, the reduction of greenhouse gas emissions is a key objective for many countries. Notably, reducing greenhouse gas emissions in households requires a transformation in individual and family lifestyles. Therefore, it is essential to promote changes in workstyles and lifestyles among citizens and consumers through various activities by national governments, local authorities, companies, and organizations. Additionally, it is crucial for companies (organizations) to undertake new initiatives, such as promoting the management and reduction of greenhouse gas emissions (mainly CO_2) generated in employees' households.

To achieve this, alongside enhancing environmental awareness and promoting environmental actions among citizens, as well as fostering behavior change movements in society, the industrial sector must further advance co-creation of new value in the environmental domain through fractal collaboration among participating companies (organizations). In companies (organizations) where the culture and values of decarbonized management are widely shared, effective sharing of tacit knowledge among employees becomes possible, thereby promoting organizational knowledge creation toward decarbonized management.

Successful companies have invested significant energy in permeating unique corporate cultures and values, based on the founders' philosophies, to the farthest reaches of their organizations. Sharing organizational culture and values creates unique systems and rules within companies, instilling distinctive ways of thinking, perspectives, and behavior patterns among employees. Therefore, the role of building a unique corporate culture for decarbonized management and promoting the sharing of values among employees falls on top leaders (CEOs and executives) of the organization, relying significantly on their centralized leadership.

Schein (1985) argues that the essence of top management leadership is not management leadership for achieving goals, but the creation, management, and destruction of organizational culture. Furthermore, Selznick (1957) emphasizes the importance of the myth-making ability of leaders. To share culture and values within an organization, it is effective to raise employee morale and convey unique visions and strategic objectives through myths and stories. Myths and stories not only promote the construction and sharing of corporate visions but also play a role in converging decision-making related to strategy formulation and execution in daily corporate activities.

What kind of centralized leadership is required for excellent companies to permeate the background and stories for decarbonized management within the company and create, establish, and reform unique organizational culture?

To deeply instill a unique corporate culture, "resonance of values" and "building trust" (Kodama, 2007) by leaders are necessary. Resonance of values and building trust gradually form as employees clash their subjective views and values through "dialectical dialogue" and "creative dialogue," discussing visions and strategic goals. Deep dialectical dialogue enables the sharing of strategic visions and goals among employees, including top management. However, realistically, individual employees interpret visions and strategic goals differently.

For example, as seen with Honda, leaders need to consistently ask fundamental questions like "Why" and "For what purpose are we doing this?" and establish this style among employees. By understanding and sharing the differing interpretations of individuals, employees develop a sense of unity in formulating and executing corporate strategies. To create new value for decarbonized management through resonance of values and building trust among employees, leaders and employees need to deeply share and implement the six strategic contexts: "Who," "What," "Why," "With whom," "When," and "How."

This requires leadership that demonstrates practical wisdom (phronesis) and collective phronesis among employees, enabling them to make the best decisions and processes, discover and acquire new values, and create new knowledge through fractal collaboration. The concept of practical wisdom itself dates back to Aristotle's concept of phronesis, meaning prudence, practical reason, and practical wisdom. In other words, practical wisdom refers to the ability of leaders to resonate values, build mutual trust, and find appropriate decisions and the best actions to execute specific strategies and create new knowledge. This phronesis forms the foundation of the holistic leadership discussed so far.

Community leaders, whether they belong to an organization as top management, middle management, or independent entrepreneurs with entrepreneurship, must quickly and interactively capture the external environment, technological changes, market structures, and customer needs surrounding their organization to achieve decarbonized management. They need the ability to continuously set visions and clarify concepts for what they need to accomplish in establishing decarbonized management at a global level.

Based on the clarified strategic concepts and the vision or strategic goals (sometimes filled with personal thoughts and beliefs) set, community leaders require holistic leadership that realizes fractal collaboration with both internal and external stakeholders, including customers, through interactions with the environment "as an ecosystem of knowledge." Achieving fractal collaboration through human networks involving "changing specific networks" (Kodama, 2006) facilitates dialogue and collaboration with core leaders inside and outside the organization, creating new knowledge.

For new knowledge creation, it is essential to form Ba of empathy and resonance of values regarding visions and strategic goals through constructive and creative dialogue with community leaders inside and outside the organization. This creates a platform of resonance of value for decarbonized management among multiple community leaders, establishing strategic partnerships with community leaders. The engine for building this new foundation of value creation for the strategic thoughts and actions of community leaders lies in phronesis and collective phronesis.

However, sharing visions and strategic goals for decarbonized management with others and constructing a "platform of resonance of values" is not easy. It requires conceptualizing complex business models, challenges, and processes, and clearly presenting them to induce the interest and motivation of others. Therefore, for community leaders, building a win–win relationship toward the future of decarbonized management is a crucial perspective.

In other words, through forming a community starting from Ba, it is necessary to create relationships that not only produce synergies from mutual core competencies but also complement each other's weaknesses. Thus, positioning others within the functions and roles of the value chain or value network is essential, not through dominance by one's own power, but by exploring business models that influence both businesses. Phronesis and collective phronesis become the engine for forming a community that continuously creates new knowledge.

Practically, community leaders must form a platform of resonance of values at the organizational level, including many community members, within a community formed from multiple internal and external companies (organizations). Based on a solid platform of resonance formed through phronesis, community leaders can further exercise holistic leadership and activate the SECI process in a spiral. Through the execution of the SECI process with such phronesis and holistic leadership by community leaders, decarbonized management becomes possible.

Until now, analytical strategic theories based on positivism have excluded the practical processes of micro human actions. However, realistically, the strategic actions of companies (organizations) are not entirely determined by objective and logical analytical strategy formulation and execution. As previously mentioned, in the modern business society, where rapid technological innovation and new ICT/AI businesses are accelerating across different stakeholders, community leaders must skillfully handle various challenges (complex internal and external power and politics, complex relationships with customers, diverse and constantly changing technologies and business models) that cannot be solved solely by logical analytical methods in strategy formulation and execution.

The leadership necessary for this is phronesis and collective phronesis and holistic leadership.

Notes

1. The author refers to companies that integrate excellent knowledge at a global level as "knowledge integration firms." For details, see Kodama (2009, 2011a).
2. The author calls the innovation system that integrates diverse core knowledge both inside and outside the company "hybrid innovation" (a system that is an intermediate form between closed innovation and open innovation, corresponding to half-open innovation). For details, see Kodama (2011b).
3. Christian (2011) often considers large-scale projects or companies not as hierarchical pyramids but as fractals, where any part, when extracted and enlarged, retains the same shape as the whole. He mentions that the levels of decision-making and artistry should be consistent at any scale.

References

Arena, M., Cross, R., Sims, J., & Uhl-Bien, M. (2017). Groundswell: Tapping the power of employee networks to fuel emergent innovation. *MIT Sloan Management Review, 58*(4), 39–47.

Axelrod, R., & Cohen, M. (1999). *Harnessing complexity: Organizational implications of a scientific frontier*. The Free Press.

Baur, J. E., Parker Ellen, B., Buckley, M. R., Ferris, G. R., Allison, T. H., McKenny, A. F., & Short, J. C. (2016). More than oneway to articulate a vision: A configurations approach to leader charismatic rhetoric and influence. *The Leadership Quarterly, 27*(1), 156–171.

Bell DeTienne, K., Dyer, G., Hoopes, C., & Harris, S. (2004). Toward a model of effective knowledge management and directions for future research: Culture, leadership, and CKOs. *Journal of Leadership & Organizational Studies, 10*(4), 26–43.

Bernard, D. (1988). *From Taylorism to Fordism: A rational madness*. Free Associated Books.

Birkinshaw, J., & Gibson, C. (2004). Building ambidexterity into an organization. *MIT Sloan Management Review, 45*(4), 47–55.

Bollinger, A. S., & Smith, R. D. (2001). Managing organizational knowledge as a strategic asset. *Journal of Knowledge Management, 5*(1), 8–18.

Bontis, N., & Fitz-enz, J. (2002). Intellectual capital ROI: A causal map of human capital antecedents and consequents. *Journal of Intellectual Capital, 3*(2), 223–247.

Brown, S. L., & Eisenhardt, K. M. (1997). The art of continuous change: Linking complexity theory and time-paced evolution in relentlessly shifting organizations. *Administrative Science Quarterly, 42*(1), 1–34.

Brown, S. L., & Eisenhardt, K. M. (1998). *Competing on the edge: Strategy as structured chaos*. Harvard Business School Press.

Bryson, J., & Crosby, B. C. (1992). *Leadership for the common good: Tackling public problems in a shared-power world*. Jossey-Bass.

Carlile, P. (2004). Transferring, translating, and transforming: An integrative framework for managing knowledge across boundaries. *Organization Science, 15*(5), 555–68.

Cegarra-Navarro, J. G., & Dewhurst, F. (2007). Linking organizational learning and customer capital through an ambidexterity context: An empirical investigation in SMEs. *International Journal of Human Resource Management, 18*(10), 1720–1735.

Chrislip, D., & Larson, C. (1994). *Collaborating leadership: How citizens and civic leaders can make a difference*. Jossey-Bass.

Christian, B. (2011). *The most human human*. Penguin Books.

Couillard, D., & Lapierre, J. (2003). Leadership, learning and resources for the high-tech firm: An integrated view of technology management. *International Journal of Technology Management, 26*(7), 767–787.
Dhiman, S. (2017). Leadership and spirituality. In *Leadership today* (pp. 139–160). Springer.
Dougherty, D. (1996). Organizing for innovation. In S. R. Clegg, C. Hardy, & W. R. Nord (Eds.), *Handbook of organization studies* (pp. 424–439). Sage.
Eisenhardt, K. M., & Tabrizi, B. N. (1995). Accelerating adaptive processes: Product innovation in the global computer industry. *Administrative Science Quarterly*, 84–110.
Fedor, D. B., Ghosh, S., Caldwell, S. D., Maurer, T. J., & Singhal, V. R. (2003). The effects of knowledge management on team members' ratings of project success and impact. *Decision Sciences, 34*(8), 513–539.
Fry, L. W. (2003). Toward a theory of spiritual leadership. *The Leadership Quarterly, 14*(6), 693–727.
Gagné, M. (2009). A model of knowledge-sharing motivation. *Human Resource Management, 48*(4), 571–589.
Gill, R. (2006). *Theory and practice of leadership.* Sage.
Goh, S. C. (1998). Toward a learning organization: The strategic building blocks. *SAM Advanced Management Journal, 63*(1), 15–22.
Govindarajan, V., & Trimble, C. (2005). *Ten Rules for strategic innovations.* Harvard Business School Press.
Greenleaf, R. (1979). *Servant leadership.* Paulist Press.
He, Z., & Wong, P. (2004). Exploration vs. exploitation: An empirical test of the ambidexterity hypothesis. *Organization Science, 15*(4), 481–494.
Ho, C. T. (2009). The relationship between knowledge management enablers and performance. *Industrial Management & Data Systems, 109*(1), 98–117.
House, R. J., & Aditya, R. N. (1997). The social scientific study of leadership: Quo vadis? *Journal of Management, 23*(5), 409–473.
Huang, Q., Davison, R. M., Liu, H., & Gu, J. (2008). The impact of leadership style on knowledge-sharing intentions in China. *Journal of Global Information Management, 16*(1), 67–91.
Inkpen, A. (1998). Learning, knowledge acquisition, and strategic alliances. *European Management Journal, 16*, 223–229.
Keister, A. C. (2014). Thriving teams and change agility: Leveraging a collective state to create organization agility. In A. Shani & D. A. Noumair (Eds.), *Research in organizational change and development* (Vol. 22, pp. 299–333). Emerald.
Kodama, M. (2002). Transforming an old economy company into a new economy success: The case of NTT DoCoMo. *Leadership & Organization Development Journal, 23*(1), 26–39.

Kodama, M. (2003). Strategic innovation in traditional big business. *Organization Studies, 24*(2), 235–268.

Kodama, M. (2004). Strategic community-based theory of firms: Case study of dialectical management at NTT DoCoMo. *Systems Research and Behavioral Science, 21*(6), 603–634.

Kodama, M. (2005). Knowledge creation through networked strategic communities: Case studies in new product development. *Long Range Planning, 38*(1), 27–49.

Kodama, M. (2006). Knowledge-based view of corporate strategy. *Technovation, 26*(12), 1390–1406.

Kodama, M. (2007). *The strategic community-based firm*. Palgrave Macmillan.

Kodama, M. (2009). Boundaries innovation and knowledge integration in the Japanese firm. *Long Range Planning, 42*(4), 463–494.

Kodama, M. (2011a). *Knowledge integration dynamics: Developing strategic innovation capability*. World Scientific.

Kodama, M. (2011b). *Interactive business communities: Accelerating corporate innovation through boundary networks*. Gower Publishing, Ltd.

Kodama, M. (2014). *Winning through boundaries innovation—Communities of boundaries generate convergence*. Peter Lang.

Kodama, M. (Ed.). (2015). *Collaborative innovation: Developing health support ecosystems* (Vol. 39). Routledge.

Kodama, M. (2017). Developing strategic innovation in large corporations—The dynamic capability view of the firm. *Knowledge and Process Management, 24*(4), 221–246.

Kodama, M. (2018). *Sustainable growth through strategic innovation: Driving congruence in capabilities*. Edward Elgar Publishing.

Kodama, M. (2020). Developing knowledge communities through video-based information networks. *Knowledge and Process Management, 27*(2), 103–122.

Kodama, M. (2021). Knowledge creation through collective phronesis. *Knowledge and Process Management, 28*(3), 223–245.

Kodama, M., & Shibata, T. (2014). Strategy transformation through strategic innovation capability—A case study of Fanuc. *R&D Management, 44*(1), 75–103.

Lakshman, C. (2005). Top executive knowledge leadership: Managing knowledge to lead change at General Electric. *Journal of Change Management, 5*, 429–446.

Lakshman, C. (2007). Organizational knowledge leadership: A grounded theory approach. *Leadership & Organization Development Journal, 28*(2), 51–75.

Levinthal, D. A., & March, J. G. (1993). The myopia of learning. *Strategic Management Journal, 14*(S2), 95–112.

Lewis, M., Dehler, G., & Green, S. (2002). Product development tensions: Exploring contrasting styles of project management. *Academy of Management Journal, 45*(3), 546–564.

Mandelbrot, B. (1983). *The fractal geometry of nature*. Freeman.

March, J. G. (1991). Exploration and exploitation in organizational learning. *Organization Science, 2*(1), 71–87.

Markides, C. (1997). Strategic innovation. *Sloan Management Review, 38*(2), 9–23.

McDonough, F. E., & Barczak, G. (1991). Speeding up new product development: The effects of leadership style and source of technology. *Journal of Product Innovation Development, 8*(2), 203–211.

Morel, B., & Ramanujam, R. (1999). Through the looking glass of complexity: The dynamics of organizations as adaptive and evolving systems. *Organization Science, 10*(3), 278–293.

Nishiguchi, T., & Beaudet, A. (2000). Fractal design: Self-organizing links in supply chain management. In G. Von Krough, I. Nonaka, & T. Nishiguchi (Eds.), *Knowledge creation; A source of value* (pp. 199–230). Macmillan.

Nonaka, I., Kodama, M., Hirose, A., & Kohlbacher, K. (2014). Dynamic fractal organizations for promoting knowledge-based transformation. *European Management Journal, 32*(1), 137–146.

Nonaka, I., & Takeuchi, H. (1995). *The knowledge-creating company*. Oxford University Press.

Nonaka, I., & Takeuchi, H. (2019). *The wise company: How companies create continuous innovation*. Oxford University Press.

Nonaka, I., & Toyama, R. (2002). A firm as a dialectical being: Towards a dynamic theory of a firm. *Industrial and Corporate Change, 11*(5), 995–1009.

Nonaka, I., & Toyama, R. (2003). The knowledge-creating theory revisited: Knowledge creation as a synthesizing process. *Knowledge Management Research & Practice, 1*(1), 2–10.

Nonaka, I., Toyama, R., & Hirata, T. (2008). *Managing flow: A process theory of the knowledge-based firm*. Palgrave Macmillan.

Nonaka, I., & Von Krogh, G. (2009). Perspective—Tacit knowledge and knowledge conversion: Controversy and advancement in organizational knowledge creation theory. *Organization Science, 20*(3), 635–652.

Obolensky, N. (2010). *Complex adaptive leadership. Embracing paradox and leadership*. Gower.

Osterlof, M., & Frey, B. (2000). Motivation, knowledge transfer, and organizational forms. *Organization Science, 11*(3), 538–550.

O'Reilly, C., III., & Tushman, M. (2004, April). The ambidextrous organization. *Harvard Business Review, 82*, 74–82.

Perry-Smith, J. E., & Mannucci, P. V. (2017). From creativity to innovation: The social network drivers of the four phases of the idea journey. *Academy of Management Review, 42*(1), 53–79.

Reinmoeller, P. (2004). The knowledge-based view of the firm and upper echelon theory: Exploring the agency of TMT. *International Journal of Learning and Intellectual Capital, 1*, 91–104.

Ribière, V. M., & Sitar, A. S. (2003). Critical role of leadership in nurturing a knowledge-supporting culture. *Knowledge Management Research & Practice, 1*(1), 39–48.

Robertson, M., & Swan, J. (2003). Control—What control? Culture and ambiguity within a knowledge intensive firm. *Journal of Management Studies, 40*, 831–858.

Rowe, W. G. (2001). Creating wealth in organizations: The role of strategic leadership. *Academy of Management Executive, 15*, 81–94.

Schein, E. H. (1985). *Organizational culture and leadership.* Jossey-Bass.

Scott, W. G. (1961). Organization theory: An overview and an appraisal. *Journal of the Academy of Management, 4*, 7–26.

Selznick, P. (1957). *Leadership in administration.* Harper and Row.

Shaked, H., & Schechter, C. (2017). Systems thinking among school middle leaders. *Educational Management Administration & Leadership, 45*(4), 699–718.

Shenhar, A. J., & Dvir, D. (1996). Toward a typological theory of project management. *Research Policy, 25*(4), 607–632.

Shibata, T., & Kodama, M. (2008). Managing technological transition from old to new technology: Case of Fanuc's successful transition. *Business Strategy Series, 9*(4), 157–162.

Singh, S. K. (2008). Role of leadership in knowledge management: A study. *Journal of Knowledge Management, 12*, 3–15.

Skyrme, D., & Amidon, D. (1997). The knowledge agenda. *Journal of Knowledge Management, 1*(1), 27–37.

Smith, W. K., & Tushman, M. L. (2005). Managing strategic contradictions: A top management model for managing innovation streams. *Organization Science, 16*(5), 522–536.

Stacey, R. (1995). The science of complexity: an alternative perspective for strategic change process. *Strategic Management Journal, 16*(6), 477–495.

Tushman, M. L., & O'Reilly, C., III. (1996). Ambidextrous organizations: Managing evolutionary and revolutionary change. *California Management Review, 38*(4), 8–30.

Uhl-Bien, M., & Arena, M. (2017). Complexity leadership: Enabling people and organizations for adaptability. *Organizational Dynamics, 46*(1), 9–20.

Uhl-Bien, M., & Arena, M. (2018). Leadership for organizational adaptability: A theoretical synthesis and integrative framework. *The Leadership Quarterly, 29*(1), 89–104.
Uhl-Bien, M., & Marion, R. (2009). Complexity leadership in bureaucratic forms of organizing: A meso model. *The Leadership Quarterly, 20*(4), 631–650.
Uhl-Bien, M., Marion, R., & McKelvey, B. (2007). Complexity leadership theory: Shifting leadership from the industrial age to the knowledge era. *The Leadership Quarterly, 18*(4), 298–318.
von Krogh, G., Nonaka, I., & Rechsteiner, L. (2012). Leadership in organizational knowledge creation: A review and framework. *Journal of Management Studies, 49*(1), 240–277.
Wren, D. (1987). *The evolution of management thought* (3rd ed.). Wiley.
Yang, J.-T. (2007). Knowledge sharing: Investigating appropriate leadership roles and collaborative culture. *Tourism Management, 28*(2), 530–543.

Index

M. Kodama, *Developing Knowledge Convergence Through Collective Phronesis*, https://doi.org/10.1007/978-981-96-4403-2

J

K

L

M

N

Q

R

S

The manufacturer's authorised representative in the EU is Springer Nature Customer Service Centre GmbH, Europaplatz 3, 69115 Heidelberg, Germany. If you have any concerns regarding our products, please contact ProductSafety@springernature.com

Printed and bound by CPI Group (UK) Ltd, Croydon, CR0 4YY
01/10/2026
02225852-0007